ADVISORY PANEL'S FOREWORD

In too many households, nutritious leftovers are "saved" in the refrigerator until they are thrown out. Not in your home, perhaps, but in millions of others.

What accounts for this saving-yet-wasting? We believe it's chiefly due to not knowing what to do with leftovers. The cookbooks most people own today are not helpful with leftovers, or it's difficult to find what help they contain. Consequently, the joys and advantages of leftovers cooking are the least known and appreciated.

Unknown to too many cooks is how to relate leftovers, or once-cooked foods, to the vast array of great dishes that require once-cooked food as the base. Among them are such culinary masterpieces as Beef Miroton, Russian Pirog, Alsatian Choucroute Garnie, and Florentine Cannelloni.

This cookbook deals with both types of leftovers cooking—with chance leftovers saved in chance amounts and with planned leftovers deliberately created in predetermined amounts. Both types are closely related through the 633 recipes given. The aim is to provide the leftovers cook with the greatest help possible:

▶ **by providing a method anyone can use to cook creatively with chance leftovers in chance amounts. The method is illustrated by "case histories."**

▶ **by making available over 600 great leftovers recipes.**

▶ **by showing how the method relates to the recipes in creating successful new dishes.**

▶ **by organizing the recipes in a new way that makes finding the right recipes easy.**

▶ **by revealing how cooking with planned leftovers permits extravagant eating without extravagant spending.**

▶ **by giving insight into the psychology of preparers of leftovers dishes and the attitudes of those who eat them.**

How the Leftovers Recipes Were Selected

This cookbook surprises some people. They never realized so many leftovers recipes existed. Thousands, of course, have appeared in food columns of magazines and newspapers, and in cookbooks. The difference between them and "regular" recipes is that all call for at least one principal ingredient to be once-cooked.

Drawing on our professional experience we advised the author on the selection and adaptation of the recipes best suited to the eating habits and lifestyles of the 1980s: We and the author kept 5 considerations in mind in making our choices. 1) Recipes for foods typically left over in most households. 2) Taste and appetite appeal. 3) Recipes that are out-of-the-ordinary, including gourmet. 4) Recipes that are economical in ease and speed of preparation, as well as cost. 5) Those recipes that best live up to these standards for each category of leftover food.

Most of the recipes meet most of these considerations. Of course, even experts can differ. So much depends on experience and taste. This cookbook is designed, chiefly, to give users of it the experience they need to create their own unique leftovers dishes. Happy cooking!

MARION GOUGH
former senior editor
HOUSE BEAUTIFUL MAGAZINE

ROBERT H. LOEB, JR.
former food editor
ESQUIRE MAGAZINE

DAPHNE E. HARDOON
author, Chinese Cooking Made Easy, published by
WOMAN'S DAY

BEATRICE OJAKANGAS
former food writer
SUNSET MAGAZINE

TWICE IS NICE

Over 600 Fabulous Recipes for Creating Delicious New Meals from Once-Cooked Foods

EDNA K. DAMERELL

COLLIER BOOKS
Macmillan Publishing Company
New York

For Karen, Diane, Holly, and Reg

Macmillan Publishing Company
866 Third Avenue, New York, N.Y. 10022
Collier Macmillan Canada, Inc.

Library of Congress Cataloging in Publication Data
Damerell, Edna K., 1927–
    Twice is nice.
    Reprint. Originally published: The 100 greatest
leftovers recipes plus 533 more. New York: Damerell Pub.,
© 1982.
    Includes index.
    1. Cookery (Leftovers)   I. Title.
TX652.D3   1984   641.5'52   83-18948
ISBN 0-02-009640-2

10 9 8 7 6 5 4 3 2 1

Printed in the United States of America

The graphics in this book were
by DiFranza Williamson Inc.

This book was previously published under the title
The 100 Greatest Leftovers Recipes Plus 533 More
by Damerell Publishing, New York.

CONTENTS

ADVISORY PANEL'S FOREWORD

AUTHOR'S INTRODUCTION

CHAPTERS

LEFTOVERS RECIPES

BASICS

AUTHOR'S INTRODUCTION

I wrote this cookbook for one reason. I always wanted but never had—*or even heard of*—a leftovers cookbook. I wanted one as a stay-at-home mother when the children were small. I wanted one even more when I took a full-time job away from home.

I learned to be a leftovers cook the hard way—by trial and error, collecting leftovers recipes as I came across them, and inventing my own. But it would have been so much easier if I'd had at my fingertips a cookbook devoted entirely to showing what dishes I could make with my leftovers of the moment, and the best way to go about it. Even as I worked on this cookbook, I looked forward to the day when I could use it myself.

When I started my research for it, to my great surprise, I came across several previously published cookbooks on leftovers. The reason that I and most other people had never heard of them was that they were never adequately advertised.

This neglect, I found, is also reflected in the loss of knowledge of leftovers cooking during the affluence of the 1950s and 1960s that encouraged the waste of practically everything, including good food. Women who came of age or grew up during those decades know less about leftovers cooking than their mothers did. Men who've taken to cooking since then are in the same boat. And so are their sons and daughters.

The time is ripe, and there is a need, for the revival of the art of leftovers cooking.

Professional & Practical

Attempting to put what I know into a cookbook was an entirely new experience for me. I therefore enlisted two kinds of professional help to make it as useful and complete as possible. First, I utilized the services of the 5-member Advisory Panel of culinary experts. Next, I involved a professional writer with expertise in organizing information graphically so that it can be located at a glance. Their professionalism plus my experience blend together into one useful whole. As the author, of course, I am solely responsible for its contents.

Original Ideas & Recipes Combined

Many of the ideas in this cookbook have never appeared anywhere else or are generally unknown. They're fresh and original. Some are apparent in the chapter headings. For example, "Mental Blocks to Leftovers Cooking" in Chapter 1. It's the ideas along with the recipes that will help turn the habit of saving-yet-wasting into saving-and-using. If the reader is already skilled with leftovers, the ideas will confirm and enhance your skills, as well as provide easy-to-find recipes conveniently at your fingertips.

Because the ideas are as important as the recipes, it is essential to read all of the editorial matter. That includes the foreword of the Advisory Panel as well as the material in each chapter and section. It makes this cookbook refreshingly different, I believe, from the many cookbooks that tend to be mere book-long recipe lists.

Edna K. Damerell

Chapter 1

MENTAL BLOCKS TO LEFTOVERS COOKING

As the Advisory Panel says in its foreword, the saving-yet-wasting of lefto-. ver foods makes little sense. But, many sensible people do it all the time.

This contradiction indicates more than a lack of knowledge. Savers-yet-wasters could, after all, learn by trial and error. They could learn from making mistakes. But certain feelings and notions keep them from making the attempt.

Lack of confidence

It's of course difficult to be confident if you're a novice at cooking, or have never tried to do much with leftovers. Confidence comes only with successful experience, which this cookbook is designed to foster.

Fear of making mistakes

Sometimes it's due to trying to live up to a perfectionist ideal. Any cooking that can turn out less than perfect is avoided at all cost, including the cost of feeling guilty for wasting good food.

Then, too, the fear is often of disapproval. Some people are so over-anxious to please a spouse and/or children or friends that they're completely inhibited.

A negative image

Unfortunately, the word "leftovers" is sometimes used disparagingly. It conjures up an image of the remains of a meal merely reheated and re-served. Except for certain dishes, nothing could be more boring. Nevertheless, it's what happens in many households and gives leftovers a bad name.

In some households, also, leftovers are consistently used up in exactly the same way. They're always made into soup, for example, or invariably reappear in curry dishes. The constant repetition is almost as boring.

This cookbook takes the positive approach, elevating leftovers cooking to the high culinary status it enjoys among sophisticated cooks. The recipes expand the cook's repertoire and the dishes made with them defy partakers to identify which ingredients are the "leftovers." Connoisseurs will know, of course. But they are aware that leftovers dishes—many of them most elegant—*require* that the principal ingredient be previously cooked.

Makes you "feel poor"

Among the uninitiated, the only reason for leftovers cooking is to save on food money. They're unaware of the other excellent reasons. Especially when income is reduced, they're blocked from using leftovers because it reminds them of reduced circumstances. But the feeling is never justified.

Some of the most ardent devotees of leftovers cooking are upper middle-class, what most people think of as "rich."

Laziness

I mention this only to say that I don't believe most savers-yet-wasters are lazy. If they were, they wouldn't take the trouble of saving leftovers in the first place.

Force of habit

All of us tend to do the same things over-and-over. If we are in the habit of throwing out "saved" leftovers, we continue to do it. But if anything can help savers-yet-wasters out of the dull rut of repetition, it's this cookbook's recipes and method for finding the needed recipe right away.

Lack of a clear concept

Much gets in the way of a clear concept of leftovers cooking. For one thing, the word "leftovers" is used in several different ways. Most of the time it means once-cooked foods saved in the refrigerator. Sometimes it includes foods that haven't been used up, cooked or uncooked. Some food writers even include pantry staples such as spaghetti and spices.

Most confusing is the "recipe" aspect. Regular cooking starts with a recipe, or a remembered recipe, and matches foods and seasonings to it. But leftovers cooking is the opposite. It starts with the foods left over. The problem has always been how to match them to useful recipes.

In the past, savers-yet-wasters have been told: "All it takes is a little imagination." But that doesn't help. Besides, it isn't true. Imagination, all by itself, can accomplish little. First, the cook must have experience of leftovers cooking and a clear concept of it. Then, and only then, can imagination be useful.

Chapters 2 and 3 develop a clear concept. They show how to take saved leftovers and match them to useful recipes. For the first time, leftovers cooking can begin to make sense even to the novice cook.

Chapters 2 and 3 do not deal with *the whole* of leftovers cooking which also encompasses deliberately creating once-cooked ingredients in planned amounts for recipes that call for them. This aspect of leftovers cooking is also hugely important and is addressed in Chapter 4.

Dealt with exclusively in the next two chapters are the unplanned, chance leftovers in chance amounts.

Chapter 2

THE CHIEF CHALLENGE
—cooking with chance leftovers in chance amounts

Using leftovers saved in the refrigerator often calls for changing *the form, the texture, the seasonings,* and sometimes even *the color or colors.* At least the form and texture should be changed. Not always, of course, but usually. The ideal is to aim for an entirely new dish having little resemblance to any from which the leftovers were saved. Which of the ingredients are twice-cooked and twice-served should remain the cook's secret unless he or she wishes to reveal it.

That, in essence, is the chief challenge. As exciting as it is, it's not easy at first for the novice or those with little experience in cooking with leftovers. But the more one learns, the easier it becomes.

So let's begin. You open the refrigerator and find several foods saved from one or more meals in varying amounts. Can you combine them successfully, changing the forms and textures? Do they call for or require changing the seasonings? Can you add other ingredients to create an appetizing new dish as tasty, if not tastier, than those from which they were saved? What you can do depends on the specifics—the actual leftovers and amounts, and number of servings required.

Getting down to specifics

This chapter provides 4 leftovers "case histories." Each deals with foods found in the refrigerator at different times. A recipe narration gives the new dish created with them. As you read, notice how the forms and textures change when combined with added ingredients and seasonings and cooked anew.

Leftovers Case History #1

▶ 1½ cups beef stew with a few whole white onions
▶ 2 wings and a leg from baked chicken
▶ 2 cups cooked noodles with sour cream sauce
▶ ½ cup cooked sliced carrots

One particular evening, I found the above leftovers in the refrigerator, saved from two previous meals. What to do with them is the classic problem faced by all who cook. When you start with the food, instead of a recipe, how do you match a recipe to the food? To begin with, one must be familiar with the types of dishes (described in the next chapter) that lend themselves to leftovers cooking. Several types of dishes could have been made with the above leftovers, but I decided on this one:

SPECIAL BEEF STROGANOFF

In a large skillet, I melted:
   2 tablespoons butter

and quickly stirred into it:
   2 tablespoons flour

I cooked 1 minute, then blended in:
   1 teaspoon tomato paste

Then, after dissolving a beef bouillon cube in boiling water, I added, stirring constantly, until sauce was thick and smooth:
   1 cup beef bouillon

I let simmer, just barely, while in another skillet, I melted:
   2 tablespoons butter

and sautéed:
   1 small onion, chopped
   1 clove garlic, minced

As soon as softened, in about 3 minutes, I added:
   8 to 10 medium mushrooms, sliced

and let cook for another 3 minutes. Meanwhile, I boned the chicken and diced the meat, which amounted to about ⅔ cup. I also cut the beef from the stew into smaller pieces so that both meats were roughly the same in size. Next, I blended into the sauce mixture:
   ▶ **the leftover stew sauce**

and stirred in the onion/mushroom mixture, and added:
   ▶ **the diced leftover meats**
   ▶ **the leftover cooked carrots**
   ▶ **the leftover noodles in sour cream sauce**

After stirring well, I let simmer to heat thoroughly for another 5 minutes. Just before serving, I added, a spoonful at a time:
   ½ cup sour cream

I served my Stroganoff in a warmed casserole dish, garnished with dabs of additional sour cream and sprinkled with parsley. It made 4 servings.

The recipe I used to help me make the above dish was for Beef Stroganoff, given in the beef section. I did not follow it exactly, which is why I called my Stroganoff "special." It did not call for my leftover chicken and carrots, although I included them because they blend well with the other ingredients. But the recipe nevertheless told me an important part of what to do with my leftovers—what fresh ingredients to add and combine with them, and how to cook. The method for quickly locating helpful recipes to use with typical leftovers is the subject of Chapter 3.

Leftovers Case History #2

▶ 1 leg, thigh, wing, and ¼ breast baked chicken
▶ 2 small baked pork chops, breaded
▶ 1 cup cooked cauliflower flowerets

This set of leftovers would go well in a casserole, but there are 8 other major types of dishes that can be made with them. With typical leftovers, the choice of what to make is frequently large. In this instance, with the help of a recipe for Hong Kong Pork, given in the pork section, I decided on this dish:

STIR FRIED PORK

Because the cooking goes rapidly, I assembled and prepared all of the ingredients in advance:

▶ the leftover pork, bread crumbs removed, and cut into thin strips
▶ the leftover chicken, boned and skinned and cut into same size strips
1 medium green pepper, seeds and membrane removed, and cut into strips
2 ribs celery, cut into diagonal slices
8 medium mushrooms, sliced
3 scallions, sliced
1 medium stalk fresh broccoli, cut into flowerets and 1-inch tender stem pieces; parboiled in salt water; drained; and held under running water for 1 or 2 minutes

Then in a mixing bowl, I combined:
2 tablespoons soy sauce
½ teaspoon sugar
1 tablespoon plus 1 teaspoon cornstarch

Added the pork/chicken strips and tossed to coat thoroughly.

In my wok (I could have used my skillet), I heated:
2 tablespoons peanut oil

When almost smoking, I added and stir fried over a medium heat for 1 minute:
1 clove garlic, crushed
2 thin slices ginger root, minced

I then discarded the garlic and added the broccoli, green pepper, celery, mushrooms, and scallions and stir fried for about 1 minute. I removed this vegetable mixture from the wok; then stir fried the pork/chicken strips in it for 1 minute. I put back the vegetable mixture and added:

▶ the leftover cauliflower
1 cup chicken broth
1 tablespoon soy sauce
1 tablespoon sherry
1 teaspoon sesame oil

and quickly brought to a boil. I reduced the heat, covered and cooked for about 2 minutes.

In a bowl, I mixed:
1½ tablespoons cornstarch
⅓ cup cold water

and added to wok and stirred until the sauce thickened. I served it immediately over hot white rice, to the 4 of us for dinner that night.

This dish took only about half an hour to prepare. Best of all, with such a dish no one ever thinks of "leftovers." The dish is accepted as new and different, unconnected with any other. That's never the case when leftovers are merely reheated and served again.

V

Leftovers Case History #3

▶ 1 cup shrimp au gratin with mushrooms
▶ ¾ cup cooked peas
▶ ¼ cup stringbeans, french cut
▶ 2 tablespoons tomato sauce

Faced with the above leftovers and little else in the way of a main ingredient on a day I wanted to prepare something special for dinner, my mind went blank. The shrimp was hardly enough to build a dish around. But in checking through my leftovers seafood recipes, one reminded me that I had an uncooked codfish fillet in the freezer. The recipe, now esconced in the seafood section, helped me make the following:

SEAFOOD-STUFFED EGGPLANT

To start, I placed in a heavy plastic food bag and immersed in cold water:

the uncooked codfish fillet

While it was thawing, with a sharp knife, I halved lengthwise, and removed and reserved the pulp from:

2 large eggplants

The shells, ¼-inch thick, I blanched in slightly salted water for 5 minutes; then drained, cut sides down, on paper towels.

Then, in a large skillet, I melted:

3 tablespoons butter

and sautéed for 3 to 4 minutes:

¼ cup chopped green pepper
¼ cup chopped scallions

together with the reserved eggplant pulp. With reduced heat, I cooked these vegetables, covered, for another 5 minutes.

In a small covered skillet, I gently poached the fish fillet 2 or 3 minutes in:

1 tablespoon butter
2 teaspoons finely chopped shallots
¼ cup dry white wine

Meanwhile, I cooked according to package directions:

1 cup instant rice

and added it to the vegetables in the large skillet together with:

▶ **the diced leftover shrimp with mushrooms**
▶ **the leftover peas**
▶ **the leftover stringbeans**
▶ **the leftover tomato sauce**

and cooked, covered, for 1 minute. Then, added the fish fillet, flaked and enough of the poaching liquid to moisten; and carefully and thoroughly mixed all together.

Next, I placed the eggplant shells in a lightly greased shallow baking dish, sprinkled them with salt and pepper, and piled in the fish/vegetable mixture, mounding the top. Next, I combined:

⅓ cup butter, melted
¾ cup bread crumbs
⅓ cup grated Parmesan cheese

and sprinkled the mixture over the eggplants. I baked them in a moderate 350° oven for about 15 minutes; then slid them under the broiler for 2 minutes to brown the tops. Made 4 servings.

I succeeded admirably in preparing "something special" for dinner that night. Stuffed vegetables are a type of dish that can do wonders to glamourize many kinds and combinations of leftovers in a relatively short time. Not only do they taste unusually delicious, they look exceptionally great when you serve them.

Leftovers Case History #4

- ▶ 3 large slices leftover meatloaf
- ▶ 1½ cups cooked cubed, unseasoned eggplant
- ▶ 1½ cups cooked rice
- ▶ ¾ cup tomato soup with milk

Meatloaf is one of the few leftovers that can be just as delicious reheated and served again. Even so, it's often desirable, for one reason or another, to create a new dish with it, making any resemblance to the original meatloaf disappear. This is what I did, with the help of portions of a recipe for Moussaka, located in the beef section:

MEATLOAF MOUSSAKA

In a large skillet, I melted:
   **1 tablespoon margarine
   and crumbled into it:**
- ▶ **the leftover meatloaf slices**

I stirred quickly for 2 or 3 minutes, then removed from the heat and reserved the meat. Next, I melted in the skillet:
   2 tablespoons margarine

and added:
   **1 large onion, chopped
   1 clove garlic, minced**

I cooked until onions were transparent, about 5 to 6 minutes. Then added:
   **10 or 12 mushrooms, sliced
   2 small zucchini, sliced
      ¼-inch thick
   1 teaspoon basil
   2 tablespoons chopped parsley**

I covered and simmered gently for about 5 minutes, stirring occasionally. Next, I added:
   **1 can (16 oz.) imported plum
   tomatoes, gently crushed
   and drained**
- ▶ **the leftover eggplant**

and simmered gently for another 5 minutes.

Next, I spread on the bottom of an 11- by 7-inch baking pan:
- ▶ **the leftover cooked rice**

Over the rice layer, I layered the reserved crumbled meat; then spooned the vegetable mixture over it.

Then I made a topping. In a saucepan, I melted:
   2 tablespoons margarine

Blended in, until smooth:
   3 tablespoons flour

Cooked for 1 minute, stirring constantly. I gradually added:
- ▶ **the leftover tomato soup
   ½ teaspoon salt
   Dash freshly grated nutmeg**

Brought almost to a boil and then removed from the heat and allowed it to cool a bit. Then I stirred in:
   **½ cup ricotta cheese (for which
      I could have substituted
      cottage cheese)
   2 medium eggs, beaten**

I spread this cheese sauce evenly over the vegetable layer. Baked in preheated 375° oven for 30 minutes. Then, I slid it briefly under the broiler to brown, and then let stand for 15 minutes. It made 6 servings for the four of us; two came back for second servings.

The leftovers cooking illustrated by this case history and the others is only "leftovers cooking" to the cook. Family and friends who eat it make no such distinction, unless you tell them. As far as they are concerned, the array of leftovers dishes you add to your cooking repertoire is just being a "good cook."

Discussion

It's obvious that leftovers cooking with chance leftovers in chance amounts is the reverse of regular cooking. Each case history starts with the foods left over instead of a recipe. Not obvious is how the new dishes incorporating the leftovers were created. The recipe narrations give end results, not how achieved. Not apparent is how the added ingredients and seasonings were selected to combine with the leftovers.

Experienced cooks will notice that parts of the narrations are very familiar. That's because they're portions of regular, and even famous recipes. They're the parts calling for the added ingredients and seasonings, and directions for how to cook them.

Other portions of the recipe narrations, however, are not familiar. We seldom see recipes calling for two kinds of meat, as in case histories #1 and #2. Beef and chicken, and pork and chicken, are excellent together, but both in one dish is too expensive for most food budgets. In leftovers cooking, however, they save money in addition to tasting great.

In other words, leftovers cooking sometimes calls for innovating—doing what the precise recipe prescriptions seldom call for. Virtually always, nevertheless, portions of certain leftovers recipes can be followed to help create new dishes. The trick is to find and use the one, or ones, that help you decide what to do with your chance leftovers of the moment.

Chapter 3

METHOD FOR FINDING THE RIGHT RECIPES

Trying to match recipes to leftovers by looking through cookbooks is often futile. It's like hunting for a needle in a haystack.

The sure and easy way is a short cut, a creative leap. It begins with the cook asking him or herself: "What type of dish do I want to make with my leftovers?" The specific leftovers must, of course, be taken into account. Some lend themselves to just one or two types of dishes but many can be used in a wide variety. The type of dish you decide on reduces the number of recipes to consider to one single type and, as we shall see, puts the useful recipes instantly at your fingertips. But first, you must be familiar with the various types.

The 9 Major Recipe Types

Out of the thousands of recipes in cookbooks, the ones that lend themselves to leftovers cooking can be grouped into just 9 major types of dishes:

1. **Casseroles**
2. **Sauced Combination Dishes**
3. **Stuffed Vegetables**
4. **Pies, Tarts, Turnovers & Quiches**
5. **Pancakes, Crêpes & Fritters**
6. **Eggs & Soufflés**
7. **Soups**
8. **Croquettes & Hash**
9. **Salads**

Not all first-rate leftovers recipes fit into these 9 major types. But since most do, fixing them firmly in mind makes leftovers easy to relate to the right recipes. To aid the eye, and the mind, we've also designed a symbol for each major type of dish and have placed the appropriate symbol next to each recipe.

 ## CASSEROLES

The casserole is a magic dish. It's just as magical today as it's been for centuries. Famous for its economy and convenience, it's the original "one-dish meal." It readily lends itself to combinations of meat, poultry, or fish with vegetables and rice, pasta, or potatoes in a simmering sauce or gravy, and all variations of them.

The one-dish meal aspect is highlighted by the casserole doing double duty as a baking dish in the oven and serving dish on the table. Typically, casserole dishes have slightly arched lids that fit snugly on squat vessels with bulging sides with handles. The variety of shapes available, however, are equally serviceable. Casserole utensils are of earthenware, glazed china, glass, or metal, and they range in size from deep enough to hold a chicken or pot roast to quite shallow. The minimum number of utensils to keep on hand for casserole cooking is 3—large and deep, medium deep and shallow.

The utensil and the ways in which it is used make it supreme for leftovers cooking. Recipes for casseroles frequently call for low baking heats of 300° to 350° and ingredients that are quick-cooking and precooked. Recipes that include rice, for instance, usually call for precooked rice. The low baking heat and tight utensil allows the different flavors of the various ingredients to blend well, so well that it's difficult to put together a "wrong" combination. It's possible, to be sure, to put tasteless combinations together; also, combinations that are too strongly flavored, especially those using, for example, cauliflower, broccoli, or liver. But the casserole recipes in this cookbook avoid these extremes and call for only delicious combinations.

Au Gratin Casseroles

"Au gratin" in the United States is usually associated with cheese. But it may also refer to a light but thorough topping or coating of fresh or dry bread crumbs, which is the origin of the term. Crushed dry cereals, cracker crumbs, or finely ground nuts are among other possible toppings. These, as well as cheese, are usually baked or broiled until brown, adding to the appetizing appearance when served, as well as enhancing flavor and taste.

Escalloped or Layered Casseroles

Some casserole recipes call for using principal ingredients, such as sliced chicken and sliced potatoes, covered with sauce and possibly a topping of cheese, in repeated layers that preserve the ingredients' shapes and textures. The layers can be two or three or as many as appropriate.

One of the best known of such dishes is one we think of as Italian. It's lasagne layered with ground beef, tomato sauce and Italian cheese. From Greece comes Moussaka—a casserole combination of layered lamb, eggplant, tomatoes, and cheese.

 SAUCED COMBINATION DISHES

Although casseroles of course have sauces, "Sauced Combination Dishes" are quite different. They're usually cooked in a skillet, wok, or dutch oven and then served *over* pasta or rice, instead of being combined with it. In addition, the ingredients and seasonings are often different and give these dishes highly characteristic flavors and tastes. Among them, reduced to simplest terms, are:

Curry:	the flavor can vary from fiercely hot to mild and can be developed in a variety of bases.
Barbecue:	spicy and distinctly American.
À La King:	a white sauce with the distinctive flavors of mushrooms and pimiento.
Italian:	hearty flavor, usually with tomatoes, garlic, and wine predominating
French:	the soul of French cooking is an infinite variety of white and stock-based sauces, often combining wine.
Chinese:	predominant is the soy sauce ingredient and the stir fry method of cooking.

STUFFED VEGETABLES

Although they are not "quickie" dishes, it's well worth the cook's effort to hollow out such vegetables as peppers, tomatoes, eggplants, cabbage, onions, winter squash, and even potatoes, to stuff with leftover food combinations. Indeed, starting with leftovers, instead of from scratch, saves preparation time and effort. Most recipes for stuffed vegetables call for precooked stuffed ingredients because the vegetable containers or shells cook faster.

Container vegetables take on novel textures and tastes that contrast nicely with the stuffed ingredients. Never eaten, of course, are the container shells of winter squash. But all, without exception, look glamourously attractive when served. Stuffed vegetable dishes are a great addition to any cook's repertoire.

PIES, TARTS, TURNOVERS, & QUICHES

What these four "naturals" for leftovers have in common is pie crust which is also the reason that some cooks are reluctant to try them. They have the notion that making good pie crust is "too hard." It isn't, but for those not brave enough to make pie crust from scratch, excellent packaged mixes and ready-to-bake frozen pie shells are available.

Pies, tarts and turnovers—like casseroles—can be filled with combinations of meat and poultry, vegetables, and starches such as rice and potatoes. Their pie crust containers contribute, of course, their own characteristic flavor and texture. Also, their sauces are thicker. Quiche, the queen of all pies, lends its egg-milk sauce and seasonings beautifully to combining with minced leftover meats and vegetables, and is deceptively easy to make.

No reason exists for anyone, including the beginning cook, not to add pies, tarts, turnovers, and quiches to his or her array of leftovers surprises. They're so mouth-watering that nobody can resist them.

That's also true of egg rolls, pinwheels, and empanadas, included in this "pies" category because they are also made with pastry crust.

PANCAKES, CRÊPES, & FRITTERS

These are "batter and fry" dishes. They're ideal for either minced leftovers combined with the batter or as filler when rolled or folded after frying. The batter is extremely simple to mix, and being heavy with egg it fries quickly. Fritter batter varies, of course, depending on whether to be pan-fried or deep-fat fried.

Crêpes, the most elegant of pancakes, are also remarkably easy to prepare. They can be made at your leisure, too, and frozen for future use. Some people prefer once-frozen to fresh-made crêpes. Depending on the leftovers and seasonings, they can be served as appetizers, the main meal, or dessert.

Pancakes, crêpes, and fritters are so delicately delicious that they really are very special treats.

XI

EGGS & SOUFFLÉS

Eggs are maids of all culinary work, including enhancing leftovers. Almost unlimited variations of leftover meats, vegetables, or fish may accompany, fold into, or fill eggs that are fried, poached, boiled, and scrambled. In omelettes, leftovers may be mixed into the egg batter, Italian style, before going into the skillet, or added to fill the omelette when cooked.

Soufflés have been called "the great glamourizers for leftover foods." The basics of a soufflé are a thick white sauce, mixed with minced or ground meat and/or vegetables, with the stiffly beaten egg whites folded into the sauce, baked, and quickly served.

Soufflés have the reputation for being temperamental. They're not really, if made right. They can even be made ahead of time, refrigerated and served later, or frozen for 2 or 3 days. And even if a soufflé "falls," it still can be delicious. It can be turned out onto a platter or left in the dish and served as, say, a savory pudding or casserole. If not called a "soufflé" no one will know it has fallen.

Included in this eggs and soufflés category are timbales, mousses, puddings, and custards. They, too, are equally delicious and easy to prepare.

SOUPS

No type of dish lends itself better to most leftovers than soups. First, there's the making of soup stocks from what are more aptly called "discards." We mean bones of beef, veal, and lamb, chicken and turkey carcasses, vegetable leavings like carrot peelings, leaves and ends of celery, and so forth. All can be simmered for hours in a slow cooker to make various kinds of stocks to save in the refrigerator or freezer for future use.

Next, soups lend themselves to all manner of leftovers that are equally suitable for other styles of dishes—casseroles, stuffed vegetables, and so forth. But soups are the perfect choice for leftovers that do not lend themselves to other types of dishes—casserole leftovers, a bland mish-mash or those with strong flavors, such as curry. Puréed through a strainer or in a food processor to make thick soups, nothing on a cold winter's day is more hearty and satisfying.

CROQUETTES & HASH

People of a certain age have memories of mother standing at an old-fashioned meat grinder and turning the handle while feeding it with the remains of the Sunday roast of ham, chicken, lamb, or beef, together with various vegetables and seasonings. Sometimes the ground ingredients were put through the grinder again to mince them. The preparations were for either croquettes or hash, two of the longstanding ways of using up leftovers.

Modern appliances make preparing croquettes and hash easier and faster, and they're still great leftovers dishes. True, croquettes made with ground or minced meat combined with thick sauce, must first be chilled before breading and deep-fat frying. The delicious result is well worth the time. Hash can be made in infinite varieties and served in a number of ways. Both belong in everyone's leftovers repertoire for their old-fashioned goodness and flavor.

Also included under "croquettes and hash," and bearing the same symbol, are loaves, patties, and balls.

SALADS

Salads are perhaps the easiest, most straightforward way of using many kinds of leftovers. Experienced cooks skilled with leftovers automatically seize opportunities to do so and don't require "recipes" so much as reminders. Beginning cooks nevertheless will find the recipes provided extremely helpful.

OTHERS

This is a special category, a catch-all section, for highly useful leftovers recipes that range from the everyday to the extraordinary, yet do not fit easily into the 9 major types of dishes.

Pin-pointing the recipe(s) that help in creating leftovers dishes

Knowing the 9 major types of leftovers dishes makes it possible to narrow down the useful recipes. Selecting the portion or portions of them to follow completes the creative leap.

Remember, it begins with asking: "What type of dish do I want to make with my leftovers?" Taking them into account, you choose from among the 9 major types.

For instance, supposing that chief among your leftovers is chicken meat, and that you decide to use it in making a stuffed vegetable dish. You look in the chicken section table of contents, see the page numbers for the five "Stuffed Vegetables" recipes, and turn to these pages. Each recipe has its symbol to make it easy to locate. Moreover, since the meat in many meat recipes is interchangeable, other useful stuffed vegetable recipes are in other ingredient sections. From among the recipes, you select the one or ones with suitable portions to follow. They tell you what fresh ingredients to add, how to combine them, and how to cook. In this way, you pin-point the recipes that help you create original dishes of your own.

SUMMARY OF THE CREATIVE LEAP

1. **Starts with deciding what type of dish to make with your leftovers.**

2. **Continues by locating recipes for that particular type under the heading of the chief leftover ingredient, or similar ingredient.**

3. **Ends with selecting the portion(s) of the recipes to follow in creating your own new dish.**

Chapter 4

THE OTHER CREATIVE CHALLENGE
—cooking with planned leftovers
in planned amounts

This chapter deals with another aspect of leftovers cooking—*planned* instead of *chance* leftovers. Although they share certain things in common, they're altogether different in origin and main purpose.

The principal reason for cooking with planned leftovers is purely culinary, although the side benefits are also important. By "purely culinary" we mean for the sake of making a widely acclaimed recipe that calls for a prescribed amount of a once-cooked principal ingredient. In famed Turkey Divan, for instance, it's the delectable turkey meat. The recipe requires it to be once-cooked. Often, too, it's first served as Roast Turkey.

In other words, you cannot serve some of the best-tasting dishes from Europe, the Near and Far East, and the Americas without a twice-cooked principal ingredient. The method of cooking and the ingredients called for dictate it and are from the world of *haute cuisine.*

These wonderful dishes are also highly practical in terms of time, effort, and money if prepared in the right way. To attempt to make Turkey Divan from scratch the same day, for example, would be impractical in most households. It takes too much time and effort and can be too expensive. But if the turkey is roasted for one meal and sufficient meat is deliberately saved for a second meal of Turkey Divan, time and effort and money are all saved.

Some of the saving is also due to buying in quantity. Especially when purchasing poultry, a large chicken or moderate-size turkey usually has a lower cost per pound than two smaller fowls of the same total weight. And when one deliberately plans to have meat left over, it's less costly to take advantage of "specials" on beef, pork, lamb, and veal to roast the first time and plan to have enough left over for a second, even gourmet meal. Thus, without being extravagant with money, you can eat extravagantly. It's easier to have that "special dinner" and remain within the food budget. All you need to do is to plan your leftovers.

Using the recipes as "planners"

All of us tend to resist advice to "plan ahead." Making plans, especially when we're busy, seems a lot of effort. But leftovers recipes, themselves, can be handy "planners." What makes them different, let's remember, is that each calls for a once-cooked principal ingredient. That's useful in planning.

As a practical matter, because meat is expensive, cooks don't always start with menus. Frequently, they start with what's most affordable. If there's a "special" on a certain kind or cut of meat, that's what they're apt to buy.

Let's suppose there's a "special" on loin of pork. It's an excellent idea then, to consult the leftovers recipes under "Pork." They act as a check list to remind you of the wonderful dishes that can be made with it. The recipe you select tells you how much pork you will need for it. Then you buy the amount you need for, let's say, Roast Loin of Pork for the first meal, plus the amount to make the second wonderful dish. You must remember, of course, that cooked meat weighs less. If the leftovers recipe calls for one pound of cooked meat, you will need more than one pound extra of uncooked meat.

Used this way, leftovers recipes help you "plan ahead" fairly effortlessly, and also save you time and money.

Chapter 5

SECRET INGREDIENTS FOR SUCCESS IN SERVING LEFTOVERS DISHES

As noted in Chapter 1, mental blocks can inhibit a cook from attempting to make leftovers dishes. Some of the same mental blocks, unfortunately, can also keep people from fully appreciating leftovers dishes when they eat them, no matter how delicious they actually are. We therefore offer 5 basic rules for ensuring acceptance of your creations. The rules simply cater to human nature.

Never Announce that Your Dish is Made With "Leftovers."

Unless your family or friends are sophisticated about cooking, "leftovers" for many people has negative connotations. It shouldn't, but it does. This barrier to enjoyment is entirely psychological. You will do your family and guests a favor if you let the "leftovers" remain the cook's secret. That way, they're free to enjoy your creations as much as they should enjoy them.

Always Give a Name to Your Dish Created With Chance Leftovers.

All dishes and recipes have names. That's true everywhere. But the dishes you create with chance leftovers don't have names until you name them. You can borrow names from the recipes in this cookbook or combine names to form new ones. Two words that particularly lend themselves to naming dishes are "supreme" and "surprise," as in "Casserole Supreme" and "Seafood Surprise." If the dish doesn't suggest a descriptive name, you can even use the names of states, countries, presidents, and so forth.

Always Make the Serving Setting Attractive.

Don't let down because your leftovers dish is inexpensive. Use the usual place settings, serving dishes, and table decorations. If the leftover dish is a casserole, use an attractive utensil that looks good on the table. Heighten attraction with color. A slice of tomato, a wedge of lemon, a sprig of parsley, or even a crisp lettuce leaf, adds a touch of color that enhances appetite appeal and sets the salivary juices flowing.

Avoid Making the Same Type of Leftovers Dish Again and Again.

If you're a novice at using leftovers creatively, you may have to repeat the same type of dish until you've mastered it. But with experience, there's no excuse for limiting yourself to just casseroles or soups, for instance. Your spouse and/or children detect the pattern; you telegraph "It's leftovers again." No matter how good and delicious the dish, it can lessen their enjoyment.

For Both "Planned" and "Chance" Leftovers, Include All 9 Major Types of Dishes in Your Repertoire.

Variety is the spice of successful cooking. Switch frequently from one type of dish to another. Also, space leftovers days apart from the meal or meals from which saved. Most leftovers don't have to be used up on successive days. There's no need to serve roast chicken one day, chicken croquettes the next, and chicken soup the third, as good and tasty as each dish is individually. That's too much sameness of the principal ingredient. Many leftovers, including chicken, keep well in the freezer and can reappear in different guises days and even weeks apart. Interspersed with other meals, each individual dish tastes fresh and different. Any connection with other meals is sometimes forgotten even by the cook.

If you vary the types of dishes—casseroles, sauced combinations, stuffed vegetables of various kinds, pies, tarts, turnovers, quiches, pancakes, crêpes, fritters, eggs, soufflés, soups, croquettes, and hash, as well as salads, and if you vary the spacing of leftovers dishes, each is deliciously fresh.

The chef's cap symbol identifies the 101 favorite recipes of the advisory panel and the author.

► This wedge points to each of the once-cooked ingredients in all of the leftovers recipes.

▸BEEF

BEEF MOUSSAKA

3 tablespoons butter or
  margarine
1 medium onion, chopped
▶ 2 cups chopped cooked beef
2 tablespoons tomato paste
3 tablespoons dry red wine
3 tablespoons chopped parsley
⅛ teaspoon cinnamon
⅛ teaspoon nutmeg
⅛ teaspoon pepper

½ teaspoon salt
2 tablespoons flour
1 cup milk
2 egg yolks
2 medium eggplants
¼ to ⅓ cup olive oil
3 tablespoons bread crumbs
4 tablespoons plus ½ cup
  Parmesan cheese

1. In a large skillet, melt 1 tablespoon butter and sauté the onion for 5 minutes over medium heat. Add the beef, tomato paste, red wine, parsley, and the seasonings. Cook 2 to 3 minutes. Remove from heat and cool.

2. Melt 2 tablespoons butter in saucepan. Blend in flour to absorb butter, cook 2 minutes, stirring. Gradually add the milk using a whisk to keep mixture smooth. Cook, stirring constantly, until sauce begins to thicken. Beat in egg yolks; cook until thickened. Set aside to cool.

3. Cut eggplant into ½-inch slices crosswise. Brown in hot olive oil on both sides. Drain on absorbent paper until ready to assemble dish.

4. Grease a 12-inch square baking dish. Arrange layer of eggplant slices on bottom. Add ½ of the meat mixture and then ½ of the white sauce. Sprinkle 1 tablespoon bread crumbs, 4 tablespoons Parmesan cheese on top. Repeat the layers in the same order, ending with the sauce. Top final layer with 2 tablespoons bread crumbs, ½ cup Parmesan.

5. Bake 40 minutes at 375°. Makes 4 servings.

MEXICAN BEEF PIE

4 strips bacon
▶ 2 cups coarsely ground cooked
  beef
1 medium onion, sliced
½ cup seedless raisins
½ cup sliced stuffed olives
2 tablespoons chopped
  pimiento

¼ cup tomato juice
▶ 1 cup cooked corn kernels
1 teaspoon salt
¼ teaspoon pepper
2 tablespoons chopped parsley
½ cup bread crumbs
1 tablespoon butter

1. Heat oven to 350°. Sauté bacon in skillet until crisp. Crumble bacon and combine with beef in a bowl and set aside. Discard all but 2 tablespoons of the bacon fat in the skillet, and sauté onion until lightly brown. Add the beef and bacon mixture, and sauté over high heat until lightly browned.

2. Combine raisins, olives, and pimiento. In a buttered 1-quart baking dish, layer the meat mixture over the bottom; pour on the tomato juice; and then layer the raisin mixture. Top with the corn and season with salt and pepper. Sprinkle with the parsley and bread crumbs; dot with butter. Bake 20 minutes. Makes 4 servings.

BEEF CASSEROLE MACEDONIA

1 cup chopped onion
1 clove garlic, minced
2 tablespoons chopped celery
2 tablespoons olive oil
► 2 cups ground roast beef
½ teaspoon salt
¼ teaspoon pepper
2 tablespoons minced parsley
1 teaspoon chopped fresh mint

¼ teaspoon cinnamon
½ bay leaf, crushed
3½ cups potatoes, peeled and
sliced thin
¼ cup tomato sauce
► 1 cup leftover gravy, thinned
Topping (see below)
¼ cup grated Parmesan cheese

1. In a large skillet, sauté onion, garlic and celery in oil until vegetables are soft, but not brown. Add the meat; cook, stirring, over medium heat until the meat is lightly browned, about 5 minutes. Add all seasonings; blend.

2. Butter 1½-quart casserole. Layer ½ the meat mixture on the bottom of the dish; then layer ½ the potato slices. Repeat the layers.

3. Combine tomato sauce with the gravy and heat thoroughly. Pour sauce over potato mixture. Bake in preheated 350° oven for 30 minutes or until most of the liquid has been absorbed. Remove from oven.

4. Make topping; pour carefully over baking dish; sprinkle with cheese. Bake 15 minutes or until custard is set and top is lightly browned. Makes 6 servings.

Topping

2 teaspoons flour
1 cup light cream

2 egg yolks, beaten
Dash paprika

Make paste with flour and some of the cream; blend until smooth. Blend paste with remaining cream, egg yolks, and paprika.

SATURDAY NIGHT CASSEROLE

½ cup chopped green pepper
½ cup sliced onion
► 3 tablespoons bacon drippings
► 2 cups finely diced or ground,
cooked beef
¼ cup chopped parsley
2 cups (16 oz.) plum tomatoes
1 teaspoon Worcestershire sauce
► 2 cups cooked rice

1 cup canned kidney beans,
drained
1 teaspoon chili powder
½ teaspoon salt
¼ teaspoon pepper
⅛ teaspoon crumbled dried
thyme
½ cup shredded Cheddar
cheese

1. In a large skillet, sauté the green pepper and onion in hot bacon drippings until soft. Add the beef and cook, stirring frequently, until brown.

2. Combine in a large mixing bowl, the parsley, tomatoes, Worcestershire sauce, rice, and kidney beans. Season with the chili powder, salt, papper, and thyme. Add the beef mixture and blend well.

3. Put into a greased 2-quart baking dish. Bake, covered, in a preheated moderate oven (350°) for about 15 minutes. Uncover, sprinkle the cheese over all, and continue baking for 15 more minutes. Makes 4 to 6 servings.

BEEF À LA BURGUNDY

2 tablespoons butter
½ pound mushrooms, sliced
½ cup chopped onions
► 1¼ cups beef gravy
½ cup dry red wine
Dash Tabasco
2 teaspoons Worcestershire
sauce

► 3 cups cooked beef, cut in 1"
cubes
► 1 cup sliced cooked carrots
½ teaspoon salt
⅛ teaspoon pepper
► 2 cups mashed potatoes
2 egg yolks
⅛ teaspoon ground rosemary
1 tablespoon chopped parsley

1. In a large skillet, melt the butter and sauté mushrooms and onions for 5 minutes. Add gravy, red wine, Tabasco and Worcestershire sauces; simmer 5 minutes. Add the beef and carrots and simmer 3 minutes. Season with salt and pepper.

2. Combine potatoes with egg yolks and rosemary in a medium-size mixing bowl, and beat well.

3. Pour beef mixture into a 1½-quart baking dish. Mound the potato mixture around the edge of the dish as a border. Bake in a preheated 375°oven for 20 minutes or until potatoes are lightly browned. Sprinkle with parsley. Makes 4 servings.

BEEF MIROTON

8 tablespoons butter or
margarine
1 cup finely chopped onion
2 tablespoons red wine vinegar
2 tablespoons flour
1 teaspoon dried thyme
1 teaspoon tomato paste
► 1½ cups beef stock, or canned
beef bouillon, undiluted
1 bouquet garni (parsley, celery
with tops, and bay leaf)

Salt
Freshly ground black pepper
► 2 cups cooked potatoes (freshly
boiled if possible), sliced
¼-inch thick
► 8 to 12 slices lean boiled beef,
cut ¼-inch thick
½ cup dry bread crumbs
2 tablespoons finely chopped
parsley

1. Heat oven to 450°. In a small heavy frying pan over moderate heat, melt 4 tablespoons of butter. Add the chopped onions and cook, stirring frequently, until they color lightly. Pour in the vinegar and boil briskly until it completely cooks away. Turn off the heat. Add the flour and mix into the onions thoroughly. Stir in the thyme and tomato paste.

2. With a whisk, beat into this roux the beef stock and, stirring constantly, bring to a boil. When the sauce is smooth and thick, lower the heat, add the bouquet, some salt and freshly ground pepper, and cover the pan. Simmer slowly for about 20 minutes, stirring occasionally. If the sauce gets too thick, add a little more stock or, if you must, water.

3. Arrange the potato slices on a flat plate and pour 2 tablespoons of warm melted butter over them. Set aside.

4. In a shallow 9-inch casserole, spread a thin layer of sauce on the bottom; lay the slices of meat in it, letting each piece overlap slightly. Spoon the remaining sauce over the meat. Place the buttered potato slices around the meat so that they form an overlapping border. Scatter the bread crumbs over the meat and moisten with remaining 2 tablespoons of melted butter.

5. Bake in the upper third of the oven for about 10 or 15 minutes, until the sauce begins to bubble and the bread crumbs lightly brown. Before serving, slide under a hot broiler to brown the potatoes. Sprinkle lightly with parsley. Makes 4 servings.

MACARONI ROMA

2 cups elbow macaroni
1 teaspoon salt
⅛ teaspoon pepper
⅛ teaspoon oregano
⅛ teaspoon basil
▶ 2 cups diced cooked beef
1 medium red onion, sliced, separated into rings

1 cup finely diced Monterey Jack cheese
⅓ cup grated Parmesan cheese
▶ 1 cup leftover gravy mixed with 1 cup half-and-half cream
1 tomato, sliced
2 tablespoons fine dry crumbs
⅛ teaspoon thyme
1 tablespoon butter

1. Cook macaroni in boiling salted water 8 minutes or until just tender. Drain; sprinkle with mixture of salt, pepper, oregano, and basil.

2. In a 1-quart baking dish, layer ½ the macaroni, ½ the beef, ½ the onion, ½ of both cheeses, and ½ the gravy/cream mixture. Repeat the layers ending with the sauce. Loosen mixture gently with knife so sauce filters through the layers.

3. Bake 30 minutes in preheated 350° oven. Remove from oven and arrange tomato slices on top. Sprinkle with combined crumbs and thyme. Dot with butter. Bake for 10 minutes longer. Makes 6 servings.

CLASSIC SHEPHERD'S PIE

▶ 2 cups cubed cooked beef
▶ 1 cup sliced cooked carrots
▶ ½ cup sliced cooked turnips
▶ ½ cup cooked peas
▶ 1 cup cooked white onions, or a 1-lb. jar, drained
1 clove garlic, pressed

1 tablespoon chopped parsley
▶ 2 cups cooked gravy
2 teaspoons Worcestershire sauce
Salt and pepper
1 egg yolk
▶ 2 cups mashed potatoes

1. In a large saucepan, combine beef, carrots, turnips, peas, onions, garlic, and parsley. Add the gravy and Worcestershire sauce and heat thoroughly. Salt and pepper to taste. Pour into a 2-quart casserole.

2. Beat the egg yolk slightly and add to the potatoes, mixing briskly to combine and to fluff the potatoes; add salt and pepper to taste. Mound potatoes around edge of casserole.

3. Bake in a preheated hot oven (425°) about 20 minutes or until gravy bubbles and potatoes brown. Makes 4 servings.

GREEK CASSEROLE

1 medium onion, chopped
1 clove garlic, minced
2 tablespoons olive oil
▶ 3 cups ground cooked beef
2 dashes cinnamon
1 can (8 oz.) tomato sauce
Margarine
¼ cup flour
2 cups milk

½ teaspoon salt
Dash of white pepper
Nutmeg
⅓ cup grated Parmesan cheese
8 ounces small elbow macaroni
2 eggs
2 cups (8 oz.) coarsely shredded
Cheddar cheese

1. In a large skillet, sauté the onion and garlic in the oil until soft. Stir in beef, cinnamon and tomato sauce and set aside.

2. Melt 3 tablespoons margarine in saucepan and stir in flour. Gradually add the milk and cook, stirring, until thickened. Season with salt, pepper, a pinch of nutmeg and the Parmesan cheese.

3. Cook macaroni in boiling salted water 10 to 12 minutes, or until tender.* Drain well and put back in pot. Break eggs into the hot macaroni and add 2 tablespoons margarine. Stir briskly with wooden spoon until well mixed.

4. Butter a shallow 2½-quart baking dish and layer ingredients as follows: put half the macaroni in dish, all the meat, half the Cheddar, the remaining macaroni, then the white sauce (whisk again before pouring). Shake dish gently to settle white sauce. Sprinkle on remaining Cheddar, dot with margarine and sprinkle with nutmeg.

5. Bake in preheated 375° oven for 1 hour. Makes 6 to 8 servings.
*If using letfover macaroni, reheat briefly in boiling water or in a microwave oven.

CALIFORNIA CASSEROLE

2 tablespoons butter or
  margarine
⅓ cup chopped onion
¼ cup chopped celery
1 teaspoon chopped parsley
▶ 2 cups ground cooked beef
1 tablespoon prepared mustard
¼ teaspoon Worcestershire sauce
Dash Tabasco

½ teaspoon salt
▶ 2 cups cooked noodles
1 cup grated sharp Cheddar
  cheese
1 egg, beaten
¾ cup light cream
⅛ teaspoon dry mustard
⅛ teaspoon pepper

1. In a medium skillet, melt butter and sauté the onion, celery, and parsley for 5 minutes. Add the beef, prepared mustard, Worcestershire and Tabasco sauces, salt, and mix well. Cook over medium heat until thoroughly heated, about 8 minutes.

2. Arrange the noodles, cheese, and meat mixture in alternate layers in a greased 9-inch square pan, ending with the cheese as the top layer.

3. Mix egg, cream, dry mustard, and pepper. Pour mixture over layers in pan. In a preheated 350° oven, bake for 30 to 40 minutes. Makes 4 servings.

WESTERN STYLE BEEF

8 thin slices roast beef
3 tablespoons butter or
  margarine
1 cup chopped onions
¼ cup chopped celery
¼ cup chopped green pepper
2 tablespoons flour

1 cup consommé
► ¼ cup leftover roast beef gravy
½ cup tomato sauce with tomato
  bits
¾ teaspoon salt
¼ teaspoon pepper
¼ cup dry bread crumbs

1. Arrange beef slices in a lightly buttered shallow casserole, overlapping them slightly.

2. Melt 2 tablespoons of butter in a large skillet. Add the onions, celery, and green pepper, and sauté until light brown, stirring frequently. Stir in flour and cook for 2 to 3 minutes. Add consommé gradually, stirring to blend. Add gravy and tomato sauce; stir constantly until thickened. Season with salt and pepper.

3. Pour sauce over meat. Sprinkle with bread crumbs; dot with remaining butter. Bake in a 450° oven 10 to 15 minutes. Makes 4 servings.

ALPINE BEEF

2 tablespoons butter or
  margarine
2 tablespoons chopped onions
2 tablespoons chopped celery
¾ teaspoon salt
¼ teaspoon pepper
¼ teaspoon paprika
2 tablespoons flour

2 cups canned tomatoes
1 teaspoon Worcestershire sauce
► 1½ cups chopped cooked beef
► 1 cup diced cooked carrots
1 teaspoon chopped parsley
► 1 cup cooked green beans
  Cheese Puffery (see below)

1. Melt butter in a Dutch oven or a deep skillet; add onion and celery and brown lightly. Stir in flour and cook for 1 minute. Add salt, pepper, paprika, tomatoes, and Worcestershire sauce. Cook 6 to 8 minutes or until slightly thickened.

2. Add beef, carrots, parsley, and beans; cook 3 minutes.

3. Pour into a buttered 2-quart casserole. Spread Cheese Puffery dough evenly over meat mixture. Bake 20 to 25 minutes. Makes 6 servings.

Cheese Puffery

1 cup flour
1½ teaspoons baking powder
½ teaspoon dry mustard
½ teaspoon salt

2 tablespoons butter
¼ cup grated sharp (Cheddar)
  cheese
¼ cup milk

Combine flour, baking powder, mustard and salt. Cut in butter until crumbly. Add cheese and milk; blend to make dough.

EGGPLANT NIÇOISE

4 tablespoons olive oil
1 clove garlic, finely chopped
1 medium onion, chopped
1 medium eggplant, peeled and cut in chunks
1 stalk celery, chopped
2 green peppers, cored and sliced
10 pitted green olives
►1½ cups diced cooked beef
4 medium tomatoes, peeled, seeded, and chopped
1 teaspoon capers
Salt and pepper
Buttered bread crumbs

1. Heat the olive oil in a large skillet and sauté the garlic and onion until lightly brown.

2. Add eggplant, celery, green peppers and olives, and cook for 10 minutes.

3. Add the diced beef, tomatoes, capers, and seasoning.

4. Transfer to a 1-quart casserole, sprinkle with bread crumbs and bake in a moderate oven (350°) for 30 minutes. Makes 4 servings.

PICADILLO PIE

1 tablespoon olive oil
½ cup finely chopped onion
1 clove garlic, crushed
► 2 cups ground cooked beef
1 can (16 oz.) tomatoes, undrained
1 can (16 oz.) whole-kernel corn, drained
1 can (3 oz.) chopped green chillies, drained
¼ cup tomato paste
¼ cup sliced black olives
½ teaspoon dried oregano leaves
1 tablespoon fresh basil or ½ teaspoon dried
1 teaspoon salt
¼ teaspoon pepper
Cornmeal Crust (see below)

1. Heat the olive oil in a large skillet and sauté the onion and garlic for about 5 minutes. Add the beef and whisk quickly for about 8 minutes. Drain off excess fat.

2. Add the tomatoes, corn, chillies, tomato paste, olives, oregano, basil, salt, and pepper; mix well. Turn into 2-quart casserole dish.

3. Preheat oven to 425°. Make the cornmeal dough:

¾ cup yellow cornmeal
1 tablespoon flour
½ teaspoon baking powder
½ teaspoon salt
1 tablespoon sugar
1 egg, beaten
⅓ cup milk
1 tablespoon vegetable oil
1 egg yolk, beaten lightly

1. Into a medium bowl, sift the cornmeal with the flour, baking powder, salt, and sugar.

2. Make a well in the center of the dry ingredients. Add egg to milk, beating to combine; pour into well all at once. Stir quickly with fork; stir in the oil.

3. Spread dough carefully over the beef mixture; pinch edge to seal all around. Brush top lightly with egg yolk combined with 1 tablespoon water. Place in oven and bake for 15 minutes or until golden brown and bubbly. Makes 6 servings.

BEEF WITH MUSTARD SAUCE

½ cup minced onion
1 tablespoon butter or
  margarine
▶ 2 cups cooked beef cut into
  ¼-inch strips
½ teaspoon salt
¼ teaspoon pepper

1 teaspoon paprika
1 can (10½ oz.) condensed
  cream of mushroom soup
3 tablespoons sherry
1 tablespoon Dijon-style mustard
½ cup sour cream
Buttered cooked noodles

1. Sauté the onion in butter in a large skillet for 5 minutes or until tender. Add the beef and brown quickly.

2. Combine the salt, pepper, paprika, and soup in a small bowl; stir until well mixed.

3. Stir into the onions and meat in skillet. Bring to boiling; lower heat. Simmer for 5 minutes, strring occasionally.

4. Combine the sherry, mustard and sour cream; stir into mixture in skillet. Heat but do not allow to boil. Serve with buttered noodles. Makes 4 servings.

ROAST BEEF AU POIVRE

▶ 4 slices very rare roast beef,
  ½-inch thick
  Salt
2 tablespoons cracked black
  pepper
¼ pound butter, softened
4 tablespoons olive oil

½ cup sifted flour
¼ cup cognac or brandy
▶ ½ cup beef stock, fresh or
  canned
2 teaspoons lemon juice
1 tablespoon minced chives or
  parsley

1. Salt each slice of beef lightly, then firmly press as much of the pepper as you can into both sides. (The flavor of the meat will be only pleasantly aromatic.) Carefully and generously spread half the butter over the pepper encrusted slices. Refrigerate between pieces of waxed paper until ready to cook, at least 1 hour. (The longer the beef mellows the more flavor it will have.)

2. Have a serving platter and plates heating in a 250° oven before you begin cooking. Also have the other ingredients ready to use.

3. Heat the olive oil in a large frying pan until it literally begins to smoke. Quickly dip the beef slices in the sifted flour, gently shake off any excess, and cook the beef a minute or two on each side. They should acquire a lightly brown crust and be thoroughly heated through. Arrange them, each slice slightly overlapping, on the heated platter, and keep warm in the oven.

4. Pour off most of the oil in the pan; to the remainder add the cognac. Bring this to a boil over high heat, allow to boil away completely; add the beef stock. Boil rapidly for 1 or 2 minutes until it has reduced to about half. Remove the pan from the heat, add the lemon juice, minced chives or parsley, and then swirl the remaining soft butter—move the pan in a circular motion until the butter melts. Add a few pinches of salt, and pour the sauce over the beef. Serve at once. Makes 4 servings.

RUSSIAN BURGERS

4 slices bacon, diced
½ cup chopped onion
1½ tablespoons flour
¼ teaspoon paprika
¾ teaspoon salt
⅛ teaspoon pepper
1 can (10½ oz.) condensed
cream of mushroom soup

⅓ cup ketchup
1 tablespoon prepared mustard
►1½ cups chopped roast beef
½ cup sour cream
1 tablespoon chopped parsley
4 hamburger buns, split

1. In a medium skillet over moderate heat, sauté the bacon and onion until lightly browned. Blend in the flour, paprika, salt, and pepper.

2. Gradually stir in the mushroom soup, ketchup, and mustard; cook for 5 minutes over low heat until smooth. Add the meat; cook over low heat, stirring frequently until thickened.

3. Fold in the sour cream and parsley; heat, stirring gently. Spoon mixture over buns. Makes 4 servings.

ORIENTAL BEEF

¼ cup sherry
¼ cup soy sauce
1 clove garlic, crushed
½ teaspoon minced fresh ginger
► 2 cups cooked beef, cut into
2" × ⅛" pieces
5 tablespoons peanut or
vegetable oil
1½ cups diagonally sliced celery

1½ cups diagonally sliced carrots,
⅛" thick
1 green pepper, cut in strips
⅓ pound mushrooms, sliced
¼ cup sliced water chestnuts
► 1 cup beef stock, homemade or
canned
2 tablespoons cornstarch
Hot cooked rice

1. In a small mixing bowl, combine the sherry, soy sauce, garlic, and ginger until well mixed. Pour over the sliced beef in the bottom of a small, shallow baking dish, coating meat thoroughly. Cover the dish with plastic wrap and marinate in the refrigerator for 1 to 2 hours.

2. In a large skillet or wok, heat 3 tablespoons of the oil. Brown the meat, reserving the marinade. Remove and set aside.

3. Add 1 tablespoon of the oil to the skillet. Sauté the celery, carrots, and green pepper until celery turns a brighter green. Remove and set aside.

4. Add the remaining 1 tablespoon of oil to the skillet. Sauté the mushrooms until golden. Add the water chestnuts, the reserved marinade, the beef stock, and the vegetables. Bring to a boil. Reduce heat; cover and simmer for 3 minutes or until vegetables are crisp-tender.

5. Stir in the beef. Combine the cornstarch with a little cold broth until smooth; stir into the hot broth. Cook until thickened.

6. Serve over hot cooked rice. Makes 4 to 6 servings.

ITALIAN-STYLE BEEF WITH SPAGHETTI

2 tablespoons olive oil
1 large onion, thinly sliced
1 cup sliced fresh mushrooms
1 clove garlic, minced
1 green pepper, cut into strips
1 can (16 oz.) whole tomatoes, drained and cut into pieces
½ can (6 oz.) tomato paste
1 can (8 oz.) tomato sauce
1 teaspoon dried oregano
1 teaspoon dried basil

1 teaspoon chopped parsley
2 beef bouillon cubes, crushed
2 teaspoons Worcestershire sauce
▶1½ to 2 cups of chopped cooked beef
1 tablespoon butter or margarine
½ package (16 oz.) of spaghetti, cooked and drained
Parmesan cheese, grated

1. Heat the oil in large skillet and sauté the onions, mushrooms, garlic and green pepper until lightly browned.

2. Stir in tomatoes, tomato paste, tomato sauce, oregano, basil, parsley, bouillon, Worcestershire sauce, and beef. Bring to boil and simmer for 30 minutes or until thickened, stirring occasionally.

3. Adjust sauce seasoning with salt and pepper, if needed. Stir butter into hot spaghetti and keep warm. Serve stew over spaghetti; sprinkle with Parmesan cheese. Makes 4 servings.

BEEF RAGOÛT SUPREME

2 tablespoons bacon drippings
½ cup chopped onion
½ cup chopped celery
10 to 12 fresh mushrooms, sliced
1 medium clove garlic, minced
2 tablespoons flour
1 teaspoon tomato paste
¾ cup dry red wine
▶ 1 cup beef stock or bouillon
½ teaspoon thyme

2 teaspoons Worcestershire sauce
1 small jar white onions, drained
▶ ½ cup cooked green peas, or carrots, green beans, broccoli flowerets, etc.
▶ 2 cups cubed cooked beef
Salt and pepper
Cooked egg noodles
2 tablespoons chopped parsley

1. In a medium skillet, heat the bacon drippings; sauté the onions, celery, mushrooms, and garlic until tender. Transfer to saucepan. Add the flour to skillet; stir to brown lightly and cook 5 minutes.

2. Stir in the tomato paste; add the wine and beef stock while stirring briskly with a whisk until the sauce is smooth and thick. Reduce the heat, add the thyme and Worcestershire sauce, and simmer for 15 minutes.

3. Add the white onions, peas and carrots, and the cubed beef. Salt and pepper to taste. Simmer for another 15 minutes to allow the flavors to blend.

4. Ladle over cooked egg noodles, and sprinkle with parsley. Makes 4 to 6 servings.

BOILED BEEF SLICES IN HORSERADISH (Sauce Albert)

1½ tablespoons butter or margarine
1½ tablespoons flour
► 1 cup beef stock
½ cup light cream
Salt and pepper

3 tablespoons prepared horseradish
1 teaspoon dry mustard
1 teaspoon sugar
1 tablespoon vinegar
► 8 to 12 slices boiled beef, about ¼" thick

1. Melt the butter in large, deep skillet; add the flour, and stir until thickened and smooth. Slowly stir in the beef stock, then the cream. Cook over low heat without boiling, stirring frequently, until sauce begins to thicken. Remove from heat.

2. Add the salt and pepper to taste, then stir in the horseradish, mustard, sugar, and vinegar. Add the beef slices and cook only until meat is well heated, about 10 minutes. Do not allow to boil. Serve with freshly cooked boiled potatoes and carrots. Makes 4 servings.

SAUERBRATEN WITH DUMPLINGS

½ cup vinegar
► 1 cup beef gravy
► ½ cup light beef broth
8 cloves
2 bay leaves
8 gingersnap cookies
1 tablespoon sugar
½ teaspoon salt

½ teaspoon Worcestershire sauce
► 8 slices cooked beef
2 eggs, beaten
1½ cups flour
½ cup water
½ teaspoon salt
¼ teaspoon baking powder
⅛ teaspoon nutmeg

1. Combine the vinegar, beef gravy, beef broth, cloves, bay leaves, gingersnaps, sugar, salt, and Worcestershire sauce in a deep skillet; bring to a boil, stirring until smooth. Add beef slices; simmer for 15 minutes to allow flavors to blend. Remove the bay leaves.

2. Put about 2 quarts of water to boil in a wide-topped pan, with 2 teaspoons of salt added, in which to boil the dumplings.

3. Combine eggs with flour, the ½ cup of water, salt, baking powder and nutmeg, and beat together well.

4. Bring water down to a simmer; drop the dough by spoonfuls, without crowding to allow room for dumplings to expand. Quickly cover the pan, with a glass pie plate if possible, and allow to simmer undisturbed for about 10 minutes. When dumplings look fluffy, insert toothpick in center. If it comes out clean, it's done. If not, continue simmering a minute or two longer.

5. Sprinkle dumplings with buttered crumbs and serve with the hot beef slices. Makes 6 servings.

COLD BOILED BEEF ITALIAN-STYLE

▶ 8 to 12 ¼-inch thick slices of cold boiled beef or pot roast
4 medium green peppers
2 tablespoons olive oil
2 cloves garlic, pressed
2 tablespoons minced scallions

12 to 16 anchovy fillets in oil, minced but not drained
1 tablespoon red wine vinegar
Salt
½ teaspoon coarsely ground black pepper

1. Arrange cold beef slices on a large oval platter. Let stand at room temperature while preparing peppers and sauce.

2 Place green peppers over direct heat of gas or electric stove. As the side exposed to the heat scorches, turn to scorch evenly on all sides. With sharp knife and using fingers also, remove scorched skin of peppers under running cold water. Cut off stems and remove seeds and membranes. Wash peppers and pat dry on paper towels. Cut into thin strips. Arrange over meat in platter.

3. Heat oil with the garlic. Add scallions and anchovies, including oil from can. Cook, stirring, over low heat about 2 minutes. Stir in vinegar, add salt and pepper. Pour over green peppers and meat. Cool but do not over-chill. Serve as buffet-supper dish or as antipasto. Makes 4 servings.

KOWLOON BEEF

1½ tablespoons butter
▶2½ to 3 cups cubed roast beef
1 medium onion, sliced thin
1 small green pepper, cut in circles
½ teaspoon curry powder
¼ teaspoon ground ginger
⅛ teaspoon ground mace
½ teaspoon sugar
1½ teaspoons Worcestershire sauce

½ teaspoon lemon juice
½ teaspoon salt
¼ teaspoon pepper
¼ teaspoon paprika
½ cup consommé
½ cup red wine, heated
1 cup sour cream
1 tablespoon prepared horseradish
1 teaspoon minced parsley
3 cups hot fluffy cooked rice

1. Heat the butter in a large skillet until very hot; add the beef and lightly brown quickly, shaking pan frequently. Transfer the beef cubes to a 1½-quart casserole, and arrange the onion, and green pepper circles on top.

2. Add to the remaining butter in the skillet the curry powder, ginger, mace, sugar, Worcestershire sauce, lemon juice, salt, pepper, paprika, consommé, and red wine. Blend well; pour the mixture into the casserole.

3. Cover and heat in 350° oven 30 to 35 minutes. Just before serving stir in sour cream and horseradish. Sprinkle with parsley. Serve at once over rice. Makes 4 to 6 servings.

BEEF WITH SALSA VERDE

2 tablespoons finely chopped shallots or scallions
2 cloves garlic, chopped
3 anchovies, drained and finely chopped, or ½ teaspoon anchovy paste
2 tablespoons capers, drained and finely chopped
4 tablespoons finely chopped parsley

3 tablespoons strained lemon juice
4 tablespoons olive oil
Freshly ground black pepper
Salt to taste
▶ 8 to 12 slices lean cooked beef, about ¼-inch thick

Note: chop all of the sauce ingredients as finely as possible. No particular flavor should predominate, as would be the case if any of the ingredients were too coarsely minced.

1. In a small mixing bowl, combine the shallots or scallions, garlic, anchovies, capers, and parsley; moisten them with the lemon juice and olive oil. Mix gently, then season quite highly with freshly ground black pepper and more discreetly with salt, because the anchovies can be quite salty. The finished sauce should have the appearance and texture of a purée.

2. Remove the beef from the refrigerator at least an hour before serving; it will have more flavor at room temperature. Serve the sauce separately. Makes 4 servings.

CURRIED BEEF

4 tablespoons margarine
1 cup chopped onion
1 apple, peeled and chopped
4 tablespoons flour
1 tablespoon curry powder
½ teaspoon ground ginger
½ teaspoon salt

▶ 2 cups beef stock or consommé
1 cup light cream
▶ 3 cups cubed cooked beef
¼ cup seedless raisins
½ lemon, juice of
1 cup rice, cooked according to package directions

1. Melt the margarine in a Dutch oven or a large saucepan and sauté the onion and apple together until tender.

2. Add the flour, curry powder, ginger, and salt; stir until blended. Gradually add the beef stock and the cream, stirring constantly. Add the beef cubes, raisins and the lemon juice. Simmer, over very low heat, for 20 minutes to thicken and blend flavors. Warm the cream and stir in slowly.

3. Serve the curried beef on top of white fluffy rice with all or some of the following accompaniments: chutney, chopped nuts, chopped hard-boiled eggs, chopped scallions, chopped cucumber, sliced bananas, grated orange rind, crumbled bacon, raisins, and grated coconut. Makes 6 servings.

Rare roast beef

When adding rare roast beef to a sauce or drippings, keep heat low and heat very slowly to avoid toughening the meat.

BEEF STROGANOFF

6 tablespoons butter
2 tablespoons flour
1 teaspoon tomato paste
▶1½ cups beef stock, home made or canned
3 tablespoons finely chopped fresh shallots or scallions
1 medium clove garlic, finely chopped
10 to 12 fresh mushrooms, thinly sliced
½ teaspoon lemon juice

3 tablespoons finely chopped dill, or 1½ teaspoons dried dill weed
▶ 4 to 6 slices roast beef, cut in thin strips (about 2½ cups)
½ cup sour cream
Cayenne to taste
Salt to taste
1 tablespoon parsley, finely chopped
Buttered noodles

1. Melt 3 tablespoons butter in large skillet. Remove from heat to stir in 2 tablespoons flour and return pan to heat. Stir constantly until flour *(roux)* is light brown; then mix in the tomato paste, and gradually add the beef stock, stirring constantly until the sauce is thick and smooth. Let simmer over very low heat for 10 minutes.

2. In another skillet, heat the remaining 3 tablespoons of butter to sizzling. Stir in shallots and garlic. Cook slowly until soft, then add the mushrooms. Sprinkle in the lemon juice, and cook, stirring, only 3 to 4 minutes. Pour the shallots/mushroom mixture into the simmering sauce, and stir in the dill. Simmer for 5 more minutes.

3. To the hot sauce, add the strips of beef, keeping the sauce to a bare simmer. Turn the meat in the sauce until heated through; do not let it cook in the sauce.

4. Stir the sour cream, a spoonful at a time, into the simmering sauce. If sauce is too thick, add more sour cream or stock. Add the cayenne and salt, if desired; stir. Sprinkle with parsley and serve with buttered noodles. Makes 4 servings.

SLOPPY JOES

3 tablespoons butter or margarine
1 large onion, chopped
1 medium green pepper, chopped
2 cloves garlic, minced
1 tablespoon Worcestershire sauce

1½ teaspoons brown sugar
1½ teaspoons dry mustard
½ teaspoon salt
1 cup ketchup
1 teaspoon vinegar
▶ 2 cups chopped cooked beef
6 hamburger buns
Butter or margarine

1. Melt the butter in large skillet; add the onion, pepper, and garlic. Cook, stirring occasionally, for 5 minutes or until tender.

2. Add the Worcestershire sauce, brown sugar, dry mustard, salt, ketchup, and vinegar; simmer, uncovered, 10 minutes to blend flavors.

3. Add the beef and simmer until hot.

4. To serve, split the buns, spread them lightly with soft butter or margarine and toast under broiler. Spoon the hot beef sauce over the buns. Makes 5 to 6 servings.

BEEF VITE

1½ tablespoons butter
1 clove garlic, cut in half
2 onions, thinly sliced
8 to 10 mushrooms, sliced
1½ tablespoons flour
½ cup white wine

1 cup beef consommé or broth
1 teaspoon Worcestershire sauce
► 8 slices leftover roast beef,
  about ¼-inch thick
½ teaspoon paprika
1 teaspoon red wine vinegar

1. Melt the butter in a large skillet and over a medium high heat, sauté the cut garlic for 2 minutes; remove. Reduce the heat. Add the onions, mushrooms, and cook for 5 minutes; sprinkle in the flour, and stir until light brown. Carefully blend in the wine, consommé, and Worcestershire sauce, and cook slowly uncovered for 15 minutes.

2. Add meat slices and the paprika. Simmer gently about 10 minutes. Do not let the sauce boil. Just before serving, stir in the vinegar. Serve with rice or buttered noodles. Makes 4 servings.

CLASSIC STUFFED EGGPLANT

4 small to medium eggplants
¼ cup olive oil
1 medium yellow onion,
  chopped
1 clove garlic, minced
►1½ to 2 cups chopped cooked
  beef
► 1 to 1½ cups cooked rice
½ teaspoon dried basil
¼ teaspoon dried marjoram
Pinch of dried thyme

2 to 4 tablespoons minced fresh
  parsley
½ cup tomato sauce
2 tablespoons tomato paste
Salt and freshly ground black
  pepper to taste
► ¾ cup beef broth, or water
3 tablespoons grated sharp
  cheese
3 tablespoons dried bread
  crumbs
3 tablespoons melted butter

1. Cut eggplants in half lengthwise. Do not peel. Brush cut sides with olive oil. Set halves, cut side up, on broiling pan and broil about 5 inches from flame for about 4 to 5 minutes, or until very brown. Remove and cool until able to handle. Using a sharp knife, scoop out the insides of each half, leaving a shell about ¼-inch thick. Chop and reserve the scooped out pulp. Place the shells in shallow baking dish.

2. In a large skillet, heat the olive oil and sauté the onions and garlic, stirring, until onion is limp. Add the eggplant pulp and cook a few minutes longer.

3. Remove from heat; stir in chopped beef, rice, basil, marjoram, thyme, parsley, tomato sauce and tomato purée; season with salt and pepper; blend well.

4. Mound stuffing into the eggplant shells. Pour the broth into the bottom of the pan and cover with aluminum foil. Place in a preheated 350° oven and bake for about 35 minutes. Remove cover; sprinkle surfaces with grated cheese and bread crumbs and drizzle with melted butter. Bake another 15 minutes until lightly brown. Makes 6 to 8 servings.

MEXICAN FIESTA PEPPERS

4 large green peppers
¼ cup olive oil
1 medium onion, chopped
¼ cup canned tomato paste
2 cloves garlic, minced
3 teaspoons chili powder
1 teaspoon salt

1 teaspoon oregano
¼ cup finely chopped peanuts
▶ 2 cups ground cooked beef
2 teaspoons flour
½ cup vegetable oil
1 can (16 oz.) red beans, heated
2 tomatoes, cut in wedges

1. Cut top off each green pepper. Discard seeds and pulp. Parboil peppers for 5 minutes in a saucepan with enough salted boiling water to cover. Drain and let cool.

2. Heat the olive oil in a skillet; add the onions, tomato paste, garlic, chili powder, salt, oregano, and peanuts. Sauté mixture over low heat, stirring constantly, for 5 minutes. Add the ground cooked beef and cook for 3 minutes longer.

3. Stuff peppers with mixture and lightly sprinkle with flour. Heat the vegetable oil in a Dutch oven or skillet. Fry the peppers in the oil, turning them carefully once, until browned on all sides.

4. Then, cover; cook slowly for 15 minutes. Put peppers in a ring on a serving platter. Heap hot red beans in the center; garnish with tomato wedges. Makes 4 servings.

STUFFED WHOLE CABBAGE

1 medium green cabbage
1 tablespoon butter or
  margarine
¼ cup minced onion
¼ cup minced green pepper
¼ pound pork-sausage meat
▶ 1 cup chopped cooked beef
2 tablespoons fresh bread
  crumbs
▶ 1 cup cooked rice

½ teaspoon salt
Dash pepper
¼ teaspoon sage
1 clove garlic, minced
1 egg, beaten
1 tablespoon tomato paste
1 carrot, pared and sliced
1 onion, thinly sliced
2 bacon slices
2 cups canned tomatoes

1. Simmer the whole cabbage for 5 minutes in boiling salted water to cover. Then, plunge the cabbage into cold water; drain well.

2. Melt butter in small skillet and sauté the minced onion, green pepper, and the sausage meat until tender, about 10 minutes. Toss in a bowl with the chopped beef, bread crumbs, cooked rice, salt, pepper, sage, garlic; mix in egg and tomato paste.

3. In bottom of 3-quart casserole, spread carrot and onion slices; on them arrange 2 lengths of string (to be used for tying cabbage). With knife, cut a 3-inch round out of the center of the drained cabbage to about 2-inches from the bottom. Press stuffing into cavity; place cabbage in casserole.

4. Top cabbage with bacon slices; with string, tie head together firmly, pulling leaves over stuffing. Around cabbage, pour tomatoes.

5. Cover casserole; bake 1½ hours in 400° oven. Serve in casserole with cabbage cut into wedges. Makes 6 servings.

STUFFED ZUCCHINI RIALTO

6 large zucchini or summer
  squash
1 tablespoon vegetable oil
  mixed with olive oil
½ cup chopped onion
¼ cup chopped mushrooms
1 clove garlic, chopped
▶ 1 cup cooked rice

▶1½ cups ground cooked beef
¼ cup chopped parsley
½ teaspoon salt
⅛ teaspoon pepper
1 egg, beaten
4 tablespoons Parmesan cheese
2 cups tomato sauce

1. Slice the zucchini or summer squash lengthwise. Scoop out the pulp leaving a ½-inch shell. Then, drop into boiling salted water for 5 minutes to parboil; drain. Chop the pulp and reserve.

2. Heat the oil in medium size skillet. Sauté onions, mushrooms, zucchini pulp, and garlic for 5 minutes. Add rice, beef, parsley and salt and pepper. Stir briskly; remove from heat, and blend in the egg and 2 tablespoons of Parmesan cheese.

3. Fill the zucchini shells with the stuffing. Arrange the stuffed shells side-by-side in a greased rectangular baking dish.

4. Pour the tomato sauce around the stuffed shells, cover the dish tightly with aluminum foil and bake at 350° for 40 to 45 minutes.

5. Sprinkle with remaining cheese when serving. Makes 6 servings.

POLISH CABBAGE BIRDS

1 large or 2 medium heads of
  cabbage
2 tablespoons bacon fat
½ cup minced onion
½ cup finely chopped
  mushrooms
1 small clove garlic, crushed

¼ cup stale bread crumbs
▶1¼ cups chopped cooked beef
1 egg
½ teaspoon salt
½ teaspoon pepper
▶ 1 to 1½ cups beef broth

Sauce

3 tablespoons butter
3 tablespoons flour
3 tablespoons tomato paste

Salt, pepper, and paprika to
taste
Pinch of sugar (optional)

1. Place whole cabbage in salted water to boil long enough to separate 10 to 12 leaves without tearing. Reserve rest of the cabbage for other meals. Cut out tough ribs to make rolling easier.

2. Heat bacon fat in a large skillet. Sauté onion, mushrooms, and garlic, for 5 minutes until onions are golden brown. Remove from heat and stir in bread crumbs. Add the meat, egg, and seasonings; mix thoroughly.

3. Divide stuffing into as many portions as there are cabbage leaves. Place stuffing in center of largest end of each leaf, roll once, fold both sides in over the center and continue rolling firmly into tight envelope; fasten with toothpick or tie with thread. If there are not enough large leaves, overlap small ones.

4. Arrange cabbage rolls in a single layer in a saucepan. Add enough beef broth to just cover the rolls, cover the saucepan and simmer over

low heat until tender, about 20 minutes. Remove rolls; keep warm. Reserve beef broth for sauce making.

5. To prepare sauce, melt the butter in a pan and blend in the flour; add tomato paste and the beef broth from the stuffed cabbage, stirring until smooth. Season to taste and let the sauce simmer for a few more minutes.

6. Arrange cabbage rolls on a hot platter, pour sauce over it, and serve with potatoes. Makes 5 to 6 servings.

STUFFED ZUCCHINI NEAPOLITAN

8 medium zucchini
►1¾ cups ground cooked beef
½ cup minced onion
1 clove garlic, minced
⅓ cup chopped walnuts
1 egg

1 can (15 oz.) tomato sauce with tomato bits
8 ounces small shell macaroni, cooked and drained
⅓ cup grated Parmesan cheese

1. Remove ends from the zucchini; use apple corer to hollow out centers, leaving ¼-inch shells. Chop the removed zucchini pulp coarsely; reserve.

2. Combine the ground beef, onion, garlic, walnuts, egg, salt, and ¼ cup tomato sauce with tomato bits in a mixing bowl.

3. Lightly fill zucchini shells with meat mixture; do not pack.

4. In skillet, heat remaining tomato sauce; add reserved zucchini pulp, and the stuffed zucchini shells. Cover; simmer 30 to 45 minutes or until zucchini shells are tender.

5. On a heated deep platter, place hot macaroni, sprinkle with ½ the Parmesan cheese and toss; arrange the stuffed zucchini on top. Pour sauce over all; sprinkle with the remaining Parmesan cheese. Makes 8 servings.

STUFFED TOMATOES RIVIERA STYLE

4 medium tomatoes
► ½ cup ground cooked beef
¼ cup finely chopped onion
1 clove garlic, minced
► ¼ cup cooked mashed potatoes, or prepared instant potatoes
1 tablespoon finely chopped parsley

½ teaspoon dried basil
¼ teaspoon salt
Freshly ground black pepper
1 egg, lightly beaten
1 tablespoon olive oil
¼ cup fine bread crumbs
2 tablespoons butter

1. Slice the top off each tomato, scoop out the pulp and chop. Invert tomato shells to drain.

2. Combine chopped tomato pulp, beef, onion, garlic, potato, parsley, basil, salt and pepper in a bowl.

3. Beat the egg and olive oil and add to tomato pulp mixture. Stuff mixture into the tomato shells.

4. Sprinkle each with breadcrumbs and top with pat of butter. Bake in a buttered baking dish in a 350° oven for 20 minutes. Serve hot. Makes 4 servings.

SUPER BEEF POT PIE

3 slices bacon, cut in 1" pieces or
   ¼ lb. salt pork, diced
½ cup chopped onions
6 to 8 mushrooms, sliced (about
   1¼ cups)
▶ 2 cups cubed cooked beef
▶ 1½ cups leftover gravy
▶ ½ cup cooked, thinly sliced
   carrots
▶ ½ cup diced cooked potatoes

▶ ½ cup cooked peas
1 teaspoon paprika
½ teaspoon crumbled basil
   Salt and freshly ground pepper
¼ teaspoon lemon juice
   Pastry for Single-Crust Pie (see
   Basics)
1 egg yolk, beaten with 1
   tablespoon milk or half-and-
   half (optional)

1. Heat oven to 425°. In a Dutch oven or saucepan, sauté bacon until it begins to turn brown; drain on towels. Discard all but 1 tablespoon bacon drippings; add onion and mushrooms, and sauté for several minutes until soft.

2. Add beef, gravy, carrots, potatoes, and peas. Stir in the paprika, basil, and the salt and freshly ground pepper, to taste, and the lemon juice. Heat, stirring occasionally, until mixture bubbles. Stir in bacon. Pour mixture into 2-quart casserole.

3. Roll out pastry and cover the casserole; crimp edges and cut out several small steam vents. Brush crust with yolk mixture. Bake for 15 minutes. Again brush surface with yolk mixture and bake additional 10 to 20 minutes or until pastry is golden. Makes 4 to 6 servings.

VERACRUZ TAMALE PIE

Cornmeal Mush

4 cups water
1 cup cornmeal
1½ teaspoons salt
¼ teaspoon pepper
½ teaspoon paprika

¼ teaspoon Tabasco
¼ teaspoon Worcestershire
   sauce
½ cup chopped ripe olives

Meat Mixture

1 tablespoon cooking oil
1 medium onion, finely chopped
½ medium green pepper, finely
   chopped
1 clove garlic, minced
1 tablespoon finely chopped
   celery

▶ 2 cups chopped cooked beef
1½ cups canned tomatoes,
   drained
1 tablespoon chili powder
   Dash nutmeg
1 tablespoon butter, melted
½ cup fine bread crumbs

1. Bring the water to a boil in a saucepan. Slowly stir in the cornmeal. Add half of the salt, and all of the pepper, paprika, Tabasco, Worcestershire sauce, and olives. Cook until thick over low heat.

2. Heat 1 tablespoon oil in a medium skillet. Add onion, green pepper, garlic, celery, and lightly brown. Stir in meat and cook 4 minutes. Add remaining salt, tomatoes, chili powder, and nutmeg; mix well. Remove from heat.

3. Grease a 2-quart casserole. Spread a thin layer of cornmeal mush on the bottom; add a layer of meat mixture, and continue alternating layers until ingredients are used, ending with cornmeal mush. Combine the melted butter with the crumbs and spread over the top. Bake in a 375° oven for 25 to 30 minutes or until well browned. Makes 6 servings.

SAVORY PERUVIAN EMPANADAS

Pastry

1½ cups flour
½ teaspoon salt
⅓ cup butter or margarine, cut in
   small pats

⅓ cup warm water
½ teaspoon lemon juice

Filling

▶ 1 tablespoon bacon drippings
▶ ¾ cup ground cooked beef
   1 small onion, minced
▶ ⅓ cup minced cooked ham
▶ 1 hard-cooked egg, chopped
   fine

2 teaspoons minced fresh
   coriander leaves, or Chinese
   parsley or regular parsley, or
   ⅓ teaspoon ground coriander
▶ 2 tablespoons beef broth
   Salt and pepper
   1 egg yolk, beaten with 1
   tablespoon water

1. Prepare pastry as follows: in a medium bowl, mix the flour, and salt. With fingers or pastry blender, work in butter until mixture resembles coarse crumbs. Mix water and lemon juice; slowly stir into flour mixture until dough forms a ball. Chill at least 30 minutes while preparing filling.

2. To prepare the filling: in a skillet, over medium heat, in hot bacon drippings, sauté the beef and the onions for 2 to 3 minutes to separate and warm the meat. Combine with the ham, egg, coriander, broth, and salt and pepper to taste.

3. On floured surface, roll out pastry to ⅛-inch thickness. Cut out 10 circles, each 5 inches in diameter, rerolling scraps if necessary. Place a heaping tablespoon of filling slightly below middle of each circle; fold circle in half over filling; pinch edges with wet tines of fork to seal.

4. Place on baking sheet; brush with yolk-water mixture. Bake in preheated 400° oven 15 minutes or until lightly browned. Makes 10.

HAMBURGER UPSIDE DOWN PIE

2 tablespoons butter or
   margarine
4 medium onions, sliced thin
1 tablespoon chopped green
   pepper
▶ 1 cup ground cooked beef

2 eggs, beaten
1 cup sour cream
½ teaspoon paprika
½ batch Buttermilk Biscuit Recipe
   (See Basics)

1. Melt butter in large skillet; add the onions, green pepper, and sauté gently, over low heat, for about 10 minutes or until onions are tender but not brown.

2. Add the ground beef, crumbling with fork, and stir briskly for 1 minute. Remove from heat. Beat the eggs, sour cream, and paprika together well.Combine with the meat mixture.

3. Roll out the pastry on a floured board to about ¼-inch thick. Press into a lightly greased 9-inch pie pan.

4. Pour the meat mixture over the biscuit pastry, sprinkle with paprika. Bake in preheated 375° oven for about 35 minutes. Serve hot, cut in wedges. Makes 6 servings.

BEEF BISCUIT ROLL

Biscuit Dough

2 cups flour
½ teaspoon salt
2 teaspoons double-
acting baking powder

¼ teaspoon rosemary
5 tablespoons butter
8 to 10 tablespoons ice water

Filling

▶ 2 cups lean, ground or
finely chopped pot roast
1 small onion, finely chopped
8 to 10 large fresh mushrooms,
finely chopped
▶ 2 to 3 tablespoons pot roast
gravy

½ to ¾ cup tomato sauce,
canned
or home made
¼ teaspoon dried basil
Salt and pepper
1 to 2 tablespoons melted butter
Tomato sauce

1. Sift flour, salt, baking powder, and rosemary into large mixing bowl. With pastry blender (or two knives) work in the butter until mixture resembles coarse-ground corn meal. Moisten with sufficient ice water to form a soft dough. Shape into a ball and refrigerate, covered, while preparing filling.

2. Combine the beef with the onion. Add mushrooms, beef gravy, and enough tomato sauce to form a thick spread. Season with basil, salt and pepper to taste.

3. Roll out the chilled dough on a lightly floured board to ¼-inch thickness, in a rectangular shape about 10-inches long. Trim edges. Spread with meat mixture and roll up (jelly-roll fashion). Moisten edges with cold water and seal.

4. Place roll, seam side down, on greased baking sheet. Brush with melted butter. Place in preheated 375° oven and bake, brushing occasionally with additional melted butter, 30 to 35 minutes or until surface is lightly browned. Slice and serve additional tomato sauce spooned over each portion. Makes 4 to 6 servings.

PLANTATION BEEF FRITTERS

1½ cups flour
1½ teaspoons baking powder
¼ teaspoon salt
Dash pepper
¼ teaspoon paprika
1 egg, well beaten
1¼ cups milk
▶1½ cups chopped cooked beef

1 tablespoon chopped parsley
1 tablespoon Worcestershire
sauce
2 teaspoons minced onion
1 tablespoon minced celery
Vegetable oil for frying
▶ ¾ cup heated leftover beef
gravy

1. In a mixing bowl, combine the flour, baking powder, salt, pepper, and paprika; set aside. Beat together the egg and milk and combine with flour mixture; blend batter until smooth.

2. In another mixing bowl, combine the chopped beef, parsley, Worcestershire sauce, onion, and celery. Fold the mixture into the batter; drop by spoonfuls into hot oil, 360°, and sauté until brown. Serve with heated gravy. Makes 4 servings.

TEXAS PANCAKE CASSEROLE

1½ cups milk
1 cup pancake mix
4 tablespoons butter, melted
2 tablespoons chopped peanuts
2 eggs, well beaten
2 tablespoons finely chopped
 onion
► 6 tablespoons bacon fat

► 2 cups finely chopped cooked
 beef
1 teaspoon salt
¼ teaspoon pepper
2 tablespoons minced parsley
½ cup sour cream
3 tablespoons grated Parmesan
 cheese
¼ teaspoon thyme

1. Add milk to pancake mix in a medium-sized bowl; stir in 1 tablespoon of the butter, peanuts, and egg. Beat well; let stand.

2. In a medium-size skillet, sauté onion in 1 tablespoon of the bacon fat. Stir in beef and cook 2 minutes. Season with salt and pepper; cool; add to the pancake batter.

3. Cook pancakes in remaining bacon fat, one at a time, in a heavy 6-inch skillet. Sprinkle each cooked pancake with parsley; roll each up, and lay in a shallow, well-greased 1½-quart baking dish, packing pancakes close together. Keep baking dish in warm oven until all pancake batter is used up.

4. Heat oven to 350°. Brush pancake rolls with the remaining butter and the sour cream and sprinkle with Parmesan cheese. Sprinkle thyme over all. Bake 10 minutes or until cheese is melted. Place under broiler a moment to lightly brown top. Makes 4 servings.

CANNELLONI WITH BEEF
AND SPINACH FILLING

Recipe for 16 to 20 Crêpes (see
 Basics)
1 cup heavy cream sauce (see
 Basics—Béchamel)
1½ cups tomato sauce, fresh (see
 Basics), or canned
4 tablespoons finely chopped
 onions
1 teaspoon finely chopped
 garlic
2 tablespoons olive oil

1 package (10 oz.) frozen
 chopped spinach, cooked and
 squeezed dry
► 1 cup finely chopped cooked
 pot roast
2 tablespoons heavy cream
7 tablespoons grated Parmesan
 cheese
2 eggs, lightly beaten
½ teaspoon salt
 Freshly ground black pepper
½ teaspoon oregano
 Butter

1. Prepare crêpes as directed in recipe.

2. Prepare the cream sauce, using 3 tablespoons flour, and season only with salt and cayenne.

3. Prepare a simple tomato sauce and season with basil.

(continued)

4. For the filling: cook the chopped onions and garlic in the olive oil for about 4 minutes, until they are soft but not brown. Add the spinach to the onions, raise the heat and, stirring constantly, cook for 2 to 3 minutes. Scrape the mixture into a mixing bowl. Add the meat, cream, 5 tablespoons of the Parmesan cheese, eggs, salt, pepper, and oregano; mix thoroughly and taste for seasoning.

5. Place a tablespoon or so of this filling on each crêpe and roll it up.

6. In a large shallow baking pan, spread a thin layer of cream sauce. Lay the cannelloni on this, side by side, and cover each one with a tablespoon or so of the tomato sauce, then spread the remaining cream sauce over them all. Sprinkle with the remaining Parmesan cheese and dot with small bits of butter.

7. Preheat the oven to 375°. Bake the uncovered cannelloni for about 20 minutes, or until they begin to bubble. Slide them quickly under a hot broiler to brown the top, and serve at once. Makes 4 to 6 servings.

 BEEF ENCHILADAS

Meat Filling

2 tablespoons vegetable oil
► 1½ cups ground cooked beef
1 clove garlic, finely chopped
1 teaspoon salt
1 tablespoon tequila, cognac, or water
1 tablespoon chili powder
1 can (16 oz.) kidney beans, undrained

Enchiladas

12 tortilas
1 cup grated sharp Cheddar cheese

Tomato Sauce

3 tablespoons vegetable oil
1 clove garlic, finely chopped
1 medium onion, chopped
¼ cup chopped green pepper
3 tablespoons flour
2 cans (16 oz. each) tomatoes, chopped with juice
1 beef bouillon cube
1 cup boiling water
2 tablespoons chopped canned green chilies
Dash ground cumin
½ teaspoon salt
Dash pepper

1. For the meat filling: in a medium skillet, heat the oil and, over low heat, sauté the meat with the garlic, salt, tequila, and chili powder until browned, about 2 minutes. Stir in the kidney beans. Set aside.

2. For the tomato sauce: in hot oil in a large skillet, sauté the garlic, onion, and green pepper for 5 minutes. Remove from heat. Add the flour and stir until smooth. Add the tomatoes and the bouillon cube dissolved in boiling water, blending well. Over medium heat, bring mixture to boiling, stirring frequently. Add the chilies, cumin, salt, and pepper; simmer uncovered, stirring occasionally, for about 10 minutes.

3. Preheat oven to 350°. Place about ¼ cup of the meat filling in the center of each tortilla; roll up. Arrange, seam side down, in a 13 × 9 × 2-inch baking dish. Pour tomato sauce over all; sprinkle with cheese. Bake 25 minutes. Makes 6 servings.

YORKSHIRE SQUARES

1 cup flour
½ teaspoon salt
1 cup milk
2 eggs, beaten
2 to 4 gratings whole nutmeg
▶ 3 cups finely chopped pot roast
2 tablespoons finely chopped onion
3 tablespoons finely chopped mushrooms

1 teaspoon minced parsley
1 teaspoon minced celery
1 teaspoon finely cut chives
½ clove garlic, minced
½ teaspoon salt
1 teaspoon Worcestershire sauce
⅛ teaspoon pepper
Pinch ground cloves
Mushroom Sauce (see below)

1. Heat oven to 425°. To make the batter, have ingredients at room temperature. In a bowl, combine flour with the salt, make a well in center and stir in milk until smooth. Add eggs and nutmeg, and beat well until large bubbles rise to the surface. Cover and set aside.

2. Combine beef, onions, mushrooms, parsley, celery, chives, garlic, salt, Worcestershire sauce, pepper, and cloves, and mix well.

3. Grease a 2½-quart casserole or a 9-inch square metal pan; heat it in oven to piping hot. Pour in half the batter. Quickly and evenly spread meat mixture over batter. Gently pour remaining batter over meat. Bake about 20 minutes or until topping has risen and begins to be firm to the touch. Reduce heat to 350° and bake 20 minutes longer. Cut in squares; serve at once with Mushroom Sauce. Makes 6 servings.

Mushroom Sauce

1½ cups fresh mushrooms, sliced or 1 can (4 oz.) sliced mushrooms, drained
1 tablespoon minced onion
1 tablespoon butter

1 can (10½ oz.) cream of mushroom soup
¼ cup milk
4 drops Worcestershire sauce

In a medium skillet, sauté mushrooms and onion in butter until light brown. Stir in mushroom soup, milk, and Worcestershire sauce. Cook over medium heat, stirring occasionally, until hot. Makes about 2 cups.

SATURDAY NIGHT SPECIAL

1 tablespoon butter
1 medium onion, chopped
2 tablespoons chopped green pepper
2 tablespoons chopped celery
1 medium tomato, peeled and sliced

▶ 4 cooked frankfurters, cut in ½-inch pieces
2 teaspoons paprika
1 teaspoon salt
⅛ teaspoon pepper
2 tablespoons sherry
4 eggs, well beaten

1. In a heavy skillet, melt the butter and sauté the onion, green pepper and celery until soft. Add the tomato, frankfurters, paprika and salt and pepper, and simmer gently over very low heat for 10 minutes.

2. Stir in the sherry and pour in the eggs, stir gently and cook over low heat until eggs are just set. Makes 4 servings.

BEEF SOUFFLÉ FINLANDIA

▶ ¾ cup finely chopped or ground
  cooked beef
1 grated onion
1 tablespoon grated raw carrots
1 anchovy fillet, drained and
  minced
3 tablespoons butter or
  margarine

3 tablespoons flour
1 cup milk
3 egg yolks at room temperature
  Salt and pepper to taste
4 egg whites

1. Preheat oven to 350°. Prepare and combine in a bowl the meat, onion, carrots and anchovies. Set aside.

2. Melt butter in a medium saucepan. Stir in the flour until all of the butter is absorbed and cook for 2 minutes. Gradually add the milk, stirring constantly. Cook over low heat until smooth and thickened, about 5 minutes. Remove from heat.

3. Beat the egg yolks until lemon colored. Gradually add 3 tablespoons of the sauce to the egg yolks, mix well and stir back into remaining sauce.

4. Add the reserved meat mixture to the sauce, stirring carefully. Season with salt and pepper, if necessary. Let cool slightly.

5. Beat egg whites until shiny and stiff but not dry. Fold ¼ of the whites into the sauce lightly but thoroughly. Fold the remaining whites in the sauce quickly and gently until most of the whites are incorporated.

6. Quickly pour into a buttered 6-cup casserole. Bake for 35 to 40 minutes until firm. Serve at once. Makes 4 servings.

RATATOUILLE PIE

¼ cup olive oil
1 medium eggplant, peeled and
  cubed
2 medium zucchini, cubed
1 cup chopped onion
1 clove garlic, chopped
3 large tomatoes, peeled and
  chopped
▶ 1 cup ground cooked beef

4 eggs
¾ cup grated Parmesan cheese
1 tablespoon minced parsley
½ teaspoon basil
½ teaspoon oregano
  Salt and pepper
¼ pound Mozzarella cheese,
  thinly sliced

1. In a deep skillet, heat the oil and sauté eggplant, zucchini, onion, and garlic until they soften, about 10 minutes. Add tomatoes, cover and simmer for 10 minutes. Add the meat and continue cooking 10 minutes longer or until vegetables are soft. Transfer to mixing bowl and let cool.

2. Beat eggs with ¼ cup Parmesan cheese, parsley, basil, and oregano. Mix with the vegetables, adding salt and pepper to taste.

3. Pour half of the mixture into greased 10-inch pie pan and top with ¼ cup more Parmesan cheese. Layer with remaining vegetables and Parmesan cheese. Top with Mozzarella cheese and bake 40 to 45 minutes or until pie is set and cheese is golden brown. Makes 4 to 6 servings.

ZUCCHINI CUSTARD SUPREME

2 tablespoons butter or
  margarine
1 medium onion, chopped
1 clove garlic, crushed
4 medium zucchini, diced
½ teaspoon curry powder
►2½ cups ground cooked beef

2 teaspoons salt
½ teaspoon pepper
2 slices white bread, in ½-inch
  cubes
4 eggs
2¾ cups milk

1. In a large skillet, melt butter over medium heat; add onion, garlic and diced zucchini; cook until onion is tender, stirring occasionally. Stir in curry powder; cook 1 minute. Add meat and cook 3 minutes longer, stirring to combine well. Add salt, pepper and bread cubes. Turn into buttered 1½-quart casserole.

2. In a small bowl, beat eggs and milk well; pour egg mixture over meat mixture in casserole.

3. Put into preheated 350° oven and bake, uncovered, for 55 to 60 minutes, until custard is set and top is golden brown. Makes 6 servings.

HUNGARIAN GOULASH SOUP (Gulyásleves)

3 tablespoons bacon drippings
2½ cups chopped onions
1 cup sliced carrots
¼ cup sliced celery
½ cup diced red bell peppers
1 tablespoon minced garlic
2 tablespoons medium-hot
  paprika
2 cups imported canned plum
  tomatoes, cut up
► ⅔ to 1 cup leftover beef gravy

2 cups potatoes, peeled and cut
  into ½-inch cubes
½ teaspoon lemon rind
1 teaspoon crushed caraway
  seed
► 3 cups beef stock, fresh or
  canned
►1½ to 2 cups cubed cooked beef
¾ to 1 cup sour cream
Freshly ground pepper
Chopped fresh parsley

1. Heat bacon drippings in large casserole over medium heat. Add onions; cook until soft but not brown, about 10 minutes. Add the carrots, celery, red pepper and garlic. Stir to combine; sauté until all vegetables are slightly softened, about 10 minutes.

2. Sprinkle in the paprika; cook another 2 minutes. Stir in the tomatoes, beef gravy, potatoes, lemon rind, caraway seed, beef stock; combine well. Bring to boiling point, reduce heat, add the beef; simmer partially covered, until potatoes and carrots are tender but still slightly firm, 20 to 30 minutes. Skim fat off surface as necessary.

3. To thicken soup, remove 1 cup of the vegetables from the soup, purée in food processor or blender, and stir purée back into soup. If soup is not thick enough, remove and purée an additional small amount of vegetables; stir back into the soup.

4. Remove from heat and stir ½ cup of the sour cream into the soup. Taste for seasoning; add pepper if necessary.

5. Serve hot in soup bowls. Top each serving with spoonful of reserved sour cream; sprinkle with chopped parsley. Makes 4 to 6 servings.

BELGIAN BEER SOUP

2 tablespoons butter or
  margarine
3 cups sliced onions
2 cups diced carrots
1 large clove garlic, minced
1 bay leaf
¼ teaspoon dried thyme
1 teaspoon salt
¼ teaspoon ground marjoram
1 quart dark beer

▶ ½ to ⅔ cup leftover meat gravy
  or juices
1½ cups sliced mushrooms
▶ 1½ to 2 cups diced cooked beef
2 medium potatoes, diced
1½ cups water
Freshly ground pepper
¾ teaspoon brown sugar
2 tablespoons chopped fresh
  parsley

1. Heat butter or margarine in large casserole over medium heat, and add the onions. Cover and cook, stirring occasionally, until onions are almost tender, about 5 minutes.

2. Combine the carrots and garlic with the onions, and cook 10 minutes. Add the bay leaf, thyme, salt, marjoram, beer, and meat juices or gravy. Heat to boiling; reduce heat. Simmer, uncovered, about 10 minutes.

3. Add the mushrooms, beef, potatoes, and enough water to cover ingredients. Heat to boiling; reduce heat. Simmer gently, partially covered, until potatoes are tender, 30 to 35 minutes.

4. Skim fat from surface and discard. Add pepper; stir in sugar, taste for seasoning. To serve, ladle into warmed soup bowls; sprinkle with chopped parsley, if desired. Makes 6 to 8 servings.

BAVARIAN SOUP

½ cup diced lean bacon
6 small white onions, chopped
3 scallions, chopped
2 tablespoons flour
▶ 6 cups beef broth, preferably
  homemade
4 medium potatoes, pared and
  diced

▶ ¾ cup diced cooked beef
¾ cup sour cream at room
  temperature
¼ cup light cream
2 egg yolks, beaten
Dash of nutmeg
1 tablespoon minced parsley
1½ teaspoons minced chervil

1. Sauté bacon for 3 minutes in a heavy saucepan. Add the white onions and scallions; cook 5 minutes or until soft but not brown.

2. Add flour and cook one minute. Gradually add the beef stock, stirring constantly. Add the diced potatoes and beef, cover and simmer for 40 minutes.

3. Mix the sour cream with the cream, egg yolks, and the nutmeg.

4. Spoon 3 tablespoons of the hot soup into the cream mixture, stirring well; then slowly stir all of the mixture back into the hot soup. Barely simmer over a very low heat for 5 to 6 minutes, stirring frequently.

5. Just before serving, add the minced parsley and chervil. Makes 8 servings.

CREOLE SOUP

2 tablespoons butter
3 tablespoons chopped onions
¼ cup chopped green pepper
¼ cup flour (scant)
► 1 quart beef broth
1 cup stewed tomatoes, drained,
or 1 cup diced fresh tomatoes

► ½ cup diced cooked beef
1 tablespoon grated horseradish
(fresh, if possible)
1 tablespoon cider vinegar
► ½ cup cooked rice

1. Melt butter in 2-quart saucepan and sauté the chopped onions and green peppers until soft, about 10 minutes.

2. Blend flour with 2 tablespoons of broth in a bowl. When smooth, add 1 cup of broth. Stir into the chopped onions and peppers in saucepan. Add the remaining broth, tomatoes and beef.

3. Simmer for 20 minutes, then add the horseradish, vinegar and rice. Simmer for 5 more minutes. Makes 6 servings.

FINNISH BEEF POTATO LOAF

► 6 cups finely chopped cooked
beef
► 3 large beets, cooked
► 4 potatoes, boiled (about 2 cups
diced)
3 eggs, beaten
¼ cup minced onions

1 tablespoon drained capers
1 teaspoon salt
½ teaspoon pepper
¼ cup butter or margarine
2 large onions, sliced
Sauce

1. Grind the meat, beets and potatoes together, using medium blade. (If you have no meat grinder, mince ingredients.) Place in a mixing bowl.

2. Add the eggs, onions, capers, salt and pepper, and mix well.

3. Turn onto a board; press firmly with hands to make into a loaf shape. (If additional binding is necessary, sprinkle lightly with flour and mix well.) Dip sharp knife into hot water and slice loaf into thick slices.

4. Melt butter in a large skillet and brown slices on both sides. Remove to warm serving platter and keep hot. When all slices are browned, sauté sliced onions in drippings in the same skillet. Remove cooked onions with a slotted spoon, and scatter over meat slices.

5. Pour sauce over all. Makes 6 large servings.

Sauce

1 tablespoon butter or
margarine
1½ tablespoons flour
1 tablespoon tomato juice

1 teaspoon prepared mustard
½ teaspoon salt
¼ teaspoon pepper
¾ cup light cream

6. In the skillet, melt butter. Stir in flour and cook 1 minute. Slowly stir in tomato juice and mustard, mixing well. Add salt, pepper and cream. Stir constantly over low heat until slightly thickened.

HEARTY BEEF-MACARONI LOAF

▶ 1½ cup finely chopped cooked
  beef
2 tablespoons minced onion
1 tablespoon minced celery
1 tablespoon minced fresh
  parsley
▶ 1½ cup cooked small elbow
  macaroni

Salt and pepper to taste
3 eggs
1½ cups milk
1 teaspoon prepared mustard
6 tablespoons grated Parmesan
  or Swiss cheese
3 tablespoons cracker or bread
  crumbs

1. In a large bowl, combine beef, onion, celery, and parsley with macaroni. Season lightly with salt and pepper. Put in buttered loaf pan.

2. Beat eggs with milk and mustard; add 3 tablespoons of the cheese.
Pour over beef mixture.

3. Set pan in larger pan; pour boiling water into the larger pan to 1-inch
depth. Bake in preheated 350° oven for 30 minutes. Combine remaining
3 tablespoons of cheese and the crumbs; sprinkle over loaf and bake
another 10 minutes, or until knife inserted near center comes out clean.
Makes 4 servings.

HEAVENLY BEEF HASH

▶ 2 cups chopped beef pot roast
▶ 2 cups chopped cooked
  potatoes
½ cup chopped onion
4 tablespoons chopped green or
  red pepper

½ teaspoon salt
¼ teaspoon pepper
2 tablespoons tomato ketchup
4 tablespoons bacon drippings
4 poached eggs

1. Combine beef, potatoes, onions, peppers, salt, pepper, and
ketchup, and blend well in a large mixing bowl.

2. Heat bacon drippings in a large, heavy skillet. Add beef mixture and
cook over medium heat for 5 minutes. With a large spatula carefully turn
mixture over, and cook 5 minutes. Turn over again, patting firmly with
spatula. Cook 5 minutes longer. When hash has a brown, crusty bottom,
transfer to a serving platter. Cut into 4 wedges.

3. Top each serving with a poached egg. Makes 4 servings.

Leftover meatloaf

... is perfect in recipes calling for ground meat. Just crumble into a skillet with a little hot margarine or oil, and warm over moderate heat for 2
to 3 minutes to perk up. Portions of leftover meatloaf, packaged in flat
slices for quick thawing, are always handy to have in the freezer.

OLD-FASHIONED BAKED HASH WITH VEGETABLES

2 tablespoons bacon drippings
½ cup diced onions
⅓ cup chopped green pepper
½ cup chopped celery
► 1 cup diced cooked potatoes
3 tablespoons diced pimientos
► 2 cups diced cooked beef
►1½ cups leftover gravy

⅓ cup tomato purée
Salt and pepper to taste
1 teaspoon Worcestershire sauce
2 ripe tomatoes, sliced
2 tablespoons butter or
margarine
¼ teaspoon basil, crumbled

1. Heat bacon drippings in skillet, and sauté onions, green pepper and celery for 2 to 3 minutes. Add potatoes, pimientos and meat, and cook for 2 minutes more.

2. In a saucepan, combine gravy, tomato purée, salt, pepper and Worcestershire sauce; heat to a boil.

3. Combine hash mixture with the gravy mixture and pour into one large casserole or divide into individual baking dishes. Top with slices of tomato dotted with butter and sprinkle with salt, pepper and basil.

4. Bake in preheated 350° oven for 20 minutes or until browned. Makes 6 servings.

BEEF PATTIES WITH CREAMED BROCCOLI

►1½ cups cubed cooked beef
► ½ cup cooked rice
½ cup minced onion
½ cup minced parsley sprigs
3 tablespoons butter or
margarine
4 tablespoons flour
1 beef bouillon cube
½ cup boiling water
1 cup milk or half-and-half
Salt and freshly ground pepper

► ½ cup cooked broccoli
1½ tablespoons dry sherry
(optional)
Flour for coating
1 egg, beaten, plus 2
tablespoons milk
1½ cups fine bread or cracker
crumbs
4 tablespoons vegetable oil, for
frying

1. Finely chop or grind beef and combine with rice, onion and parsley in a mixing bowl; set aside.

2. In small saucepan, melt butter; add 4 tablespoons flour and cook, stirring, for 3 minutes. Dissolve bouillon cube in boiling water; stir gradually into flour mixture, cook one minute. Add ½ cup milk and cook, stirring until thickened, about 5 minutes. Mix ½ cup of the sauce into beef mixture, blending thoroughly; add salt and pepper to taste. Chill.

3. To remaining ½ cup sauce, add remaining ½ cup milk and broccoli; heat gently until hot. Stir in sherry; keep hot.

4. Shape meat/rice mixture into 6 thick patties; roll in flour, then in beaten egg, and finally in bread crumbs. Fry in hot oil until brown on both sides. Serve patties topped with the creamed broccoli. Makes 6 servings.

ELEGANT BEEF HASH

¼ cup butter or margarine
½ cup finely chopped onions
¼ cup finely chopped green
  pepper
¼ cup finely chopped celery
½ cup chopped mushrooms
► 4 cups cubed cooked roast beef

► 2 cups diced cooked potatoes
¼ teaspoon marjoram
¼ teaspoon thyme
2 tablespoons chopped parsley
½ cup red wine
½ cup heavy cream

1. Melt 3 tablespoons butter in large skillet. Sauté onions, green pepper, celery and mushrooms for 5 minutes, until vegetables are crisp-tender. Stir in beef, potatoes, marjoram, thyme, and parsley.

2. Stir in wine and cream. Turn into a greased 1½-quart casserole.

3. Put into preheated 350° oven and bake for 30 minutes or until lightly browned. Makes 6 servings.

ROAST BEEF AND VEGETABLE SALAD
IN MUSTARD MAYONNAISE

1¼ pounds celery root (celeriac),
  cut into 4 slices and peeled
1 cup mayonnaise, freshly made
  (see Basics), or commercial
2 teaspoons Dijon-type mustard
⅓ teaspoon dry mustard
1 teaspoon lemon juice
¼ cup heavy cream
  Salt to taste
  Cayenne to taste
½ cup red onion rings

½ cup diced blanched
  carrots
► 1½ to 2 cups cooked rare roast
  beef, trimmed and cut into
  julienne strips
  Romaine or Boston lettuce
1 egg, hard-cooked and
  coarsely chopped
1 tablespoon chopped
  parsley

1. Blanch the peeled celery root slices by plunging them into boiling water that contains ¼ cup lemon juice. Leave in boiling water for 1 to 2 minutes. Remove and submerge immediately in cold water. Remove and dry the root slices. Cut each into julienne strips ⅛" thick and 1" long, about 2 cups, and set aside.

2. Combine the mayonnaise with the mustards and lemon juice, increasing the amounts of mustard to make as highly seasoned a dressing as you will enjoy. Thin it by beating in the heavy cream a tablespoon at a time until the sauce will run slowly off a spoon. Taste for seasoning; add as much salt and cayenne as needed.

3. In a large mixing bowl, combine the celeriac, onion rings, carrots and roast beef with the mustard mayonnaise until thoroughly coated. Cover the bowl and set aside for one hour before serving, stirring occasionally. Refrigerate, if necessary, but serve the salad at room temperature, if possible.

4. To serve, spoon onto crisp lettuce. Sprinkle the top with the coarsely chopped egg and with chopped parsley. Makes 4 servings.

BEEF-POTATO SALAD

- ▶ 2 cups diced cooked beef
- ▶ 2 cups diced cooked potatoes
  ½ green pepper, chopped
  ⅓ cup diced celery
  ½ cup chopped dill pickles
  1 small onion, cut in rings

- ▶ 1 cup cooked peas
  2 hard-cooked eggs
  1 cup mayonnaise
  2 teaspoons Dijon-type mustard
  ¼ teaspoon salt
  Crisp salad greens

1. In a large bowl, combine the beef, potatoes, green peppers, celery, pickles, onions, peas, and eggs.

2. Mix the mayonnaise with mustard and salt; blend thoroughly. Pour dressing over meat and vegetable mixture, and toss lightly. Cover and chill for several hours.Serve on crisp salad greens. Makes 4 servings.

BOILED BEEF AND VEGETABLE PLATTER WITH SOUR CREAM DRESSING

- ▶ 8 to 12 slices cold boiled beef or
  pot roast, about ¼-inch thick
  ½ cup oil and vinegar dressing
  ½ cup mayonnaise
  ½ cup sour cream
  1 teaspoon chopped dill pickle,
  drained
  1 teaspoon lemon juice
- ▶ 6 small potatoes, boiled and
  thinly sliced (about 2 cups)

- ▶ 3 medium beets, cooked and
  thinly sliced (about 2 cups)
- ▶ 2 cups cooked stringbeans,
  Frenched or in 1-inch pieces
- ▶ 4 medium carrots, cooked,
  diced or sliced (about 2 cups)
  4 hard-cooked eggs, quartered
  Tomato wedges
  2 scallions, chopped
  Sprigs of parsley

1. Arrange the slices of beef in the center of a large round platter. Spoon half the dressing over the slices.

2. Combine the mayonnaise, sour cream, pickles, lemon juice, and blend well. Place in a serving dish and refrigerate.

3. Around the meat, place in alternate mounds the potatoes, beets, string beans, carrots, eggs, and tomato wedges.

4. Sprinkle the entire arrangement first with minced scallions; then with the remaining oil and vinegar dressing. Let stand at room temperature for about ½ hour before serving. (The dish should be served cool but not chilled.) Garnish with sprigs of parsley. Serve mayonnaise dressing separately. Makes 4 to 6 servings.

BEEF SALAD JAPANESE-STYLE

▶ 2 cups diced pot roast
▶ 1 cup cooked rice
  ½ cup sliced water chestnuts
  ½ cup peeled and chopped
    cucumber
  1 scallion, chopped

¾ cup sliced celery, cut on the
  diagonal
1 cup mayonnaise
1½ teaspoons Dijon-type mustard
  Crisp lettuce leaves
2 hard-cooked eggs, sliced
  Sprigs of parsley

In a large mixing bowl, combine the meat with the rice, water chestnuts, cucumbers, scallions, and celery. Mix separately the mayonnaise with the mustard; add to the meat mixture and toss lightly. Place onto crisp lettuce leaves. Garnish with egg slices and parsley. Makes 4 servings.

CLASSIC BEEF VINAIGRETTE

3 tablespoons red wine vinegar
½ teaspoon salt
  Freshly ground black pepper
1 teaspoon Dijon-type mustard
½ cup olive oil
2 tablespoons capers, drained
  and coarsely chopped
1 small clove garlic, finely
  chopped

3 tablespoons finely
  chopped parsley
▶ 6 to 8 slices cooked pot roast
  ¼-inch thick; or 2½ to 3 cups
  pot roast, cubed
½ cup thinly sliced onions

1. In a small mixing bowl, combine the vinegar, salt, 2 or 3 grindings of black pepper, and the mustard, and mix thoroughly. Beat in the olive oil. Add the capers, garlic, and 2 tablespoons of the parsley.

2. Arrange the slices or cubes of beef in a shallow casserole large enough to hold the meat in one layer. Scatter the sliced onions over them. Beat the dressing ingredients well to combine them thoroughly, then pour the dressing into the casserole. Make sure that the onions and the meat are moistened thoroughly. Marinate at room temperature for at least 2 to 3 hours before serving.

3. Arrange the meat on a serving platter with the onion slices scattered on top and a sprinkling of more parsley. Serve with a good potato salad. Makes 4 to 6 servings.

To serve sliced once-cooked meat, without reheating, always bring to room temperature first. Otherwise, the "cold" masks the delicate flavor.

POT ROAST PÂTÉ

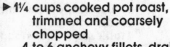

▶ 1¼ cups cooked pot roast,
   trimmed and coarsely
   chopped
   4 to 6 anchovy fillets, drained
   and chopped
▶ ½ to ¾ cup thin pot roast gravy
   or beef stock

¼ pound sweet butter, softened
1 teaspoon finely grated onion
¾ teaspoon lemon juice
Salt to taste
Freshly ground black pepper

1. In the jar of an electric blender, combine the pot roast, anchovies, and ½ cup of gravy or stock. Purée at high speed, stopping the machine occasionally to scrape the sides with a rubber spatula, adding liquid when necessary to produce a smooth, fairly fluid purée.

2. Cream the butter in a mixing bowl by beating with a wooden spoon until smooth and light in color. Mix a spoonful at a time into the meat purée, and continue to beat the mixture until the butter and meat are completely combined. Add the grated onion, lemon juice, salt and pepper.

3. Spoon the pâté into a small crock—preferably earthenware— cover tightly, and refrigerate for at least 4 hours, or until pâté is firm. Serve on hot buttered toast or French or black bread with cocktails or beer. Makes 6 to 8 servings.

JELLIED BEEF MOLD

2 tablespoons chopped
   celery with leaves
1 medium onion, stuck
   with one clove
1 clove garlic, chopped
1 bay leaf
2 tablespoons chopped parsley
   Dash of ground thyme
1 teaspoon dried tarragon

4 peppercorns
¼ teaspoon salt
▶ 2¾ cups beef stock, from the
   boiled beef
2 envelopes unflavored gelatin
¼ cup cold water
½ cup Madeira wine
▶ 3 cups finely diced cold boiled
   beef

1. In a large saucepan, combine the celery, onion, garlic, bay leaf, parsley, seasonings, and stock; simmer for about 20 minutes. Cool slightly and strain carefully.

2. Sprinkle the gelatin on cold water to soften. Let stand 2 to 3 minutes. Add the stock and stir until dissolved. Add the Madeira wine and refrigerate until mixture begins to thicken.

3. Add the meat and pour into a lightly greased loaf pan. Refrigerate until firm. Dip mold briefly in hot water. Unmold onto serving platter. Cut into slices and serve. Makes 6 servings.

DEVILED ROAST BEEF BONES

▶ 12 rib roast beef bones
  2 tablespoons cider vinegar
  ½ cup prepared mustard
  2 tablespoons molasses
  ½ cup Worcestershire sauce

2 teaspoons dry mustard
1 teaspoon Tabasco
1 tablespoon brown sugar
1 teaspoon salt
¼ teaspoon curry powder

1. When carving rib roasts, get in the habit of deliberately leaving some meat on them. Wrap in foil and accumulate in freezer. When you have 12 ribs, defrost.

2. Combine the remaining ingredients in a small bowl and blend well. Brush each rib generously with mixture. Place on a baking sheet in a preheated 400° oven and bake for 10 minutes. Brush each rib again, and continue baking another 10 to 15 minutes until ribs are glazed. Makes 4 to 6 servings.

DEVILED BEEF SLICES (Boeuf Diable)

  3 tablespoons red wine vinegar
  ½ teaspoon dry mustard
  ½ teaspoon salt
  Black pepper, freshly ground
  ½ cup olive oil
  1 large clove garlic, sliced
▶ 8 to 12 slices cooked beef,
  about ¼-inch thick
  3 egg yolks

¾ cup prepared mustard,
  preferably Dijon-type
1¾ cups fine, dry bread crumbs
3 tablespoons vegetable oil
2 tablespoons butter or
  margarine
2½ tablespoons finely
  chopped parsley
1 lemon, wedged

1. In a small bowl mix the wine vinegar, dry mustard, salt, and a few grindings of black pepper; slowly beat in the olive oil and add the sliced garlic. Pour this marinade over the beef slices arranged in a single layer in a glass or enamel baking dish. Make sure marinade completely covers the meat. Steep for one hour; then remove and pat each piece dry with paper toweling.

2. In a small bowl stir the egg yolks briefly, then beat in the mustard 1 tablespoon at a time. Should be the consistency of heavy cream.

3. Put the bread crumbs on waxed paper. Spread each slice of meat heavily with the mustard mixture, then lay it on the crumbs. With a spatula pat the crumbs onto both sides of the slices until solidly coated; then place them side by side on a platter lined with waxed paper. Cover with more waxed paper and refrigerate for at least ½ hour before sautéing.

4. To sauté, heat the oil and butter in a large heavy frying pan. When the foam subsides, add the meat and sauté briskly to a golden-brown on each side, turning the slices over carefully, and adding more butter and oil to the pan as needed. Put each slice of meat as it is finished on a heated platter and keep warm in a 250° oven until ready to serve.

5. Sprinkle lightly with finely chopped parsley and serve with wedges of lemon. Makes 4 servings.

PÂTÉ OF BEEF IN CROUSTADE
(Stuffed French or Vienna Bread)

▶ 2 cups ground cooked beef, cold
3 tablespoons minced onion
3 tablespoons minced parsley
2 small pickles, finely chopped
2 hard-cooked eggs, chopped
Dash of hot pepper sauce
1 tablespoon Worcestershire sauce
Mayonnaise
1 large loaf well-crusted French or Vienna bread
Butter

1. In a large bowl, mix ground beef with the minced onion and parsley, the chopped pickles and eggs; season with the pepper and Worcestershire sauces; mix thoroughly. Combine well with enough mayonnaise to make a stiff paste.

2. Cut both ends from the bread. Hollow out the loaf, using a fork and working from both ends, leaving a shell about ½-inch thick. Brush the interior well with soft butter and then force the meat mixture into the bread firmly so that it has no air holes in it. Wrap in foil and keep in refrigerator for several hours before slicing. Makes 6 servings.

ROAST BEEF TARTARE

▶ 2 cups diced rare roast beef
2 egg yolks
⅓ cup finely chopped scallions
1 clove garlic, finely chopped
1 tablespoon Worcestershire sauce
Tabasco to taste
2 tablespoons finely chopped parsley
1½ tablespoons capers, drained
1 teaspoon lemon juice
½ teaspoon salt
Black pepper, freshly ground
8 anchovy fillets
4 egg yolks (optional)
Black bread or buttered toast

1. Dice the red, rare center of the roast beef with a very sharp knife as finely as possible without mashing it. Do not try to grind it; the meat will disintegrate.

2. In a mixing bowl, gently mix together the meat, egg yolks, scallions, garlic, Worcestershire sauce, Tabasco, 1 tablespoon parsley, capers, lemon juice, salt, and pepper. Taste for seasoning and form the beef into 4 plump mounds.

3. Serve each mound on individual plates. Sprinkle with chopped parsley or garnish with 2 anchovy fillets or with an egg yolk in the center of each mound. Accompany the tartare with squares of black bread, or hot buttered toast, and cold beer. Makes 4 servings.

RISOTTO BEEF TORINO

¼ cup olive oil
¼ cup chopped onion
2 cloves garlic, crushed
2 cups raw rice
½ pound Italian sweet or hot
   sausage, sliced
▶ ½ cup chopped or ground
   cooked beef

1 teaspoon salt
¼ teaspoon pepper
⅛ teaspoon saffron
½ teaspoon oregano
2 tablespoons chopped parsley
▶ 5 cups chicken or beef broth
   Grated Parmesan cheese

1. Heat the olive oil in a 2½ quart casserole; sauté the onion and garlic for 5 minutes.

2. Stir in the rice and sausage; sauté over medium heat, stirring frequently, until sausage is browned.

3. Add the beef. Stir in salt and pepper, saffron, oregano, parsley, and broth. Bring to a boil; cover; simmer, stirring occasionally, for 20 minutes. Serve with the grated cheese. Makes 8 servings.

SPINACH, ORANGE, AND CORNED BEEF SALAD

1 tablespoon grated onion
1 teaspoon salt
½ teaspoon ground black
   pepper
1 tablespoon Dijon-type
   mustard
2 tablespoons wine vinegar
1 teaspoon lemon juice
⅔ cup olive and vegetable oils
   mixed

1 pound fresh young spinach
   leaves, washed and dried
3 navel oranges, peeled,
   trimmed and sectioned
▶ 2 cups cooked corned beef,
   cut into strips ½-inch wide
   and 1½ inches long

1. Combine the grated onion, salt, pepper, mustard, vinegar, and lemon juice in a small mixing bowl. Mix into a smooth paste. With a wire whisk beat in, little by little, the ⅔ cup of oil. Continue to beat until the dressing thickens. (All of the foregoing steps may also be done in a blender.)

2. Combine the spinach leaves, orange sections, and corned beef in a chilled bowl. Pour the dressing over mixture and toss thoroughly. Allow to stand a short while before serving on chilled plates. Makes 4 servings.

Seasoning

Because all once-cooked foods have had some kind of seasoning, it is important to taste as you cook, adding more seasoning only as needed.

CORNED BEEF TURNOVERS WITH MUSHROOM SAUCE

▶ ½ cup minced cooked corned beef
1 can (10½ oz.) cream of mushroom soup
1 small onion, grated
½ teaspoon prepared mustard
2 sprigs parsley, chopped
Salt and pepper

Pastry for turnovers (see Basics; use 1½ cups flour), or, use 2 frozen pie shells
2 tablespoons milk or cream
⅓ cup milk
¼ can (4 oz.) mushroom pieces
½ teaspoon Worcestershire sauce

1. Combine in mixing bowl the corned beef, ¼ cup of the soup, the onion, mustard, and the parsley; add salt and pepper to taste.

2. Roll the pastry into a rectangle (16" × 8") on floured board. Cut into eight 4-inch squares. Spoon meat mixture onto the center of each square. Moisten edges with water and fold over in triangles. Crimp edges with fork; brush tops with milk. Put on cookie sheet; bake in preheated hot oven (425°) for about 20 minutes.

3. Empty remaining soup from can into saucepan and combine with the milk; stirring to blend. Add the mushroom pieces and Worcestershire sauce. Serve as the sauce for the turnovers. Makes 4 servings.

CORNED BEEF AND NOODLE CASSEROLE

1 can (10-¾ oz.) cream of chicken soup
1 cup milk
1 cup shredded Cheddar cheese
1 teaspoon Dijon-type mustard

▶ 2 cups diced cooked corned beef
½ cup chopped onion
2 cups cooked egg noodles
Bread crumbs

Blend soup, milk, cheese, and mustard in a large bowl. Add corned beef, onion, and noodles, and mix well. Place in a buttered 1½-quart baking dish. Top with bread crumbs. Bake at 350° for 45 minutes. Make 4 servings.

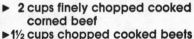

OLD-FASHIONED RED FLANNEL HASH

▶ 2 cups finely chopped cooked corned beef
▶ 1½ cups chopped cooked beets
▶ 3 cups chopped cooked potatoes
2 tablespoons finely chopped onion
1 teaspoon salt

½ teaspoon onion salt
⅛ teaspoon pepper
1 teaspoon Worcestershire sauce
3 tablespoons light cream
¼ cup bacon drippings
Poached or fried eggs

1. In a large bowl combine the corned beef, beets, potatoes, onion, the salts, pepper, and Worcestershire sauce. Add cream and mix lightly.

2. Melt bacon drippings in a heavy skillet. Spread meat mixture evenly in bottom; cook over a low heat without stirring for 30 minutes. Loosen

(continued)

around edges with a spatula; shake skillet occasionally to prevent mixture from sticking.

3. When crust has formed on bottom, make certain hash is not sticking to the pan and turn over quickly. Or, make a shallow cut across the hash, tip the skillet and slide the hash out onto a platter folding it in half like an omelet. Top each serving with a poached or fried egg. Makes 4 servings.

 ## POTATO AND CORNED BEEF SALAD

5 large potatoes to be cooked, peeled and sliced
▶ 2 tablespoons beef or chicken stock, heated
1 teaspoon salt
½ teaspoon dry mustard
½ teaspoon prepared mustard
Freshly ground black pepper
2 tablespoons white wine vinegar

5 tablespoons olive oil
▶ 1½ cups cooked corned beef, julienned
2 tablespoons finely chopped scallions or chives
1 tablespoon finely chopped parsley
Watercress

1. Cook the potatoes just before mixing the salad. Put them in a large mixing bowl and, while they are still hot, pour the hot stock over them. Stir gently until the stock is absorbed. Transfer to salad bowl.

2. In a small dish, mix together the salt, mustards, gratings of black pepper, the vinegar, and the olive oil, adding gradually. Beat well after each addition to blend well. Add to the potatoes. Stir in the corned beef and scallions and parsley. Surround with sprays of crisp watercress. The salad will be at its best if served at room temperature. Makes 4 servings.

Cutting terms

"ground"—through a grinder
"shred"—into very thin, small pieces
"mince"—in very small pieces about ⅛" across
    (can be used in place of "ground")
"chop"—in small pieces from ⅛" to ¼" across
"cube"—in large pieces from ½" to ¾" across
"julienne"—into thin matchlike strips, about ⅛" by 2"

TYROLIAN TONGUE

2 kosher-style gherkins, finely
  chopped
3 scallions, finely chopped
1 teaspoon finely chopped
  parsley
1 teaspoon finely chopped
  capers
⅓ cup bread crumbs

⅓ cup dry white wine
¼ teaspon salt
⅛ teaspoon white pepper
3 tablespoons butter, melted
▶ 12 thin slices cooked tongue
  Hot buttered noodles
2 tablespoons chopped parsley

1. Combine the gherkins, scallions, parsley, capers, bread crumbs, wine, salt and pepper in a small mixing bowl.

2. In the bottom of a shallow, buttered, 1½-quart baking dish, pour 1½ tablespoons butter. Next, spread ½ the gherkin mix, on top of which arrange the slices of tongue. Cover with the remaining gherkin mix and top with the rest of the butter.

3. Bake 20 minutes in a 350° oven. Serve with hot buttered noodles sprinkled with chopped parsley. Makes 4 servings.

TONGUE WITH FRUIT AND ALMOND SAUCE

¼ cup red wine vinegar
3 tablespoons sugar
▶ 1 cup braising liquid from the
  tongue, or beef bouillon
1 tablespoon cornstarch
  dissolved in 2 tablespoons
  Madeira or cold water
⅛ teaspoon ground cinnamon
⅛ teaspoon ground cloves

8 prunes, pitted and
  chopped
¼ cup raisins
¼ cup slivered almonds,
  blanched
1 tablespoon shredded
  orange rind
3 lemon slices
▶ 12 slices braised tongue

1. Mix the vinegar and sugar together in a small enamel saucepan and slowly bring it to a boil. Let it boil without stirring for about 5 minutes until it becomes a thick, heavy syrup and begins to caramelize, turning a dark mahogany brown. Remove pan from heat. Pour into it the cup of braising liquid. Bring the stock to a boil and stir with a spoon to dissolve the caramel completely.

2. Stir in the cornstarch-Madeira mixture and cook over moderate heat until the sauce thickens and becomes clear. Add the spices, the prunes, raisins, almonds, orange rind, and lemon slices and simmer over a very low heat for about 5 minutes.

3. Reheat the sliced tongue in its own braising liquid or in a little beef or chicken stock; drain. Arrange the slices overlapping slightly down the center of a small heated platter. Pour the fruit sauce over the tongue and serve at once. Makes 4 servings.

TONGUE HASH

- ▶ 2 cups coarsely chopped cooked tongue
- ▶ 2 cups coarsely chopped cooked potatoes
  - ½ cup minced onion
  - 2 teaspoons minced parsley
  - 2 teaspoons minced celery
- ▶ ¼ to ⅓ cup tongue broth
  - 2 teaspoons prepared mustard
  - ½ teaspoon marjoram
  - ⅛ teaspoon thyme
  - ½ teaspoon salt
  - ⅛ teaspoon pepper

1. Combine tongue, potatoes, onion, parsley, and celery in a medium heavy skillet. Pour over enough broth to moisten through. Cook over medium heat for 5 minutes.

2. Add mustard, marjoram, thyme, salt, and pepper and blend in. Cover; reduce heat and simmer 20 minutes or until thoroughly hot. Serve at once. Makes 4 servings.

TASTY TONGUE MOLD

- 1 tablespoon unflavored gelatin
- ▶ ½ cup broth
  - ½ cup white wine
  - ¼ cup prepared horseradish, drained
  - ½ cup mayonnaise
  - ½ teaspoon dry mustard
  - Dash Tabasco
- ▶ 2 cups finely chopped cooked tongue
  - ¼ cup minced green pepper
  - 1 tablespoon minced onion
  - 1 teaspoon minced pimiento
  - 1 teaspoon minced celery
  - Lettuce or watercress

1. In a bowl, soak gelatin in ¼ cup of the cold broth. Heat remaining broth in a saucepan and dissolve gelatin in it; add wine. Cool off to luke-warm.

2. Mix the horseradish with the mayonnaise, dry mustard, and Tabasco. Combine tongue, green pepper, onion, pimiento and celery with the mayonnaise mixture.

3. Stir into gelatin mixture. Turn into a 5-cup mold and chill until set. Serve over a bed of lettuce or watercress. Makes 6 servings.

►CHICKEN

VIENNESE CHICKEN

¼ cup butter
1 large onion, finely chopped
1 green pepper, cut into thin strips
1 pimiento, cut into thin strips
½ pound fresh mushrooms, sliced
2 tablespoons flour
▶ 1 cup chicken stock
1 teaspoon paprika

1 teaspoon salt
¼ cup canned tomatoes, chopped and well drained
▶ 2 cups diced cooked chicken
1 package (8 oz.) medium egg noodles, cooked
½ cup sour cream
½ cup grated Cheddar cheese

1. In a large skillet, melt the butter and cook the onion, green pepper, pimiento, and mushrooms over low heat until tender. Stir in the flour, blending well, and cook for 2 minutes. Add the chicken stock gradually and cook, stirring occasionally until thickened. Season with paprika and salt.

2. Add the tomato, chicken, noodles, and sour cream to the sauce. Turn into a buttered 3-quart casserole, sprinkle with the grated cheese, and bake in a preheated 350° oven for 20 minutes or until bubbling. Makes 6 to 8 servings.

BAKED CHICKEN PARMESAN

1½ tablespoons olive oil
6 tablespoons unsalted butter
⅓ pound mushrooms, coarsely chopped
⅓ cup roasted canned red peppers, drained and chopped
1 large onion, finely chopped
2 medium carrots, finely chopped
1 large stalk celery, finely chopped
1 large clove garlic, minced
¼ teaspoon dried rosemary, crumbled
¾ cup dry white wine

▶ 2¼ cups minced cooked chicken
1½ teaspoons salt
Freshly ground pepper
▶ ¾ cup chicken stock or broth
¼ cup dry sherry
4 tablespoons all-purpose flour
2½ cups milk
1 cup freshly grated Parmesan cheese
▶ 6 ounces fine egg noodles, cooked
▶ 2 slices baked ham, or prosciutto, shredded
¾ cup Mozzarella cheese, shredded

1. In a large skillet, over medium heat, combine 1 tablespoon of the oil and 1 tablespoon of the butter, and sauté mushrooms until lightly browned, about 2 minutes. Remove from pan to a bowl. Add the red peppers to the bowl; toss until mixed.

2. Heat remaining oil and 1 tablespoon of butter; add the onion, carrots, celery, and garlic, and sauté gently about 10 minutes. Add rosemary, ½ cup white wine and the chicken; cook until heated, about 5 minutes. Season with 1 teaspoon of the salt, and pepper to taste. Remove from heat.

3. Combine the stock, sherry, and remaining white wine in a small pan, heat to boiling and simmer gently for 5 minutes.

4. Melt remaining butter in medium saucepan, stir in the flour, stirring constantly, and cook for 3 minutes. Slowly add the milk, and simmer, stirring frequently, until thick and smooth, about 5 minutes. Remove from heat; stir in the broth mixture, ½ cup of the Parmesan cheese and salt and pepper to taste.

5. Heat oven to 400°. Spread a little sauce on the bottom of a 1½-quart baking dish. Layer ⅓ of the noodles first, then, ½ the chicken and mushroom mixtures, and ½ the ham, then ⅓ of the sauce and Parmesan and Mozzarella cheeses. Repeat the layering, ending with the remaining ⅓ of the noodles, sauce, and cheeses. Bake until bubbling and lightly browned, about 30 minutes. Let stand 15 minutes before serving. Makes 6 servings.

BASQUE CHICKEN AND RICE

1 pound hot Italian sausages
▶ 1 cup chicken stock, homemade or canned
1 strip orange peel, 1" x 3"
¼ cup olive oil
2 large green peppers, seeded and cut into strips ¼" x 1½"
1 clove garlic, finely chopped
6 fresh ripe tomatoes, peeled, and coarsely chopped, or 2 cups canned plum tomatoes, chopped
2 teaspoons imported sweet paprika

1 teaspoon oregano, dried
Salt to taste
Freshly ground black pepper
▶ 5 cups cooked rice
1 tablespoon butter or margarine
▶ 8 to 10 substantial pieces cooked chicken
1 tablespoon finely chopped parsley

1. In a small frying pan, cover the sausages wth chicken stock. Add the orange peel, let the sausages simmer for about 5 minutes, then prick them with a knife in 2 or 3 places to allow the fat to escape. Pierce them again after 5 more minutes of cooking, then remove from the pan and let drain on paper towel. Reserve the cooking stock but skim it of fat.

2. Heat the olive oil in the pan and cook the green peppers over moderate heat for about 10 minutes or until tender. Add the garlic, cook for 1 or 2 minutes without browning, then add the thoroughly drained tomatoes. Mix in the paprika and oregano; salt and pepper to taste; cook quickly for about 5 minutes, stirring frequently, taking care not to let the vegetables burn. When most of the liquid is cooked away, remove from heat.

3. Arrange the cooked rice in a lightly buttered 3- or 4-quart casserole. Pour over it ½ cup of reserved chicken/sausage stock. Place the chicken pieces on top and spread the tomato/pepper sauce around and in between them. Slice the sausage into ½-inch pieces and arrange around the edge of the casserole. Bring to a boil on top of stove, then bake in the preheated 350° oven for about 20 minutes. Sprinkle with the parsley. Makes 4 to 6 servings.

CHICKEN LORENZO

1 tablespoon butter
► 8 cooked lasagna noodles
1 tablespoon chopped onion
6 mushrooms, chopped
1 clove garlic, chopped
1 tablespoon olive oil

► ¾ cup ground cooked chicken
⅛ teaspoon ground thyme
Dash ground rosemary
1 tablespoon heavy cream
2 tablespoons grated Parmesan cheese

1. Heat the butter in a frying pan; add the noodles to soften. Remove and reserve.

2. Sauté the onion, mushrooms and garlic in the olive oil and brown lightly. Add the chicken, thyme and rosemary and combine with the cream to bind. Allow to cool.

3. Spread each noodle with about 1 tablespoon of the filling and roll up. Place in a greased baking pan and sprinkle with the cheese. Place in a 350° oven until cheese is melted. Serve with tomato sauce (see Basics). Makes 4 servings.

GRATIN OF CHICKEN

4 tablespoons butter or margarine
4 tablespoons flour
► 1 cup chicken stock, homemade or canned
¼ cup dry white wine
½ to ¾ cup heavy cream
½ teaspoon dried tarragon

Salt to taste
Cayenne to taste
1 teaspoon Dijon-type mustard
¼ cup grated Swiss cheese
► 6 to 8 large pieces, or 4 large breasts, of chicken, cooked
⅓ cup bread crumbs

1. Melt 3 tablespoons of the butter in a small saucepan, remove from heat, and mix in flour. Stir this **roux** until smooth, add the chicken stock and wine and beat together with a whisk to combine. Return the pan to the heat, and cook, stirring constantly, until the sauce thickens. Simmer slowly for about 5 minutes, stirring occasionally. The sauce should be quite thick. Thin it with ½ cup of the heavy cream; if still too thick add the remaining cream, 1 tablespoon at a time, until the sauce runs slugglishly off the spoon. Add the tarragon, salt, cayenne, mustard and Swiss cheese and stir until well blended. Simmer a moment or two to melt the cheese, and taste again for salt. The sauce should be well seasoned.

2. Spread a thin layer of the sauce on the bottom of a shallow baking dish and arrange the chicken pieces in one layer. Sprinkle each lightly with salt, then with a large spoon coat the pieces thoroughly, one by one, with the remaining sauce. Sprinkle the bread crumbs over the top and dot with the remaining butter.

3. Preheat the oven to 375°. Bake for about 20 minutes, until the sauce begins to bubble and the chicken is heated through. Slide under the broiler to brown the surface lightly, then serve at once. Makes 4 servings.

CHICKEN FLORENTINE

1 tablespoon olive oil
1 tablespoon butter
▶ 3 cups cubed cooked chicken
2 cups canned Marinara Sauce
½ cup dry red wine
▶1½ cups chicken stock
1 cup uncooked long grain rice
⅓ cup sliced, pitted black olives
2 packages (10 oz. each) frozen

chopped spinach, cooked and
pressed dry
1 cup ricotta or cottage cheese
2 eggs, beaten
½ teaspoon crushed marjoram
½ teaspoon salt
¼ teaspoon nutmeg
¼ cup grated Parmesan cheese

1. Heat oil and butter in a large skillet; add chicken cubes and sauté quickly until barely brown. Remove chicken from pan and set aside.

2. In a bowl, combine the Marinara Sauce and the wine. Take 1 cup of this mixture and pour into the skillet, adding chicken stock, rice, and olives. Stir thoroughly, scraping the bottom of the skillet. Put into a heavy casserole and bring to a boil; set on a trivet and, over a very low heat, simmer for about 20 minutes or until the rice is tender. Stir the chicken into the rice using a large fork, and combine well.

3. Combine the spinach, ricotta, eggs, marjoram, salt, and nutmeg in a saucepan and heat thoroughly. Spoon the mixture around the edge of the casserole. Pour the remaining sauce/wine mixture over the center. Sprinkle with the cheese and bake in 425° oven, uncovered, for 10 minutes. Makes 6 servings.

CHICKEN ROYALE

2 cans (10½ oz. each) cream of
chicken soup
▶ 2 cups cubed cooked chicken
⅛ teaspoon dried basil
⅛ teaspoon dried rosemary
3 ounces heavy cream
½ cup sherry or Madeira

▶ 2 cups cooked medium noodles
▶ 2 cups cooked broccoli
flowerets
½ pound grated Swiss or
Cheddar cheese
¼ cup slivered, blanched
almonds

1. Empty into the blender the contents of the cans of chicken soup; and blend for 1 minute at high speed. Pour into a saucepan and add the chicken cubes, basil, rosemary, cream, and sherry; heat thoroughly.

2. Spread the noodles in the bottom of a shallow, 3-quart casserole, arrange the broccoli pieces over the noodles and pour the chicken sauce over all. Sprinkle with the grated cheese and the almonds. Bake in 350° oven for 15 minutes. Slide under broiler for 2 minutes to melt cheese and brown slightly. Makes 4 servings.

CHICKEN TETRAZZINI

5 tablespoons butter or
  margarine
2 cups thinly sliced mushrooms
1 medium green pepper, thinly
  sliced
⅓ cup sliced pimiento
▶ 2 cups diced cooked chicken
3 tablespoons flour
2 cups light cream

▶ ½ cup chicken broth
1 teaspoon salt
½ teaspoon white pepper
2 egg yolks
▶ 6 ounces fine spaghetti, cooked
⅛ teaspoon freshly grated
  nutmeg
2 tablespoons dry white wine
Grated Parmesan cheese

1. In a large skillet, melt 2 tablespoons butter, and add the mushrooms and green pepper; sauté until tender, about 5 minutes. Add pimiento and chicken and heat for 3 minutes. Remove from heat.

2. Melt 3 tablespoons butter in a medium saucepan; add flour and stir to a smooth paste. Slowly add the cream and chicken broth, and cook over low heat, stirring constantly, until mixture is smooth and thickened. Season with salt and pepper. Add a small amount of sauce to the egg yolks, mix well and pour slowly back into the saucepan, stirring constantly. Add the chicken mixture, the spaghetti, and the nutmeg and stir well. Remove from heat and add the wine.

3. Put the mixture into a buttered 3-quart casserole. Sprinkle the top with grated Parmesan cheese, and bake in a preheated 375° oven for about 15 minutes or until lightly brown. Makes 6 servings.

PAELLA SEVILLE

6 small sausages: fresh pork
  chorizos, hot or sweet Italian
  sausages
3 tablespoons olive oil
2 tablespoons butter or
  margarine
1 large onion, chopped
1 large clove garlic, chopped
1 medium green pepper and 1
  medium red pepper, seeded
  and cut into 1" x 1½" pieces
1 cup raw rice
1 cup canned tomatoes,
  drained and coarsely
  chopped, or 3 fresh tomatoes,
  chopped

▶ 1 to 1½ cups chicken stock,
  homemade or canned, heated
¼ teaspoon powdered saffron
Salt
Freshly ground black pepper
▶ 2 to 2½ cups cooked chicken,
  cut into 2-inch chunks
1 package frozen artichoke
  hearts, defrosted
8 to 12 large uncooked shrimp,
  shelled and deveined
1 dozen small cherrystone clams,
  scrubbed, or mussels,
  scrubbed and bearded
1 tablespoon finely chopped
  parsley
Pimiento strips (optional)

1. In a shallow frying pan cover the sausages with cold water and cook at a rapid boil, uncovered, piercing them occasionally to allow their fat to escape. When the water has cooked away, turn the heat down and slowly brown the sausages in the remaining fat. Remove from pan and drain on paper toweling. Cut the sausages into 2-inch lengths and reserve.

2. Preheat the oven to 350°. Heat the oil and butter in a heavy 3-quart casserole or a paellera, slowly cook the chopped onion and garlic for

about 3 or 4 minutes. Add the green and red pepper strips and cook for about 15 minutes longer. Stir in the rice and cook, stirring constantly, until most of the grains turn slightly opaque or white. Don't let them burn. Stir in the chopped tomatoes and 1 cup of the hot chicken stock, in which you have first dissolved the saffron. Season highly with salt and pepper.

3. Bring the casserole to a boil on top of the stove, then bake in the oven for about 15 minutes. Remove the casserole from the oven; if the mixture seems dry, moisten with the remaining ½ cup of heated stock. In the rice bury the chicken, artichoke hearts, shrimp, and clams. Cover the casserole tightly, return to the oven, and let it cook until the bivalves open. Sprinkle the top with finely chopped parsley and garnish the paella platter with strips of pimiento. Makes 4 to 6 servings.

CHICKEN RATATOUILLE AU GRATIN

1 tablespoon olive oil	⅛ teaspoon ground fennel
1 medium onion, thinly sliced	2 ounces part-skim Mozzarella
1 small clove garlic, minced	cheese, shredded
▶ 2 cups diced cooked chicken	2 tablespoons chopped parsley
▶ 2 cups Ratatouille	Hot cooked rice

1. Heat oil in large skillet with ovenproof handle. Sauté onion and garlic in oil over moderate heat until onion is tender, about 1 minute. Stir in the chicken, cover, and heat for 5 minutes. Divide mixture and pan juices into four individual or one large baking dish. Preheat oven to 350°.

2. Place Ratatouille in a saucepan, stir in the ground fennel, and heat thoroughly. Spread over the onion/chicken mixture; sprinkle with the cheese and bake for 15 minutes. Sprinkle with parsley before serving over hot fluffy rice. Makes 4 servings.

TRIPLE DELIGHT CASSEROLE

1 package (6 oz.) long grain rice and wild rice mixture	½ teaspoon salt
	1 clove garlic, crushed
1 package (10 oz.) frozen chopped broccoli, partially defrosted	⅛ teaspoon nutmeg
	▶ 2 cups diced cooked chicken
	2 eggs, separated
1 can (10½ oz.) cream of mushroom soup	2 tablespoons butter

1. Cook rice according to package directions but for only 15 minutes. Break apart broccoli and spread on top of rice; mix thoroughly and continue cooking until rice and broccoli are tender and liquid has been absorbed. Remove from heat and allow to cool.

2. Stir together the soup, salt, garlic, nutmeg, chicken and lightly beaten egg yolks. Combine this mixture thoroughly with the rice.

3. Beat egg whites until stiff but not dry; gently fold into rice mixture. Thoroughly butter a 2-quart deep casserole or soufflé dish. With a very light hand spoon the casserole mixture into the prepared dish and bake in a preheated 350° oven for 30 minutes. Makes 6 servings.

SOUTHERN CASSEROLE

¼ cup butter
¼ cup flour
▶ 1 cup chicken broth
1½ cups milk
½ cup light cream
½ teaspoon salt
⅛ teaspoon pepper
⅛ teaspoon ground ginger
¼ teaspoon nutmeg
▶ 2 cups cooked rice
▶ 3 cups diced cooked chicken

1½ cups sliced mushrooms, sautéed lightly with 2 tablespoons of chopped onions
½ cup chopped walnuts
¼ cup blanched almonds, toasted and chopped
2 cups fresh bread crumbs, buttered
½ teaspoon paprika

1. Melt the butter in a large heavy skillet; add the flour and cook 1 minute; stir to a smooth paste. Gradually stir in the chicken broth, milk, and cream, until smooth. Simmer until thickened. Add the salt, pepper, ginger, and nutmeg.

2. Preheat oven to 350°. Layer ½ the rice in a buttered 2-quart baking dish; then layer ½ the chicken, ½ the cream sauce, the mushroom/onion mixture, and the chopped nuts. Repeat the layers, and sprinkle bread crumbs and the paprika over the top layer. Bake 35 minutes or until browned. Makes 6 servings.

CREAMED CHICKEN RING WITH BUTTERED PEA PURÉE

7 to 8 tablespoons butter
4 tablespoons flour
1 cup light cream
Salt and pepper to taste
▶ 3 cups diced cooked chicken
1 can (2½ oz.) mushrooms, drained and chopped

¼ cup dry sherry
2 tablespoons minced parsley
1 tablespoon minced scallion
6 eggs, lightly beaten
½ cup water
2 packages (10½ oz. each) frozen peas

1. Melt 4 tablespoons of the butter in a saucepan over medium heat. Stir in the flour and cook until *roux* is smooth and thickened. Stir in cream, salt and pepper to taste, and simmer sauce 15 to 20 minutes until sauce tastes rich and smooth. Let sauce cool to lukewarm.

2. Combine cream sauce with chicken, mushrooms, sherry, parsley, scallion, and eggs, and additional salt and pepper to taste, in large mixing bowl.

3. Thoroughly butter a 7- to 8-cup ring mold. Pour chicken mixture into mold, and set mold into a larger pan filled with hot water. Bake in a preheated 375° oven until firm, about 30 to 40 minutes.

4. Bring water to boil; add peas, let water come back to boil and cook peas for 30 seconds. Thoroughly drain peas; purée with 2 tablespoons of the butter, using a food processor, blender, or food mill. Season purée with salt and pepper to taste.

5. Unmold chicken ring onto serving platter. Spoon pea purée into center. Makes 4 to 6 servings.

STIR FRY CHICKEN WITH ZUCCHINI

¼ cup peanut oil
½ cup sliced onion
⅓ cup celery, sliced on diagonal
1 clove garlic, crushed
2 thin slices fresh ginger root,
  minced
8 to 10 mushrooms, sliced thin
1 can water chestnuts, drained,
  cut in strips

1 medium zucchini, sliced thin
▶ 1 cup chicken broth
▶1½ cups slivered cooked chicken
1 tablespoon sherry
2 teaspoons cornstarch
2 tablespoons soy sauce
Hot white rice

1. In a heavy skillet or wok, heat 2 tablespoons of oil over high heat until just smoking. Stir fry the onion, celery, garlic, and ginger root quickly for 2 minutes. Remove from pan.

2. Add 1 tablespoon oil; allow to heat. Add mushrooms and water chestnuts; cook for 1 minute. Remove. Add 1 tablespoon oil; allow to heat, then add zucchini. Cook briskly for 3 minutes to brown.

3. Drain all oil from pan. Add ¼ cup chicken broth to pan, cover, lower heat, and steam for 2 to 3 minutes. Return the cooked vegetables to pan. Add the chicken, remaining chicken broth, and sherry. Bring to boil over high heat.

4. Combine cornstarch and soy sauce, add to pan, stirring briskly, to thicken. If too thick, add a bit more broth. If too thin, add a bit more cornstarch thinned with cold broth or water. Serve with white fluffy rice. Makes 4 servings.

CHOP SUEY

3 tablespoons cooking oil
2 cups shredded Chinese
  cabbage
1 cup sliced celery
1 medium onion, sliced
1 green pepper, seeds and
  membrane removed, coarsely
  chopped
6 to 8 mushrooms, sliced
2 scallions, sliced
2 chicken bouillon cubes,
  crumbled

1 cup boiling water
1 cup bean sprouts, drained
½ cup sliced water chestnuts
3 tablespoons soy sauce
▶ 1 cup cooked chicken, cut into
  strips
1½ tablespoons cornstarch,
  blended with ¼ cup cold
  water
▶ 2 cups cooked rice

1. In a large skillet or wok, heat the oil and stir fry the cabbage, celery, and onion for 4 minutes; add the green pepper, mushrooms, and scallions, and stir fry for 2 to 3 minutes.

2. Dissolve the bouillon cubes in the boiling water. Add to the skillet, with the bean sprouts, water chestnuts, soy sauce, and the chicken, and bring to a boil.

3. Quickly blend the cornstarch sauce into the chicken mixture; cook until clear and thickened, about 2 minutes. Serve on rice. Makes 4 servings.

GOLDEN CHICKEN ON ASPARAGUS

3 tablespoons butter or
  margarine
3 tablespoons flour
1¼ cups milk
¼ cup cream
  Salt and pepper to taste
½ cup grated Gruyère or
  Cheddar cheese

1 teaspoon prepared mustard
► 2 cups diced cooked chicken
1 (10 oz.) package frozen kernel
  corn, cooked
2 (10 oz.) packages frozen
  asparagus spears, cooked
► 2 hard-cooked eggs
2 tomatoes

1. In a saucepan melt butter or margarine. Stir in flour and cook 1 minute. Gradually blend in milk and cream. Cook over low heat, stirring constantly, until sauce is smooth and thickened. Season with salt and pepper to taste.

2. Add grated cheese and mustard; stir until melted. Stir in chicken and corn and keep warm over low heat.

3. Arrange asparagus spears on serving platter. Shell hard-cooked eggs. Chop whites finely. Add to chicken mixture.

4. Spoon chicken over asparagus. Garnish with finely sieved egg yolks and tomato slices. Makes 4 to 6 servings.

HAWAIIAN CHICKEN ALMOND

2 tablespoons peanut or
  vegetable oil
½ cup sliced water chestnuts
½ cup sliced celery
½ cup sliced green pepper
2 cups chicken bouillon
3 tablespoons soy sauce
1 tablespoon vinegar

1 tablespoon brown sugar
► 2 cups diced cooked chicken
1 cup drained pineapple cubes
1½ tablespoons cornstarch
3 tablespoons cold water
½ cup toasted, slivered almonds
  Hot cooked rice

1. Heat the oil in a large skillet or wok. Cook the water chestnuts, celery, and green pepper for 5 minutes, stirring frequently.

2. Combine the chicken bouillon, soy sauce, and vinegar; stir in the brown sugar until dissolved. Add to the vegetables in the skillet, and combine thoroughly. Add the chicken and pineapple cubes, and bring to a boil.

3. Blend the cornstarch with the cold water. Add to the skillet and cook, stirring constantly, until thickened. Sprinkle with almonds. Serve with hot, cooked rice. Makes 4 to 6 servings.

CHICKEN VERONIQUE

3 tablespoons butter
3 tablespoons flour
1½ cups milk
⅓ cup white wine
1 cup small seedless green grapes

▶ 2 whole cooked chicken breasts, or 4 cups of large chunks
¼ cup heavy cream, whipped
Salt and pepper to taste

1. Melt butter in a saucepan. Blend in the flour and cook 3 minutes; do not allow to brown. Slowly add the milk, stirring constantly until well-blended, and cook slowly over low heat for about 10 minutes, until thickened and smooth.

2. Heat the wine, and simmer the grapes and chicken for 2 to 3 minutes.

3. Fold whipped cream into the hot sauce, and season with salt and pepper to taste.

4. Arrange the chicken and grapes on a serving platter, and spoon the sauce over all. Makes 4 servings.

BATON ROUGE CHICKEN CREOLE

5 tablespoons butter or chicken fat
2 tablespoons chopped onion
2 tablespoons chopped green pepper
10 sliced mushrooms or 1 can (2 oz.), drained
3 tablespoons flour
¼ teaspoon salt
¼ teaspoon paprika

½ cup tomato purée or strained tomatoes
▶ 1 cup chicken broth
¼ teaspoon garlic powder
1 teaspoon lemon juice
½ teaspoon horseradish
10 stuffed olives, sliced
▶ 2 cups diced cooked chicken
Hot cooked rice
1 cup sour cream

1. Melt the butter in a large skillet, and sauté the onion and green pepper for 2 minutes; add the mushrooms and cook 4 minutes longer. Stir in the flour, salt and paprika blending well, and cook for 3 minutes, stirring frequently.

2. Slowly add the tomato purée and the chicken broth, stirring constantly to blend well. Bring to boil, then add the garlic powder, lemon juice, horseradish and olives, reduce the heat, add the chicken and simmer until smooth and thickened.

3. Press the hot rice into a buttered ring mold and wait about five minutes before turning out onto a serving plate. Pour chicken creole mixture into the center and over the sides. Top with the sour cream. Makes 4 to 6 servings.

BRUNSWICK STEW

3 tablespoons cooking oil
2 medium onions, chopped
2 medium potatoes, peeled and diced
2 carrots, peeled and diced
► ½ cup chicken broth
1 can (16 oz.) tomatoes
½ cup water
1 package (10 oz.) frozen whole kernel corn

1 package (10 oz.) frozen lima beans
½ cup sliced celery
1 tablespoon Worcestershire sauce
½ teaspoon salt
¼ teaspoon black pepper
Dash Tabasco
¼ teaspoon rosemary, crumbled
1 bay leaf
► 2 cups cubed cooked chicken

Heat the oil in a large saucepan; sauté the onions until soft. Add the potatoes, carrots, chicken broth, tomatoes, water, corn, beans, celery, Worcestershire sauce, salt, pepper, Tabasco, rosemary, and bay leaf. Simmer, covered, 20 to 25 minutes or until vegetables are tender. Add the chicken and heat thoroughly, about 5 minutes. Makes 4 to 6 servings.

CHICKEN CACCIATORE WITH SPAGHETTI

2 tablespoons olive oil
1 medium onion, chopped
1 medium green pepper, chopped
1 clove garlic, minced
1 can (16 oz.) Italian plum tomatoes with basil (2 cups), drained and chopped
1 can (8 oz.) tomato sauce
½ cup red wine

½ teaspoon celery seed
½ teaspoon oregano
1 teaspoon salt
Freshly ground black pepper, to taste
► 6 to 8 pieces cooked chicken, or 2 cups, cubed
1 package (16 oz.) thin spaghetti
½ cup grated Parmesan cheese

1. Heat the oil in a large heavy saucepan. Add onion, green pepper, and garlic. Cook, stirring, over medium heat until onion is limp but not browned. Add tomatoes, tomatoe sauce, and wine and combine well. Season with celery seed, oregano, salt, and pepper. Turn heat to low, and simmer sauce gently for about 15 minutes, stirring occasionally. Add chicken pieces and cook a final 10 minutes, or until chicken is thoroughly heated.

2. Cook spaghetti according to package directions for *al dente*. Drain well, and place on large platter. Place chicken pieces in center, cover with some of the sauce, and sprinkle with Parmesan cheese. Serve any remaining sauce separately. Makes 4 servings.

BARBECUED CHICKEN ON ROLL

2 tablespoons melted butter
2 tablespoons finely chopped
  onion
1 tablespoon finely chopped
  green pepper
3 tablespoons flour
1 can (8 oz.) tomato sauce
1 cup water
▶ 2 cups diced cooked chicken

2 tablespoons lemon juice
2 teaspoons salt
¼ teaspoon pepper
2 tablespoons sugar
1 tablespoon prepared
  horseradish
1 tablespoon prepared mustard
6 to 8 hamburger rolls

1. Heat butter in a heavy skillet and sauté the onion and green pepper for about 5 minutes. Blend in flour and cook for 1 minute. Gradually add the tomato sauce and water and bring to boil, stirring constantly until thickened.

2. Add the chicken, lemon juice, salt, pepper, sugar, horseradish, and mustard. Cover and simmer slowly for 15 minutes. Serve on split, toasted and buttered hamburger rolls. Makes 6 to 8 servings.

CHICKEN INDIENNE CURRY

3 tablespoons butter or
  margarine
1 small onion, sliced
3 tablespoons flour
1 teaspoon to 1 tablespoon curry
  powder, to taste
¾ cup milk
▶ ¾ cup chicken stock

Salt and pepper, to taste
1 egg yolk
½ teaspoon ground ginger
1½ tablespoons dry vermouth
  (optional)
2 tablespoons chutney
3 tablespoons raisins
▶ 3 cups cubed cooked chicken

1. Melt the butter in a skillet, and sauté the onion for 3 minutes. Stir in the flour and curry powder and blend thoroughly; cook for 1 to 2 minutes. Slowly stir in the milk and chicken stock, and cook, stirring constantly, until sauce is smooth and thickened. Salt and pepper to taste.

2. When ready to serve, beat the egg yolk; mix 2 to 3 tablespoons of the sauce into the yolk and slowly pour the mixture back into the sauce. Add the ginger, vermouth, chutney, raisins and the chicken to the sauce and combine well. Heat thoroughly, but do not boil.

3. Serve with hot fluffy rice and any or all of these accompaniments: more chutney and raisins, chopped apple, chopped onion, sieved hard-cooked egg, chopped peanuts and/or slivered almonds, thinly-sliced cucumber, crumbled crisp bacon. Makes 4 to 6 servings.

CALABRIAN CHICKEN

3 tablespoons olive oil
▶ 2 cups cubed cooked chicken
▶ 1 cup cubed cooked ham
2 cloves garlic, minced
½ cup dry white wine
2 green peppers, cut into rings
1 cup sliced mushrooms

2 medium onions, chopped
1 zucchini, sliced (about 8 oz.)
1 can (16 oz.) tomatoes
1 bay leaf
½ teaspoon dried marjoram
1 tablespoon chopped parsley

1. Heat oil in a large skillet; brown chicken and ham lightly. Remove from pan and drain. Add the garlic and wine to the pan; cook until wine is reduced by half.

2. Add green peppers, mushrooms, onions, zucchini, tomatoes, bay leaf, marjoram, and parsley. Simmer for 10 to 12 minutes.

3. Add chicken and ham; stir to blend. Cook until heated through, about 10 to 15 minutes. Makes 4 servings.

CHICKEN À LA KING

1 can (10½ oz.) condensed
  cream of chicken soup
½ cup cream
1 can (3 oz.) broiled sliced
  mushrooms
¼ cup chopped pimiento

▶ 1 cup cooked peas
▶ 1½ cups finely diced cooked
  chicken
2 tablespoons sherry
6 waffles or baked pastry shells
Chopped parsley

1. In a saucepan, mix the cream of chicken soup with the cream until smooth. Add the mushrooms, pimiento and peas and stir until thoroughly blended. Add the chicken. Stir gently until heated. Add the sherry.

2. Serve on waffles or pastry shells. Garnish with chopped parsley. Makes 6 servings.

SWEET AND SOUR CHICKEN

1 can (20 oz.) pineapple chunks,
  juice drained and reserved
½ cup brown sugar, packed
2 tablespoons cornstarch
½ teaspoon ground ginger
½ cup cider vinegar
¼ cup soy sauce

1¼ cups green pepper strips
1 cup sliced onion
½ cup sliced celery
1 cup sliced pared carrots
▶ 2 cups cubed cooked chicken
  Hot cooked rice

1. Combine reserved pineapple juice with enough water to make 2½ cups. Mix the brown sugar, cornstarch and ginger in a large skillet. Gradually stir in the reserved liquid, vinegar, and soy sauce. Place over high heat and cook, stirring constantly, until mixture comes to a boil, about 6 minutes.

2. Add pineapple chunks, green pepper, onion, celery, carrots, and chicken. Reduce heat to low. Cover and simmer 10 minutes or until the vegetables are crisp-tender. Serve with rice. Makes 6 servings.

CHICKEN AND MUSHROOMS

1 teaspoon salt
¼ teaspoon white pepper
1 tablespoon cornstarch
▶ 3 cups cubed cooked chicken
¼ cup oil
2 thin slices fresh ginger root, minced

2 cups small fresh button mushrooms
1 green pepper, seeded and cut into strips 1½ inches long
1 tablespoon cornstarch dissolved in ⅓ cup chicken broth

1. Mix salt, pepper, and cornstarch. Add chicken cubes and toss to coat.

2. Heat the oil in a large skillet or wok until very hot. Add ginger root and stir fry ½ minute. Add chicken and stir fry 1 minute to brown slightly. Remove from pan. Add mushrooms and green pepper and stir fry 1½ minutes. Return chicken to pan.

3. Add cornstarch mixture and stir until thickened. Serve immediately. Makes 4 servings.

CHICKEN MONTEREY

6 tablespoons butter
2 acorn squash
1 cup water
1 can (10½ oz.) condensed cream of chicken soup
2 tablespoons dry sherry
▶ 2 cups diced cooked chicken

▶ 1 cup cooked green peas
2 tablespoons chopped parsley
1 tablespoon lemon juice
½ teaspoon salt
⅛ teaspoon pepper
½ cup grated Swiss cheese
1 cup fresh bread crumbs

1. Melt 2 tablespoons of butter. Cut the squash in half, remove seeds and brush with melted butter. Place squash, cut side up, in roasting pan with water; cover pan tightly with aluminum foil. Bake the squash in a preheated 350° oven for 45 minutes or until they are very tender; remove from oven and keep warm. (Do not turn oven off.)

2. Combine the soup and sherry, bring to a boil and remove from heat. Stir in the chicken, peas, parsley, lemon juice, salt, pepper and cheese.

3. Melt remaining butter in skillet; set aside two tablespoons of the butter. Add the bread crumbs to butter in skillet and cook, stirring often, over medium heat until crumbs are golden.

4. Heap the chicken mixture into center of each squash half; sprinkle chicken-filled center with bread crumbs; brush reserved melted butter over exposed border rim of each squash half.

5. Place the squash halves back into the roasting pan, add a little water to bottom of pan if it is absolutely dry; and bake 20 minutes or until heated through. Makes 4 servings.

CHICKEN AND CRAB STUFFED ACORN SQUASH

3 medium acorn squash
½ teaspoon salt
2 tablespoons butter
2 cups sour cream
▶ 1½ cups diced cooked chicken

▶ 1 cup cooked crabmeat, diced or flaked
2 tablespoons dry Madeira wine
½ cup grated Swiss cheese

1. Wash the acorn squash and cut in half lengthwise. Remove seeds and fibers. Place cut sides down on buttered baking sheet. Bake at 350° for 35 to 40 minutes. Turn cut sides up, sprinkle with salt, dot with butter, and continue baking for 15 to 20 minutes, or until squash is tender.

2. Meanwhile, place sour cream in a saucepan; mix in the diced cooked chicken, crabmeat, and Madeira. Heat over low heat just to serving temperature.

3. Fill squash halves with chicken/crabmeat mixture; sprinkle with Swiss cheese and serve immediately. Makes 6 servings.

HONOLULU STUFFED SQUASH

2 large acorn squash
1 can (12½ oz.) pineapple tidbits, drained; reserve syrup
2 tablespoons honey
½ teaspoon cinnamon

⅛ teaspoon freshly grated nutmeg
½ cup chopped walnuts
▶ 1 cup diced cooked chicken

1. Wash the acorn squash and cut in half, lengthwise. Remove seeds and fibers. Place cut side down on buttered baking sheet. Bake at 350° for 35 to 40 minutes. Turn cut sides up.

2. Mix the drained pineapple tidbits with honey, cinnamon, nutmeg, chopped walnuts, chicken, and enough pineapple juice to moisten. Spoon into acorn squash halves. Return to oven and bake 15 minutes or until squash is tender. Makes 4 servings.

Heating terms

"simmer"—over the lowest possible heat
"cook"—over moderate to low heat
"sauté"—(quickly) over moderate to high heat
"boil" and "stir fry"—over high heat

ONIONS STUFFED WITH CHICKEN

6 large mild onions, peeled
3 tablespoons butter or
  margarine
½ cup chopped mushrooms
▶ ½ cup chopped cooked chicken
1 cup soft bread crumbs

Salt and pepper
Cayenne
½ cup chicken bouillon
Paprika
½ cup sour cream

1. Parboil onions for 15 minutes. Scoop out centers leaving a ¼-inch shell to be stuffed. Chop the centers and sauté in melted butter with the mushrooms for 2 or 3 minutes, then combine with the chicken, bread crumbs, salt and pepper, and the cayenne.

2. Stuff the onions. Put in buttered baking pan. Pour the bouillon into the pan around the onions; sprinkle the onions with paprika. Cover and bake in preheated 375° oven for about 30 minutes. Remove cover for the last 10 minutes to permit the onions to brown. Remove the onions to a serving dish. Add the sour cream to the pan and stir to blend. Serve over the onions. Makes 6 servings.

CURRIED CHICKEN IN PEPPER CUPS

6 medium green peppers
▶ 1½ cups cooked rice
▶ 1½ cups diced cooked chicken
½ cup chopped celery
¼ cup minced onion
2 tablespoons chopped
  pimiento

¾ cup mayonnaise
¼ cup sour cream
1 teaspoon curry powder
½ teaspoon salt
Dash pepper

1. Remove the tops and seeds from the green peppers; partially cook in small amount of boiling salted water, about 5 minutes. Drain.

2. Mix rice with chicken, celery, onion, and pimiento. Combine the mayonnaise, sour cream, curry powder, salt and pepper. Add to the rice mixture and toss lightly.

3. Fill peppers and place in greased 10 × 6 × 1½-inch baking dish; pour small amount of water around peppers. Bake in moderate oven (350°) for 30 minutes. Makes 6 servings.

Remember: turkey may be substituted for chicken in chicken recipes, and vice versa.

DEEP DISH CHICKEN PIE

1 cup plus 2 tablespoons flour
1 teaspoon baking powder
½ teaspoon salt
▶ 1 cup mashed cooked sweet
   potatoes, cooled
2 tablespoons butter, melted
1 egg, well beaten
▶ 3 cups diced cooked chicken
▶ 1 cup diced cooked carrots

▶ 6 small white onions, boiled and
   halved
▶ 1 cup cooked green peas
1 tablespoon chopped parsley
½ teaspoon poultry seasoning
½ teaspoon oregano
⅛ teaspoon pepper
⅛ teaspoon paprika
▶ 1 cup chicken gravy
▶ 1 cup chicken broth

1. To make the dough, combine 1 cup flour, baking powder, and salt. In a bowl combine the sweet potatoes, butter, and egg. Stir in dry ingredients. Chill thoroughly, covered, at least 1 hour.

2. Put the chicken in a shallow 1½-quart baking dish. Sprinkle with the carrots, onions, peas and parsley.

3. Combine 2 tablespoons of the flour with the poultry seasoning, oregano, pepper and paprika in a saucepan. Gradually stir in the chicken gravy and broth. Bring to a boil. Cook, stirring constantly, for 2 minutes. Pour sauce over chicken mixture.

4. Roll out dough ¼-inch thick on a lightly floured board; cut a little larger than the baking dish. Place over baking dish and flute edge. Bake 40 minutes or until top is lightly browned. Makes 6 servings.

RUSSIAN CHICKEN PIE

10 tablespoons butter
6 tablespoons flour
▶ 2 cups chicken stock,
   homemade
¾ cup heavy cream
1 teaspoon fresh lemon juice
Salt and pepper to taste
¼ pound mushrooms, finely
   chopped

4 tablespoons Madeira
▶ 2 cups cubed cooked chicken
▶1½ cups cooked rice
▶ 4 hard-cooked eggs, chopped
4 tablespoons finely chopped
   fresh dill, or 2 teaspoons dried
   dill
1 recipe pastry crust (see Basics)

1. Melt 6 tablespoons of the butter in a large saucepan and stir in the flour. Cook for 1 minute. Add the chicken stock and bring to a boil. Lower heat to simmer and add ½ cup cream. Cook for 1 minute more. Add the lemon juice, and salt and pepper to taste.

2. Melt 2 tablespoons of the butter in a small frying pan and add the mushrooms; sauté for 1 minute. Cook over low heat, stirring, for about 10 minutes. Pour in the Madeira, raise the heat and cook the wine away. Add the chicken and mix well.

3. In the bottom of a large greased baking dish, spread the rice. Scatter over it the chopped eggs and half the dill. Arrange the chicken mixture evenly over the eggs, then cover with 1½ cups of the cooked sauce. Sprinkle with the remaining dill. Dot with remaining 2 tablespoons butter. Cover with the pastry crust. Bake in a 375° oven for 45 minutes, or until crust is golden brown. Serve with remaining sauce, thinned with remaining cream. Makes 6 servings.

BAYOU CHICKEN AND OYSTER PIE

¼ cup butter or margarine
¼ cup finely chopped onion
⅓ cup finely chopped celery
3 tablespoons flour
⅛ teaspoon paprika
¼ teaspoon curry powder
¼ teaspoon salt
⅛ teaspoon pepper
1 pint oysters, freshly shucked, liquor reserved

▶ ½ cup (approximately) chicken broth
1 cup cream
¼ cup finely chopped parsley
1 pimiento, chopped
▶ 2 hard-cooked eggs, chopped
▶ 3 cups diced cooked chicken
Baking Powder Biscuit dough (below)

1. In a saucepan, melt the butter; stir in the onion and celery and sauté until vegetables are tender. Add the flour, paprika, curry powder, salt, and pepper and cook 1 minute.

2. Measure the reserved oyster liquor and add enough chicken broth to make 1 cup; stir into the saucepan mixture along with cream. Cook sauce over low heat, stirring frequently, until it is thickened and smooth.

3. Lower heat to a bare simmer; add oysters, parsley, pimiento, eggs, and chicken to sauce and cook about 2 minutes, just until oysters begin to plump. Pour mixture into a buttered 2-quart casserole. Set aside.

4. Prepare the Baking Powder Biscuit dough with:

1¾ cups flour
2 teaspoons baking powder
1 teaspoon salt
1 teaspoon sugar
½ teaspoon baking soda

½ teaspoon sage
½ teaspoon cream of tartar
¼ cup lard or 5 tablespoons butter
⅔ to ¾ cup buttermilk

Sift before measuring the dry ingredients. Mix the flour, baking powder, salt, sugar, baking soda, sage, and cream of tartar. Cut in the lard with a pastry knife until the mixture resembles corn meal. Add the buttermilk all at once, and mix gently with a fork until a soft dough is formed. Turn onto a floured board and knead lightly for ½ minute.

5. Roll dough out about ½-inch thick to fit the top of the casserole. Place on top of the chicken mixture. Bake casserole in a preheated 450° oven for 15 to 20 minutes or until golden. Makes 6 servings.

CURRIED CHICKEN PIE

▶ 1½ cups leftover stuffing
4 tablespoons butter, melted
½ cup milk
1 can (10½ oz.) condensed cream of chicken soup
▶ 1½ cups cubed cooked chicken

▶ 1 cup cooked peas
⅓ cup chopped fresh mushrooms
1 tablespoon minced onion
1 teaspoon curry powder
¼ cup raisins, soaked in hot water 15 minutes

1. Combine the stuffing, buttter and 1 to 2 tablespoons water in a medium bowl. Set aside ⅓ cup. Press the remaining stuffing into a 9-inch pie plate.

2. Stir the milk into soup; add the chicken, peas, mushrooms, onion, curry powder and raisins. Cook for about 5 minutes, over low heat to blend flavors. Turn into the stuffing shell. Top with the reserved ⅓ cup stuffing. Bake in 425° oven for 10 minutes. Makes 6 servings.

CALIFORNIA CHICKEN PIE

1½ cups sifted enriched flour
½ teaspoon salt
½ cup shortening
½ cup shredded Cheddar
   cheese
4 to 5 tablespoons cold water
▶ 2 cups diced cooked chicken

1 can (9 oz.) pineapple tidbits,
   drained
1 cup chopped walnuts
½ cup sliced celery
1 cup sour cream
⅔ cup mayonnaise
6 ripe olives

1. To prepare the pastry shell, mix the flour and salt. Cut in the shortening and ⅓ cup cheese with pastry blender or 2 knives until mixture resembles coarse corn meal. Sprinkle with the water, 1 tablespoon at a time, mixing lightly with a fork until all the dry ingredients are moistened; turn dough on to a floured board and roll out the pastry to a 9" round; transfer to the 8" piepan and ease loosely into place. With a fork, prick the shell close and deep on bottom and sides. Bake in preheated very hot (450°) oven for 12 to 15 minutes, or until golden-brown. Cool the shell.

2. Combine the chicken, pineapple, nuts, and celery. Blend the sour cream and mayonnaise and add ⅔ cup to chicken mixture; mix well. Spoon into the pastry shell. Top with the remaining sour cream mixture and sprinkle with reserved cheese. Chill. Trim with ripe olive slices. Makes 6 servings.

CHICKEN PASTIES

2 tablespoons mayonnaise
4 tablespoons sour cream
2 eggs, lightly beaten
▶ 2 cups minced cooked chicken
4 tablespoons minced onions
1 cup shredded Monterey Jack,
   Mozzarella, or Swiss cheese
½ teaspoon dried tarragon

2 tablespoons minced fresh
   parsley
Pastry for 2-crust pie, chilled
(see Basics)
1 egg yolk beaten with 1
   tablespoon milk or half-and-
   half cream

1. Combine the mayonnaise, sour cream and the eggs, blending well. Add the chicken, onion, cheese, tarragon, and parsley. Divide into 8 portions.

2. Divide the pastry into 8 pieces. On a lightly-floured board, roll out the dough to about ⅛" thickness into a 6-inch round; place one portion of the filling on half of the round; brush edges with water; fold the dough over the filling and press the edges together; crimp with a fork. Repeat with the remaining pastry and filling.

3. Brush tops with yolk mixture and cut small vent holes in each. Carefully place the filled pastries on an ungreased baking sheet and bake at 400° for 20 to 25 minutes or until golden brown. Serve hot or cold. Makes 8.

SOUTHERN CHICKEN BISCUITS

1½ cups flour
½ teaspoon salt
4 teaspoons baking powder
¼ teaspoon nutmeg
2 tablespoons shortening
► ¾ cup mashed potatoes
► ¾ cup diced cooked chicken
¼ cup shredded Cheddar
cheese

¼ cup chopped mushrooms
1 egg
¼ cup milk
Melted butter
1 tablespoon minced parsley
1 tablespoon minced chives

1. In a mixing bowl, combine the flour, salt, baking powder, and nutmeg. Cut in the shortening and mashed potatoes; blend until flour mixture is the size of peas. Add the chicken, cheese, and mushrooms. Mix the egg with the milk; add to flour mixture and stir until blended. Knead dough lightly on floured board. Pat to ¾-inch thickness.

2. Cut into 3-inch squares, then into triangles. Place on a greased baking sheet and bake at 450° for 10 minutes. Brush with melted butter and sprinkle with parsley and chives; bake 5 minutes longer. Makes 4 servings.

COUNTRY CHICKEN PIE

2 cups packaged baking mix
½ cup cold water
3 to 4 tablespoons butter
1 cup thinly sliced mushrooms
¼ cup chopped green pepper
½ cup thinly sliced green onions
1 jar (2 oz.) pimiento, drained
and chopped
►1½ cups diced cooked chicken

1 cup (4 oz.) shredded Cheddar
cheese
1 cup sour cream
⅓ cup mayonnaise
3 eggs, beaten
1 teaspoon garlic salt
⅛ teaspoon pepper
½ teaspoon dry mustard

1. Combine the baking mix and water until a soft dough forms; beat vigorously 20 strokes. Gently smooth the dough into a ball on a floured board and knead 5 times. Roll the dough into a rectangle, 14-x 10-inches. Place dough in a rectangular, well-buttered baking dish 13- x 9- x 2-inches, so edges of dough are ½ inch up sides of dish.

2. Melt 2 tablespoons of the butter in a skillet. Sauté mushrooms and green pepper until liquid in pan has evaporated and vegetables are tender. Add green onions and cook, stirring, another minute.

3. Combine cooked vegetables with pimiento, chicken, cheese, sour cream, mayonnaise, eggs, garlic salt, pepper, and mustard. Mix thoroughly and spread mixture evenly over prepared dough.

4. Bake pie in preheated 425° oven until edges are golden and knife inserted in center comes out clean, about 25 minutes. Cut into squares. Makes 6 to 8 servings.

CHICKEN-SPINACH QUICHE

Piecrust mix for one 9-inch
piecrust
3 tablespoons butter or
margarine
3 scallions, minced
3 eggs
2 cups half-and-half cream
1 teaspoon salt

⅛ teaspoon pepper
Freshly grated nutmeg
1 cup shredded Swiss cheese
1 package (10 oz.) frozen
chopped spinach, cooked and
squeezed dry
▶ 1 cup diced cooked chicken

1. Prepare piecrust mix as label directs; use to line 9-inch pie plate. Spread crust with 1 tablespoon softened butter or margarine. Preheat oven to 425°.

2. In a small saucepan, over medium heat, melt 2 tablespoons butter; add the scallions and cook for 3 to 4 minutes or until tender, stirring occasionally. Remove saucepan from heat; set aside.

3. In a medium bowl, beat the eggs well with the half-and-half, salt, pepper, and several gratings of nutmeg. Add the cheese, spinach, chicken, and scallions, and mix thoroughly. Pour into the piecrust. Bake 15 minutes. Reduce the heat to 325° and bake 30 minutes longer or until knife inserted in center comes out clean. Makes 6 servings.

RUSSIAN CHICKEN TURNOVERS

6 slices stale white bread, crusts
removed
▶ 1 cup ground or minced cooked
chicken, chilled
1 small clove garlic, crushed
2 tablespoons chopped onion
1 tablespoon chopped parsley
1 tablespoon chopped celery
¼ cup chopped stuffed green
olives

1 egg yolk, slightly beaten with 1
tablespoon cream
1 tablespoon lemon juice
Dash hot pepper sauce
¼ teaspoon dried rosemary
⅛ teaspoon ground ginger
Salt and pepper to taste
1 package pie crust mix

1. Break up the bread, soak in water for 1 minute and squeeze dry. Mix in a bowl with the chicken, garlic, onion, parsley, celery and olives. Combine the egg yolk/cream with the lemon juice; add to the chicken mixture and season with rosemary, ginger, salt and pepper.

2. Prepare the pie crust mix according to directions on the package. On a floured board roll dough into a large rectangle to a ⅛-inch thickness. Cut into 8 six-inch squares.

3. Divide the filling among the squares, placing it in one corner of each. Brush the edges with water, fold into triangles and crimp edges with a fork. Brush tops with milk or unbeaten egg white. Bake in a preheated 400° oven 12 to 15 minutes. Makes 8 large turnovers.

CHICKEN-TAMALE PIE

7 tablespoons butter or
margarine
1 onion, chopped
2 cloves garlic, chopped
3 teaspoons chili powder
1 teaspoon ground coriander
► 4 cups cooked chicken, cut in
large pieces

1 cup sliced pitted ripe olives
1 can (10 oz.) tomato purée
► 6 cups chicken broth
Salt and pepper to taste
2 cups cornmeal
1½ cups shredded Cheddar
cheese

1. Melt 2 tablespoons butter in large skillet. Sauté onion and garlic until tender. Stir in chili powder and coriander. Cook 1 minute. Add chicken, olives, tomato purée, ½ cup chicken broth and salt and pepper to taste. Cover; simmer 15 minutes.

2. Bring 5½ cups chicken broth to a boil; slowly stir in cornmeal. Add 3 tablespoons butter; cook, stirring constantly, 5 minutes. Add salt to taste.

3. Butter 3-quart casserole; line it with half of cornmeal mush. Pour in chicken mixture; sprinkle with cheese and cover with rest of mush. Bake in a preheated 300° oven for 1¼ hours. Makes 6 hearty servings.

CHICKEN-FILLED CRÊPES IN CHEESE SAUCE

3 eggs
1½ cups milk
1 cup plus 2 tablespoons flour
¾ teaspoon salt
5 tablespoons butter or
margarine
¼ teaspoon pepper
Dash Tabasco
1 cup shredded Swiss cheese

1 small onion, chopped
►1¼ cups chopped cooked
chicken
►1½ cups cooked rice
► ½ cup cooked peas
½ teaspoon leaf rosemary
½ teaspoon leaf thyme
¼ teaspoon dry mustard

1. Place the eggs, ½ cup of the milk, 1 cup of the flour, ¼ teaspoon of the salt, and 2 tablespoons of the butter, melted, in a blender or food processor and whirl until smooth. Refrigerate batter at least 1 hour. Heat a 6-inch skillet until hot; rub the bottom with butter to film. Pour enough batter in to coat the bottom; tilt the skillet to spread batter evenly over the bottom. Cook until lightly browned, flip and cook the other side. Turn crêpes out on wax paper until ready to use.

2. Melt 2 tablespoons of the butter in a small saucepan. Blend in the remaining flour, ¼ teaspoon of the salt, and the pepper; cook 1 minute. Add milk; cook, stirring constantly, until mixture thickens and bubbles. Remove from heat; add Tabasco and cheese, stirring until melted; reserve.

3. In a large skillet, sauté onion in remaining butter until tender. Add chicken, rice, peas, rosemary, thyme, mustard, and the remaining salt and pepper. Add ⅔ of the cheese sauce, stirring until blended.

4. Spoon a heaping tablespoonful of the chicken mixture on each crêpe; roll up. Repeat until all crêpes are filled. Arrange crêpes in a shallow baking dish and spoon remaining cheese sauce over crêpes. Bake at 375° for 15 minutes, or until sauce is bubbly and lightly browned. Makes 6 servings.

CHICKEN FRITTERS

2 teaspoons butter
4 medium shallots, thinly sliced
1 clove garlic, pressed
¼ teaspoon salt
½ teaspoon freshly ground
 pepper
1 teaspoon ground ginger

¼ teaspoon freshly grated
 nutmeg
►1½ cups finely chopped cooked
 chicken
2 eggs, beaten
1 tablespoon cornstarch
¼ cup peanut oil or corn oil

1. Melt butter in a heavy large skillet over medium heat; sauté the shallots and garlic until golden. Stir in salt, pepper, ginger, and nutmeg, blending well. In a mixing bowl, combine the chicken, eggs, cornstarch, and shallot mixture; blend well.

2. Heat oil in heavy large skillet or wok over medium-high heat. Add chicken mixture to oil by heaping teaspoons (do not crowd) and brown on both sides. Remove with slotted spoon and drain well on paper towel. Makes 4 servings.

CHICKEN CRÊPES À LA RUSSE

3 tablespoons butter
1 tablespoon flour
½ cup light cream
½ teaspoon salt
⅛ teaspoon pepper
► 1 cup chopped cooked chicken

¼ cup chopped almonds
¼ cup chopped mushrooms,
 sautéed in 1 teaspoon butter
8 cooked crêpes (see Basics)
½ cup sour cream
¼ cup grated Parmesan cheese

1. Heat oven to 375°. In a medium-sized skillet, melt 1 tablespoon of butter and blend in the flour. Cook and stir 1 minute. Add cream gradually, stirring constantly, and bring to a boil. Add salt and pepper. Cook until sauce is smooth and thick, about 5 to 10 minutes.

2. Add chicken, almonds and mushrooms; mix well. Top each crêpe with a generous tablespoonful of chicken mixture, roll up and arrange side by side in a greased, shallow 2-quart baking dish. Top each crêpe with a dollop of sour cream. Sprinkle with cheese and dot with the remaining butter. Bake 20 minutes, or until cheese is melted. Makes 4 servings.

Combining meats

Some of these recipes call for up to 2 cups of once-cooked chicken. The amount may be more than you have on hand. If so, you can add other leftover meats such as pork or ham. They combine extremely well with chicken.

CHICKEN POTATO PANCAKES

3 eggs, lightly beaten
3 cups shredded raw potatoes,
  thoroughly drained
▶1½ cups finely minced cooked
  chicken
2 tablespoons finely minced
  onion

2 tablespoons finely minced
  parsley
1½ teaspoons salt
¼ teaspoon pepper
1½ tablespoons flour
Warm applesauce

1. Combine eggs, potatoes, chicken, onion, parsley, salt, pepper, and flour in large bowl and mix well.

2. Lightly grease a griddle and place over medium heat. When griddle is hot, drop batter by ¼-cup measure onto griddle and spread batter so that pancakes are about 4 inches in diameter. Cook 3 to 4 minutes, turn, and cook until light golden.

3. Transfer pancakes to plates, cover, and keep warm; repeat until all the batter is used. Serve with warm applesauce. Makes 15 pancakes.

CHICKEN PUFFS

▶ 2 cups finely chopped cooked
  chicken
¼ cup finely chopped celery
2 tablespoons minced onion
2 tablespoons chopped
  pimiento
⅓ cup mayonnaise

2 tablespoons dry white wine
¼ teaspoon salt
Dash pepper
⅔ cup water
1 recipe puff shells (see Basics)
Watercress

1. Stir together the chicken, celery, onion, pimiento, mayonnaise, wine, salt, and pepper in a medium mixing bowl and chill.

2. To make the puffs: drop the prepared dough from a rounded teaspoon onto ungreased baking sheet, and sprinkle lightly with a few drops of water. Bake in 425° oven for 20 to 25 minutes until puffed, golden brown, and dry.

3. Transfer puffs to rack; cool slowly away from draft. Split and fill with chicken mixture and top with a few sprigs of watercress. Makes 8 to 10 servings as an hors d'oeuvre.

In leftovers cooking

...tables of ingredient substitutions and weight and volume equivalents are often helpful. You will find such tables in the back of this cookbook following the "Basics" recipes section.

CHICKEN ENCHILADAS

1 cup chopped onion
1 clove garlic, minced
1 can (4 oz.) chili peppers,
  drained, seeded and chopped
1 tablespoon corn oil
2½ cups tomato purée
½ cup water
½ cup raisins, soaked in hot
  water 15 minutes

¼ cup chopped pitted black
  olives
½ teaspoon salt
¼ teaspoon cumin
1 package (9 oz.) refrigerated,
  canned or frozen tortillas
► 1 cup chopped cooked chicken
1 cup sour cream
1 cup shredded Cheddar
  cheese

1. In a large saucepan, sauté onion, garlic and chili peppers in oil until tender, about 3 minutes. Add tomato purée, water, raisins, olives, ¼ teaspoon of the salt and the cumin; bring to boiling, lower heat and simmer 30 minutes.

2. Soften tortillas, following label directions.

3. Combine chicken, sour cream, ¾ cup of the cheese and remaining salt in a medium-sized bowl. Spoon a rounded tablespoon of the chicken mixture in center of each tortilla; roll up. Place filled tortillas, seam-side down, in a greased rectangular baking dish. Spoon sauce over top; sprinkle with remaining cheese. Bake in a moderate 350° oven for 20 minutes. Makes 4 servings.

CHICKEN SOUFFLÉ

3 tablespoons butter
1 small onion, minced
3 tablespoons flour
1 cup hot milk
4 egg yolks
► 1 cup finely diced cooked
  chicken

½ teaspoon salt
  Dash cayenne pepper
2 tablespoons minced parsley
2 tablespoons minced chives
5 egg whites
1 tablespoon lemon juice

1. Lightly grease a 6-cup soufflé dish using ½ tablespoon butter.

2. Melt remaining butter in saucepan, sauté onion until soft, and stir in flour. Add milk gradually. Cook over low heat, stirring constantly, until sauce is thick and smooth. Remove pan from heat.

3. Cool soufflé mixture slightly, then beat in egg yolks, one at a time. Add chicken, salt, pepper, parsley and chives. Set aside until at room temperature.

4. Meanwhile, beat egg whites until frothy, add lemon juice gradually, and continue beating until whites are thick enough to hold a point when beater is raised. Fold ¼ of egg whites thoroughly into yolk mixture. Fold remaining whites gently into yolk mixture; it need not be perfectly blended.

5. Pour into prepared dish. Bake in 350° oven until the soufflé is well puffed and richly browned, about 45 minutes. Serve at once. Makes 4 servings.

CHICKEN-HAM MOUSSE LOAF

¾ cup milk
▶ ¾ cup chicken stock
1 envelope unflavored gelatin
2 egg yolks
▶ 1 cup ground cooked ham
¾ teaspoon paprika
1 pimiento, chopped
Onion salt

Salt and pepper
1 cup heavy cream
2 teaspoons vegetable oil,
approximately
▶ 1 cup ground cooked chicken
1 tablespoon prepared
horseradish
1 tablespoon minced parsley

1. Put the milk and stock in top part of double boiler; sprinkle the gelatin on liquids to soften. Beat in egg yolks. Cook over boiling water, stirring constantly, until mixture is slightly thickened and coats a metal spoon. Put half (about ¾ cup) mixture in each of two bowls and cool.

2. To one bowl, add the ham, paprika, pimiento, onion salt and salt and pepper to taste; whip ½ cup heavy cream in small bowl until stiff, and fold into ham mixture. Pour into 3½-cup lightly oiled loaf pan and chill until firm.

3. To second bowl, add the chicken, horseradish, parsley and salt and pepper to taste. When ham layer is firm, whip remaining cream and fold into chicken mixture. Pour chicken mixture over ham layer and chill until firm. To serve, unmold and cut into slices. Makes 4 to 6 servings.

BAKED CHICKEN AND VEGETABLE OMELET

4 tablespoons butter
2 large onions, minced
3 garlic cloves minced
1 pound zucchini, diced
9 eggs
1 teaspoon salt
⅜ teaspoon pepper
1 can (16 oz.) peeled tomatoes,
drained, finely chopped

3 tablespoons Parmesan cheese
2 tablespoons fresh minced
parsley
▶1½ cups minced cooked chicken
½ teaspoon dried tarragon
½ teaspoon dried basil
¾ cup tomato sauce or spaghetti
sauce, preferably homemade

1. Melt 2 tablespoons butter in skillet, sauté onion, garlic and zucchini until vegetables are tender and liquid has evaporated. Allow to cool and beat in 3 eggs, ½ teaspoon salt, ⅛ teaspoon pepper and set aside.

2. Beat 3 eggs; combine with tomatoes, Parmesan cheese, parsley and ⅛ teaspoon pepper and set aside.

3. Beat 3 eggs and blend in chicken, tarragon, basil, ½ teaspoon salt and ⅛ teaspoon pepper.

4. Thoroughly butter a deep 2-quart casserole or soufflé dish with remaining butter. Pour in zucchini mixture, then the tomato mixture, then the chicken mixture. Cover casserole with aluminum foil and bake at 375° for 30 minutes. Remove foil and continue to bake for another 10 minutes or until top is light golden and omelet is firmly set (testing with skewer). Let rest 10 minutes before cutting into wedges to serve. Spoon a little tomato sauce over each wedge. Makes 6 to 8 servings.

BROCCOLI AND CHICKEN FRITTATA

3 tablespoons olive oil
▶ 1½ cups chopped cooked
 broccoli
1½ cups sliced mushrooms
1 clove garlic, minced
½ cup minced onion
2 tablespoons diced green
 pepper

▶ 1 cup cooked chicken, sliced
 into julienne strips
6 eggs, beaten
 Salt to taste
½ teaspoon freshly ground black
 pepper
½ cup shredded Monterey Jack
 cheese
¼ cup grated Parmesan cheese

1. In a medium-size skillet, heat the oil and stir in the broccoli, mushrooms, garlic, onion, and green pepper; cover and cook for 3 minutes. Mix together in a bowl, the chicken, eggs, salt, pepper, and shredded cheese. Remove the skillet from the heat and stir in the egg mixture.

2. Bake for 20 minutes at 350°. Top with the Parmesan cheese and place under the broiler until the top is brown. Makes 4 servings.

CREAMED CHICKEN OMELET

½ cup heavy cream
▶ 1 cup diced cooked chicken
1 can (10½ oz.) condensed
 cream of chicken soup
1 teaspoon Worcestershire sauce
4 tablespoons chopped parsley
2 tablespoons grated Swiss
 cheese

4 drops Tabasco
½ cup chopped black olives
8 eggs, beaten
½ teaspoon salt
½ teaspoon white pepper
2 tablespoons butter

1. Heat 3 tablespoons of the cream with the chicken, soup, Worcestershire sauce, 2 tablespoons of the parsley, the Swiss cheese, Tabasco, and olives. Cover and keep warm.

2. Combine the eggs with the remaining cream, salt and pepper. Heat the butter in a medium heavy skillet and pour in egg mixture. Cook, lifting edges with a spatula to allow uncooked egg to run under.

3. When omelet is done, cover half with some of the hot chicken mixture; fold over and slide onto a heated platter. Top with the remaining chicken mixture. Sprinkle with the remaining parsley and serve immediately. Makes 4 servings.

"Julienne strips"

... or "julienned" refer to the shape and size into which meat, poultry, and vegetables are to be cut. Julienne strips are matchlike shapes, approximately ⅛" wide by 2" in length.

CHICKEN AND CORN CUSTARD

- ▶ 1 cup diced cooked chicken
  2 cups cooked whole kernel
  corn (drain, if using canned)
- ▶ 2 cups cooked rice
  1 cup shredded Cheddar
  cheese

½ green pepper minced
1 teaspoon minced onion
4 eggs, beaten
1½ cups milk
Salt and pepper to taste
Dash nutmeg

1. Mix the chicken, corn, rice, cheese, green pepper and onion. Combine the eggs with the milk; season with salt, pepper, and nutmeg. Carefully stir in the chicken mixture; combine thoroughly.

2. Put in a buttered shallow 1½-quart baking dish. Bake in a 325° oven for 1 hour, or until firm. Makes 4 servings.

CHICKEN-ALMOND MOUSSE

- ▶ 3 egg yolks, slightly beaten
  ⅛ teaspoon onion salt
  ¼ teaspoon celery salt
  ¼ teaspoon paprika
- ▶ 1 cup chicken stock, homemade
  or canned
  1 envelope unflavored gelatin

¼ cup cold water
- ▶ 2 cups minced cooked chicken
  ½ cup chopped toasted almonds
  ½ cup seedless white grapes
  ½ teaspoon grated red onion
  1 cup heavy cream, whipped

1. In the top of a double boiler, combine the egg yolks, onion salt, celery salt, and paprika. Pour the stock over the mixture and, stirring constantly, cook over hot water until thickened.

2. In a bowl, sprinkle gelatin over cold water, and allow to soften for 5 minutes. Add to the egg yolk mixture and cook, stirring until dissolved. Remove from the heat.

3. Add the chicken, almonds, grapes and onion. Cool to lukewarm; fold in whipped cream. Pour into a 5-cup mold and chill until firm. Unmold on a chilled platter. Serve with mayonnaise. Makes 6 servings.

CHICKEN EGG DROP SOUP

- ▶ 4 cups chicken stock
  1 to 2 teaspoons soy sauce (or to
  taste)
  3 tablespoons water
  2 tablespoons cornstarch

2 eggs, at room temperature,
  lightly beaten
- ▶ ½ to 1 cup cooked chicken, cut
  in julienne strips

1. Place chicken stock in saucepan. Combine soy sauce, water, and cornstarch, and stir into chicken stock; bring soup to boil, then simmer until thickened.

2. Pour eggs into soup slowly, stirring constantly in a wide circle with a fork to make long threads.

3. Pour soup into bowls; sprinkle chicken over the top. Makes 4 servings.

MULLIGATAWNY SOUP

4 tablespoons butter
2 medium onions, diced
1 carrot, diced
1 stalk celery, diced
2 apples, peeled and diced
3 tablespoons flour
1 tablespoon curry powder
⅛ teaspoon each mace and
   ground cloves

▶ 4 cups chicken broth
  1 can (16 oz.) peeled tomatoes,
    drained, chopped
  ½ cup cream
▶ 1 cup cubed cooked chicken
▶ 1 cup cooked rice
  Salt and pepper

1. Melt butter in a large saucepan. Add onion, carrot, celery and apples; sauté until very tender.

2. Stir into vegetables, the flour, curry powder, mace and cloves, and cook 2 minutes.

3. Add broth, tomatoes and cream to pan and bring to a boil. Lower heat and simmer soup 20 minutes. Add chicken, rice and salt and pepper to taste. Simmer until chicken is warmed through. Makes 4 to 6 servings.

CURRIED CREAM OF CHICKEN SOUP

2 tablespoons butter
1 medium onion, sliced
3 cups sliced, peeled apples
2 tablespoons flour
2 to 3 teaspoons curry powder
  Salt to taste

▶ 4 cups chicken stock,
    homemade or canned
  1 cup dry white wine
  2 cups light cream
▶ 1 cup chopped cooked chicken
  ½ cup raisins, soaked in hot
    water for 15 minutes

1. Melt butter in a large saucepan; add onion and apple, and sauté until soft but not brown. Combine flour, curry and salt; blend into sautéed mixture. Gradually add stock, stirring constantly over medium heat. Add wine. Simmer, stirring often, 10 minutes. Cool.

2. Purée mixture through a food mill or in the container of a blender. Return to saucepan; stir in cream, and add chicken and raisins. Serve hot or cold. Makes 8 servings.

CHICKEN ONION SOUP

4 tablespoons butter
6 cups thinly sliced onions
1 clove garlic, minced
3 tablespoons flour
► 3 cups rich chicken broth
2 cups light cream

► 1 cup diced cooked chicken
½ teaspoon salt (or more to taste)
¼ teaspoon pepper
Toasted croutons for garnish
Grated Parmesan cheese

1. Melt the butter in a heavy saucepan; add the onions and garlic, and cook slowly, until onions are very tender and light golden brown.

2. Sprinkle flour over onions, stir well; slowly pour in chicken broth, cream, chicken, salt, and pepper. Cook until soup tastes rich and is thickened, about 30 minutes. Serve garnished with croutons and sprinkle with Parmesan cheese. Makes about 6 servings.

CHICKEN GUMBO SOUP

3 slices bacon, or 1 ounce salt pork, diced
½ cup finely chopped onions
¼ cup thinly sliced celery
¼ cup finely chopped green pepper
1 teaspoon finely chopped garlic
1 package (10½ oz.) frozen okra, defrosted
1 can (16 oz.) solid-pack tomatoes, coarsely chopped

► 4 cups chicken stock
1 bay leaf
►1½ to 2 cups diced cooked chicken
Salt and pepper to taste
A few drops Tabasco
2 teaspoons *filé* powder
► 1 cup hot cooked rice
2 tablespoons finely chopped parsley

1. In a large heavy saucepan, cook bacon over medium heat until almost crisp. Add the onion, celery, green pepper, and garlic to saucepan and cook, stirring, until vegetables are tender. Add the okra, lower heat and simmer mixture another 5 minutes.

2. Add tomatoes, stock, and bay leaf to pan; simmer 30 minutes. Stir in chicken, and salt, pepper, and Tabasco. When chicken pieces are warmed through, remove pan from heat and stir in filé powder. Spoon hot rice into 4 bowls, ladle soup over the rice, sprinkle with parsley and serve. Makes 4 servings.

CHICKEN BISQUE

3 tablespoons butter or
  margarine
3 tablespoons flour
3 cups chicken broth
1 tablespoon tomato paste
½ cup dry white wine
▶ 1½ cups shredded cooked
  chicken

1 cup light cream
3 tablespoons sherry
⅛ teaspoon nutmeg
½ teaspoon salt
⅛ teaspoon pepper
1 tablespoon chopped parsley
1 teaspoon chopped chives

1. Melt the butter in a skillet; stir in the flour. Add the broth, tomato paste and wine; cook, stirring constantly, until mixture boils and thickens. Lower heat and simmer 5 minutes.

2. Add chicken, cream, sherry, nutmeg, salt and pepper. Heat, pour into the soup bowls, and garnish each serving with a sprinkling of parsley and chives. Makes 4 to 6 servings.

CHICKEN CROQUETTES

4 tablespoons butter
4 tablespoons flour
  Salt and pepper to taste
▶ 1 cup chicken stock, homemade
  or canned
¼ cup heavy cream
▶ 2 cups minced cooked chicken
2 tablespoons sherry
1 egg, lightly beaten

1 tablespoon dried tarragon
1 tablespoon chopped chives
1 tablespoon chopped parsley
1 tablespoon chopped celery
1 egg
2 tablespoons water
1 cup fine dry breadcrumbs
  Vegetable oil for deep frying

1. In a medium saucepan, melt the butter and blend in the flour. Cook for 1 minute. Add salt, pepper and chicken stock; bring to a boil. Reduce heat to a simmer, add heavy cream; cook for 5 minutes, stirring.

2. Add the chicken, sherry, beaten egg, tarragon, chives, parsley and celery; mix well and cook until mixture comes to a boil. Cool quickly; chill at least one hour.

3. Shape ¼-cup portions of chicken mixture into pear-shaped croquettes. Beat remaining egg and water together. Dip each croquette into breadcrumbs, then beaten egg, and again in breadcrumbs. Chill 30 minutes. Heat oil in a deep pan to 380°. Fry croquettes until golden brown. Drain on paper toweling. Makes 4 servings.

In recipes calling for "cream"

People who prefer less rich dishes can substitute milk, or even evaporated milk for some or all of the cream. The flavor and texture, of course, will be somewhat different but the recipes should "work" equally well.

LOUISIANA CHICKEN LOAF WITH ALMOND-MUSHROOM SAUCE

- 2 cups warm chicken broth
  3 eggs, lightly beaten
- 2 cups chopped cooked
  chicken
  1½ cups soft bread crumbs
  1 teaspoon salt
  ¾ teaspoon paprika
  ¼ teaspoon dried rosemary
  1 teaspoon Worcestershire sauce
  ⅓ cup minced celery
  ¼ cup chopped green pepper

1 tablespoon minced parsley
2 teaspoons grated onion
2½ teaspoons lemon juice
½ pound mushrooms
1 small clove garlic, crushed
¼ cup melted butter
¼ cup flour
- 2 cups chicken stock or bouillon
⅛ teaspoon white pepper
½ cup slivered almonds
1 can cranberry sauce

1. In a large mixing bowl, pour the broth over the eggs, stirring constantly. Add the chicken and bread crumbs; mix well. Add the salt, ¼ teaspoon paprika, rosemary, Worcestershire sauce, celery, green pepper, parsley, onion and 1½ teaspoons lemon juice; mix well. Grease a 9 x 5 x 2¾-inch loaf pan; pat chicken mixture evenly into it. Set in pan of hot water; bake at 350° for 1½ hours or until knife inserted comes out clean.

2. Chop mushroom stems, and slice caps thin. Sauté caps and stems with the garlic in 2 tablespoons of butter in a skillet until tender. Sprinkle with flour and blend well. Gradually stir in the stock, stirring constantly until it thickens. Season with remaining paprika and pepper; stir in the remaining lemon juice and almonds. Unmold the chicken loaf, garnish with slices of cranberry sauce, and serve the sauce on the side. Makes 8 servings.

CREAMED CHICKEN HASH

- 2 cups minced cooked chicken
  1½ cups heavy cream
- ½ cup diced boiled potatoes
  2 tablespoons minced onion
  1 tablespoon parsley
  3 tablespoons butter

3 tablespoons flour
½ teaspoon salt
⅛ teaspoon cayenne
4 tablespoons grated Parmesan
  cheese
2 tablespoons bread crumbs

1. In the top of a double boiler or in a saucepan, combine the chicken with ½ cup of the cream, the potato, onion, and parsley and cook for about 15 minutes. Stir occasionally until the cream is completely absorbed. Transfer the chicken to a mixing bowl.

2. In a small saucepan, melt 2 tablespoons of the butter; remove from heat and add the flour. Stir with a wooden spoon until smooth. Pour in the remaining cream and stir with a wire whisk. Return the pan to the heat and, still stirring, bring the sauce almost to the boil. Simmer as slowly as possible for about 5 minutes, then quickly bring to a boil for about 10 seconds, stirring constantly. Stir in the salt and cayenne. Combine the sauce with the chicken mixture.

3. Pour the chicken into a baking dish; sprinkle with cheese and bread crumbs. Broil until crumbs are brown. Makes 4 to 6 servings.

CHICKEN COCKTAIL CROQUETTES

3 tablespoons butter, melted
¾ cup flour
▶ 2 cups chicken stock, fresh or
  canned
4 egg yolks
2 tablespoons heavy cream
1 teaspoon salt
¼ teaspoon cayenne
2 tablespoons lemon juice
1½ tablespoons finely chopped
  shallots or scallions
½ cup finely chopped
  mushrooms

2 tablespoons Madeira or sherry
▶ 1½ cups (packed down) finely
  chopped cooked chicken
1 tablespoon finely chopped
  parsley
▶ ¼ cup shredded cooked carrots
1 tablespoon cornstarch
2 tablespoons chopped fresh
  dill, or ½ teaspoon dill weed
2 eggs, lightly beaten with 1½
  tablespoons vegetable oil
½ cup bread crumbs, combined
  with ½ cup ground almonds

1. In a small saucepan, mix 2 tablespoons of the butter with 3 table-spoons of the flour. Pour in ¾ cup of the stock and stir with a whisk until the flour dissolves. Over medium heat, stir the sauce constantly; bring to a boil and simmer for 1 or 2 minutes. Combine 1 egg yolk with the cream, then pour the egg mixture into the sauce and, continually stirring, bring to a boil again for 10 seconds. Turn off the heat and season with ½ tea-spoon of the salt, ⅛ teaspoon of the cayenne, and 1 teaspoon of the lemon juice.

2. Melt the remaining butter in a small frying pan and add the chopped shallots; sauté for about 1 minute without letting them color, then mix in the mushrooms. Stirring occasionally, cook the mixture until the mush-rooms are dry but not brown. Pour in the Madeira, raise the heat and, stirring constantly, cook the wine away entirely.

3. In a mixing bowl, combine the sauce with the chicken, the mush-rooms, parsley, and carrots. Taste for seasoning and add lemon juice or salt, if needed. Cover tightly and chill for 2 hours or overnight.

4. In the top of a double boiler, combine the remaining egg yolks with the cornstarch and the remaining salt and cayenne. Beat with a wire whisk; add the remaining stock. Cook directly over heat, stirring con-stantly, until it begins to thicken. Stir in 1 tablespoon of the lemon juice and the dill. Keep warm.

5. Form the chicken mixture into 1-inch balls, roll in the remaining flour, then dip into the egg mixture. Coat completely with bread crumb/ al-mond mixture and chill again. Deep fry the balls a few at a time, for 1 or 2 minutes, until they're a delicate golden brown. Drain on paper towels. Pierce each ball with a toothpick and serve with the warm lemon sauce. Makes 6 to 8 servings as an hors d'oeuvre.

DELTA CHICKEN BALLS

2 tablespoons finely chopped scallions
2 tablespoons butter
▶ 1 cup finely chopped cooked chicken
1 can (8 oz.) finely chopped clams, drained
4 egg yolks
1 tablespoon parsley

1 teaspoon lemon juice
¼ cup heavy cream
¼ teaspoon salt
½ teaspoon Tabasco
1 tablespoon finely chopped celery
½ cup dry bread crumbs
½ cup ground pecans

1. Sauté scallions in butter until transparent. In a mixing bowl, add the scallions to the chicken, clams, 2 egg yolks, parsley, lemon juice, 2 tablespoons of the heavy cream, salt, Tabasco, and celery; mix well. Shape into ¾-inch balls; chill 1 hour.

2. Beat the remaining egg yolks with remaining cream. Combine bread crumbs with pecans. Dip balls in egg yolk mixture; roll in crumbs and pecan mixture; chill 1 hour. Fry a few balls at a time in deep fat, at 375°. Cook until delicately browned on all sides; drain on absorbent paper. Makes 6 servings.

CHICKEN HASH

1 medium-size onion, chopped (½ cup)
¼ cup chopped green pepper
3 tablespoons olive oil
▶ 4 coarsely chopped cooked potatoes
▶ 1 cup diced cooked carrots

▶ 2 cups chopped cooked chicken
⅓ cup light cream
½ teaspoon salt
⅛ teaspoon pepper
1 tomato, cut in wedges
▶ ½ cup cooked peas

1. Sauté onion and green pepper in 1 tablespoon of oil in a large skillet until tender. Combine with potatoes, carrots, chicken, cream, salt and pepper in a large bowl. Heat the rest of the oil in the same skillet; spoon in hash mixture. Pat down in skillet; cook uncovered, 10 minutes over moderate heat without stirring. Cover and cook over low heat until brown.

2. Loosen from bottom; flip over onto serving platter. Arrange tomato wedges to make a circle on top of hash; fill center with cooked green peas. Makes 4 servings.

CHICKEN PATTIES

▶ 2 cups ground cooked chicken
¾ cup dry bread crumbs
3 tablespoons mayonnaise
1 tablespoon minced parsley
1 tablespoon dry sherry

2 teaspoons grated onion
Salt and pepper to taste
1 egg
¼ cup water
¼ cup butter

1. Mix together in a large bowl, the chicken, bread crumbs, mayonnaise, parsley, sherry, onion, salt, pepper, egg and water.

2. With your hands, shape the chicken mixture by tablespoonfuls into 1½-inch round patties. Heat butter over medium heat in a large skillet. Cook the patties until golden brown on both sides. Makes 4 servings.

CHICKEN AND RICE LOAF

▶ 2 cups finely chopped cooked
  chicken
▶ 2 cups cooked rice
  ¼ cup chopped celery leaves
  ½ cup diced red pepper
  2 tablespoons grated onion

▶ ½ cup chopped cooked string
  beans
  2 teaspoons lemon juice
  ¾ cup mayonnaise
  ¼ cup milk or vegetable broth
  Salt and pepper to taste

1. Mix together the chicken, rice, celery leaves, red pepper, onion, string beans, lemon juice, mayonnaise and milk. Mix well; salt and pepper to taste.

2. Grease a loaf pan and pour the chicken mixture into it. Bake at 350° for 1½ hours. Makes 4 servings.

CHICKEN TEA SANDWICH LOAF

▶ 3 cups chopped cooked
  chicken
  1 cup minced celery
  1 teaspoon grated onion
  ⅓ cup chopped green pepper
  1 cup mayonnaise
  Salt and pepper
  18 slices soft white bread

  ½ cup butter or margarine,
  softened
  ⅔ cup crumbled blue cheese
  (about 4 ounces)
  1 package (3 oz.) cream
  cheese, softened
  1 tablespoon milk
  Watercress

1. Mix together the chicken, celery, onion, green pepper and mayonnaise. Season to taste with salt and pepper. Trim crusts from bread and place 3 slices in a row on sheet of foil or wax paper. Butter slices on one side and spread with filling. Keep layering with buttered bread and filling.

2. Press loaf firmly together. Beat together the blue and cream cheeses, and milk until smooth. Spread on top and sides of loaf. Chill for several hours, or overnight. Cut into slices or triangles and garnish with watercress. Makes 6 to 8 servings.

ORIENTAL CHICKEN CROQUETTES

  6 tablespoon butter
  6 tablespoons flour
▶ 1 cup chicken broth
  1 cup light cream
  ½ teaspoon salt
  Dash pepper
  ¼ cup minced onion
  1 large clove garlic, minced
  1 tablespoon minced parsley

  ¼ teaspoon ground ginger
▶ ½ cup chopped cooked carrots
▶ 3 cups chopped cooked
  chicken
  1 cup finely chopped blanched
  almonds
  2 cups cracker crumbs
  1 egg, well beaten
  Cooked rice

1. Melt butter in a medium skillet and blend in flour; slowly add the broth and cream, stirring constantly until thickened. Season with the salt, pepper, onion, garlic, parsley, and ginger. Mix in the carrots and chicken. Remove from heat and cool. Chill several hours or overnight.

2. Shape chilled mixture into 8 croquettes. Add almonds to cracker crumbs and mix well. Roll croquettes in the crumbs, then in the beaten egg, then in crumbs again. Deep fry until golden brown. Serve with rice. Makes 4 servings.

CHICKEN AND RICE SALAD

¼ pound thinly sliced fresh
   mushrooms
4 tablespoons lemon juice
½ teaspoon dried oregano
½ teaspoon finely chopped
   garlic
3 tablespoons olive oil
   Freshly ground black pepper
▶ 2 cups cooked rice
½ cup fennel or celery, cut into
   julienne strips 1 inch by ½ inch

1 teaspoon salt
▶ 2 cups cold cubed cooked
   chicken
1 medium cucumber, diced
2 tablespoons finely chopped
   parsley
Tomatoes, peeled and sliced
Black olives
Watercress

1. Cut the stems off and thinly slice the mushroom caps; mix them with the lemon juice in a glass mixing bowl. After the mushrooms have absorbed the juice, add the oregano, garlic, olive oil, and a few grindings of black pepper. Marinate for at least 2 hours, stirring occasionally.

2. In a large mixing bowl, using a fork, combine the rice and the mushrooms with the marinade, the fennel, salt, chicken, cucumber and 1 tablespoon of the parsley. Mix together gently and taste for seasoning. Refrigerate for at least 1 hour before serving. Pile loosely in the center of a platter and surround with sliced peeled tomatoes, black olives, and watercress. Dust the top of the salad with remaining parsley. Makes 4 to 6 servings.

PARTY CHICKEN MOLDS

1 envelope unflavored gelatin
1 cup mayonnaise
▶ 2 cups diced cooked chicken
¾ cup chopped unpared
   cucumber
¼ cup minced green pepper
⅓ cup diced celery
3 tablespoons minced onion

3 tablespoons chopped stuffed
   green olives
2 tablespoons lemon juice
½ teaspoon salt
¼ teaspoon paprika
1 cup heavy cream, whipped
Watercress

1. Soften the gelatin in ¼ cup cold water in a small mixing bowl. Place the bowl in a pan of hot water until gelatin dissolves completely, stirring occasionally. Stir the gelatin into the mayonnaise, then add the chicken, cucumber, green pepper, celery, onion, olives, lemon juice, salt, and paprika. Gently fold in the whipped cream.

2. Spoon the mixture into 8 small molds or custard cups. Chill until firm. Unmold on chilled plates, lined with watercress. Makes 8 servings.

CHICKEN AND RICE SALAD WITH TUNA MAYONNAISE

1 whole egg plus 1 yolk
1 teaspoon salt
⅛ teaspoon cayenne
1¼ cups olive oil, or ½ olive oil
  and ½ vegetable oil
1 can (3½ oz.) tunafish, drained
2 flat anchovy fillets, drained
  and coarsely chopped
1 tablespoon plus 1 teaspoon
  lemon juice
► 2 cups cold diced cooked
  chicken
► 3 cups cooked rice

3 tablespoons white wine
  vinegar
2 tablespoons coarsely chopped
  pimiento
¾ cup tiny cold cooked peas
  (canned or frozen)
Salt and freshly ground black
  pepper
Parsley sprigs or watercress
Tomatoes, sliced
Black olives (Mediterranean
  varieties)

1. In a blender or food processor, blend together the egg and yolk, ½ teaspoon of the salt, and the cayenne. In a thin stream, pour 1 cup of the oil into the eggs. Turn off the blender. Mash the tunafish and anchovies in a small bowl, then add to the mayonnaise; blend the mixture long enough to combine the fish and mayonnaise into a smooth, thick mass. Stir in 1 tablespoon of the lemon juice; if it is too thick, thin it with a little more lemon juice. Scrape the mayonnaise into a bowl and cover. Two hours before serving, thoroughly combine the mayonnaise with the chicken and cover tightly.

2. Steam the rice in a colander over hot water for a few minutes; transfer the rice to a large mixing bowl and let it cool to lukewarm. Using a fork, stir in the vinegar, pimiento, peas, the remaining 1 teaspoon of lemon juice, and season with salt and pepper to taste.

3. Press the rice mixture into an oiled 1-quart ring mold, chill for a half-hour, and unmold on a round platter. Fill center with the mayonnaise-coated chicken and sprinkle with parsley. Garnish with sliced tomatoes and black olives. Makes 4 to 6 servings.

SUPREME CHICKEN SALAD

► 3 cups cubed cooked chicken,
  white meat preferred
► 1½ cups cooked broccoli
  flowerets
  ¾ cup coarsely chopped walnuts
  1¼ cups halved seedless grapes

1 cup mayonnaise
2 teaspoons lemon juice
⅓ cup sour cream
Salt and white pepper to taste
Lettuce leaves

1. In a large glass bowl, combine the chicken, broccoli, walnuts, and grapes. Mix together the mayonnaise, lemon juice, and sour cream; pour over the chicken mixture and blend well. Add salt and white pepper to taste. Chill for at least 2 hours.

2. Line a serving platter with lettuce leaves and pile the salad lightly over them. Makes 4 to 6 servings.

CHICKEN AND RICE SALAD ITALIANO

▶ 3 cups cooked rice, room
  temperature
2 pimientos, cut into strips
1 green pepper, cut into strips
⅔ cup chopped red onion
1 teaspoon dried or 2
  tablespoons minced fresh basil
18 large black pitted olives,
  sliced

▶1½ cups cooked chicken, cut into
  julienne strips
¾ cup olive oil
¼ cup white wine vinegar
2 garlic cloves, crushed
¼ teaspoon pepper
¼ teaspoon salt
¼ cup Parmesan cheese

1. Combine rice, pimiento, green pepper, onion, basil, olives and chicken in large bowl; toss and set aside.

2. In a jar, combine the olive oil, vinegar, garlic, pepper, salt and cheese. Shake or stir together vigorously and toss with salad. Serve at room temperature. Makes 6 servings.

CLASSIC CHICKEN SALAD

▶ 2 cups diced cooked chicken
1 cup chopped celery
1 tablespoon lemon juice
1 small onion, minced
1 medium green pepper,
  minced
Salt and pepper to taste

¾ cup mayonnaise
¼ cup chopped pickle
2 tablespoons parsley
▶ 3 hard-cooked eggs, chopped
6 large ripe tomatoes
Lettuce leaves

1. Combine the chicken, celery, lemon juice, onion and green pepper; season to taste. Mix the mayonnaise with the chopped pickles and parsley, and blend well into the chicken mixture. Fold in egg. Chill.

2. Cut the tops off the tomatoes, scoop out the pulp, sprinkle with salt and drain upside down on a towel. Arrange on 6 plates on lettuce leaves; fill the tomatoes with the chicken salad. Makes 6 servings.

ORIENTAL CHICKEN SALAD

▶2½ cups cooked chicken, cut in
  julienne strips
1 cup shredded radishes,
  drained on absorbent toweling
¼ cup minced scallions
½ cup drained diced water
  chestnuts
¼ cup minced celery
2 tablespoons soy sauce

¼ cup vegetable oil
1 tablespoon peanut butter
1 to 2 tablespoons honey
1 teaspoon vinegar
½ teaspoon ground ginger
4 cups shredded lettuce
½ cup chopped dry-roasted
  peanuts

1. Combine chicken, radishes, scallions, water chestnuts, and celery in a large bowl, and toss thoroughly.

2. Combine soy sauce, oil, peanut butter, honey, vinegar, ginger. Stir until well blended, and toss with salad ingredients.

3. Arrange bed of lettuce on serving dish; heap salad in center. Sprinkle peanuts over chicken salad. Makes 4 servings.

SWISS CHICKEN SALAD

▶ 1½ cups cubed cooked chicken
⅓ cup diced Swiss cheese
▶ ⅓ cup diced cooked tongue or
  ham
  1 medium onion, minced
  ¼ cup chopped green pepper
  1 cup chopped celery
▶ ¼ cup diced cooked string
  beans

1 cup mayonnaise
¼ teaspoon salt
¼ teaspoon dried tarragon
⅛ teaspoon black pepper
½ teaspoon prepared mustard
6 slices toast points
6 lettuce leaves
Pitted black olives
Sprigs of parsley

1. Mix together the chicken, cheese, tongue, onion, green pepper, celery and string beans. Combine the mayonnaise with the salt, tarragon, pepper, and mustard. Pour over the chicken salad and blend well.

2. Put toast points on individual plates; arrange lettuce leaves over top and lightly pile on the salad. Garnish with olives and parsley. Makes 6 servings.

SALMAGUNDI SALAD

▶ 2 cups sliced cold cooked
  potatoes
▶ 1½ cups sliced cold cooked beets
  ½ cup grated raw carrot
▶ 2 cups finely diced cooked
  chicken
  ½ cup diced raw tart apple
  6 anchovy fillets, minced

¼ teaspoon sugar
1 teaspoon dried dill weed
¼ cup chopped parsley
1½ cups mayonnaise
¼ teaspoon pepper
Sour cream
Cherry tomatoes
▶ Hard-cooked eggs, sliced

1. In a bowl, mix together the potatoes, beets, carrot, chicken, apple, and anchovies. With a wire whisk, blend together the sugar, dill, parsley, mayonnaise, and pepper. Combine the sauce with the chicken mixture; mix well.

2. In the center of the salad, make a depression with the back of a large spoon; fill with sour cream. Layer, alternating, around the sides of the bowl, the tomatoes and egg slices. Makes 6 servings.

SALAD OLIVER

▶ 3 large cooked potatoes, diced
▶ 1 cup cooked peas
▶ 1½ cups diced cooked chicken
  1 tart apple, diced
  ⅓ cup mayonnaise
  ⅓ cup sour cream

½ cup diced dill pickle
3 scallions, chopped
1 teaspoon Worcestershire sauce
▶ 2 hard-cooked eggs, chopped
  Salt and pepper to taste

Combine all ingredients in a large bowl; toss until well blended. Refrigerate, covered, until chilled, about 2 hours. Makes 6 servings.

SPANISH CHICKEN WITH RICE

2 tablespoons olive oil
1 large onion, chopped
1 garlic clove, minced
1 medium green pepper, minced
1 cup uncooked long-grain rice
► 2 cups diced cooked chicken
► 1 cup chicken stock or bouillon
2 cups canned tomatoes

⅓ cup sherry
¼ teaspoon pepper
Pinch of ground saffron
½ teaspoon paprika
2 whole cloves
1 crumbled bay leaf
► 1 cup cooked peas
1 pimiento, cut in strips

1. In a skillet, heat the olive oil; add onion, garlic, and green pepper, and brown for about 3 minutes. Add the rice and cook, stirring, for 5 minutes longer.

2. Add the chicken meat and stock, tomatoes with liquid, sherry, pepper, saffron, paprika, cloves, and bay leaf. Bring to boil, cover and simmer for 30 minutes or until rice is tender and liquid is completely absorbed.

3. Remove from heat, add peas, and let stand for 5 minutes before serving. Garnish with pimiento strips. Makes 4 to 6 servings.

CHICKEN IN MAYONNAISE COLLÉE

2 tablespoons unflavored gelatin
¼ cup cold water
¼ cup Madeira wine
2 cups mayonnaise
½ teaspoon curry powder

► 8 substantial pieces of cooked chicken, skinned
4 ripe olives
1 pimiento

1. Sprinkle gelatin in the water in top of a double boiler or saucepan. Place over simmering water, stir until gelatin is dissolved. Remove from heat and add the Madeira. Stir in the mayonnaise and curry powder.

2. Put the pieces of chicken on a platter. Spoon the gelatin mixture over the chicken. Slice the olives and pimiento into strips and arrange in attractive designs over each piece. Refrigerate for 1 hour or overnight. Makes 4 servings.

TOASTED CHICKEN-CHEESE SANDWICHES

4 slices of toast
► 4 slices of cooked chicken
8 slices of tomato
½ cup sliced mushrooms

½ cup finely crumbled blue cheese
1 egg, beaten
4 crisply cooked bacon strips, halved

1. On each toast slice, put a slice of chicken and top with slices of tomato and mushrooms. Mix together the cheese and egg.

2. Spread the cheese on top of the tomato and top each with bacon. Broil until cheese is melted. Makes 4 sandwiches.

CURRIED CHICKEN SPREAD

▶ 1½ cups ground cooked chicken
  ½ cup finely minced celery
▶ 2 hard-cooked eggs, finely
    chopped
  1 jar (2 oz.) pimiento, drained,
    chopped
  1 tablespoon minced onion
  1 small clove garlic, minced

½ teaspoon fresh lemon juice
½ teaspoon curry powder or to
    taste
½ teaspoon salt
⅛ teaspoon allspice
⅛ teaspoon cayenne
¾ cup mayonnaise

1. Combine ingredients and mix thoroughly. Cover and chill overnight.

2. Great for fancy sandwiches garnished with watercress; or spread on toasted, buttered French bread rounds garnished with a sprinkle of fresh minced parsley. Makes 2½ cups.

WESSEX CHICKEN SANDWICHES

▶ 3 cups diced cooked chicken
  1½ cups chopped celery
  3 large scallions, minced
  1 cup grated sharp Cheddar
    cheese
  ¼ cup chopped stuffed green
    olives

▶ 2 hard-cooked eggs, chopped
  ½ cup finely chopped walnuts
  ½ teaspoon salt
  ¼ teaspoon pepper
  1 cup mayonnaise
  8 slices bread

1. Mix together the chicken, celery, scallions, cheese, olives, eggs, and walnuts. Season with salt and pepper; add mayonnaise and blend well.

2. Arrange bread on a broiler pan; spread with chicken mixture. Broil 5 inches from heat until golden. Makes 8 servings.

CHICKEN LIVERS WITH RICE PARMESAN

  6 tablespoons butter
  2 tablespoons olive oil
  1 pound fresh chicken livers
    Salt and freshly ground black
    pepper to taste
  3 tablespoons brandy or
    bourbon

  4 cups thinly sliced onions
  2 fresh eggs, lightly beaten
  ¼ cup milk
  ⅔ cup grated Parmesan cheese
▶ 4½ to 5 cups warm cooked rice,
    buttered and seasoned
    Dry bread crumbs

1. Heat 2 tablespoons butter with 1 tablespoon olive oil until butter melts; add chicken livers and cook uncovered over high heat. When livers change color, add salt, pepper and brandy; cover, lower heat and cook for five minutes. Let livers cool; remove from pan and dice into ½-inch cubes. Set aside with pan juices.

2. Wipe pan clean. Melt 2 tablespoons butter with 1 tablespoon olive oil and sauté the onions until they are very tender. Remove from pan with slotted spoon and set aside. (Discard pan juices).

3. Butter a deep 3-quart casserole. Spoon into dish, half the livers and their juices.

4. Beat eggs and milk together and combine with onions. Pour half this mixture over the livers.

5. Stir the Parmesan cheese into the rice, and spread half the rice over the onion layer.

6. Repeat the layers using up all the ingredients. Sprinkle bread crumbs over upper layer of rice, and bake casserole in a 450° oven for 15 minutes. Makes 6 servings.

 # SAVORY CHICKEN LIVERS AND RICE

¼ cup soy sauce
½ teaspoon ground ginger
1 clove garlic, crushed
¼ cup firmly packed light brown sugar
¾ pound chicken livers, cut in quarters

6 slices bacon, chopped
¾ cup uncooked long-grain rice
▶ 2 cups chicken stock (homemade or canned; do not use bouillon cubes)
1 cup chopped water chestnuts
½ cup chopped scallions

1. Combine soy sauce, ginger, garlic and sugar in a small bowl; add chicken livers; stir to mix. Let marinate while preparing rest of recipe.

2. Cook bacon in a large skillet until just crisp; drain on paper toweling. Pour off bacon fat; reserve 3 tablespoons.

3. Measure 1 tablespoon of the bacon fat into a medium-size saucepan. Add the rice and cook over medium heat until slightly brown. Add the stock and cook 15 to 20 minutes or until rice is tender.

4. Drain the livers, reserving marinade; sauté the water chestnuts and livers in remaining bacon fat until livers are fairly pink in the center, or to taste, (about 3 to 5 minutes).

5. Spoon rice onto serving platter; with slotted spoon remove livers from pan and arrange over rice. Into the pan in which livers were just cooked, pour reserved marinade. Bring to boil, add scallions, cook 1 minute more, and pour over livers. Makes 4 servings.

 # CHOPPED CHICKEN LIVER

½ pound chicken livers
¼ cup chicken fat
1 medium onion, diced
▶ 1 hard-cooked egg

½ teaspoon salt
¼ teaspoon pepper
¼ teaspoon dried thyme

1. In a skillet, sauté livers in chicken fat for 5 minutes, or until pink color is gone. Add onion, sauté for 2 more minutes.

2. Into the container of a blender, add the cooked livers with the drippings in the pan, the egg, salt, pepper and thyme. Blend for about 10 seconds, or until coarsely chopped. Chill and serve with crackers as an appetizer.

CHICKEN LIVER PASTRIES

1 cup sifted flour
½ teaspoon salt
4 ounces (1 stick) cold butter, cut into small pieces
3 tablespoons sour cream
4 tablespoons butter
1 small onion, chopped
½ pound chicken livers, washed and drained

½ teaspoon salt
⅛ teaspoon freshly ground black pepper
½ cup finely minced, peeled apple
1 egg white
1 egg yolk
1 tablespoon water

1. Make the pastry: Combine flour and salt in a bowl. Work butter in by hand until mixture resembles coarse crumbs. Add sour cream and mix until a ball of dough forms. Cover with plastic wrap and refrigerate at least 2 hours.

2. Make the filling: Melt the butter in a skillet. Sauté the onion 5 minutes. Add the livers and sauté about 5 minutes, or until just barely pink in the center; drain. Chop or grind until smooth. Add salt, pepper, and apple.

3. To assemble: Roll out dough, preferably as thin as ⅛-inch thick. (If dough is too hard, let sit for 5 minutes to soften slightly.) Cut into rounds with 2-inch biscuit cutter. Place about 1 teaspoon of filling on each round. Fold over dough and seal edges with egg white. Beat egg yolk and water together. Brush tops of pastries with yolk. Bake in a preheated 425° oven for 12 to 15 minutes or until browned. Makes 20 to 30 pastries.

What to do with too little

You will find at times that the quantity of a leftover ingredient called for by a recipe is greater than the quantity you have on hand. In that case, you have the choice of several alternatives depending, of course, on the main ingredient:

1. You can freeze the leftover and save to use at a later date with additional leftovers.
2. You can cut the recipe in half to prepare a smaller quantity of the dish.
3. You can supplement the leftover by quickly cooking an additional quantity, or by adding previously frozen leftovers to it (as in Case History #3).
4. You can make up the difference by combining with another meat or vegetable saved in the refrigerator from another meal (as in all of the Case Histories).

▶TURKEY

TURKEY TETRAZZINI

½ cup butter or margarine
½ cup all-purpose flour
1 teaspoon salt
Dash nutmeg
Dash cayenne
2 cups milk
▶ 1 cup chicken broth, homemade
or canned
2 egg yolks
½ cup light cream

¼ cup dry sherry
8 ounces thin spaghetti, cooked
according to package
directions
▶ 4 cups diced cooked turkey
1 cup sliced mushrooms,
sautéed in 1½ tablespoons
butter
1 cup grated Parmesan cheese

1. Melt ½ cup butter in medium-size saucepan. Stir in flour, salt, nutmeg, and cayenne until smooth. Cook for 3 minutes. Gradually stir in milk and chicken broth; bring to boiling, stirring constantly. Boil gently, stirring constantly, 2 minutes, until thickened. Remove from heat.

2. In small bowl, beat egg yolks with cream. Gently beat in a little of the hot mixture. Return the mixture to saucepan; cook over low heat, stirring constantly, until sauce is hot—do not let it boil. Remove from heat. Add sherry and stir.

3. Add 2 cups of the sauce just made to the cooked spaghetti; toss until well blended. Add turkey and mushrooms to the remaining sauce.

4. Turn spaghetti into a 12 x 8 x 2-inch baking dish. Spoon turkey mixture over top. Sprinkle with cheese. Bake, covered, in a 350° oven for 25 to 30 minutes, or until piping hot. Makes 6 servings.

TURKEY ROLL-UPS

½ cup chopped onion
5 tablespoons butter or
margarine
▶2½ cups minced cooked potatoes
2 packages (10½ oz. each)
frozen spinach, cooked,
pressed almost dry, and
chopped

¼ teaspoon white pepper
▶ 12 large thin slices cooked turkey
▶1½ cups turkey gravy, warmed
(homemade or packaged)
½ cup sour cream
1 teaspoon Worcestershire sauce
½ cup slivered toasted almonds

1. In a skillet, sauté onion in 2 tablespoons of the butter until transparent. Remove from heat and add potatoes, spinach, and pepper. Toss together lightly.

2. Spoon some of the potato mixture in the center of each turkey slice; fold ends over and secure with wooden pick. Place roll-ups in a buttered 1½-quart casserole.

3. Combine gravy, sour cream, and Worcestershire sauce; pour over roll-ups. Bake in a preheated 350° oven for 25 minutes or until roll-ups are heated through. Baste occasionally with pan juices.

4. Melt 3 tablespoons of the butter in a small skillet; stir in almonds. Sprinkle over roll-ups. Makes 6 servings.

TURKEY SCALLOP

⅓ cup uncooked rice
▶ 2 cups turkey or chicken broth,
 homemade or canned
2 tablespoons butter
½ cup chopped green pepper
⅓ cup chopped onion
1 tablespoon minced celery

▶2½ cups diced cooked turkey
½ teaspoon salt
¼ teaspoon celery salt
⅛ teaspoon poultry seasoning
2 eggs, well beaten
Mushroom Sauce (see below)

1. Cook rice in broth 10 minutes or until partially tender. Drain and reserve both rice and broth.

2. Melt butter in a medium-size skillet and sauté the green pepper, onion, and celery for 5 minutes. Mix the vegetables, rice, turkey, salt, celery salt, and poultry seasoning together in a large bowl. Combine the reserved broth with the beaten eggs and stir into the turkey mixture, blending well.

3. Turn into a greased 1-quart baking dish. Bake in a preheated 325° oven for 40 to 45 minutes or until set. Serve hot with Mushroom Sauce. Makes 4 servings.

Mushroom Sauce

½ cup minced onion
3 tablespoons butter
3 tablespoons flour
▶ 1 cup turkey or chicken broth

½ cup heavy cream
1 cup sliced mushrooms,
 sautéed in 1 tablespoon butter

In a deep skillet, sauté onion in butter until soft but not brown. Blend in flour. Stir in broth and heavy cream. Cook, stirring constantly, over medium heat until thick. Add mushrooms. Heat thoroughly. Makes 2½ cups.

TURKEY MACARONI

▶ ½ cup turkey or chicken broth,
 homemade or canned
1 can (10½ oz.) cream of
 mushroom soup
1 tablespoon steak sauce
½ teaspoon Worcestershire sauce
1 cup shredded Cheddar
 cheese
½ cup sliced fresh mushrooms,
 sautéed in 1 tablespoon butter
 for 5 minutes

8 ounces macaroni, cooked
 according to package
 directions
▶ 2 cups diced cooked turkey
2 tablespoons slivered almonds
2 tablespoons chopped pecans
¼ cup grated Romano cheese

1. In a saucepan, combine broth, mushroom soup, steak sauce, and Worcestershire sauce; stir in Cheddar cheese, mushrooms, macaroni, turkey, almonds, and pecans.

2. Pour into a 1½-quart baking dish; sprinkle with Romano cheese. Bake in a preheated 350° oven for 30 minutes. Makes 4 servings.

TURKEY FLORENTINE IN SCALLOP SHELLS

▶ 2 cups chopped cooked
  spinach
1 tablespoon Madeira, or sherry
4 tablespoons butter
4 tablespoons flour
▶ 1½ cups turkey or chicken stock
⅓ cup heavy cream
⅛ teaspoon cayenne
½ teaspoon nutmeg

Salt
2½ tablespoons grated Parmesan
  cheese
2½ tablespoons grated Swiss
  cheese
▶ 2 cups diced cooked breast of
  turkey
4 teaspoons dry bread crumbs

1. Into a bowl, purée the spinach through a food mill or force through a coarse sieve (not a blender). Stir in the Madeira. Melt 3 tablespoons of butter in a saucepan and stir in the flour. Mix to a smooth paste, then add the stock. Stir constantly with a wire whisk and bring sauce to a boil. Cook until thick and smooth. Simmer for 5 minutes, then stir in the cream; add the cayenne, nutmeg, and salt to taste. Mix 3 tablespoons of the sauce with the spinach. Stir into the remaining sauce 2 tablespoons each of the Parmesan and Swiss cheese. Cook for one minute or until the cheese is melted.

2. Butter lightly four scallop shells. Spoon in the spinach purée. Arrange the turkey on top and spoon the remaining sauce over it. Sprinkle with bread crumbs and the rest of the cheeses. Dot lightly with remaining butter.

3. Bake for 15 minutes in 375° oven or until mixture bubbles; brown the tops briefly under a hot broiler. Makes 4 servings.

MEXICAN TURKEY MOLE

2 green peppers, seeded and
  roughly chopped
2 small or 1 large onion, peeled
  and roughly chopped
2 cans (16 oz. each) tomatoes,
  roughly chopped
1 can (4 oz.) pimiento, drained
½ cup pecans
¼ cup vegetable oil or lard
2 jalapeño chilies, fresh or
  canned, seeded and chopped

1 teaspoon salt
¼ teaspoon Tabasco
⅛ teaspoon ground cinnamon
⅛ teaspoon ground cloves
  Few dashes Worcestershire
  sauce
¼ cup fine dry bread crumbs
1 ounce (1 square) unsweetened
  chocolate, grated
▶ 8 large slices cooked turkey

1. Into the container of an electric blender, put green peppers, onion, tomatoes (with their juice), pimiento and pecans; blend until smooth.

2. Heat oil or lard in a large, heavy skillet. Add blended mixture, jalapeño chilies, salt, Tabasco, cinnamon, cloves and Worcestershire and bring to a boil over medium heat. Reduce heat, partially cover and simmer 30 minutes. Stir in bread crumbs and chocolate. Stir over medium heat until chocolate is melted.

3. In a 2½-quart casserole make alternate layers of turkey slices and sauce mixture. Bake in a preheated 350° oven for 20 minutes. Makes 8 servings.

DIVINE TURKEY CASSEROLE

▶ 2½ cups chopped cooked
    broccoli or asparagus, or 2½
    cups cooked peas, or any
    combination of the three to
    make 2½ cups
2 tablespoons butter
2 tablespoons flour
1 teaspoon salt

½ teaspoon pepper
1 cup milk
¾ cups grated Swiss cheese
▶ 2 cups diced cooked turkey
½ cup soft bread crumbs
¼ cup grated Parmesan Cheese
1 tablespoon butter, melted

1. In a 7-by-11-inch baking dish, spread the cooked vegetables.

2. In a medium-sized saucepan, melt the 2 tablespoons butter; blend in flour, salt and pepper; cook for 1 minute. Add milk; cook, stirring constantly, until mixture thickens, about 5 minutes. Add Swiss cheese and stir until melted. Remove from heat, and stir in the turkey.

3. Spoon the turkey mixture over vegetables. Mix together bread crumbs, Parmesan cheese and 1 tablespoon melted butter; sprinkle over the top of the casserole. Bake at 350° for 20 to 25 minutes, or until heated through. Makes 6 servings.

TURKEY AU GRATIN

½ cup finely chopped onion
2 tablespoons finely chopped
    shallots or scallions
½ teaspoon finely chopped
    garlic
3 tablespoons butter
2 tablespoons white wine
    vinegar
½ cup peeled, seeded, and
    chopped tomato
1 teaspoon tomato paste
▶ ¾ cup homemade turkey or
    chicken broth, or canned
    chicken broth

½ teaspoon sugar
1 small bay leaf
    Salt to taste
    Black pepper to taste
▶ 2 tablespoons turkey gravy
    (optional)
1 tablespoon capers, drained
▶ 4 to 8 pieces of roast turkey
½ cup dry bread crumbs
2 tablespoons finely chopped
    parsley

1. In a medium skillet, lightly brown the onion, shallots, and the garlic in 2 tablespoons of the butter. Pour the vinegar into the pan, raise the heat, and stirring constantly, boil the vinegar completely away. Add the chopped tomato and tomato paste, and stir in the broth. Bring to a boil, and immediately reduce the heat to barely simmering. Add the sugar and bay leaf and season with salt and pepper. Cook the sauce slowly, uncovered, for about 20 minutes, or until it is very thick. Stir in the turkey gravy and the capers.

2. Preheat the broiler. Add the turkey to the simmering sauce and simmer slowly for about 5 minutes, until the turkey is heated through. Transfer the hot turkey to a small shallow baking dish, spread the sauce over it, and sprinkle with the bread crumbs. Dot with the remaining butter, in small pieces, and brown quickly under the broiler. Sprinkle with chopped parsley. Makes 4 servings.

TURKEY RAGOÛT

4 tablespoons butter or
   margarine
1 large onion, sliced
2 medium-size zucchini, sliced
   (about 3 cups)
½ cup sliced celery
► 4 cups cooked turkey, in large
   chunks (about 1½-inch)
½ pound small fresh mushrooms
► 1 cup cooked carrots, sliced in
   circles

⅔ cup dry white wine
► ⅔ cup strong homemade chicken
   broth, or canned condensed
   broth
1 can (10½ oz.) condensed
   cream of celery soup
1 can (10½ oz.) condensed
   cream of chicken soup
½ teaspoon dried thyme
½ teaspoon dried marjoram
Chopped parsley

1. In a large, heavy skillet melt the butter and sauté the onion, zucchini, and celery until almost tender and lightly browned. Mix with turkey in a 3-quart casserole. In the same skillet, brown mushrooms adding more butter if needed. Add to the mixture in the casserole along with the carrots.

2. Stir wine into the drippings in the skillet, then add the chicken broth, celery soup, chicken soup, thyme, and marjoram. Bring to a boil, stirring. Pour wine mixture over turkey and vegetables, and mix lightly.

3. Bake, covered, 1 hour, or until bubbling in center. Sprinkle with chopped parsley before serving. Makes 6 servings.

TURKEY DIVAN

¼ cup butter or margarine
¼ cup flour
1 chicken bouillon cube
1½ cups boiling water
2 tablespoons sherry or Madeira
   Dash nutmeg
½ cup heavy cream, whipped

¾ cup grated Parmesan cheese
►2½ cups broccoli spears, cooked
   and drained
► 5 large slices cooked turkey
   breast
¼ cup grated Cheddar cheese

1. Melt butter in a medium saucepan over low heat. Blend in flour and cook, stirring constantly, until smooth and bubbly. Remove from heat. Dissolve chicken bouillon cube in boiling water. Gradually stir broth into flour mixture. Heat to boiling, stirring constantly, and boil one minute. Remove from heat.

2. Stir in the sherry and nutmeg; gently fold in the whipped cream and ½ cup of the Parmesan cheese. Place the cooked broccoli in a shallow heat-proof baking dish. Top with the slices of turkey and pour sauce over all. Place in 350° oven for 15 minutes to heat through.

3. Remove from oven; sprinkle with the remaining Parmesan cheese and the Cheddar cheese. Place baking dish under the broiler, 3 to 5 inches from heat and broil until cheese is bubbly and lightly browned. Makes 4 servings.

TURKEY PAPRIKASH

4 tablespoons butter
½ cup finely chopped onion
1 medium green pepper, cut into very thin slivers (about ¾ cup)
1 tablespoon flour
1 tablespoon paprika
►1½ cups turkey stock or canned chicken stock
⅛ teaspoon sugar

Salt
1 egg yolk
½ cup sour cream
► 2 cups diced cooked turkey
¼ teaspoon lemon juice
2 tablespoons finely chopped fresh dill or parsley
Cooked noodles with butter

1. Melt the butter in a large saucepan and add the onion. Cook over low heat, stirring occasionally, until they color lightly. Stir in the green pepper and cook 3 to 5 minutes longer. Remove from heat. Combine the flour and paprika and stir into the onion and pepper slowly. Beat in the stock with a wire whisk; return the pan to the heat, and still beating, bring the sauce to a boil, until thick and smooth. Reduce heat, add the sugar and a little salt and cook slowly for 10 minutes.

2. Mix the egg yolk with the sour cream and stir it into the simmering sauce gradually; don't let it boil. When the sauce is hot, fold in the turkey, and season with the lemon juice and more salt, if needed. Heat the turkey through without letting the sauce boil. Sprinkle with dill or parsley and serve with the hot noodles. Makes 4 servings.

BOMBAY TURKEY

¼ cup butter
½ cup chopped onion
1 clove garlic, minced
1 stalk celery, diced
3 carrots, finely chopped
1 tart apple, pared and diced
2 tablespoons flour
1 tablespoon curry powder
1 teaspoon salt

¼ teaspoon dry mustard
⅛ teaspoon sage
►1¾ cups homemade chicken broth or 1 can (13¾ oz.) broth
1 bay leaf
► 3 cups diced cooked turkey
½ cup light cream
6 tablespoons chopped chutney
► 3 cups hot cooked rice

1. Melt the butter in a 3-quart saucepan. Add the onions, garlic, celery, carrots and apple and sauté until tender. Mix in the flour, curry, salt, mustard and sage. Cook over low heat, stirring constantly, until the mixture starts to bubble.

2. Stir in the broth and add the bay leaf. Bring to a boil, stirring constantly, until the mixture thickens. Add the turkey, light cream and 2 tablespoons of the chutney. Simmer gently until the turkey is heated through.

3. Mix the remaining chutney with the hot cooked rice. Spoon the rice onto a platter to make a ring. Spoon the turkey mixture into the center of the ring. Makes 6 to 8 servings.

TURKEY AND BEEF IN MUSHROOM SAUCE

5 tablespoons butter
2 tablespoons all-purpose flour
2 cups light cream
1 can (4 oz.) mushroom buttons, drained
¼ teaspoon ground nutmeg
Dash of cayenne

Salt and pepper
2 tablespoons dry white wine
6 slices of bread
▶ 6 slices of leftover rare roast beef ¼-inch thick
▶ 6 slices of breast of roast turkey
Paprika

1. In a skillet, melt 2 tablespoons of butter and blend in the flour. Gradually stir in the cream and cook over low heat until thickened. Add mushrooms, nutmeg, and cayenne pepper. Season to taste with salt and pepper. Stir in the wine.

2. Cut bread into rounds, butter, and sauté until lightly browned. Keep hot. Quickly sauté beef on both sides in the remaining butter.

3. Place slices of fried bread on plates. Top each slice with beef and turkey. Cover with mushroom sauce and sprinkle with paprika. Makes 6 servings.

TURKEY CURRY

2 tablespoons butter
1 cup finely chopped onion
½ cup finely chopped celery
1 small tart apple, peeled, cored, and finely chopped
½ teaspoon finely chopped garlic
⅛ teaspoon crushed red peppers
2 tablespoons flour
3 tablespoons curry powder
1 teaspoon tomato paste

▶ 2 cups turkey or chicken stock, homemade or canned
½ cup heavy cream
1 teaspoon lime juice
Salt
▶ 2 to 3 cups cubed cooked turkey
Boiled rice
Raisins, soaked in cognac or Madeira
Almonds, toasted and slivered

1. In a large heavy frying pan melt the butter, and sauté the onion and celery until they are soft. Mix in the chopped apple, garlic, and crushed red peppers and continue to cook until the apple is soft. Remove from the heat.

2. In a small bowl combine the flour and curry powder. Add to the mixture in the frying pan, stir in the tomato paste, and mash into a smooth paste. Stirring constantly, cook over low heat for about 3 minutes. Slowly pour in the turkey stock and cream, beating gently with a whisk until thick and smooth. Simmer for about 20 minutes with the pan partially covered.

3. Strain the sauce through a fine sieve, pressing down on the vegetables with the back of a large spoon to extract all their juices, then return the strained sauce to the frying pan. Stir in the lime juice and salt to taste; thin the sauce, if necessary, with a little more cream or stock. Heat the turkey in the sauce over low heat. Serve with plain boiled rice, garnished with raisins and almonds. Makes 4 to 6 servings.

TURKEY À LA KING

5 tablespoons butter or
    margarine
1 cup chopped onion
1 cup sliced celery
⅓ cup finely chopped green
    pepper
½ teaspoon dried basil leaves
¼ teaspoon dried thyme leaves
¼ cup all-purpose flour
2 cups milk

2 chicken bouillon cubes
► 2 cups cubed cooked turkey
½ cup mayonnaise
1 jar (2 oz.) diced pimientos,
    drained
½ teaspoon salt
2 dashes Tabasco
2 tablespoons dry sherry or
    Madeira
Hot Biscuits (see Basics)

1. In 2½-quart saucepan, melt 2 tablespoons butter over medium heat.
Add onions, celery, green pepper, basil, and thyme. Cook, stirring constantly, for 4 minutes; remove vegetables and set aside.

2. In the same saucepan, melt remaining 3 tablespoons butter. Stir in
flour; cook for 3 minutes. Add the milk and bouillon; cook, stirring, until
mixture thickens. Add the vegetables, turkey, mayonnaise, pimientos,
salt, Tabasco, and sherry. Cook until heated through. Serve over hot biscuits. Makes 4 to 6 servings.

TURKEY NEWBURG

4 tablespoons butter or
    margarine
1 teaspoon finely chopped
    onion
¼ cup sliced mushroom
3 tablespoons flour
1½ cups light cream
1 chicken bouillon cube,
    crumbled

Dash pepper
½ teaspoon chervil or tarragon
1 tablespoon chopped parsley
1 tablespoon chopped pimiento
2 to 4 tablespoons dry sherry
► 8 slices cooked turkey
8 slices French bread, lightly
    toasted

1. Melt the butter in a 1-quart saucepan. Add the onion and mushrooms
and sauté gently until most of the liquid has evaporated. Stir in the flour.
Blend in the cream, stirring constantly. Add the crumbled bouillon cube,
pepper, and chervil. Cook, over low heat, stirring constantly, until the
mixture thickens. Add the parsley, pimiento, and sherry; heat gently.

2. Warm the turkey slices by placing them in a microwave oven for a few
seconds, or by simmering them gently in the sauce for a minute or two.
Place the turkey slices on the toasted French bread; top with sauce.
Makes 4 servings.

To keep tender

Turkey meat should be added to a sauce for 5 to 6 minutes only at the
end of the cooking time, so that it doesn't become tough or stringy. It
can *bake* longer in a sauce, however.

TURKEY IN BRANDY CREAM

¼ cup chopped onions
1 can (6 oz.) sliced mushrooms, drained
½ cup diced green pepper
½ cup butter or margarine
7 tablespoons flour
¾ teaspoon salt
¼ teaspoon celery salt
Pepper to taste

⅛ teaspoon paprika
▶ 2 cups turkey or chicken broth
1½ cups light cream
½ cup heavy cream
▶ 2 cups cubed cooked turkey
¼ cup chopped pimiento
2 tablespoons brandy or port
8 baked pastry shells

1. In a skillet, or saucepan, sauté onions, mushrooms and green pepper in butter for 10 minutes. Lower heat. Blend in flour, salts, pepper, and paprika. Simmer, stirring constantly, until mixture is hot.

2. Slowly stir in broth and creams. Heat mixture to boiling, stirring constantly; boil 1 minute. Add turkey, pimiento, and brandy and continue to cook until mixture is hot. Spoon into pastry shells. Makes 8 servings.

TURKEY ELEGANTE

4 tablespoons butter or margarine
1 large Bermuda onion, chopped fine
1 can (6 oz.) broiled mushroom crowns, drained
1 can condensed cream of tomato soup

▶ ⅓ cup strong coffee beverage
1 cup sour cream
▶ 1½ pounds thick sliced cooked turkey (approximately)
1 pound small macaroni shells, cooked, tossed with butter and parsley

1. Heat 2 tablespoons butter in a medium skillet, add onion and cook just until tender. Stir in drained mushrooms and continue to cook just until almost all the liquid in the pan has evaporated.

2. Stir in soup and coffee and cook until sauce is hot, and slightly thickened. Remove skillet from heat and stir in sour cream.

3. Melt remaining butter in a chafing dish and gently warm turkey slices. Pour sauce over turkey and allow to barely simmer. Do not allow to come to a boil. Serve with prepared macaroni shells. Makes 6 servings.

TURKEY MARSALA

4 to 6 tablespoon butter or margarine
▶ 8 slices (¼ inch thick) cooked turkey
⅛ teaspoon pepper

8 thin slices prosciutto ham
1 package (8 oz.) Mozzarella cheese, cut in 8 slices
½ cup Marsala wine
2 tablespoons minced parsley

1. Heat 4 tablespoons butter in large skillet. Gently sauté the turkey slices, a few at a time, just until light golden, (about one minute on each side). Remove and keep warm. Add more butter to the skillet as needed.

2. Overlap the sautéed slices in the skillet. Sprinkle with pepper. Place a slice of ham, and a slice of cheese on each slice of turkey. Pour the Marsala over all. Simmer, covered, 3 to 5 minutes, or until heated through and cheese is melted. Sprinkle with parsley. Serve in skillet. Makes 4 servings.

TURKEY À L'ORANGE

1 tablespoon butter
¼ cup finely minced onion
2 tablespoons orange
  marmalade
1 teaspoon grated lemon rind
½ teaspoon grated orange rind
⅛ teaspoon salt

1 to 2 tablespoons lemon juice
1 tablespoon cornstarch
¾ cup white wine or chicken
  stock
▶ 4 thick slices cooked turkey
  (about 1 pound)

1. Heat butter in a skillet; sauté onion until tender. Add marmalade, lemon rind, orange rind, salt, and 1 tablespoon lemon juice; simmer 5 minutes.

2. Dissolve the cornstarch in 2 tablespoons of the wine, then add the rest of the wine. Stir cornstarch mixture into sauce and cook, stirring constantly, until sauce is clear and thickened. Add more lemon juice if desired.

3. Turn heat down to barely a simmer. Add turkey slices to sauce in skillet; cook, covered, just until turkey is heated through (about 3 to 4 minutes). Makes 4 servings.

LEMON TURKEY SCALLOPPINE

▶ 8 thin slices cooked breast of
  turkey
  Flour seasoned with salt and
  pepper
4 tablespoons butter or
  margarine
1 tablespoon olive oil
¼ cup dry white wine

▶ ½ cup turkey or chicken broth
1 tablespoon lemon juice
2 scallions, minced
1 clove garlic, minced
2 tablespoons minced fresh
  parsley
½ teaspoon tarragon
½ lemon, thinly sliced

1. Dip the turkey in seasoned flour and shake off excess. Heat butter and oil in a large heavy skillet and cook turkey until golden on both sides. Transfer to a plate and reserve.

2. Pour off fat; stir the wine into the pan drippings. Add the chicken broth, lemon juice, scallions, garlic, parsley, and tarragon and simmer 5 minutes. Return turkey to skillet, cover, and simmer 3 minutes. Serve immediately, garnished with lemon slices. Makes 4 servings.

TURKEY FRUIT CURRY

½ cup chopped onion
½ cup butter or margarine
7 tablespoons flour
2 teaspoons curry powder
1 teaspoon salt

▶ 4 cups turkey or chicken broth
▶ 3 cups cubed cooked turkey
1 cup pineapple tidbits, drained
½ cup raisins
  Hot cooked rice

1. In a large skillet sauté onion in butter until soft. Blend in flour, curry powder, and salt. Slowly add broth; stir over low heat until thickened.

2. Add turkey, pineapple and raisins; heat until warmed through. Serve over hot rice. Makes 6 servings.

TURKEY POT PIES

1½ cups flour
1 envelope cheese sauce mix
½ teaspoon salt
½ teaspoon paprika
½ cup shortening
5 to 6 tablespoons cold water
3 tablespoons butter

1 cup sliced celery
1 cup sliced mushrooms
½ cup diced onion
▶ 2 cups leftover turkey gravy
▶ 3 cups diced cooked turkey
¼ teaspoon rosemary
⅛ teaspoon thyme

1. In a mixing bowl, combine flour, cheese sauce mix, salt, and paprika. With a pastry blender or two forks, cut shortening into dry ingredients until mixture resembles corn meal. Add just enough water to moisten flour particles and press dough together. Divide into 6 portions. On a floured surface, roll each portion ⅛-inch thick. Place pastry sheets on an ungreased baking sheet and cut each to fit the diameter of individual serving dishes. Flute edges. Carefully cut a small star in center of each pastry sheet; remove center dough. Prick pastry. Bake in a 425° oven 10 to 15 minutes or until brown. Cool on rack.

2. Melt butter in a small skillet and sauté celery, mushrooms, and onion for 10 minutes, until soft.

3. In a saucepan combine gravy, turkey, vegetables, rosemary, and thyme. Heat until bubbly hot. Divide evenly among the 6 individual serving dishes. Top with baked crust rounds. When ready to serve, heat in a 350° oven 10 minutes or until heated through. Makes 6 servings.

BATTER-FRIED ALMOND TURKEY

1 cup flour
1 teaspoon baking powder
½ teaspoon salt
⅛ teaspoon pepper
1 egg, lightly beaten
¾ cup milk

1 to 2 teaspoons Dijon mustard
▶ 6 large slices cold cooked turkey
Shortening for deep-fat frying
¼ cup butter
½ cup sliced almonds

1. In a mixing bowl, combine flour, baking powder, salt, and pepper. Combine egg, milk, and mustard; stir into dry ingredients to make a batter. Dip a few turkey slices in batter. Deep-fry in shortening heated to 365° until golden brown. Drain on absorbent paper; keep warm. Repeat with remaining slices.

2. Melt butter in a small saucepan; add almonds and sauté until golden. Remove almonds from butter with slotted spoon and sprinkle over turkey slices. Makes 6 servings.

TURKEY NOODLE SOUP

1 tablespoon butter
2 carrots, peeled and sliced thin
2 stalks celery, sliced thin
(crosswise)
1 cup sliced fresh mushrooms
1 small red pepper, seeded and
diced
1 small green pepper, seeded
and diced

▶ 2 quarts turkey stock
4 ounces fine egg noodles
▶ 1 to 2 cups diced cooked turkey
½ cup chopped parsley
½ cup grated Parmesan cheese
¼ teaspoon white pepper
Salt to taste

1. Melt butter in medium skillet. Add carrots, celery, mushrooms, and red and green peppers; sauté 10 minutes.

2. Put the turkey stock in large saucepan, add sautéed vegetables and simmer 15 minutes. Add noodles to soup; cook 10 minutes. Add turkey and cook 5 minutes longer.

3. Remove soup from heat. Stir in parsley and Parmesan cheese. Season with pepper and salt. Makes about 8 servings.

TURKEY CORN CHOWDER

¼ pound lean bacon, diced
1 cup chopped onion
3 cups diced potatoes
1 cup diced celery
½ teaspoon salt
⅛ teaspoon pepper

▶ 6 cups chicken or turkey broth,
homemade or canned
1 can (16 oz.) cream-style corn
1 can (13 oz.) evaporated milk
▶1½ cups diced cooked turkey
½ teaspoon marjoram
½ teaspoon thyme

1. In large saucepan, sauté the bacon until crisp; remove from pan. Cook the onion in bacon fat until soft, about 5 minutes.

2. Add the potatoes, celery, salt, pepper, broth, and bacon; simmer over low heat for 20 mintues, or until potatoes are tender. Stir in the corn, milk, turkey, marjoram, and thyme. Heat until warmed through. Makes 6 servings.

TURKEY CHOWDER

2 tablespoons butter
1 cup minced onion
¼ cup minced celery
6 mushrooms, chopped
▶ 4 cups turkey or chicken broth,
homemade or canned
¼ cup uncooked rice

1 teaspoon salt
½ teaspoon pepper
▶ ¾ cup diced cooked turkey
2 cups milk
1 cup light cream
2 tablespoons minced parsley

1. In a large saucepan, melt butter and sauté onion, celery and mushrooms for 5 minutes. Add broth, rice, salt and pepper. Bring to a boil; cook 30 minutes, or until rice is cooked.

2. Add turkey, milk and cream; heat through, but do not boil. Sprinkle parsley on each serving. Makes 6 servings.

CREAMY TURKEY NOODLE SOUP

▶ 8 cups turkey or chicken broth, homemade or canned
¾ cup quartered, thinly sliced carrots
½ cup sliced celery, including some leaves
½ cup chopped green pepper
½ cup chopped onion
1 clove garlic, minced
½ teaspoon dried or ground marjoram

Salt and freshly ground pepper
1 cup uncooked noodles (broken in pieces, if desired)
▶1½ cups diced cooked turkey
¼ cup all-purpose flour
1½ cups milk
2 tablespoons butter or margarine (optional)

1. Place broth in large kettle; add carrots, celery, green pepper, onion, garlic, marjoram, and salt and pepper to taste. Cook until vegetables are crisp-tender (about 20 minutes); add noodles and turkey, and cook until almost done (about 10 more minutes).

2. Whisk together flour and ½ cup milk. Then, add remaining milk and stir into soup mixture; boil gently for 3 minutes. Stir in optional butter or margarine. Taste and adjust seasoning. Makes 6 to 8 servings.

TURKEY HASH CASSEROLE

4 tablespoons butter
¾ cup minced celery
¼ cup minced green pepper
½ cup finely diced mushrooms
2 tablespoons flour
2 cups milk

▶ 2 tablespoons stuffing from roasted turkey, crumbled
▶ 2 cups chopped cooked turkey
2 tablespoons brandy
2 tablespoons fine dry bread crumbs
2 tablespoons melted butter

1. Melt 2 tablespoons of the butter in a large saucepan. Add celery, green pepper, and mushrooms. Cook, stirring, over low heat for 5 minutes. Remove from heat.

2. Melt the remaining 2 tablespoons butter in a skillet; blend in flour; cook for 1 minute. Add milk; cook, stirring constantly, until mixture thickens, about 5 minutes.

3. Add sauce and turkey stuffing to vegetables. Stir, breaking up stuffing so that it becomes part of sauce. Add turkey and brandy; blend, and pour mixture into a shallow baking pan or into 6 individual baking dishes.

4. Sprinkle with bread crumbs and melted butter. Bake in preheated 350° oven for 15 to 20 minutes, or until heated through. Makes 6 servings.

TURKEY HASH

2 tablespoon butter
1 tablespoon vegetable oil
2 cups sliced fresh mushrooms
1 cup diced onion
1 cup sliced celery
½ cup thinly sliced carrots
½ cup diced green pepper
▶ 1½ cups chopped cooked turkey
▶ 1 cup chopped cooked
  potatoes

▶ 1 cup chicken stock, homemade
  or canned
1 teaspoon crumbled thyme
1 teaspoon minced parsley
½ teaspoon dry mustard
½ teaspoon salt
  Pepper to taste
4 eggs

1. In a large skillet, melt the butter and add the vegetable oil, mushrooms, onion, celery, carrots, and green pepper. Sauté until vegetables are crisp-tender.

2. Add the turkey and potatoes; stir and cook 1 minute. Add the stock, thyme, parsley, mustard, salt, and pepper. Simmer 15 minutes. Serve with poached eggs. Makes 4 servings.

TURKEY-RICE COCKTAIL TIDBITS

▶ 2 cups cooked rice
  ½ cup minced celery
  ½ cup chopped almonds
  2 tablespoons minced onion
  ¾ teaspoon salt
  ¾ teaspoon poultry seasoning

  Dash of pepper
▶ 2 cups minced cooked turkey
  ¼ cup butter, melted
  2 eggs, lightly beaten
  ¾ cup fine dry bread crumbs

1. Preheat oven to 425°. In a bowl, combine rice, celery, almonds, onion, salt, poultry seasoning, pepper, and turkey.

2. Stir in butter and eggs. Shape into 2-inch balls; roll in crumbs.

3. Arrange in baking pan; bake in preheated oven for 30 minutes or until crisp. Makes about 20 balls.

BROILED TURKEY SALAD

2 teaspoons minced onion
1 tablespoon fresh lemon juice
▶ 2 cups diced cooked turkey
  ½ teaspoon salt
  ⅛ teaspoon pepper
  ½ cup mayonnaise

1½ cups finely diced celery
¼ cup canned buttered
  chopped almonds
2 cups fine bread crumbs
1 cup grated Cheddar cheese

1. In a bowl mix together the onions, lemon juice, turkey, salt, pepper, mayonnaise, celery, and almonds. Chill.

2. Put mixture into a 9-inch pie pan. Combine the bread crumbs with the cheese and completely cover the top. Put under the broiler just until top is golden. Garnish with watercress and sliced tomatoes. Makes 4 servings.

TURKEY CRANBERRY SQUARES

2 envelopes unflavored gelatin
1 can (16 oz.) whole cranberry
  sauce
1 can (8 oz.) crushed pineapple
1 can California walnuts, half
  cup broken
4 tablespoons lemon juice

1 cup mayonnaise
½ cup water
¾ teaspoon salt
▶ 2 cups diced cooked turkey
½ cup diced celery
2 tablespoons parsley

1. In a small bowl, soften 1 package of gelatin in ¼ cup cold water. Place the bowl in a pan of hot water until the gelatin is dissolved. Add to the gelatin the cranberry sauce, pineapple, broken walnuts and 1 tablespoon lemon juice. Pour into a 10 x 6 x 1½-inch pan; chill until firm.

2. Soften the remaining package of gelatin as directed above. Blend in the mayonnaise, water, the remaining lemon juice, and salt, then mix in the turkey, celery and parsley. Pour over cranberry layer and chill until set.

3. Just before serving, cut into 6 or 8 squares. Place each square on lettuce. Garnish with a dollop of mayonnaise and the walnut halves. Makes 6 to 8 servings.

TURKEY MOUSSE

1 envelope unflavored gelatin
▶ 1½ cups turkey stock
▶ 1½ cups ground cooked turkey
½ teaspoon curry powder
¼ cup mayonnaise
1 teaspoon celery salt
2 teaspoons grated onion

1 teaspoon finely chopped
  celery
Salt
White pepper
¾ cup heavy cream, whipped
Lettuce leaves
Jellied cranberry sauce slices

1. In the top of a double boiler, dissolve gelatin in ½ cup cold turkey stock. In a bowl, combine the remaining stock with the turkey, curry powder, mayonnaise, celery salt, onion, and celery. Add the dissolved gelatin; mix well. Season with salt and white pepper to taste. Chill until thick and syrupy.

2. Beat chilled mixture until light and foamy; fold in the whipped cream. Pour mixture into a 1-quart mold. Chill overnight or until firm.

3. Unmold on top of the lettuce leaves arranged on a serving platter. Garnish with the jellied cranberry sauce slices. Makes 6 servings.

Low calorie salads

Because well-chilled evaporated skim milk more than doubles in volume when whipped, it can be substituted for whipped cream in molded salads and desserts that contain gelatin.

TURKEY-STUFFED BAKED APPLES

▶ 1 cup diced cooked turkey
½ cup chopped raw mushrooms
¼ cup diced green pepper
2 tablespoons finely chopped
   walnuts
¼ cup white wine
½ teaspoon salt

¼ teaspoon freshly ground black
   pepper
6 large Rome apples
▶ 3 to 4 cups chicken stock
Lettuce
Mayonnaise

1. In a bowl, combine turkey, mushrooms, green pepper, walnuts, wine, salt, and pepper. Blend well.

2. Core apples and remove some of the fruit, leaving thick apple shells. Pare the top third of the skins.

3. Place apples in baking dish and heap turkey mixture into centers. Cover bottom of dish with about ½-inch of stock. Cover dish and bake apples in a preheated 375° oven until they are tender but not broken. Baste several times with pan juices while baking.

4. Remove apples from pan with slotted spoon and refrigerate until well-chilled. Place on a bed of finely chopped lettuce and serve with mayonnaise. Makes 6 servings.

TURKEY RICE SALAD

½ teaspoon salt
½ teaspoon ground black
   pepper
½ teaspoon tarragon
¼ cup white wine vinegar
⅔ cup olive oil
▶ 3 cups cooked rice, warm
¼ cup finely chopped green
   pepper
3 tablespoons finely chopped
   pimiento
½ cup mayonniase

⅛ teaspoon cayenne pepper
2 teaspoons Dijon mustard
▶ 2 cups diced cooked turkey
▶ 2 hard-cooked eggs, chilled and
   thinly sliced
1 tablespoon finely chopped
   fresh chives or scallion tops
1 tablespoon finely chopped
   parsley
French or Italian bread,
   warm

1. In a mixing bowl, combine the salt, the freshly ground pepper and tarragon into the vinegar. With a wire whisk slowly beat in the olive oil. Pour the dressing over the warm rice and toss it thoroughly. Add the chopped green pepper and pimiento. Toss again and taste for seasoning. Add more salt and pepper if needed.

2. In another mixing bowl combine the mayonnaise with the cayenne pepper and mustard. Fold the diced turkey into this and make sure each piece is well coated. Let the turkey marinate at room temperature in the mayonnaise for about 1 hour.

3. Chill a 1½-quart glass salad bowl. Arrange the cold rice on the bottom of the bowl, spread the turkey over it and garnish the top with overlapping slices of cold hard-cooked eggs. Sprinkle with the chives and parsley and serve with warm French or Italian bread. Makes 4 servings.

SAVORY TURKEY SALAD

- ▶ 4 cups cooked macaroni
- ▶ 3 cups cubed cooked turkey
  1 carrot, grated
  1 cup diced celery
  1 medium onion, thinly sliced
  ½ cup sliced radishes
  ½ cup diced green pepper
  ½ cup sliced green olives
  ½ cup chopped parsley

2 tomatoes, cut into eighths
▶ 1 cup cooked peas or broccoli
  flowerets
1½ cups cubed Swiss cheese
1½ cups mayonnaise
¼ cup lemon juice
⅓ cup sugar
1 teaspoon salt
⅛ teaspoon pepper

1. In large bowl, toss macaroni, turkey, vegetables, and cheese.

2. In a separate bowl, blend mayonnaise, lemon juice, sugar, salt, and pepper. Pour over salad and blend well. Chill several hours or overnight. Makes 8 servings.

TURKEY PILAF

6 slices bacon
1 large green pepper, chopped
1 medium onion, chopped
1 tablespoon minced celery
1 package (10 oz.) frozen cut
  okra, thawed
1 teaspoon salt
2 cups uncooked rice

▶ 4½ cups turkey or chicken broth,
  homemade or canned
1 can (14 oz.) whole plum
  tomatoes, drained and
  chopped
Dash Tabasco
¼ teaspoon Worcestershire sauce
▶ 3 cups diced cooked turkey

1. In a large saucepan, sauté bacon until golden; remove bacon and break into pieces. Leave bacon drippings in the saucepan. Add green pepper, onion, celery, okra, and salt and sauté 5 minutes.

2. Add rice and stir over low heat for 2 minutes. Add bacon, broth, tomatoes, Tabasco, and Worcestershire sauce, and bring to a boil. Transfer to a 2-quart casserole, cover tightly and put into a 350° oven for 20 minutes. Remove from the oven, gently stir in the turkey, return to oven and bake for 10 more minutes. Fluff up rice with fork before serving. Makes 6 servings.

GREEK TURKEY SANDWICHES

½ cup sour cream
1 tablespoon prepared
  horseradish
½ teaspoon dill
4 pita bread

▶ 1 cup thinly sliced turkey
1 cup shredded Cheddar
  cheese
1 medium tomato, sliced and
  cut in strips

In a small bowl, mix the sour cream with the horseradish and dill. Warm the pita bread. Split open and in the pocket put the turkey, cheese, and tomato. Spoon the sauce over the turkey. Makes 4 servings.

HOT TURKEY SANDWICHES
WITH MUSHROOM SAUCE

2 cans (10½ oz. each) cream of
  mushroom soup
½ cup milk
1 teaspoon Worcestershire sauce
8 slices white bread, toasted

▶ 8 to 10 slices cooked turkey
½ cup shredded sharp Cheddar
  cheese
8 slices bacon, partially cooked

1. In a sauce pan, mix soup with the milk and Worcestershire sauce and heat thoroughly, stirring until smooth.

2. On each of four plates, put one whole slice of toast in the middle with a half piece of toast on either side. Cover the toast with the turkey. Spoon sauce over turkey; sprinkle with cheese and bacon.

3. Put under the broiler until cheese is melted. Makes 4 servings.

Five or six sumptuous meals, each fresh and different, from one 12-pound turkey

Pound for pound, turkey is often the "best buy." It's not just for Thanksgiving anymore. Even for a small family, it is highly practical to roast a 12-pound turkey, feast on part of it, then freeze the rest for 4 or 5 additional meals.

Just strip the turkey of all leftover meat and package it in meal-size portions by parts with recipes in mind, i.e. the legs for Turkey Curry, a breast for Turkey à l'Orange, the thighs and wings for Turkey Tetrazzini, and so forth.

Then, simmer the carcass for the delicious broth (see Basics) and enjoy still another hearty meal of Creamy Turkey Noodle Soup, with the extra broth frozen in pint portions for use in various sauces.

Freezing, moreover, lets you space the meals days and weeks apart.

"COOKED" MEATS

In all ingredient listings, "cooked" meat means only that the meat be once-cooked—roasted, baked, braised, broiled, stewed, or boiled.

With the exception of recipes caling for "rare" meat—roast beef, for example—variously cooked meats are interchangeable in most recipes.

Remember that meats which have been dry-cooked (roasted, baked, broiled) have a firmer texture than moist-cooked meats, such as pot roast. Unless the meat is ground up, they should preferably be used in sauced recipes or recipes that call for a shorter cooking time.

Remember, too, that moist-cooked meats usually have more flavor than dry-cooked. Seasonings for each should be adjusted accordingly.

"BROWNING" CUBED MEATS

When using meats that have been previously roasted or broiled, you can brown the cubes lightly for 3 to 4 mintes in butter or oil before adding to the sauced mixture, to give the meat a crisping that will add a nice flavor. This can also be done with pot-roasted or braised meat, but brown only for a moment or two.

▶HAM

CREOLE HAM AND EGGS

8 tablespoons butter or
 margarine
2 tablespoons flour
1 cup milk
2 tablespoons chopped onion
2 tablespoons chopped green
 pepper
2 tablespoons chopped red
 pepper

1 teaspoon chili powder
1 clove garlic, minced
1 can (16 oz.) tomatoes,
 chopped and drained
▶ 4 eggs, hard-cooked and sliced
▶ 1 cup diced cooked ham
1 cup shredded cheese
½ cup soft bread crumbs

1. Melt 2 tablespoons butter in saucepan. Stir in flour and cook for 1 minute. Gradually stir in the milk; cook, stirring constantly, until sauce is thickened and smooth. Set aside.

2. Heat 4 tablespoons butter in another saucepan; sauté onion, peppers, chili powder and garlic for 7 to 8 minutes. Add tomatoes; bring to boil. Cook over low heat for about 20 minutes, or until thick. Stir into white sauce.

3. Arrange alternate layers of sauce, sliced eggs, ham and cheese in buttered casserole. (The top layer should be cheese). Top with breadcrumbs, dot with butter. Bake casserole in a preheated 350° oven for 20 minutes. Serve on toast. Makes 4 servings.

JAMBALAYA

▶ 3 tablespoons bacon fat,
 lard or butter
1 cup minced onion
2 green peppers, cut into thin
 strips
1 cup uncooked rice
▶1½ cups chicken stock,
 homemade or canned
1 can (15 ounces) tomatoes,
 drained and chopped
1 teaspoon minced garlic

1 teaspoon dried thyme
1 teaspoon chili powder
1 teaspoon salt
½ teaspoon pepper
½ teaspoon turmeric
▶ 6 small cooked sausages, or 1¼
 cups minced cooked pork
▶ 2 cups cubed cooked ham
12 fresh oysters (optional)
2 tablespoons minced parsley

1. In a large casserole, melt the bacon fat, and sauté the onions and green pepper until vegetables are soft, about 10 minutes. Stir in the rice, cook and stir for 2 minutes.

2. Add the stock, tomatoes, garlic, thyme, chili powder, salt, pepper and tumeric; stir and bring to a boil. Add the sausages (or the pork) and the ham to the casserole and stir. Cover tightly and cook in a 350° oven for 25 minutes, or until the liquid has been completely absorbed.

3. 10 minutes before the end of the cooking time, add the shucked oysters to the casserole. Sprinkle parsley on top just before serving. Makes 6 servings.

HAM DI PARMA

1 package (8 oz.) spaghetti,
  cooked
¾ cup grated Parmesan cheese
⅓ cup butter or margarine
2 cups mushrooms, sliced
3 tablespoons grated onion
¼ cup flour

2 cups cream
¾ cup dry white wine
▶ 2 cups cooked ham, cut in strips
⅓ cup sliced green olives
1 pimiento, cut in thin strips
¼ teaspoon dried oregano
⅛ teaspoon black pepper

1. Toss the cooked spaghetti with ½ cup of the Parmesan cheese and keep warm.

2. Melt butter in a large skillet; add mushrooms and onion. Cook over medium heat 5 minutes, stirring occasionally. With slotted spoon, remove mushrooms; set aside.

3. Blend the flour into butter in skillet. Remove from heat and gradually add cream, stirring constantly. Continue to stir and bring mixture to boiling. Cook 1 minute longer. Blend in wine, mushrooms, ham, olives, pimiento, oregano, and pepper.

4. Put hot spaghetti in a large flame-proof baking dish. Spoon hot creamed-ham mixture over spaghetti and sprinkle with remaining ¼ cup Parmesan cheese.

5. Broil 4 to 6 inches from heat source until lightly browned and thoroughly heated. If desired, garnish with olive slices and parsley sprigs. Makes 6 to 8 servings.

CAULIFLOWER-HAM AU GRATIN

3 cups flowerets of cauliflower
5 tablespoons butter or
  margarine
¼ cup sliced onion
1 cup sliced mushrooms
⅓ cup flour

1 cup milk
1 cup diced Cheddar cheese
½ cup sour cream
▶ 2 cups cubed cooked ham
1 cup soft bread crumbs

1. In a skillet, cook the cauliflowerets, covered, in boiling salted water until crisp-tender; drain. Place cauliflowerets in bottom of buttered 2-quart casserole.

2. In medium saucepan, melt 4 tablespoons of the butter. Add onion and mushrooms and sauté until tender. Add flour; cook 1 minute, stirring constantly. Add milk; cook over low heat until sauce is thickened. Stir in cheese and sour cream until blended; add ham.

3. Pour into buttered 2-quart casserole, over cauliflowerets. Combine remaining 1 tablespoon butter with bread crumbs; sprinkle over top of casserole. Bake in preheated 350° oven for 20 minutes or until crumbs are lightly browned. Makes 4 servings.

HAM AND CORN CASSEROLE

▶2½ cups ground or minced
  cooked ham
▶ 4 cups cooked, drained corn
  1 cup soft bread crumbs
  ¼ cup grated onion
  2 teaspoons prepared mustard
  1½ cups milk
  2 eggs, beaten

1 tablespoon horseradish
  (optional)
3 medium tomatoes, cut in thick
  slices
Salt
Pepper
2 tablespoons melted butter

1. Spread the ham in the bottom of a greased 12- × 8-inch, or a 9-inch square baking dish.

2. Mix the corn, bread crumbs, onion, mustard, milk, eggs, and horse-radish. Pour over the ham. Arrange the tomato slices on top. Sprinkle with salt and pepper and brush with butter. Bake for 45 minutes to 1 hour in a preheated 350° oven. Makes 6 to 8 servings.

ALSATIAN CHOUCROUTE GARNIE

  2 pounds sauerkraut
  1¼ cups finely chopped onion
▶ 3 tablespoons bacon fat
  ½ cup finely chopped carrot
  6 large mushrooms, sliced
  ½ teaspoon finely chopped
   garlic
  2 tablespoons flour
  2 medium tart apples, peeled,
   cored, and coarsely chopped
  12 Juniper berries (wrapped in
   cheesecloth), or ¼ cup gin
▶1½ to 2 cups chicken stock
  1¼ cups dry white wine

½ pound piece of salt pork, lean
  and mildly cured
1 1-pound Kielbasa sausage, cut
  in 1-inch pieces
A bouquet of 4 sprigs parsley,
  2 celery tops with leaves, and 1
  small bay leaf, tied together
  with string
Salt
Freshly ground black pepper
▶ 6 to 8 slices ham, cut about
  ¼-inch thick
  Boiled potatoes

1. Drain the sauerkraut in a colander, wash well under cold running water and soak in cold water for 10 to 20 minutes. Squeeze out excess moisture and put into a 4- or 6-quart casserole (with a heavy tight fitting cover) over low heat.

2. In a skillet, cook the onion in the bacon fat for 2 minutes; add the car-rots, mushrooms, and garlic and cook for 5 minutes. Stir in the flour and cook another 2 minutes before adding to the casserole.

3. Add the apples, juniper berries (or gin), stock, and wine, and stir the mixture thoroughly. Push the salt pork, Kielbasa, and bouquet into the mixture and salt and pepper to taste. Cover, bring liquid to a boil, and place in a preheated 325° oven to cook for 45 to 60 minutes.

4. A half hour before serving, stir the sauerkraut mixture well and bury the ham slices in the middle.

5. To serve, mound the *choucroute* in the center of a large serving plat-ter, arrange the ham slices over it, and surround with plain boiled pota-toes. Pass it with a variety of mustards, pickles, and cold beer. Makes 6 to 8 servings.

HAM GOUGÈRE

1 cup water
¾ cup butter or margarine
Pinch salt and pepper
1 cup plus 1½ tablespoons sifted
flour
4 eggs
½ cup diced, sharp Cheddar
cheese
1 cup chopped onion
2 cups sliced mushrooms

▶ 1 cup chicken broth, homemade
or canned
2 cups peeled, seeded, diced
tomatoes
▶1½ cups julienned cooked ham
1 teaspoon salt
¼ teaspoon pepper
2 tablespoons shredded
Cheddar cheese
2 tablespoons chopped parsley

1. Heat the water, ½ cup butter, and the salt and pepper in a large saucepan until the butter melts. Turn up the heat and bring water to boiling. Add the 1 cup flour all at once and stir vigorously until mixture forms a ball in the center of the pan.

2. Allow mixture to cool for 5 minutes. Add the eggs one at a time, beating well with a wooden spoon after each addition. Each egg must be completely absorbed before the next one is added. Stir in the diced cheese.

3. Melt 4 tablespoons of the butter in a large skillet; sauté the onion until soft but not browned. Add the mushrooms and continue cooking 2 minutes. Sprinkle with the remaining flour; mix and cook an additional 2 minutes. Add the chicken broth. Bring to a boil, stirring constantly. Simmer 4 minutes.

4. Remove the sauce from the heat and add the tomato and the ham. Season with the salt and pepper.

5. Preheat the oven to 400°. Butter a 10- to 11-inch ovenproof skillet, pie pan, or shallow baking dish. Spoon the dough in a ring around the edge, leaving the center open. Pour the ham mixture into the center and sprinkle all over with the cheese. Bake for 40 minutes or until gougère is puffed and brown and the ham mixture is bubbling. Sprinkle with parsley and serve at once, cut into wedges as for a pie. Makes 6 servings.

HAM-POTATO-CHEESE SCALLOP

1 can (10½ oz.) cream of
mushroom soup
½ cup milk
1 cup shredded Swiss cheese
½ cup sliced scallions
¼ cup chopped green pepper
2 teaspoon dried dillweed

4 large potatoes, pared and
sliced
4 tablespoons butter or
margarine
▶ 3 cups diced cooked ham
1 cup fine soft bread crumbs
Paprika

1. In a medium bowl, combine soup, milk, cheese, scallions, green pepper, and dillweed. Set aside.

2. Put ⅓ of potatoes in a buttered 2½-quart casserole and add half the ham. Top with half the sauce mixture. Repeat the layers, ending with a layer of potatoes.

3. Melt remaining butter and mix with crumbs. Sprinkle on casserole and bake in a preheated 350° oven about 45 minutes. Sprinkle with paprika. Makes 6 servings.

HAM AND CORNBREAD CASSEROLE

Sauce

▶ 2 cups cubed cooked ham
  (½-inch cubes)
1 package (10 oz.) frozen mixed
  vegetables, cooked
¾ cup ketchup
½ cup water
2 tablespoons minced onions
2 tablespoons brown sugar
⅛ teaspoon pepper
1½ teaspoons Worcestershire
  sauce

Corn Bread

1 cup cornmeal
1 cup sifted all-purpose flour
3 tablespoons sugar
4 teaspoons baking powder
1 teaspoon salt
1 cup milk
1 egg
¼ cup butter or margarine
  melted

1. Preheat the oven to 425°. Combine the ham, vegetables, ketchup, water, onion, brown sugar, pepper, and Worcestershire sauce in a saucepan, and heat to boiling, stirring occasionally to prevent sticking.

2. Sift the cornmeal, flour, sugar, baking powder, and salt into a mixing bowl. Add the milk, egg, and melted butter; mix until all ingredients are well combined.

3. Pour the hot ham mixture into a greased 2-quart baking dish, spreading it evenly. Pour the cornmeal batter over the ham mixture and spread it to the edges of the baking dish. Bake for 30 to 35 minutes. To serve, cut corn bread into serving-size pieces, and place them on plates. Spoon the ham mixture over the cornbread. Makes 6 servings.

EGGPLANT-HAM BAKE

1 medium onion, chopped
⅓ cup chopped celery
¼ cup chopped green pepper
1 clove garlic, halved
3 tablespoons butter or
  margarine
1 tablespoon chopped parsley
1 cup sour cream
1 teaspoon salt
1 egg, slightly beaten

2 tablespoons milk
⅛ teaspoon pepper
¾ cup fine dry bread crumbs
1 medium-size eggplant, pared
  and cut into ½" slices
⅓ cup vegetable oil
▶ 12 thin slices cooked ham
¼ pound Muenster or Mozzarella
  cheese, thinly sliced

1. Sauté the onion, celery, green pepper, and garlic in butter just until tender; put into a small bowl and remove the garlic; slowly stir in the parsley, sour cream, and ½ teaspoon of the salt.

2. Combine the egg, milk, remaining salt, and pepper in a shallow dish. Place the bread crumbs in a second dish. Dip the eggplant in the egg mixture, then in the crumbs; brown in the vegetable oil about 3 minutes on each side.

3. Line the bottom of a large shallow baking dish with ½ of the eggplant slices. Spread ½ of the sour cream mixture over the eggplant in the bottom of the dish; top with 6 ham slices and ½ the cheese; repeat layers; cover pan with aluminum foil. Bake in a preheated 350° oven about 25 minutes, or until bubbly; uncover and bake 5 more minutes to brown. Makes 6 servings.

HAM AND MACARONI CASSEROLE

2 tablespoons butter or
  margarine
1 small onion, minced
1 can (3 oz.) chopped
  mushrooms, drained
2 tablespoons chopped green
  pepper
1¼ cups elbow macaroni, cooked
2 tablespoons chopped stuffed
  olives

1 cup grated sharp Cheddar
  cheese
► 1 cup diced cooked ham
1 teaspoon salt
¼ teaspoon pepper
1 cup sour cream
¼ cup milk
½ cup buttered soft bread
  crumbs
Paprika

1. Heat the butter in a large skillet and cook the onion, mushrooms, and green pepper for 2 to 3 minutes. Combine in a bowl with the macaroni, olives, cheese, ham, salt, and pepper. Mix the sour cream and milk together and add to the macaroni mixture.

2. Preheat oven to 350°. Mix well and put in shallow buttered 1½-quart baking dish. Sprinkle with crumbs and paprika. Bake for about 30 minutes. Makes 6 servings.

HAM FLORENTINE

¼ cup finely chopped shallots or
  scallions
½ cup white wine vinegar
1 tablespoon dried tarragon
½ bay leaf
4 whole black peppercorns
2 sprigs parsley
► ½ cup chicken stock, homemade
  or canned
2 egg yolks

½ cup heavy cream
Salt
⅛ teaspoon white pepper
3 tablespoons butter
1 tablespoon vegetable oil
► 6 to 8 slices cooked ham, cut
  about ¼-inch thick
2 packages (10½ oz.) frozen
  chopped spinach

1. In a small saucepan, mix together the shallots, vinegar, 1 teaspoon of the tarragon, bay leaf, peppercorns, and parsley. Bring to a boil, then reduce the liquid to about a tablespoonful. Strain into a small bowl, pressing down on the shallots and herbs before throwing them away.

2. In a saucepan, heat the chicken stock and keep warm. In a bowl, beat the egg yolks lightly and mix with the heavy cream. Slowly add the hot stock to the cream mixture, then return it to a saucepan. Add the reduced vinegar and cook the sauce over moderate heat until it slowly begins to thicken; stir constantly. Don't let it boil or it will curdle. When it has thickened enough to coat the back of a spoon very heavily, remove from the heat, taste for salt, add the white pepper, and mix in the remaining tarragon.

3. In a heavy frying pan over moderate heat, melt the butter, add the oil and heat the ham slices. Cook the spinach; drain and squeeze almost dry. On a serving platter, arrange the spinach, layer the ham slices on top, and pour the sauce over all; serve immediately. Makes 4 to 6 servings.

HAM À LA KING

3 tablespoons chopped green
  pepper
½ cup sliced mushrooms
3 tablespoons butter
1½ tablespoons all-purpose flour
1½ cups light cream
½ teaspoon salt

Dash of paprika
▶ 2 cups diced cooked ham
1½ tablespoons chopped
  pimiento
2 egg yolks
2 tablespoons sherry

1. Sauté the green pepper and mushrooms in butter, in a deep skillet, for 2 to 3 minutes. Stir in the flour.

2. Gradually stir in the cream and cook until thickened, stirring constantly. Season with salt and paprika. Add ham and pimiento and cook over low heat for 2 minutes, stirring constantly.

3. In a small bowl, beat the egg yolks slightly; stir in some of the hot sauce. Stir the egg mixture back into the sauce. Cook for 1 minute longer over low heat, stirring constantly.

4. Remove from heat and stir in sherry. Serve on rice, noodles, or in heated pastry shells. Makes 4 to 6 servings.

SPAGHETTI CARBONARA

4 strips bacon
2 tablespoons olive oil
2 tablespoons butter
1 clove garlic, crushed
▶ 2 cups julienned strips of ham
  (about ½ pound)

1 package (16 oz.) spaghetti,
  cooked and drained
⅓ cup grated Parmesan cheese
¼ cup chopped parsley
½ teaspoon salt
¼ teaspoon pepper
3 eggs, beaten

1. Brown bacon in a skillet; drain, crumble, and reserve. Pour off fat; add oil, butter, garlic, and ham to skillet. Sauté lightly.

2. Add the cooked spaghetti, the reserved bacon, cheese, parsley, salt and pepper to the skillet; stir well. Turn off heat. Pour eggs over the mixture and quickly toss to coat spaghetti evenly. Decorate with parsley. Serve at once. Makes 4 to 5 servings.

HAM IN CREAM SAUCE

¼ cup butter or margarine
6 scallions, chopped fine
¼ cup all-purpose flour
¾ cup milk
¾ cup light cream
2 tablespoons tomato sauce

¼ cup white wine
Dash ground cloves
Salt and pepper
▶ 8 thin slices baked or boiled
  ham, cut in julienne strips

1. In a saucepan, melt the butter and sauté the scallions for 5 minutes. Blend in flour; add milk and cream and stir constantly until thickened. Stir in the tomato sauce, wine, cloves, salt and pepper to taste and simmer over very low heat for 5 minutes.

2. Place the ham strips in the bottom of a shallow broiler-proof dish. Pour the sauce over the ham and place under the broiler until top is slightly browned and bubbly. Makes 4 servings.

HAM ROLL-UPS

1 cup small curd, creamy
  cottage cheese
1 egg
1 cup sour cream
¼ cup minced onions
▶ ½ cup drained, chopped cooked
  spinach

½ teaspoon dry mustard
¼ teasponn salt
▶ 8 large slices ham, trimmed
Prepared mustard
1 can (10½ oz.) condensed
  cream of mushroom soup

1. Put the cottage cheese and the egg in a blender or food processor and process 5 seconds. Remove to a mixing bowl and blend in ¾ cup of the sour cream, the onions, spinach, dry mustard, and salt.

2. Lightly spread the ham slices with prepared mustard and place about 2 tablespoons filling on each slice of ham. Roll and tuck in the edges. Put in a shallow baking dish.

3. Combine the soup and the remaining sour cream. Pour over the ham rolls and bake in a preheated 375° oven about 25 minutes or until hot. Makes 4 servings.

MANICOTTI WITH MUSHROOMS AND HAM

4 tablespoons butter
¼ cup chopped onion
1 pound mushrooms, coarsely
  chopped
¾ to 1 cup grated Parmesan
  cheese

½ pound packaged manicotti
  (pasta tubes)
▶ 1½ to 2 cups diced cooked ham
2 cups hot Cream Sauce (see
  Basics)

1. Heat the butter in a large skillet. Add the onion and mushrooms, and sauté over high heat for about 5 minutes. Remove from the pan and cool. Stir in 2 tablespoons of the cheese.

2. Cook the manicotti in boiling salted water according to the package directions. Drain, rinse in cold water, and drain again very thoroughly.

3. Preheat the oven to 350°. Butter a broad, shallow baking dish. Stuff each pasta tube with some of the mushroom filling and arrange them in the baking dish.

4. Distribute the diced ham over the manicotti. Stir 4 tablespoons of the cheese into the hot Cream Sauce, and pour the sauce over the ham. Sprinkle the remaining cheese over the top. Bake until brown and bubbling. Makes 6 servings.

HAM IN RAISIN SAUCE

⅓ cup raisins
2 cups water
1 cup firmly packed dark brown
  sugar
2 tablespoons cornstarch
  Dash of salt

½ teaspoon ground ginger
¼ teaspoon ground mustard
2 tablespoons cider vinegar
▶ 2 cups diced baked ham
3 cups wide noodles, cooked
  and drained

1. In a saucepan, cook the raisins in the water for 5 minutes, over medium-low heat. In a bowl, combine the brown sugar, cornstarch, salt, ginger, mustard, and vinegar and add to the raisins; cook until slightly thickened. Add the ham and heat thoroughly.

2. Place the noodles on a deep serving platter, and pour the ham and raisin sauce over the center. Makes 4 servings.

FRESH TOMATO AND HAM SAUCE

¼ cup olive oil
1 clove garlic, crushed
2 medium tomatoes, cut into thin
  wedges
½ medium green pepper,
  seeded and cut into strips
6 to 8 scallions, diced

▶ 1 cup julienned cooked ham
½ teaspoon dried or 2
  tablespoons minced fresh basil
  Salt and pepper to taste
1 pound cooked spaghetti
⅓ cup grated Parmesan cheese

1. Heat the oil in a heavy skillet; add garlic and sauté until golden. Remove the garlic and cook the tomato slices and green peppers in the oil until they are warm; mix in the scallions, ham and basil; salt and pepper to taste. Simmer until ham is thoroughly heated.

2. Serve over spaghetti, sprinkled with parmesan cheese. Makes 4 servings.

STUFFED ONIONS

6 Bermuda onions, peeled
1 tablespoon finely chopped
  celery
2 tablespoons butter
▶ 1 cup ground cooked ham
½ cup sour cream
2 tablespoons chopped parsley

¼ teaspoon dried marjoram or
  sage
1 cup soft bread crumbs
  Salt and pepper
  Cayenne
1 cup meat bouillon or
  consommé

1. Boil the onions for 10 minutes in boiling salted water. Scoop out and chop the centers. Sauté the chopped onion and celery in the butter until tender.

2. Mix with the ham, sour cream, parsley, marjoram, and bread crumbs. Season with salt, pepper, and cayenne.

3. Preheat the oven to 400°. Stuff the onions with the mixture. Place in a baking dish and pour the bouillon on the bottom. Bake for 45 minutes. Makes 6 servings.

HAM-STUFFED MUSHROOM CAPS

1 pound large mushrooms
¼ cup olive oil
¼ cup minced onion
1 garlic clove, minced
2 tablespoons dry white wine
▶ ½ cup finely chopped cooked ham

½ cup fine dry bread crumbs
¼ cup grated Parmesan cheese
1 egg
2 tablespoons chopped parsley
½ teaspoon oregano
½ teaspoon salt
Freshly ground black pepper

1. Remove stems from mushrooms and spoon out a little of the inside of the cap to make a pocket for stuffing. Chop enough of the mushroom stems to make ½ cup. Heat the oil in a skillet; add the mushroom caps and toss them in the oil just long enough to coat them. Remove caps from pan and set aside.

2. Add chopped mushroom stems, onion, garlic, and wine to pan. Cook over low heat for 10 minutes, until mixture has cooked almost to a pulp. Remove pan from heat and stir in ham, bread crumbs, cheese, egg, parsley, oregano, salt, and pepper.

3. Spoon the mixture into the mushroom caps. Arrange caps in a baking dish and drizzle a little oil over them. Bake in a 325° oven for 30 minutes. Makes 4 servings.

STUFFED SQUASH

6 medium summer squash
¼ cup butter
1 tablespoon minced onion
1 clove garlic, chopped
▶ 1 cup chopped cooked ham
▶ ¼ cup chopped cooked shrimp
1 cup dry bread crumbs

1 egg, beaten
¼ teaspoon dried thyme
2 tablespoons chopped parsley
Salt and pepper to taste
⅓ cup chopped chives
Pimiento
Parsley sprigs

1. Cook the squash in boiling salted water until they are tender enough to be pierced. Cut squash into halves and scoop out the pulp, being careful not to break the shells. Mash the pulp and reserve.

2. Melt 3 tablespoons of the butter in a heavy skillet and add the reserved pulp, onion, and garlic. Cook over medium heat, stirring occasionally, until the onions are limp, about 5 minutes. Remove from heat. In a bowl, combine the vegetables with the ham, shrimp, bread crumbs, egg, thyme, parsley, and salt and pepper to taste.

3. Pile the stuffing into the squash shells, mounding it high. Sprinkle with additional bread crumbs, dot with the remaining butter, and sprinkle with the chives. Bake in a 350° oven for about 25 minutes, or until the topping is browned. Garnish with a strip of pimiento and a parsley sprig. Makes 6 servings.

HAM-STUFFED TOMATOES

4 large ripe tomatoes
► 1½ cups cooked long-grain rice
► 1 cup diced cooked ham
   1 small carrot, minced
► ¼ cup cooked peas
   1 tablespoon finely chopped
    parsley

⅓ cup white wine vinegar
⅔ cup vegetable oil
¼ teaspoon salt
⅛ teaspoon pepper
Lettuce

1. Cut the tomatoes into 6 or 8 pieces with a sharp knife, cutting half way down. With a spoon, scoop out seeds and pulp. Carefully turn upside down on paper towels to drain.

2. Combine the cooked rice with the ham, carrot, peas, and parsley in a bowl. Mix the vinegar, oil, salt, and pepper in a screw top jar, shake well. Pour ⅔ cup of the dressing over the rice mixture; toss until ingredients are coated.

3. Stuff the ham/rice filling into the drained tomatoes and chill. Serve in crisp lettuce leaves with the remaining dressing. Makes 4 servings.

BAKED STUFFED YAMS

4 large yams
8 slices bacon, cooked crisp
► 1 cup chopped cooked spinach
3 tablespoons milk
2 tablespoons butter or
   margarine

2 tablespoons chopped onion
1 egg
► ½ cup ground cooked ham
1 teaspoon salt
¼ teaspoon pepper
¼ cup grated Parmesan cheese

1. After washing and drying the yams, prick them several times with a fork and bake at 400° for 45 minutes or until soft. Remove from the oven and cut ⅓ of the top off; scoop out the center and mash in a large mixing bowl.

2. Crumble 6 slices of bacon. Add the bacon, spinach, milk, butter, onion, egg, ham, salt and pepper to the mashed yams; beat until smooth. Spoon the mixture into the yam shells. Crumble the remaining bacon over the yams. Sprinkle with Parmesan cheese and bake in 350° oven for 30 minutes. Makes 4 servings.

HAM AND EGG PIE

1 unbaked 9-inch pie shell or 6
   tart shells (see Basics)
1 raw egg white, lightly beaten
► 1 cup minced cooked ham
► 3 hard-cooked eggs, chopped

3 raw egg yolks
1 cup heavy cream
Salt
Pepper
Nutmeg

1. Brush the inside of the pie shell with the egg white and let it dry. Preheat the oven to 375°.

2. In a medium bowl, mix together the ham, hard-cooked eggs, egg yolks, and cream. Season to taste with salt, pepper and nutmeg.

3. Fill the pie shell. Bake until the filling is set and lightly browned, about 35 to 45 minutes. Serve hot or cold. Makes 6 servings.

HAM AND YAM PIE

¼ cup butter or margarine, softened
1 tablespoon light brown sugar
3 eggs, separated
3 tablespoons flour
2 tablespoons lemon juice
3 tablespoons chopped scallions
3 tablespoons chopped parsley
½ teaspoon dried basil
¼ teaspoon salt
► 2 cups mashed cooked yams
►1½ cups diced cooked ham
1 cup tart apples, pared and chopped
1 pastry shell (9-inch) unbaked (see Basics)

1. Cream together the butter and sugar in a large bowl. Beat in the egg yolks, flour, lemon juice, scallions, parsley, basil, salt and yams. Stir in the ham and chopped apple. Beat egg whites to stiff peaks and fold gently into the ham mixture.

2. Turn into pie shell and bake at 375° for 1 hour or until a knife comes out clean from the center. Let stand for 10 minutes and serve. Makes 6 servings.

VEGETABLE-HAM SOUFFLÉ PIE

1 cup sliced carrots
1 large onion, cut in thick slices
1 cup sliced mushrooms
1 medium zucchini, cut into 2" × ¼" sticks
► ¼ pound cooked ham, ¼-inch thick and cut into 1-inch strips
½ teaspoon salt
¼ teaspoon pepper
½ teaspoon crumbled leaf marjoram
3 tablespoons butter or margarine
3 tablespoons flour
¾ cup half-and-half cream
½ cup (2 oz.) shredded Swiss cheese
3 eggs, separated
1 single pie crust, baked (see Basics)

1. Cook the carrots, onion, mushrooms, and zucchini in boiling salted water for 5 minutes or until crisp-tender; drain. Turn into large bowl; add ham, salt, pepper and marjoram; mix lightly.

2. Melt the butter in a medium-size saucepan; blend in flour; cook 1 minute. Stir the half-and-half slowly into the saucepan. Cook, stirring constantly, until mixture thickens. Remove from heat; stir in the cheese until melted. Let the sauce cool while beating eggs.

3. Beat the egg whites in a small bowl with electric mixer until soft peaks form.

4. Beat egg yolks until light in a medium-size bowl. Beat in cooled cheese sauce. Measure ¼ cup of the cheese mixture; stir into vegetables. Fold remaining cheese mixture into beaten egg whites until no streaks of white remain.

5. Spoon vegetable mixture into cooled pie shell. Carefully spoon soufflé mixture over vegetables, spreading to edge of pastry to seal in vegetables.

6. Bake in a preheated 375° oven for 20 minutes, or until soufflé top has puffed and is lightly browned. Serve at once. Makes 6 servings.

HAM AND CHEESE QUICHE

Pie dough for 9-inch Single-Crust Pie (see Basics)
½ cup thinly sliced leeks, scallions or onions
1 clove garlic, minced
2 tablespoons butter
¾ cup diced Swiss or Cheddar cheese

▶ 1 cup diced cooked ham
3 eggs, beaten
1½ cups half-and-half cream
½ teaspoon salt
¼ teaspoon pepper
Ground nutmeg

1. Prepare and prebake the pie shell in a 425° oven until firm but not browned. Remove from oven, set aside, and reduce oven heat to 350°.

2. In a small skillet, sauté the leeks and garlic in butter for 2 minutes, stirring. Spread the onion mixture over the bottom of the pie shell. Combine the cheese and ham and sprinkle over the onion mixture.

3. Mix the beaten eggs, half-and-half, salt, and pepper. Pour into the pie shell and sprinkle the top with nutmeg. Bake for 35 to 45 minutes or until knife inserted near the center comes out clean. Remove from oven and let stand for 10 minutes before cutting into wedges. Makes 4 servings.

HAM BISCUIT ROLL WITH CHEESE SAUCE

¼ cup butter
¼ cup flour
2 cups milk
▶ 1½ to 2 cups ground or minced cooked ham
3 tablespoons finely chopped onion

¼ teaspoon salt
⅛ teaspoon pepper
¼ teaspoon dry mustard
Biscuit dough (recipe using 2 cups flour) (see Basics)
¾ cup grated Cheddar cheese

1. Melt the butter in a 1-quart saucepan. Stir in the flour. Gradually stir in the milk. Bring to a simmer, stirring constantly, until the sauce thickens.

2. In a bowl, mix together the ham and onion. Stir in about ½ cup of the white sauce, or just enough to make a thick paste. Season with the salt, pepper, and dry mustard.

3. Preheat the oven to 450°. Roll out the biscuit dough into a rectangle about 12 × 10 inches. Spread with ham mixture. Roll up from 10-inch end like a jelly roll. Cut in 1-inch slices and put, cut side down, on greased cookie sheet. Bake in oven for 15 to 20 minutes.

4. Stir the cheese into the remaining 1½ cups cream sauce. Season to taste with salt, pepper, and dry mustard if desired. Spoon the cheese sauce over the biscuits at serving time. Makes 6 servings.

Frozen pie shells

If time or inclination dictates the use of packaged frozen pie shells, remember that they are often smaller than the recipe calls for. Take care not to pour in too much filling. Any excess filling can be used in buttered custard cups or ramekins, and baked at the same time.

HAM AND SHRIMP QUICHE

½ cup sliced scallions
⅓ cup sliced leeks
1 9-inch baked pie shell (see Basics)
▶ ¾ cup diced cooked shrimp
½ cup diced Gruyère cheese
½ cup diced mild Cheddar cheese
▶ ½ cup finely diced baked ham

3 eggs
½ teaspoon salt
⅛ teaspoon pepper
⅛ teaspoon ground nutmeg
1 cup light cream, scalded and slightly cooled
½ cup heavy cream, scalded and slightly cooled

1. In boiling salted water, parboil the scallions and leeks for 5 minutes and drain.

2. Cover the center of the pie shell with the shrimp. Arrange the cheeses around the shrimp. Layer the ham over the cheese and shrimp, and sprinkle with the scallions and leeks.

3. In a bowl, beat the eggs with the salt, pepper and nutmeg until foamy, then carefully add the scalded creams and blend well. Pour slowly over mixture in pie shell. Bake in a 375° oven for 35 minutes or until center is firm. Cool for 10 minutes. Makes 6 servings.

HAM AND SPINACH RICOTTA PIE

1 package (10 oz.) frozen chopped spinach, cooked
1 10-inch pie shell, unbaked (see Basics)
¾ cup sliced mushrooms
▶ ¾ cup finely diced cooked ham

4 eggs
2 cups milk
1 cup ricotta or small curd, cottage cheese
1 teaspoon salt
¼ teaspoon pepper

1. Squeeze out the excess moisture in the spinach and sprinkle it evenly over the bottom of the pie shell. Add the mushrooms and ham.

2. In a mixing bowl, beat the eggs, milk, ricotta, salt, and pepper until smooth. Pour into pie shell over the spinach mixture. Bake in preheated 350° oven for 40 to 45 minutes until light brown and firm to the touch. Makes 6 servings.

HAM AND EGG PIROSHKI

2 tablespoons butter
½ cup minced onion
▶ ½ cup finely chopped cooked ham
▶ 2 hard-cooked eggs, chopped
1 tablespoon chopped parsley

1 teaspoon dried dillweed
2 to 4 tablespoons sour cream
Pie dough enough for 3 9-inch pie shells (see Basics)
1 raw egg

1. Melt the butter in a small pan, add the onion, and sauté just until translucent. Cool the onions slightly. Add the ham, eggs, parsley, and dillweed. Stir in just enough sour cream to bind this mixture together.

2. Preheat the oven to 400°. Roll out the pie dough on a floured board. With a 2½- or 3-inch round cookie cutter, cut out circles of dough.

(continued)

3. Place about 2 teaspoons of the ham filling in the center of each circle. Brush the edges of the dough lightly with water, fold the circles in half, and press the edges together firmly to seal them. Place on a baking sheet and bake until browned. Makes 24 Piroshki.

BAKED HAM PASTRIES NIÇOISE

4 anchovies, washed, dried and chopped
▶ ½ cup ground cooked ham
1 clove garlic, minced
1 tablespoon grated onion
½ teaspoon black pepper
1 tablespoon chopped parsley
2 tablespoons brandy

2 tablespoons olive oil
1 egg yolk
1 cup sifted flour
½ teaspoon salt
½ cup butter
3 tablespoons sour cream
1 egg yolk
2 tablespoons water

1. In a bowl, mix together the anchovies, ham, garlic, onion, pepper, parsley, brandy, oil, and egg yolk until smooth. Set aside.

2. Sift the flour and salt into a bowl. Work in the butter by hand. Add the sour cream, mixing until a ball of dough is formed. Chill for at least 2 hours.

3. Preheat the oven to 425°. Roll out the dough as thin as possible and cut into rounds with a cookie cutter. Place a teaspoon of the ham mixture on each round. Fold over the dough and seal the edges by pressing with a fork. Mix the egg yolk and water and brush the tops of the pastries with this mixture. Bake for 15 minutes or until browned. Makes about 30 pastries.

HAM AND TOMATO PIE

1 prebaked 9-inch pie shell (see Basics)
2 teaspoons Dijon mustard
▶ 2 cups coarsely ground or chopped cooked ham
2 tablespoons minced parsley
1 small garlic clove, pressed
3 tablespoons minced celery
¼ cup minced onion

2 tomatoes, peeled, cored, and thickly sliced
Salt and pepper to taste
2 cups shredded sharp Cheddar cheese
⅓ cup mayonnaise
¼ cup cracker crumbs
½ teaspoon dried basil

1. In a prebaked pie shell, spread the mustard and allow to dry.

2. In a small bowl, mix the ham with 1 tablespoon parsley, garlic, 2 tablespoons celery, and 2 tablespoons onion; spread in the pie shell. Layer overlapping tomato slices on top and sprinkle lightly with salt and pepper and the remaining parsley, celery, and onion.

3. In a small bowl, blend together the cheese, mayonnaise, cracker crumbs, and basil; spread over the filling in pie shell. Bake in a 400° oven for 30 or 40 minutes, until hot and bubbly. Makes 4 to 6 servings.

HAM AND MUSHROOM CRÊPES

12 large mushrooms, sliced
3 tablespoons butter or
  margarine
8 crêpes (see Basics)
▶ 1 cup minced cooked ham
3 tablespoons mayonnaise
3 tablespoons sour cream
1½ teaspoons prepared
  horseradish

½ teaspoon Dijon mustard
1 tablespoon minced fresh
  parsley
Salt and freshly ground pepper
  to taste
½ cup shredded Swiss or other
  cheese

1. Heat the oven to 350°. In a small skillet, sauté the mushrooms in 2 tablespoons of the butter or margarine, stirring, over high heat until lightly browned. Lay the crêpes on a flat surface and divide the mushrooms equally among them.

2. Lightly sauté ham in the same skillet with the remaining butter. In a bowl, mix ham, mayonnaise, sour cream, horseradish, mustard, parsley, and salt and pepper to taste. Place an equal amount on each crêpe. Roll up the crêpes and place, seam side down, in a greased 11- by 7-inch baking dish. Bake for 20 minutes. Sprinkle with the cheese and place under the broiler for 1 or 2 minutes, until the cheese is melted. Makes 4 servings.

HAM-FILLED CRÊPE TORTE

1 cup cold milk
1 cup cold water
4 eggs
1 teaspoon salt
2 cups sifted flour
6 tablespoons melted butter

▶ 4 cups minced cooked ham
4 eggs, separated
1 cup sour cream
Salt
¼ cup bread crumbs

1. Beat together the milk, water, eggs, and salt in a large bowl. Add the flour gradually, beating constantly until smooth. Add 4 tablespoons of the melted butter. Refrigerate the batter for at least 1 hour.

2. Lightly grease a 7-inch crêpe pan or skillet ,heat until it is almost smoking, and pour in just enough of the batter to coat the bottom lightly. Tilt the pan to be sure that the batter covers the bottom of the pan. Brown the crêpe lightly on one side. Turn and brown the other side. Continue making crêpes until batter is used. The crêpes may be made ahead of time, wrapped, and refrigerated.

3. Mix the ham, egg yolks, and sour cream. Whip the egg whites until stiff and fold into the ham mixture. Season with salt.

4. Preheat the oven to 350°. Place one crêpe in a shallow baking dish and spread with a little of the ham mixture. Continue layering crêpes and filling until all the crêpes are used. Mix the remaining 2 tablespoons of butter with the crumbs and sprinkle on top. Bake until hot and browned, about 30 to 40 minutes. Makes 8 servings.

CORN AND HAM PATTIES

2 cups flour
2 teaspoons baking powder
1 teaspoon salt
   Dash pepper
2 eggs

1¼ cups milk
1 cup whole kernel corn
   (drained, if from a can)
▶ 1 cup minced cooked ham
   Vegetable oil for frying

1. Sift together flour with baking powder, salt, and pepper. In a mixing bowl, beat eggs with milk; add dry ingredients and stir just until smooth. Fold in corn and ham.

2. Pour oil to a depth of ¼ inch into a medium-size frying pan, and heat. Spoon ¼ cupfuls of batter into the oil. Cook until patties are golden brown on one side (about 5 minutes); turn and brown the other side. Makes 6 servings.

CORN CAKES WITH HAM

2 cups cream-style canned corn
▶ ½ cup minced cooked ham
2 tablespoons flour
1 teaspoon baking powder
1 teaspoon sugar

¾ teaspoon salt
   Dash of pepper
1 tablespoon melted butter
1 tablespoon cream
2 eggs, separated

1. In a large bowl, mix together all ingredients except the eggs. In a small bowl, beat the egg yolks until thick and lemon-colored. Stir the yolks into the corn/ham mixture.

2. Whip the egg whites with an electric mixer or a wire whisk until they are stiff. Fold the whites into the corn/ham mixture.

3. For each cake, drop 2 tablespoons of the batter onto a hot, lightly greased griddle, and brown on both sides. Makes 4 to 6 servings.

SPICED HAM FRITTERS

1 cup water
1 cup flour
2 eggs
1 teaspoon curry powder (more taste)
⅛ teaspoon ground coriander
▶ ¾ cup finely ground cooked ham

3 to 4 cups vegetable oil
   (approximately)
2 to 3 cups applesauce
   (combined if desired, with
   ground cinnamon, allspice,
   ginger, and coriander to taste)

1. Bring water to a rapid boil in a saucepan. Stir in the flour and continue to stir vigorously until mixture leaves sides of pan; decrease heat. Beat in the eggs, one at a time, beating vigorously after each addition. Remove from heat. Stir in curry powder, coriander, and ham.

2. Heat 2 inches of vegetable oil in a deep skillet to 375°; drop the ham batter into hot oil by tablespoonfuls. Cook until golden on both sides. Drain on absorbent paper and keep warm in a 250° oven until all the batter is used. Serve with the applesauce. Makes 4 servings.

HAM AND CHEESE FRITTERS

▶ 1 cup chopped cooked ham
¾ cup grated Cheddar cheese
2 tablespoons grated onion
1 egg

¼ cup dry cracker crumbs or
   bread crumbs
½ cup milk
1 cup crushed cornflakes
Oil for deep frying

1. Combine the ham, cheese, onion, egg, and crumbs in a bowl; mix well. Shape the mixture into 1½-inch balls. Dip the balls into milk; then coat with cornflakes.

2. Pour about 3 inches of oil into a heavy saucepan or deep fryer and heat it until very hot but not smoking, or until a frying thermometer reads 365°. Fry the balls for about 4 minutes or until golden brown. Drain on paper towels. Serve at once. Makes 16 balls.

APPLESAUCE AND HAM PANCAKES

1 cup packaged pancake mix
½ cup milk
1 egg, lightly beaten
1 tablespoon melted butter or
   margarine
½ cup applesauce

⅛ teaspoon cinnamon
▶ ½ cup finely chopped cooked
   ham
Maple syrup
⅓ cup raisins (optional)

1. Place the pancake mix in a mixing bowl; add the milk, egg, melted butter, applesauce, and cinammon. Stir gently until just mixed. Stir in the ham.

2. For each pancake, drop 2 tablespoonfuls of the batter onto a hot, lightly greased skillet. Brown on both sides. Serve with maple syrup and garnish with raisins, if desired. Makes 4 servings, 3 pancakes per serving.

EGGS FOO YUNG

1 tablespoon sherry or water
2 teaspoons cornstarch
3 teaspoons soy sauce
   (approximately)
▶ 1 cup chicken broth
½ teaspoon sugar
3 teaspoons ketchup
2 to 3 tablespoons peanut or
   vegetable oil

½ cup chopped water chestnuts
¼ cup chopped scallions
¼ cup chopped bamboo shoots
½ cup bean sprouts
▶ ½ cup slivered cooked ham
6 eggs, lightly beaten

1. Combine sherry and cornstarch in small saucepan. Add 2 teaspoons soy sauce (or more to taste), chicken broth, sugar and ketchup. Cook over medium heat until sauce is clear and thick. Set aside and keep warm.

2. Heat 2 tablespoons oil in a large skillet. Combine water chestnuts, scallions, bamboo shoots, bean sprouts, ham, and 1 teaspoon soy

(*continued*)

sauce; and stir fry for 2 minutes. Remove from pan; stir eggs into vegetables. Pour egg/vegetable mixture by ⅓ cup measure into skillet and cook, pancake style, until one side is set, then turn and cook the other side. Keep "pancakes" warm as they are done. Repeat until all the egg mixture is used.

3. Serve with warm sauce spooned over pancakes. Makes 4 to 6 servings.

HAM MOUSSE

1 envelope unflavored gelatin
¼ cup cold water
¾ cup milk
2 egg yolks
¾ teaspoon salt
1 teaspoon dry mustard

▶ 2 cups ground or finely chopped cooked ham
½ teaspoon minced onion
¼ cup mayonnaise
½ cup heavy cream, whipped
Watercress

1. Stir the gelatin into the cold water and let soften. Heat the milk to lukewarm. Beat in the egg yolks, salt, and mustard. Cook in top of a double boiler, over simmering water, stirring constantly, until mixture thickens slightly and coats a metal spoon. Remove from heat.

2. Add the gelatin and stir until dissolved. Cool until almost set. Stir in the ham, onion, and mayonnaise; fold in the whipped cream. Pour mixture into a lightly oiled 1-quart mold. Chill until firm; unmold on a platter, and garnish with watercress. Makes 4 to 6 servings.

BROCCOLI AND HAM PUFF

2 tablespoons chopped onion
3 tablespoons butter or margarine
3 tablespoons flour
½ teaspoon salt
Dash pepper
1 cup milk

4 eggs, separated, plus 1 extra egg white
1 teaspoon prepared mustard
▶ 1 cup chopped cooked broccoli
▶ 1 cup minced cooked ham
¼ cup grated Parmesan cheese

1. In a medium-size saucepan, sauté onion in the butter, stirring occasionally, until translucent. Stir in flour, salt, and pepper; cook 1 minute. Stir in milk until mixture is smooth. Cook, stirring constantly, about 5 minutes.

2. Beat egg yolks in a small bowl; stir in a little of the hot mixture; return blended mixture to saucepan. Cook over low heat, stirring constantly, 2 minutes.

3. Off the heat, stir the mustard, broccoli, ham, and cheese into the hot mixture.

4. Beat egg whites in a large bowl until soft peaks form. Gently fold broccoli mixture into whites until no streaks of white remain. Spoon into a lightly greased 1½-quart soufflé or other straight-sided dish.

5. Bake in preheated 350° oven for 35 minutes or until browned and puffed and a knife inserted 1 inch from edge comes out clean. Serve at once. Makes 4 servings.

HAM FRITTATA ITALIENNE

5 tablespoons olive oil
2 large Bermuda onions, thinly
   sliced
1 jar (4 oz.) roasted peppers
► ½ cup cubed baked ham
7 eggs
¾ teaspoon salt
⅛ teaspoon freshly ground black
   pepper
   Dash of Tabasco sauce or to
   taste

⅓ cup fresh bread crumbs
2 tablespoons minced fresh
   parsley
2 tablespoons freshly grated
   Parmesan cheese
1 medium garlic clove, minced
3 large ripe tomatoes (about 1
   pound) cut into ¼-inch slices

1. In a heavy 10-inch skillet with an ovenproof handle, heat 2 table-spoons of the oil. Add the onions and sauté over high heat until lightly browned. Reduce the heat, cover the skillet and cook until soft and golden brown, stirring frequently, about 15 minutes. Add the roasted peppers and the ham to the skillet with the onions and cook for 2 minutes.

2. In a large bowl, beat the eggs with the salt, pepper and Tabasco sauce until well blended. Scrape the vegetables and ham into the bowl with the eggs; fold gently to mix. Add 2 more tablespoons of oil to the skillet and place over moderate heat. Pour in the egg mixture and cook for 2 minutes, or until the eggs are lightly set on the bottom. Bake in a preheated 350° oven, uncovered, for 15 to 20 minutes, or until eggs are set.

3. While the frittata is baking, prepare the topping. In a small bowl, toss the bread crumbs, parsley, Parmesan, garlic and remaining oil until well blended. When the frittata is done, remove the skillet from the oven and increase the temperature to broil. Cover the frittata with overlapping slices of tomato and sprinkle the bread-crumb topping evenly over the tomatoes. Broil about 4 inches from the heat until tomatoes are heated through and the bread crumbs are golden brown, 3 to 5 minutes. Cut the frittata into wedges and serve directly from the skillet. Makes 4 servings.

BAKED HAM AND EGGS

1 small onion, chopped
1 small green pepper, chopped
4 to 5 tablespoons butter
►3½ to 4 cups minced baked ham

8 eggs
4 teaspoons cream
Salt and pepper to taste

1. In a saucepan, sauté the onion and green pepper in 2 tablespoons of the butter until soft but not browned. Add ham and blend well.

2. Thoroughly butter 4 ramekins or individual soufflé dishes. Spoon the ham mixture into the ramekins. Break 2 eggs into each and spoon 1 tea-spoon of the cream over the surface. Dot with slivers of the remaining butter, and sprinkle with salt and pepper. Bake in a preheated 350° oven until eggs have set (about 12 minutes). Makes 4 servings.

HAM AND ONION FRITTATA

4 eggs, lightly beaten
¼ cup milk
▶ 1 cup chopped cooked ham
▶ 1 cup chopped cooked
   potatoes
  1 cup shredded Cheddar
  cheese

2 tablespoons chopped green
  pepper
1 can (2.8 oz.) French-fried
  onions
2 tablespoons butter or
  margarine

1. In a large bowl, combine the eggs and milk and mix well. Stir in the ham, potatoes, cheese, green pepper, and half the onions.

2. Preheat the oven to 350°. Melt the butter in a 10-inch ovenproof skillet or omelet pan over low heat. Pour the egg mixture into the skillet. Place in the oven and bake 20 minutes. Top with remaining onions; continue baking 5 minutes or until the onions are lightly browned. Makes 4 to 6 servings.

HAM AND EGGS MADEIRA

3 tablespoons butter
1 tablespoon minced scallions or
  shallots
3 tablespoons flour
1 cup canned condensed
  consommé
½ cup dry Madeira wine

Salt
Pepper
1 tablespoon butter, oil, or ham
  fat
▶ 4 slices cooked ham
4 eggs

1. Melt the butter in a small saucepan. Add the scallions and sauté lightly for one minute. Stir in the flour. Gradually add the consommé, stirring constantly. Bring to a boil and cook until thickened. Add the Madeira, simmer 5 minutes, and season with salt and pepper.

2. Heat the butter, oil, or fat in a frying pan. Fry the ham slices just until hot, and put them on 4 plates.

3. Fry the eggs in the same pan. Place the eggs on the ham slices and spoon the hot sauce over the top. Makes 4 servings.

EGGS BENEDICT

2 egg yolks, beaten until lemony
3 tablespoons lemon juice
¼ teaspoon salt
⅔ cup butter, cut into thick slices
  Pinch white pepper

8 poached eggs
▶ 8 thin slices cooked ham
4 English muffins
1 tablespoon chopped parsley
  (optional)

1. Place egg yolks, lemon juice, and salt in a small saucepan; blend together using a wooden spoon. Add half the butter slices to the pan.

2. Place saucepan over low heat and stir quickly until butter is melted and sauce is thickened. Add the remaining slices of butter; cook, stirring constantly, until butter is melted. Season with white pepper to taste. If sauce is not used immediately, reheat *gently* over warm water.

3. Prepare the poached eggs, while the ham slices sauté in the remaining butter. Split the muffins and toast.

4. Place 1 ham slice on each muffin half. Top with 1 poached egg. Spoon the sauce over all. Sprinkle with parsley if desired. Serve immediately. Makes 4 to 8 servings.

HAM RING WITH SHERRY

2 eggs, separated
▶ 2 cups finely ground, cooked ham
1 tablespoon finely chopped onion
⅛ teaspoon nutmeg
Dash cayenne

½ teaspoon minced parsley
1 tablespoon minced pimiento
1 cup heavy cream
2 tablespoons dry sherry or Madeira
▶1½ cups cooked green peas, well buttered

1. In a bowl, combine well-beaten egg yolks with ham, onion, nutmeg, cayenne, parsley, pimiento, cream, and sherry. Beat egg whites until stiff but not dry. Gently fold into ham mixture. Turn into a well-greased 1½-quart ring mold.

2. Set mold in a pan of hot water. Bake in a 300° oven for 35 minutes or until top is firm to the touch. Remove from oven; let stand 3 to 4 minutes. Unmold on heated serving platter. Fill center with green peas. Serve at once. Makes 6 servings.

CAJUN HAM GUMBO

4 bacon strips
½ cup chopped scallions
1 clove garlic, minced
5 tablespoons flour
3 cups water
▶ ½ cup chicken stock
1 cup dry white wine
½ teaspoon thyme
2 tablespoons parsley
⅛ teaspoon cayenne
2 cans (16 oz. each) whole tomatoes, undrained, coarsely chopped

1 bay leaf
1 package (10 oz.) frozen okra
▶ 2 cups cubed cooked ham
1 pound uncooked medium shrimp, peeled, deveined, split lengthwise
1 package (6 oz.) frozen Alaska king crab meat (optional)
▶1¼ cups hot cooked rice
Salt and pepper to taste

1. In a large, heavy skillet sauté bacon until crisp. Remove, chop coarsely, and set aside. In bacon drippings, sauté scallions and garlic until golden. Sprinkle in the flour and stir until blended. Gradually add water, chicken stock, and wine, stirring until smooth. Add thyme, parsley, cayenne, tomatoes, bay leaf, okra, and ham. Cover and simmer 30 minutes over very low heat, stirring occasionally.

2. Add shrimp and crab meat and simmer, uncovered, 10 minutes or until shrimp is tender. Remove bay leaf. Serve in soup bowls, first spooning rice into each. Sprinkle each with bacon bits. Makes 6 servings.

HAM AND GARBANZO SOUP

3 tablespoons butter
½ cup finely chopped onions
½ cup finely chopped carrots
¼ cup finely chopped celery
► 6 cups chicken stock
► Ham bone (optional)
6 sprigs parsley and 1 small bay leaf, tied together with string
1 can (20 oz.) garbanzos (chick-peas), drained and rinsed in cold water

►1½ cups cooked ham, cut into small cubes
1 package (10 oz.) frozen lima beans, defrosted
2 medium potatoes, peeled and cut into 1-inch cubes
Salt
Black pepper
1 tablespoon finely chopped parsley

1. Melt the butter in a heavy 3- or 4-quart soup pot over moderate heat. Add the chopped onions, carrots, and celery and cook, stirring almost constantly, until the vegetables are wilted but not brown. Pour in the chicken stock; add the ham bone and the parsley sprigs and bay leaf. Bring to a boil; then lower the heat and, with the pot half covered, simmer slowly for about ½ hour.

2. Add the garbanzos, the ham, the lima beans, and the cubed potatoes and continue to simmer until the potatoes are tender. Remove the ham bone and the bundle of parsley sprigs and bay leaf. Season the soup with salt and pepper to taste. Serve sprinkled with chopped parsley. Makes 4 to 6 servings.

ROBUST HAM AND CABBAGE SOUP

2 tablespoons vegetable oil
►1½ cups cubed cooked ham
1 cup diced onion
½ small head cabbage, coarsely shredded
1 large carrot, coarsely shredded
► 4 cups turkey or chicken broth homemade or canned

1½ cups tomato juice
½ teaspoon sugar
½ teaspoon lemon juice
Salt and pepper to taste
½ teaspoon dried summer savory,
2 whole cloves
2 tablespoons minced fresh parsley

1. Heat vegetable oil in large heavy kettle or skillet; sauté ham over medium high heat for 5 minutes, stirring constantly, until lightly browned. Remove with a slotted spoon and set aside.

2. Reduce heat to medium; add onion to oil and sauté for 5 minutes, stirring. Add cabbage and carrot; sauté for 5 minutes, stirring.

3. Pour in broth, tomato juice, sugar, lemon juice, pepper, salt, savory, and cloves. Bring to a boil. Cover and simmer for 30 minutes until vegetables are tender, stirring occasionally. Add ham and simmer another 15 minutes. Serve with a sprinkling of parsley. Makes 4 to 6 servings.

HAM AND BEAN SOUP

1 pound dried kidney beans	1 teaspoon minced parsley
3 quarts water	4 whole cloves
► 1 meaty ham bone, cracked	1 bay leaf
½ cup chopped onion	1 garlic clove, pressed
½ cup chopped celery	1 teaspoon salt
½ cup chopped carrot	¼ teaspoon pepper
¼ teaspoon dry mustard	Pinch of dried thyme
Dash of Worcestershire sauce	

1. In a large pot, place the beans and water; bring to a hard boil over moderate heat. Remove from heat; cover and let stand 1 hour. Add the ham bone, onion, celery, carrot, mustard, Worcestershire sauce, parsley, cloves, bay leaf, garlic, salt, pepper, and thyme. Simmer 2 hours or until beans are very tender.

2. Remove the ham bone from the soup; cut off any meat remaining on the bone, cube and set aside. Remove the bay leaf. Purée the mixture through a food mill or in a blender. Return the soup to the pot; add the cubed ham and reheat. Makes 8 to 10 servings.

MINNESOTA PEA SOUP

1 package (1 lb.) split green peas	1 large clove garlic, pressed
► Leftover ham bones	1 bay leaf
½ cup diced celery	1 tablespoon salt
¼ cup diced onion	¼ teaspoon pepper
½ cup diced carrots	5 cups water
¼ cup chopped leeks	4 cups canned mixed vegetable juice

1. In a large heavy kettle, combine together the peas, ham bones, celery, onion, carrots, leeks, garlic, bay leaf, salt, pepper, water, and 2 cups of the vegetable juice; bring to a boil. Reduce heat and simmer, stirring occasionally, for 2 hours or until peas are mushy.

2. Remove the bones and bay leaf. Cut off any lean meat from bones and return it to soup. Stir in remaining 2 cups vegetable juice and heat just to boiling. Makes 6 to 8 servings.

HAM HASH

► 4 medium potatoes, peeled and cooked	►1½ cups diced cooked ham
1 small onion	¼ teaspoon salt
½ green pepper	⅛ teaspoon pepper
► ½ cup cooked carrots	Dash of dried thyme
	3 tablespoons butter

1. Put through a food chopper using the coarse blade, or chop very fine and mix well the potatoes, onion, green pepper, carrots, ham, and seasonings.

2. Melt the butter in a skillet and add the hash. Cook until well browned, stirring frequently. Makes 4 servings.

BAKED HAM BALLS

▶ 1 pound ground cooked ham
½ cup minced onion
½ teaspoon pepper
2 eggs, lightly beaten
⅓ cup butter
⅓ cup all-purpose flour
▶1⅓ cups chicken stock
2⅔ cups sour cream

¾ teaspoon each: dried
marjoram and dillweed
Salt to taste
2 tablespoons fresh minced
parsley
Hot cooked saffron-flavored or
plain buttered rice
Watercress sprigs (optional)

1. Combine the ham, onions, pepper and eggs and shape into balls, allowing about ¼ cup of mixture for each ball. Arrange ham balls in a lightly greased baking pan. Bake in a preheated 400 degree oven for 35 minutes.

2. Meanwhile, prepare sauce in a medium saucepan. Melt ⅓ cup butter; blend in flour. Beat in chicken stock and stir until mixture is smooth. Add sour cream, marjoram, dillweed and salt; cook, stirring constantly, until sauce is thickened. Gently simmer sauce another 10 minutes.

3. Serve the ham balls with the sour cream sauce, over rice. Sprinkle with minced parsley. Makes 4 to 6 servings.

GLAZED HAM LOAF

2 tablespoons butter
1 small onion, chopped
1 tablespoon chopped celery
1 medium carrot, grated
▶ 3 cups ground cooked ham
½ cup soft bread crumbs
▶ ½ cup mashed potatoes,
homemade or instant,
reconstituted
1 egg, lightly beaten

1 tablespoon chopped parsley
1 teaspoon prepared mustard
¼ teaspoon salt
⅛ teaspoon paprika
8 whole cloves
2 tablespoons frozen
concentrated orange juice
2 tablespoons honey
1 can (8½ oz.) pineapple slices

1. Melt 1 tablespoon of the butter in a skillet. Sauté onion, celery, and carrot for 5 minutes; let cool. Combine onion mixture with ham, bread crumbs, potatoes, egg and parsley in a large bowl. Toss lightly to mix; stir in mustard, salt and paprika. Mound ham mixture into a loaf shape in a greased shallow baking pan; stud top with cloves.

2. Mix orange juice and honey together. Brush about one third of this mixture over ham loaf. Bake loaf in a preheated 400 degree oven for 20 minutes. Brush some of the remaining orange-honey mixture on loaf; bake 20 minutes longer or until loaf is richly glazed. Carefully transfer loaf onto a heated platter; keep warm.

3. Lightly grease a cookie sheet. Place pineapple slices on cookie sheet, brush with remaining orange-honey glaze and broil just until the edges of the pineapple begin to color. Garnish ham loaf and platter with pineapple slices. Makes 6 servings.

HAM LOAF DIJON

1 slightly beaten egg
1 cup soft bread crumbs
1 can (8½ oz.) applesauce
2½ tablespoons chopped onion
2 teaspoons Dijon-style mustard
2 teaspoons parsley

¼ teaspoon salt
Dash pepper
8 ounces bulk pork sausage
▶ 8 ounces ground cooked ham
1 tablespoon brown sugar
1 tablespoon vinegar

1. In a bowl, combine the egg, crumbs, ½ cup applesauce, onion, 1 teaspoon mustard, the parsley, salt, and pepper. Add the sausage and ham and mix.

2. Shape into a round loaf in a baking pan. With a spoon, make a depression in top of loaf. Combine the remaining applesauce and mustard in a bowl with the brown sugar and vinegar; pour into the depression. Bake in 350° oven for 1 hour. Makes 4 servings.

HAM POTATO PATTIES

▶ 2 cups ground or finely chopped
  cooked ham
▶ 1 cup mashed potatoes
2 tablespoons finely chopped
  onion
2 tablespoons chopped parsley

⅛ teaspoon cayenne
1 tablespoon milk
1 egg
½ cup fine dry bread crumbs
3 tablespoons vegetable oil

1. In a medium bowl, combine the ground ham, mashed potatoes, onion, parsley and cayenne. Chill about 1 hour. Shape into 12 patties.

2. Beat the milk and the egg together in a pie plate. Dip the patties in the egg mixture and then in the crumbs. Heat the oil in a skillet and fry the patties until golden. Drain on absorbent paper and serve hot. Makes 4 servings.

DUTCH HAM LOAF

▶ 3 cups ground cooked ham
2 tablespoons finely chopped
  onion
½ cup cracker crumbs
½ cup milk
¼ cup cream
1 teaspoon prepared mustard
1 egg
▶1½ cups cooked rice

4 tablespoons minced parsley
1½ tablespoons minced celery
  leaves
1 tablespoon butter, melted
Dash pepper
¾ cup sour cream
1 tablespoon drained prepared
  horseradish

1. In a medium bowl, mix together the ham, onion, cracker crumbs, milk, cream, mustard, and egg and blend thoroughly. In a separate bowl, mix the rice with the parsley, celery leaves, butter, and pepper. Spread half the ham mixture in a 9 × 5 × 2¾-inch loaf pan. Spread rice over ham, and top with remaining ham mixture.

2. In a 350° oven, bake 35 to 40 minutes. Combine the sour cream with horseradish; serve with ham loaf. Makes 6 servings.

HAM-CORNBREAD RING

1 cup sifted all-purpose flour
¼ cup sugar
2 teaspoons baking powder
½ teaspoon baking soda
¼ teaspoon salt
¾ cup cornmeal
1 egg
1 cup sour cream
¼ cup milk

2 tablespoons butter or
  margarine, melted
► 1 cup ground cooked ham
2½ cups hot Cream Sauce (see
  Basics)
¼ cup chopped pimiento,
  drained
2 packages (10 oz. each) frozen
  green peas, cooked and
  drained

1. Preheat the oven to 425°. Grease a 6-cup ring mold. Sift the flour, sugar, baking powder, baking soda, and salt into a large bowl; stir in the cornmeal.

2. Beat the egg slightly in a medium-size bowl. Stir in the sour cream, milk, butter, and ham. Pour this mixture into the flour mixture, stirring just until combined. Pour the batter into the greased ring mold.

3. Bake in the preheated oven for 20 minutes or until the top springs back when lightly pressed with your fingertip.

4. While cornbread bakes, prepare or reheat the Cream Sauce. Stir in the chopped pimiento and the cooked peas.

5. When the cornbread is done, let it cool about 5 minutes. Cut around the edges of the mold with a thin knife to loosen the bread; then unmold it onto a heated platter. Spoon the creamed peas into the center. Makes 6 to 8 servings.

CHEF'S SALAD

1 cup olive oil
¼ cup wine vinegar
¼ cup lemon juice
1 tablespoon anchovy paste
½ teaspoon salt
½ teaspoon coarsely ground
  pepper
½ teaspoon dried thyme
1 clove garlic, pressed
2 heads Belgian endive
1 bunch romaine lettuce
1 small head iceberg lettuce,
  broken up

2 tablespoons snipped parsley
½ teaspoon dried basil
¼ teaspoon dried oregano
► ½ cup cooked ham, cut in
  julienne strips
► ½ cup cooked tongue, cut in
  julienne strips
► ½ cup cooked white chicken
  meat, cut in julienne strips
¼ pound Swiss cheese, cut in
  julienne strips

1. In a jar, put the olive oil, vinegar, lemon juice, anchovy paste, salt, pepper, thyme, and garlic. Cover tightly and shake until mixed. Chill.

2. Tear endive, romaine, and lettuce into bite-size pieces into a salad bowl. Season with parsley, basil, and oregano; toss with dressing until well coated. Arrange the meats and cheese on top. Serve at once. Makes 6 servings.

WILTED LETTUCE SALAD WITH HAM AND EGG

1 small head romaine lettuce
▶ 3 hard-cooked eggs, chopped
3 scallions, chopped
6 tablespoons bacon fat, or ham fat

▶ ½ cup diced baked ham
2 tablespoons wine vinegar
Black pepper

1. Wash and dry the lettuce and break it into bite-size pieces. Place the lettuce, eggs, and scallions in a large bowl.

2. Heat the bacon fat or ham fat in a skillet. Add the ham and stir over low heat until heated through.

3. Add the vinegar and pepper to taste. Stir once or twice and pour the ham mixture over the lettuce. Toss the salad to mix the ingredients and serve at once. Makes 4 to 6 servings.

HAM SALAD MOLD

2 envelopes unflavored gelatin
¾ cup water
1 cup pineapple juice, canned
1 tablespoon fresh lemon juice
½ teaspoon salt
1 tablespoon prepared mustard
1 teaspoon sugar

1 teaspoon paprika
1½ cups mayonnaise
1 cup finely diced celery
3 tablespoons chopped scallions
¼ cup chopped green pepper
▶ 1 cup finely diced cooked ham
Lettuce leaves

1. Soften gelatin in ¼ cup water. In a saucepan, bring the remaining ½ cup of water to a boil and dissolve the gelatin completely. Add the pineapple and lemon juices, salt, mustard, sugar, and paprika. Beat in the mayonnaise and chill until thickened.

2. Fold celery, scallions, green peppers and ham into the mayonnaise. Pour into a 6-cup mold and chill until firm. Line a serving plate with lettuce leaves and unmold the salad. Makes 6 servings.

GARDEN HAM SALAD

½ cup lemon-flavored yogurt
½ cup sour cream
2 tablespoons tarragon vinegar
2 tablespoons milk
1 tablespoon snipped parsley
1 tablespoon Dijon-style mustard
1 teaspoon celery seed
Salt
Dash pepper

2 cups torn romaine lettuce
2 cups torn bibb lettuce
½ head cauliflower, broken into flowerets
▶ 2 cups diced cooked ham
1 cup alfalfa sprouts or bean sprouts
½ small red onion, sliced and separated into rings

1. In a small bowl combine the yogurt, sour cream, vinegar, milk, parsley, mustard, celery seed, salt, and pepper till well blended. Cover and chill.

2. In a large salad bowl toss together the romaine, bibb lettuce, cauliflower, ham, sprouts, and onion slices. Serve with dressing. Makes 4 servings.

HAM FRUIT SALAD

2 teaspoons grated orange rind
1 teaspoon grated lemon rind
½ cup orange and lemon juice,
   mixed
1 egg, beaten
   Dash of salt
½ cup sugar
▶ 1 cup diced cooked ham

½ cup diced peeled orange
½ cup diced unpeeled apple
¾ cup diced pineapple tidbits
½ cup diced banana
½ cup walnuts
   Lettuce leaves
¼ cup sour cream

1. In a heavy saucepan, mix the orange and lemon rinds with the juice, egg, salt, and sugar. Bring to a boil, stirring. Cool; then chill.

2. Mix the ham with the orange, apple, pineapple, banana, and walnuts. Line a serving plate with lettuce leaves and spoon the ham mixture on top.

3. Fold the sour cream into the dressing and pour over the salad. Serve the remaining dressing on the side. Makes 4 to 6 servings.

HOLIDAY HAM MOLD

1 cup seedless raisins
1 quart sweet cider
4 whole cloves
¼ cup brown sugar, firmly
   packed
2 envelopes unflavored gelatin
3 tablespoons water
1 tablespoon lemon juice
½ teaspoon salt
   Dash cayenne

   Pinch nutmeg
▶2¼ cups minced cooked ham
½ cup finely chopped walnuts
   Lettuce leaves
▶ 1 cup cooked peas
▶ 1 cup cooked carrots
¼ cup mayonnaise
1 teaspoon prepared
   horseradish
2 tablespoons chopped parsley

1. In a saucepan, soak raisins in cider for 30 minutes. Add cloves and brown sugar; heat mixture slowly to boiling. Remove from heat and remove cloves. In a large bowl, soak the gelatin in combined water and lemon juice for 3 minutes. Add the cider mixture and stir until gelatin is dissolved. Add salt, cayenne, and nutmeg. Chill until mixture begins to thicken, then stir in ham and walnuts. Pour mixture into an 8-cup ring mold and chill until firm.

2. Unmold on a chilled platter lined with lettuce leaves. Mix the cooked vegetables with mayonnaise and horseradish and spoon into center of mold. Garnish with parsley. Makes 6 servings.

CHILLED HAM MOLD

1 package (3 oz.) lemon-
　flavored gelatin
1 cup boiling water
½ cup dry white wine
4 tablespoons lemon juice
½ cup mayonnaise
¼ teaspoon salt

⅛ teaspoon pepper
½ teaspoon dry mustard
► 1 cup ground cooked ham
2 tablespoons vegetable oil
　Mixed greens
　Thin rounds of French bread,
　toasted and lightly buttered

1. Dissolve the gelatin in boiling water in medium-size mixing bowl. Add wine, lemon juice, mayonnaise, salt, pepper, and mustard. Beat mixture with a rotary beater until well blended. Pour into a small pan and refrigerate until mixture is firm around edges and soft in the middle (about 20 to 25 minutes).

2. Turn the mixture into a bowl and whip until fluffy; fold in ham and pour into a very lightly oiled decorative mold. Chill until firm, about 30 minutes to an hour; unmold. Garnish with mixed greens and serve with French bread rounds. Makes 4 servings.

CAULIFLOWER SALAD WITH HAM AND AVOCADO

1 small head of cauliflower
3 tablespoons olive oil
1 tablespoon wine vinegar
1 teaspoon salt
　Pepper
½ cup mayonnaise
2 tablespoons light cream

1 teaspoon lemon juice
► 1 cup chopped cooked ham
¼ cup minced parsley
　Lettuce leaves
1 avocado, sliced and dipped
　in lemon juice

1. Break the cauliflower into flowerets. Simmer in a saucepan in salted water until just tender. Drain well. Place the cauliflower in a bowl and while it is still hot, pour over it a mixture of the oil, vinegar, salt and pepper. Chill for several hours.

2. In another bowl, mix together the mayonnaise, cream and lemon juice until well blended. Add the ham and parsley and combine thoroughly. On a serving platter or bowl, arrange a layer of lettuce leaves. Place the ham mixture in the center. Drain the cauliflower and arrange in clusters around ham mixture, garnishing with the avocado slices. Makes 6 servings.

RUSSIAN SALAD

¾ cup olive oil
¼ cup wine vinegar
1 clove garlic
¼ teaspoon dried thyme
¾ teaspoon salt
¼ teaspoon pepper
7 cups crisp shredded cabbage
►1½ cups drained, cooked string beans

5 cups sliced cucumber
►1½ cups drained, cooked or canned peas
►1½ cups sliced cooked potatoes
►1½ cups drained, cooked or canned sliced beets
► 1 cup julienne strips cooked ham
1 cup sour cream

1. In blender, combine olive oil, vinegar, garlic, thyme, salt, and pepper; blend 10 seconds.

2. In a large bowl, mix the vegetables and the ham; chill thoroughly. Pour the dressing over the salad and marinate 1 hour.

3. Before serving, add the sour cream; toss. Season to taste. Makes 8 to 10 servings.

PIPERADE BASQUE

5 tablespoons olive oil
½ cup finely chopped onion
½ teaspoon finely chopped garlic
2 small peppers (preferably 1 green and 1 red), seeded and cut into 1" × 1½" strips
1 pound ripe tomatoes, peeled, cubed, and drained
1 tablespoon minced fresh basil or 1 teaspoon dried basil
⅛ teaspoon Tabasco, or ⅛ teaspoon cayenne (or to taste)

1 tablespoon butter
► 1 cup cooked ham, cut into julienne strips
5 eggs
½ teaspoon salt
⅛ teaspoon freshly ground black pepper
1 tablespoon finely chopped parsley
1 tablespoon fresh snipped chives

1. Prepare the sauce: heat 4 tablespoons olive oil in a heavy 8-inch frying pan. Add the onion, garlic, and peppers, and cook over moderate heat, stirring frequently, until the onions are soft but not brown. The peppers will still be a bit crisp. Add the tomatoes, basil, and Tabasco to the pan; raise the heat and cook the sauce, stirring constantly until all the moisture from the tomatoes has evaporated from the pan. Be careful that the vegetables don't burn. Remove pan from heat, cover tightly and keep warm.

2. Heat the remaining olive oil and the butter in a heavy frying pan, and sauté the ham strips until they are heated through. Remove the ham with a slotted spoon, set aside, and keep warm.

3. Allow the fat in the frying pan to cool to lukewarm. Lightly beat the eggs with salt and pepper and pour into skillet. Over low heat, stir the eggs until they begin to form soft, creamy curds. Remove from the heat when they are just beginning to set, and gently spread over the vegetables. Let some of the colorful vegetables show through. Scatter the ham over the top of the piperade, sprinkle with the parsley and chives and serve at once. Makes 4 servings.

JAMBON PERSILLÉ

▶ 3 cups chicken broth,
   homemade or canned
   1 cup dry white wine
   1 small onion, diced
   1 teaspoon dried tarragon
   4 sprigs parsley
   2 celery tops with leaves
   1 small bay leaf
   10 whole black peppercorns

▶ 3 cups cooked ham, cut into
   2-inch chunks
   1 envelope unflavored gelatin
   ¼ cup cold water
   2 teaspoons wine vinegar
   Salt
   6 tablespoons finely chopped
   parsley
   Sauce Moutarde (see below)

1. Combine the broth, wine, onion, tarragon, parsley sprigs, celery tops, bay leaf, peppercorns, and ham in an enamel or stainless-steel saucepan. Bring to a boil, then lower the heat and simmer slowly, with the pan half covered, for 20 to 30 minutes, or until the ham is quite soft but not falling apart. Remove the ham with a slotted spoon and put into a 1-quart mold or bowl. Press the ham firmly into the mold with the back of a large spoon and set aside to cool.

2. Strain the cooking liquid through a fine sieve into a 2- or 3-quart deep saucepan, and discard the onion, herbs, and peppercorns. Bring the liquid to a boil and cook rapidly, uncovered, until it has cooked down to 2½ cups. Add the gelatin to ¼ cup of cold water and let it soften for 5 minutes. Add it to the reduced stock and stir until it dissolves. Add the vinegar and salt to taste.

3. When the liquid is cool but not set, pour 1 cup of it over the ham in the mold; shake the mold gently so the aspic seeps through and permeates the ham. Chill thoroughly. Chill the remaining liquid in the refrigerator until it becomes syrupy but not set. (If it sets, melt again, then recool it). Stir the chopped parsley into the gelatin mixture and pour it into the mold. Refrigerate until set. Unmold onto a platter and serve with Sauce Moutarde. This is perfect for a buffet or special summer picnic. Makes 6 servings.

Sauce Moutarde

Mix ½ cup Dijon mustard with ½ cup very finely chopped sweet and sour mixed gherkins.

COLD ROAST FRESH HAM WITH HONEYDEW MELON

▶ 4 to 8 thin slices cold roast ham
   or pork
   Salt
   12 black olives
   Lemon or lime quarters

8 ½-inch thick slices of chilled
ripe honeydew melon, with
rinds cut off
Freshly ground black pepper

Trim the slices of fresh ham or pork of all their fat and arrange them on a chilled platter. Sprinkle the meat lightly with salt. Arrange the olives and lemon or lime quarters around the outside of the platter.

Arrange the melon slices attractively over the meat and sprinkle with black pepper. Makes 4 servings.

HAM DUMPLINGS

▶ 1 cup ground lean cooked ham
¾ cup all-purpose flour
¼ teaspoon salt
1 teaspoon baking powder
⅓ cup milk

½ teaspoon dried thyme
½ teaspoon rubbed sage
⅛ teaspoon ground mace
▶ 2 quarts broth or stock

1. In a bowl, mix the ham with the flour, salt, baking powder, milk, and seasonings.

2. In a large saucepan, bring broth to a rapid boil. Drop the ham mixture by teaspoonfuls into the broth. Cover and simmer until dumplings are cooked, about 10 minutes. Makes 4 servings.

MONTE CRISTO SANDWICHES

2 eggs
2 tablespoons flour
½ cup milk
1 teaspoon salt
⅛ teaspoon pepper
⅛ teaspoon paprika
8 slices white bread, buttered

▶ 4 slices cooked ham
▶ 4 thin slices cooked chicken
4 slices Swiss cheese
⅓ cup butter
¼ cup sour cream
Brown sugar

1. In a blender or in a mixing bowl, combine the eggs, flour, milk, salt, pepper, and paprika and mix until smooth. Arrange on 4 slices of bread 1 slice each of ham, chicken, and cheese. Cover with the remaining bread slices.

2. Dip the sandwiches into the egg mixture, coating both sides well. Melt the butter in a large heavy skillet over moderate heat. Brown the sandwiches on both sides. Serve at once topped with sour cream and sprinkle with brown sugar. Makes 4 servings.

BAKED HAM AND EGG SANDWICHES

▶ 1 cup chopped cooked ham
½ cup diced Cheddar cheese
2 tablespoons chopped onions
▶ 2 hard-cooked eggs, chopped
2 tablespoons chopped green
olives

4 tablespoons mayonnaise
3 tablespoons chili sauce or
ketchup
8 sandwich buns, buttered

Preheat the oven to 400°. In a bowl, combine all ingredients except buns. Spread this mixture on the buns; wrap tightly in foil. Bake 15 to 18 minutes. Makes 8 servings.

WAFFLEWICHES

½ cup grated Swiss or Gruyère
  cheese
¼ cup mayonnaise
⅛ teaspoon pressed garlic
1½ tablespoons minced onion
▶ ½ cup chopped cooked ham

¼ teaspoon dried basil
  Pinch of salt
1½ cups packaged pancake or
  waffle mix, or 12 4½-inch
  prepared waffles

1. In a medium bowl, mix together the cheese, mayonnaise, garlic, onion, ham, basil and salt.

2. Prepare 12 waffles according to the directions on the mix package, or use prepared waffles. Spread the ham and cheese mixture evenly on 6 of the waffles and top with the remaining waffles. Makes 6 servings.

HAM SOUFFLÉ SANDWICHES

1 package (10 oz.) frozen
  asparagus spears
▶ 4 slices cooked ham
4 slices white bread, toasted
⅔ cup mayonnaise
¼ cup grated sharp Cheddar
  cheese

¼ cup sliced stuffed green olives
¼ teaspoon salt
2 tablespoons finely chopped
  green pepper
2 egg whites

1. Cook the asparagus spears according to the package directions; drain and set aside. Preheat the broiler. Line a broiler pan with aluminum foil. Place 1 slice of ham on each slice of toast, and arrange them on the broiler pan. Place 2 or 3 asparagus spears on each slice of ham.

2. In a medium bowl, mix together the mayonnaise, cheese, olives, salt, and green pepper. Whip the egg whites until they are stiff but not dry. Fold them into the mayonnaise mixture. Top each sandwich with some of this mixture and spread it evenly to the edges. Broil 4 inches from the heat for 5 minutes, or until golden brown. Makes 4 servings.

HOT HAM SALAD SANDWICHES PIQUANTE

▶ ¾ cup ground cooked ham
¾ cup shredded Cheddar
  cheese
2 tablespoons grated onion
⅓ cup grated carrot
1 tablespoon sweet pickle relish
1 tablespoon chili sauce
3 tablespoons mayonnaise

2 teaspoons prepared mustard
  Dash of garlic salt
  Dash of celery salt
  Dash of pepper
  Dash of cayenne
¼ teaspoon sugar
6 French rolls

1. In a bowl combine the ham, cheese, onion, carrot and relish, until evenly blended. In a small bowl, mix the chili sauce, mayonnaise, mustard and seasonings thoroughly. Combine the two mixtures and blend.

2. Cut the rolls in half horizontally. Hollow them out by scooping out part of the centers. Fill the rolls with the ham mixture. Wrap the sandwiches separately in aluminum foil. Bake in a preheated 400° oven for 20 minutes. Serve hot. Makes 6 servings.

CROQUE-MONSIEUR

1 cup grated Swiss cheese
5 to 7 tablespoons heavy cream
Salt
Cayenne
16 slices white bread

▶ 8 thin slices cooked ham, trimmed to about same size as bread
3 eggs, lightly beaten
4 to 6 tablespoons butter

1. In a small bowl mash the grated Swiss cheese with 2 to 4 tablespoons of the cream or just enough to make a thick, smooth paste. Season to taste with salt and cayenne. Spread the cheese evenly on all 16 slices of bread, leaving about ⅛ inch of rim exposed. Cover 8 of the pieces of bread with slices of ham, and top each with the remaining cheese-spread bread. Press each sandwich together firmly. If desired, trim off the crusts with a sharp knife.

2. Combine the eggs and 3 tablespoons of the cream in a broad, shallow bowl and mix well. Dip each sandwich into the egg mixture and let it soak for a few seconds. Heat the butter in a large, heavy frying pan over moderate heat. Fry the sandwiches, turning them once, until both sides are browned and the cheese is melted. Makes 8 servings.

PITA SANDWICHES WITH HAM AND CHICK PEAS

2 tablespoons sesame seeds (optional)
1 envelope onion soup mix
2 cups sour cream
1 can (1 lb., 4 oz.) chick peas, drained, rinsed and chopped
▶1¼ cups diced baked ham

¼ cup sliced scallions, (include some green tops)
1 tablespoon lemon juice
1 clove garlic, minced
3 cups shredded lettuce
6 small loaves pita bread, halved to form pockets

1. Toast the sesame seeds in a small dry skillet until golden brown, stirring constantly. Combine soup mix, sour cream, chick peas, ham, scallions, lemon juice, garlic, and sesame seeds in a large mixing bowl; cover and chill several hours.

2. To assemble sandwiches, tuck a little lettuce into each pita pocket, spoon in some filling and top with a little more lettuce. Makes 6 servings.

DEVILED HAM SPREAD

▶ 1 cup ground cooked ham
3 tablespoons mayonnaise
1 tablespoon chili sauce
2 teaspoons Dijon mustard

Hot pepper sauce to taste
1 to 2 tablespoons chopped sweet pickle
2 tablespoons minced celery

Combine all ingredients in a bowl and mix well. Taste and add salt, if necessary. Use as a spread for sandwiches or crackers. Makes about 1½ cups.

▸PORK

SPICY PORK AND RICE CASSEROLE

3 tablespoons olive oil
1¼ cups finely chopped onion
2 cloves garlic, minced
½ cup minced green pepper
¾ cup uncooked rice
1½ cups sliced fresh mushrooms
▶1¾ cups turkey or chicken broth
▶ 2 cups cubed cooked pork
½ cup tomato sauce

½ teaspoon salt
½ teaspoon ground coriander
¼ teaspoon ground cumin
Pinch of cayenne
½ teaspoon ground turmeric
Freshly ground pepper to taste
1 package (10 oz.) frozen peas,
thawed

1. Heat the olive oil in a large skillet, and sauté the onion, garlic, and green pepper until they're limp. Add the rice and cook, stirring, until rice becomes milky and opaque; add mushrooms and cook until soft. Stir in broth, pork, tomato sauce, salt, coriander, cumin, cayenne, turmeric, and pepper to taste; bring to a boil.

2. Spoon into a well-greased shallow 2-quart casserole; cover and bake 30 minutes at 350°. Remove from the oven and stir in peas. Return to oven and bake for 10 to 15 minutes longer, until peas are cooked and moisture is absorbed. Makes 4 to 6 servings.

LAYERED STUFFED-CABBAGE CASSEROLE

8 strips bacon, diced
1½ pounds green cabbage,
cored, finely shredded (about
6 cups)
2 cups minced onion
2 tablespoons butter or
margarine
▶1¼ cups ground cooked beef
▶1¼ cups ground cooked pork
1 teaspoon salt
Freshly ground pepper

1 can (16 oz.) whole tomatoes,
undrained
1 cup water
⅓ cup fresh lemon juice
¼ cup (packed) dark brown
sugar
2 teaspoons caraway seeds
½ cup raw long-grain rice
1 to 1½ cups sour cream, at
room temperature

1. Cook bacon in a large heavy skillet over medium heat until crisp. Remove bacon and drain on paper toweling; reserve. Pour off all but 3 tablespoons fat and add the cabbage and 1 cup of the onion; sauté until cabbage is wilted and begins to brown. Transfer mixture to medium bowl; reserve.

2. Melt the butter and add the meats and the rest of the onion. Stir, breaking up lumps, until the onion is translucent. Add salt, and pepper to taste; remove the meat mixture to a bowl.

3. Purée the tomatoes in a food processor or blender until smooth. Pour the purée into the skillet and add water, lemon juice, brown sugar, and caraway seeds. Heat over medium heat, scraping the bottom with a wooden spoon, until it boils.

4. In a 3-quart flameproof casserole or dutch oven, spread ⅓ of the cabbage mixture over the bottom. Top with half of the meat mixture and sprinkle with ½ of the rice. Repeat, ending with a layer of cabbage and onion. Pour the sauce over the casserole, cover, and cook over low heat for 45 minutes. Just before serving. spread the sour cream over the top and sprinkle with the bacon bits. Makes 6 to 8 servings.

PORK-YAM MASH

4 tablespoons butter or
  margarine
½ cup chopped onion
► 2 cups chopped cooked pork
► 2 cups mashed cooked yams
⅓ cup evaporated milk or cream
¼ teaspoon dry mustard

½ teaspoon cinnamon
¼ teaspoon salt
1 cup crushed pineapple,
  drained
2 tablespoons brown sugar
½ cup chopped walnuts

1. Melt the butter in a medium skillet and sauté the onion until soft. Stir in the pork; add yams, milk, mustard, cinnamon, and salt. Simmer uncovered, for 10 minutes.

2. Turn the pork mixture into a buttered shallow 1½-quart baking dish. Spread the pineapple over the pork mixture; sprinkle with the brown sugar and top with the nuts. Heat oven to 350°. Bake for 15 to 20 minutes or until sugar melts. Makes 4 servings.

PORK CASSEROLE

2 slices bacon
1 large onion, chopped
1 can (16 oz.) stewed tomatoes
► 1 cup cooked peas
► 1 cup diced cooked carrots

► 2 cups diced cooked pork
  Salt and pepper to taste
½ cup buttered soft bread
  crumbs

1. In a large skillet, cook the bacon until crisp; remove bacon and crumble. In the bacon fat, brown the onion; add the tomatoes, peas, carrots, pork, salt and pepper, and let cook for 2 minutes, uncovered. Remove from heat and sprinkle the bacon, then the bread crumbs over the top.

2. Bake at 425° for 15 minutes or until crumbs are brown. Makes 4 servings.

LAST-MINUTE CASSOULET

2 tablespoons vegetable oil or
  bacon drippings
1 cup sliced celery
½ cup chopped onion
½ cup chopped green pepper
1 clove garlic, minced
► 1 cup sliced cooked sausages

► 2 cups diced cooked pork
1 can (8 oz.) tomato sauce
1 can (16 oz.) pork and beans
1 can (16 oz.) lima beans,
  drained
  Salt and pepper to taste

In a medium-size skillet, heat the vegetable oil or bacon drippings and sauté the celery, onion, green pepper, and garlic for 5 minutes. Add the sausage and pork and cook for 2 minutes longer. Stir in the tomato sauce, pork and beans, lima beans, and salt and pepper to taste. Simmer, uncovered, 30 minutes or longer. Flavor improves with long, gentle heating. Makes 4 to 6 servings.

BASQUE PORK AND CHICKEN

▶ 1¼ cups diced cooked pork
▶ 1¼ cups diced cooked chicken
  1 teaspoon chopped chives or
    shallots
  ⅓ cup mayonnaise
  ¼ cup chopped stuffed green
    olives

3 black pitted olives, finely
  chopped
1 teaspoon lemon juice
1 teaspoon lime juice
Pinch salt
2 egg whites, stiffly beaten

1. Mix the pork, chicken, and chives together and divide among 4 heatproof ramekins or custard cups. Broil 3 to 4 inches from heat for 5 minutes. In a medium-size bowl, combine the mayonnaise, the olives, the lemon and lime juices, and salt. Mix thoroughly. Fold gently into the beaten egg whites.

2. Spoon the egg mixture over the pork and chicken and broil until the top is puffed and lightly browned. Makes 4 servings.

FRUITED PORK CASSEROLE

  1 cup dried apricots
  ¼ cup raisins
    Boiling water
  2 tablespoons butter

▶ 2 cups cubed cooked pork
▶ 1 cup diced cooked carrots
  ½ cup consommé
  ¼ cup brown sugar

1. Cover the apricots and raisins with the boiling water and let stand overnight. Force mixture through a sieve or purée in an electric blender. Melt the butter in a skillet and quickly sauté the pork.

2. In a 2-quart baking pan, put in the pork and cover with the carrots; top with the fruit purée. Pour the consommé over all; cover and bake 20 minutes at 350°. Uncover and sprinkle with brown sugar; bake 15 minutes longer. Makes 4 servings.

SAVORY PORK AND PINEAPPLE CASSEROLE

▶ 2 cups diced roast pork
  1 medium onion, minced
  2 cups diced canned sweet
    potatoes
  1 can (9 oz.) pineapple spears
  ½ teaspoon prepared mustard

½ teaspoon wine vinegar
  Salt and pepper to taste
2 tablespoons brown sugar
2 tablespoons butter or
  margarine

1. In the bottom of a shallow casserole, arrange the pork, onion, and sweet potatoes. Drain the pineapple; add enough water to the syrup to make ½ cup liquid. Mix the liquid with the mustard and vinegar, and pour over the meat mixture. Salt and pepper to taste.

2. Layer the pineapple over the meat. Sprinkle with brown sugar and dot with butter. Bake at 350° for 30 minutes, basting occasionally. Makes 4 servings.

SCALLOPED POTATOES WITH PORK

4 cups peeled and sliced potatoes
▶ 1 pound sliced, cooked smoked pork
2 tablespoons flour
Pepper to taste
1 medium onion, minced
2 tablespoons butter
2 cups hot milk
2 medium tomatoes, sliced
¼ cup buttered bread crumbs
½ cup grated Cheddar cheese

1. Arrange half of the potatoes in the bottom of a well-buttered 2-quart casserole; cover with the third of the pork. Sprinkle with 1 tablespoon of the flour, pepper, and half the minced onion. Dot with 1 tablespoon of butter. Add a little more than half the remaining potatoes in the next layer; cover with the same amount of the remaining pork. Top with the last of the potatoes and pork. Sprinkle with the remaining flour, onion, and pepper to taste; dot with the remaining butter.

2. Pour milk over the top and cover with the tomato slices. Cover and bake at 350° for 30 minutes. Uncover, sprinkle with the buttered crumbs and the cheese, and bake 30 minutes longer or until potatoes are tender and top is browned. Makes 6 to 8 servings.

PORK AND PEPPER MOUSSAKA

¼ cup olive oil
4 large green peppers, cut into thin strips
1½ cups sliced onions
1 teaspoon salt
½ teaspoon pepper
▶2½ cups ground cooked pork
1 teaspoon minced garlic
1 tablespoon tomato paste
1 teaspoon dried oregano
1½ cups freshly-grated Parmesan cheese
3 tablespoons butter
¼ cup flour
3 cups milk
2 eggs
▶ 2 cups cooked rice

1. In a large skillet, heat half of the oil over medium heat. Add green peppers, onions, salt and pepper; sauté until vegetables are soft, about 1 minute. Transfer to a small bowl.

2. In the same skillet, heat the remaining oil over medium heat. Add pork, garlic, tomato paste, oregano, ½ cup of the Parmesan; sauté for 5 to 10 minutes, until ingredients are well blended.

3. In a medium-sized saucepan, melt butter over medium heat. Add flour; cook for 1 minute. Add milk; cook, stirring constantly, until mixture thickens, about 5 minutes.

4. In a small bowl, beat eggs; whisk in about ½ cup of the hot sauce. Gradually stir egg mixture back into remaining sauce; cook over very low heat for 1 minute (do not boil). Add ½ cup Parmesan.

5. In a greased 1½-quart casserole or 8-inch square baking dish, spread rice evenly. Layer about ½ of the sauce over the rice, make another layer of the pepper/onion mixture, then another of the pork mixture; finish with the remaining sauce. Sprinkle with remaining ½ cup cheese. Bake 30 minutes at 350°. Makes 4 to 6 servings.

TEXAS PORK PIE

- 2 cups diced cooked pork
  ¼ cup chopped green pepper
  ¼ cup chopped onion
  2 tablespoons chopped celery
  3 large mushrooms, chopped
- 1 tablespoon bacon drippings or oil
- 2 cups cooked drained whole-kernel corn
  2 cups tomato sauce
  ½ teaspoon dried sage
  Salt

Pepper
1 to 3 teaspoons chili powder, optional
¾ cup corn meal
¾ cup flour
2 teaspoons baking powder
¾ teaspoon salt
1 tablespoon sugar
1 egg, well beaten
¾ cup milk
¼ teaspoon Worcestershire sauce
3 tablespoons melted butter

1. Brown the pork, pepper, onion, celery, and mushrooms in bacon drippings. Stir in corn, tomato sauce, and sage. Season to taste with salt, pepper and chili powder. Pour into a 2-quart baking dish.

2. Mix the corn meal, flour, baking powder, salt, and sugar in a bowl. Stir together the egg, milk, Worcestershire sauce, and melted butter. Add to the corn meal mixture and stir just until the dry ingredients are completely moistened.

3. Pour the batter over the pork mixture. Bake in a preheated 400° oven for 30 to 35 minutes. Makes 6 to 8 servings.

MEMPHIS PORK WITH BISCUITS

2 cans (20 oz. each) stewed tomatoes
3 tablespoons quick-cooking tapioca
1 teaspoon salt
¼ teaspoon paprika
¼ teaspoon dried thyme
¼ teaspoon dried basil
1 tablespoon sugar

2 teaspoons Worcestershire sauce
2 tablespoons butter or margarine
¾ cup chopped onion
¾ cup thinly sliced celery
1 small clove garlic, minced
- 2 cups cubed cooked pork
  Baking Powder Biscuit dough, (see Basics)

1. Drain the juice from the tomatoes into a medium saucepan. Add the tapioca, salt, paprika, thyme, basil, sugar, and Worcestershire sauce. Simmer slowly until sauce is clear, stirring constantly.

2. Melt the butter in a medium skillet; add onion, garlic, and celery and sauté 5 minutes, stirring frequently. Add pork, tomatoes, and sauce and heat just to boiling point. Turn into a greased 1-quart baking dish.

3. Roll biscuit dough to ½-inch thickness and cut into rounds with a biscuit cutter. Cover top of pork mixture with biscuits. Bake 20 to 25 minutes at 400°. Makes 4 servings.

BUDAPEST PORK AND CABBAGE BAKE

½ medium cabbage (about 1½ lbs.) shredded
½ cup water
½ cup whipping cream
Salt and freshly ground pepper, to taste
1 teaspoon caraway seed

½ teaspoon paprika
▶ 4 to 6 slices cooked pork, julienne cut
▶ 1 cup potatoes, boiled, peeled, and sliced
½ cup grated Swiss cheese

1. In a heavy skillet over high heat, cover and boil cabbage in the water until the water has evaporated completely, being careful not to burn. Add the cream, salt, pepper, caraway seed, and paprika; bring to a boil and cook, uncovered, for 5 minutes, stirring frequently.

2. Place half of the cabbage mixture in a lightly greased 9-inch baking dish, layer on pork and potatoes, and cover with the remaining cabbage mixture. Top with cheese and bake at 350° for 25 to 30 minutes until cabbage is done. Makes 4 servings.

HUNGARIAN PORK CASSEROLE

2 tablespoons butter
1 small onion, minced
▶ 2 cups ground smoked pork
¼ cup fine dry bread crumbs
1 cup sauerkraut, rinsed under cold water and drained well

1 carton (16 oz.) creamed cottage cheese
½ teaspoon dried basil
½ teaspoon salt
Dash pepper
3 eggs
Paprika

1. Melt butter in a skillet and sauté the onion and pork together, stirring, for 3 minutes. Sprinkle in the bread crumbs. In the bottom of a greased 1½-quart baking dish, spread the pork mixture, top with the sauerkraut.

2. Beat the cottage cheese until smooth; add the basil, salt, and pepper. Beat in the eggs one at a time, and pour the sauce over the sauerkraut. Sprinkle with paprika and bake at 375° for 35 to 40 minutes. Makes 4 servings.

PORK AND VEGETABLE SKILLET DINNER

3 tablespoons butter or margarine
1 medium onion, sliced
1 can (10½ oz.) condensed cream of mushroom soup
½ cup milk
1 teaspoon Worcestershire sauce

⅛ teaspoon Tabasco
▶ 2 cups diced cooked pork
▶ 1 cup diced cooked potatoes
▶ ½ cup diced cooked carrots
▶ ½ cup cooked peas
1 teaspoon paprika
4 slices of toast

1. In a heavy skillet, melt the butter and sauté the onion until translucent. Pour in the soup, milk, Worcestershire sauce, and Tabasco. Stir until smooth. Add the pork, potatoes, carrots, peas, and paprika; blend well.

2. Cook over low heat for 10 minutes, stirring often. Serve over toast. Makes 4 servings.

SWEET BALINESE CURRY

- 2 cups cubed cooked pork
  ½ cup chopped scallion
- ½ cup diced cooked carrots
  ¼ cup chopped green pepper
  1 tablespoon minced parsley
  2 medium apples, pared and
  diced
  1 large banana, diced
  ½ cup raisins
  2 dried figs, chopped (optional)

1½ tablespoons lemon juice
1 tablespoon honey
- 1 cup thinned gravy, leftover
  from a roast; or ¾ cup beef
  stock, homemade or canned
  1 to 2 tablespoons curry powder
  to taste
  Dash of nutmeg
  Hot fluffy rice
  ½ cup chutney

1. In a large skillet, combine pork, scallions, carrot, green pepper, parsley, apples, banana, raisins, figs, lemon juice, and honey. Add gravy or stock to meat mixture. Blend in curry powder and nutmeg.

2. Cover and simmer 30 minutes, stirring occasionally. Remove cover and simmer 5 minutes longer. Serve over hot rice. Garnish with chutney. Makes 4 servings.

PORK TRIANON

- 4 to 8 slices cooked pork, ¼"
  thick
  4 to 8 slices Swiss cheese
  1 cup dried apple rings, soaked
  in hot water for ½ hour and
  drained

2 tablespoons butter
- 2 cups cooked sweet-sour red
  cabbage, homemade or from
  a jar
  1 tablespoon light brown sugar
  1 teaspoon caraway seed

1. On each thin slice of pork, place 1 slice of cheese and 1 apple ring; roll up, and secure with a wooden toothpick.

2. Melt butter in a heavy skillet; add meat rolls and brown evenly on all sides. Mix cabbage, sugar, and caraway seed. Remove meat rolls from skillet and keep warm. Place cabbage mixture in skillet; simmer 10 minutes. Place cabbage on platter and top with meat rolls. (Remove wooden toothpicks before serving.) Makes 4 servings.

POLISH PORK AND POTATO STEW (Bigos)

2 pounds fresh or canned
  sauerkraut
- 2 cups beef or chicken stock,
  homemade or canned
  2 cups (one 16 oz. can) tomatoes
  1 large onion, chopped
  1 large apple, peeled and
  chopped
- 1 tablespoon bacon fat
  1 pound kielbasa sausage

- 2 cups diced cooked pork
  1 tablespoon sugar
  1 tablespoon flour
  Salt to taste
  Dash of black pepper and
  cayenne
  1 cup sliced mushrooms,
  sautéed in 1 teaspoon
  vegetable oil
- 4 cooked potatoes, cubed

1. Drain and rinse sauerkraut. Put in heavy pot with stock and liquid from tomatoes; simmer 5 minutes.

2. Sauté tomatoes, onion and apple in bacon fat for 3 to 5 minutes. Cut kielbasa into 1-inch chunks and add to vegetables with pork meat; simmer for 10 minutes. Add sugar, flour, salt, pepper and cayenne to vegetable-meat mixture; stir. Add mushrooms and stir; cook until slightly thickened. Add to sauerkraut.

3. Simmer mixture for 1 hour, adding more stock if it becomes dry. Refrigerate overnight. When ready to use, stir in potatoes and reheat slowly. Makes 6 to 8 servings.

CHOP SUEY

▶ 1½ cups chicken or beef stock
1 cup diced celery
½ cup diced green pepper
1 large onion, sliced
▶ 3 cups julienned cooked pork
▶ 1 cup cooked green beans, cut to 1-inch lengths
▶ 1 cup cooked peas

¼ cup sliced water chestnuts
2 to 3 tablespoons soy sauce to taste
2 cups bean sprouts, or 1 can (16 oz.) bean sprouts, drained
1 tablespoon cornstarch
2 tablespoons water
Hot fluffy rice

1. In a medium-sized saucepan, bring ½ cup of the stock to a boil; add celery and cook 5 minutes. Add green pepper and onion; cook for 3 more minutes.

2. Add pork, green beans, peas, water chestnuts, remaining stock and soy sauce. Stir and bring to a boil. Add bean sprouts, stir again, and cook for 3 minutes. In a cup, mix cornstarch with the water, add to the saucepan, and cook until thickened. Serve with rice. Makes 6 servings.

ASIAN CURRY

¼ cup butter
1 large Bermuda onion, finely chopped
1 to 2 tablespoons curry powder to taste
½ teaspoon celery salt
¼ teaspoon salt
¼ teaspoon pepper
⅛ teaspoon ground cloves

⅛ teaspoon ground nutmeg
⅛ teaspoon dried thyme
▶ 2 cups chicken stock, homemade or canned
¾ cup heavy cream
1½ tablespoons cornstarch
▶ 3 cups diced cooked pork
½ cup chopped peanuts

1. Melt butter in a heavy skillet; cook onion in butter until it becomes translucent or about 5 minutes. Add curry powder, celery salt, salt, pepper, cloves, nutmeg and thyme; simmer 5 minutes. Add stock and simmer 10 minutes. Strain through a fine sieve into a large saucepan.

2. Bring the sauce to a boil and gradually stir in ½ cup of the cream. Dissolve the cornstarch in the remaining cream and gradually stir into the sauce; simmer until the sauce is smooth and thickened. Add the meat; simmer 5 to 10 minutes until heated through. Garnish with peanuts. Makes 8 servings.

SOUTH-OF-THE-BORDER SKILLET SUPPER

3 tablespoons lard or shortening
▶ 3 cups cubed cooked pork
1 large onion, sliced
1 can (16 oz.) tomatoes
1 can (8 oz.) tomato sauce
¼ cup diced celery
¼ cup chopped parsley
1 teaspoon salt

1 teaspoon sugar
½ teaspoon chili powder, or more to taste
Pepper to taste
½ cup sliced stuffed green olives (optional)
1 package (8 oz.) noodles, cooked

1. In a large skillet, melt the lard and sauté the pork and onions until the pork is browned, about 5 minutes.

2. Stir in the tomatoes, tomato sauce, celery, parsley, salt, sugar, chili powder, and pepper. Heat to boiling; cover the skillet, reduce the heat, and simmer for 15 minutes. Stir in the olives and heat through. Serve with noodles. Makes 6 servings.

STIR FRIED PORK AND ZUCCHINI

1½ teaspoons cornstarch
½ teaspoon sugar
▶ ¼ cup chicken stock, homemade or canned
2 tablespoons soy sauce
1 tablespoon dry sherry

▶ 1½ cups cubed cooked pork
4 tablespoons corn oil
4 cups cubed zucchini (and/or any other green vegetable such as celery, asparagus, broccoli, green beans, etc.)

1. Combine the cornstarch, sugar, stock, soy sauce, and sherry. Add the pork and mix well. Set aside.

2. Heat the oil in a large skillet or wok. Stir-fry the zucchini for 4 to 5 minutes. Remove the pork from its marinade and stir-fry over high heat for 2 minutes. Add the marinade to pan, mix well, and heat through. Serve with white rice, if you wish. Makes 4 servings.

PORK AND BEAN CHILI

½ cup minced onion
4 tablespoons chili powder
3 tablespoons tomato paste
2 cloves garlic, minced
¾ teaspoon salt
¾ teaspoon dried oregano
¾ teaspoon ground cumin

2 cups water
▶ 2 to 2½ cups diced cooked pork
1 can (15 oz.) pinto beans, drained
3 to 4 cups hot cooked rice
Grated Cheddar cheese
Chopped scallions (optional)

Combine the onion, chili powder, tomato paste, garlic, salt, oregano, and cumin in a saucepan. Stir in the water; bring to a boil, lower heat, and simmer until reduced to 1½ cups, about 10 minutes. Stir in the pork and pinto beans. Cover and simmer for 15 minutes. Serve over rice. Garnish with grated cheese and chopped scallions. Makes 4 servings.

SWEET AND SOUR PORK

▶ 2 cups cubed cooked pork
3 tablespoons soy sauce
½ cup red wine vinegar
4 tablespoons brown sugar
▶ 1 cup chicken stock, homemade
or canned
2 green peppers, cut into 1-inch
squares
2 carrots, cut into julienne strips
(½" wide × 2" long)

2 teaspoons cornstarch
¾ cup pineapple chunks,
drained
⅓ cup flour
½ teaspoon ground ginger
4 tablespoons water
1 egg
Peanut oil for deep frying

1. Marinate the pork in 2 tablespoons of soy sauce for ½ hour, stirring from time to time.

2. In a saucepan, combine the vinegar, brown sugar and ¾ cup of the stock. Bring to a boil and reduce by half. Add green pepper and carrots and cook for 5 minutes over medium heat. In a cup, mix together the 2 teaspoons cornstarch and remaining ¼ cup stock and stir it into the hot sauce; cook for 2 minutes. Add the remaining soy sauce and the pineapple. Remove from heat; keep warm.

3. Make a batter by mixing together the flour, ginger, water and egg; beat until smooth. Add the pork to the batter; stir gently. Lift the pork cubes out of the batter with a slotted spoon and fry until brown, in a deep skillet, in peanut oil which has been heated to 375°.

4. Serve the crisp pork cubes on a platter with the sauce poured over the top. Makes 4 servings.

HONG KONG PORK

2 tablespoons vegetable oil
1 medium clove garlic
1 scallion, thinly sliced
1 tablespoon grated fresh ginger
or 1 teaspoon ground ginger
2 medium green peppers, cubed
3 large mushrooms, thinly sliced
Salt and pepper to taste

½ cup sliced water chestnuts
▶ 1 cup finely chopped cooked
pork
1 teaspoon sugar
1 tablespoon soy sauce or Hoisin
sauce
▶ 3 tablespoons chicken stock
2 teaspoons cornstarch blended
with 1 tablespoon water

1. Heat a skillet or wok over medium-high heat; add oil and sauté garlic, scallion, and ginger until lightly browned. Remove garlic; add green peppers; sauté until wilted. Add mushrooms, simmer 5 minutes and season with salt and pepper.

2. Add water chestnuts, pork, sugar, soy sauce, stock, and cook 4 minutes longer. Blend in the cornstarch and cook until mixture thickens. Makes 4 servings.

PORK IN ORANGE SAUCE

1 tablespoon grated orange
  peel
3 tablespoons frozen
  concentrated orange juice,
  thawed
▶ ⅓ cup beef or chicken stock,
  homemade or canned
2 tablespoons soy sauce

2 teaspoons cornstarch
1 teaspoon sugar
1 teaspoon grated fresh ginger
2 large carrots, thinly sliced
2 stalks celery, chopped
2 tablespoons cooking oil
▶ 2 cups cubed cooked pork
¼ cup cashews

1. Combine the orange peel, orange juice, stock, soy sauce, cornstarch and sugar; set aside. In wok or large skillet stir-fry ginger, carrots and celery in hot oil about 4 minutes or until crisp-tender. Remove from wok with slotted spoon, and set aside.

2. Stir-fry pork 2 to 3 minutes or till browned. (Add more oil, if necessary.) Add orange juice mixture and cashews. Cook and stir till thickened and bubbly. Return vegetables to wok. Cover and heat through 1 minute. Serve over ice. Makes 4 to 6 servings.

STIR FRY PORK AND VEGETABLES

2 tablespoons peanut oil
3 stalks celery, sliced diagonally
3 medium onions, sliced thin
1 large carrot, sliced diagonally
  as thin as possible
1 medium white turnip (cut into
  julienne strips)
▶ ¼ cup chicken stock, homemade
  or canned

10 water chestnuts, slivered
▶ 2 cups diced cooked pork
½ pound fresh spinach, chopped
1 cup snow peas, fresh or frozen
  (thawed)
½ cup julienned bamboo shoots
2 tablespoons soy sauce, mixed
  with 1 teaspoon cornstarch if
  you like a thicker sauce

1. In a large skillet or a wok, heat the oil over medium heat and add the celery, onions, carrot and turnip. Stir and sauté for 2 minutes. Add stock, stir to blend; cover and steam for 4 minutes.

2. Add water chestnuts and pork; stir again. Cover and cook 4 minutes more. Add the spinach, snow peas, bamboo shoots and soy sauce. Stir, cover and steam for a minute or so more. Serve with hot white rice. Makes 4 servings.

"Reducing" a gravy or sauce

Thicken a gravy or sauce, and increase the flavor, by "reducing" the liquid. Place the pan over low heat, remove the cover, and allow some of the liquid to evaporate. Remember that the greater the surface area exposed, the shorter the time needed to "reduce" the liquid.

PORK IN APPLE GRAVY

5 tablespoons butter
2 tablespoons flour
1 cup milk
1 cup chopped peeled tart
apples

¼ teaspoon ground nutmeg
¼ cup chopped chives
Salt and pepper to taste
▶ 8 slices cooked pork
½ cup sour cream

1. In a small saucepan, melt 1 tablespoon of the butter, stir in 1 table-spoon of the flour, and cook for 1 minute. Gradually add milk and stir constantly until smooth and thickened, about 5 minutes.

2. Melt 2 tablespoons of the butter in a saucepan and sauté the apple until golden. Sprinkle in the remaining flour and cook for 2 minutes, until slightly thick. Gradually stir in the sauce, nutmeg, and chives; simmer for 5 minutes, remove from heat. Season with salt and pepper.

3. In a skillet melt the remaining butter. Quickly sauté the pork slices. Mix the sour cream into the sauce and pour over the pork slices; bring to a simmer and heat gently until meat is heated through. Do not let sauce boil. Makes 4 servings.

PORK IN OLIVE SAUCE

2 tablespoons olive oil
1 tablespoon chopped onion
2 tablespoons all-purpose flour
▶ 1 cup beef stock, homemade or
canned
1 tablespoon fresh lemon juice
2 tablespoons brown sugar

½ teaspoon paprika
½ teaspoon salt
▶ 3 cups cooked pork, cut in
julienne strips
½ cup sliced pimiento-stuffed
olives

1. In a large saucepan, heat olive oil and sauté onion for 1 minute; stir in flour; cook and stir about 1 minute. Add stock, lemon juice, brown sugar, paprika and salt. Blend thoroughly. Cook over low heat for 5 minutes, stirring constantly.

2. Put meat in sauce. Cook, covered, over low heat until meat is heated through, 5 to 10 minutes. Stir occasionally. Add olives and cook for 5 minutes longer, or until heated. Makes 4 servings.

ORIENTAL PORK AND APRICOTS

1½ cups boiling water
½ package (8 oz.) dried apricots
▶ 4 cups cubed cooked pork
1 tablespoon butter
2½ tablespoons soy sauce

Dash of Tabasco
⅛ teaspoon pepper
6 scallions cut in 2-inch pieces
1 tablespoon chopped parsley

1. Pour boiling water over apricots and let stand for at least ½ hour. Brown meat in butter in a medium-sized skillet until well browned on all sides. Add soy sauce, Tabasco, pepper and half the apricot liquid. Cover and simmer 10 minutes.

2. Add scallions, apricots, and more apricot liquid, if necessary. Simmer 10 minutes longer, sprinkle with parsley and serve with rice, if you wish. Makes 6 servings.

ZUCCHINI STUFFED WITH PORK

6 large zucchini, ends trimmed
6 tablespoons butter
1 cup minced onion
2 cups chopped mushrooms
2 teaspoons dried thyme
  Salt and pepper to taste

▶ 2 cups minced cooked pork
1 cup Cream Sauce (see Basics)
6 tablespoons grated Parmesan
  cheese
⅓ cup minced parsley (garnish)

1. Blanch the zucchini in boiling water for about 10 minutes. Cut off the top ⅓ of the zucchinis lengthwise; scoop pulp from top and bottom, being careful not to tear bottom shells. Invert bottom portion to drain and discard tops. Squeeze as much moisture as possible from the pulp, then mince.

2. Melt the butter in a large skillet. Add onion and cook until soft. Stir in mushrooms and thyme; sauté 5 minutes and add salt and pepper to taste. Add minced zucchini pulp and simmer 5 minutes. Stir in the pork and Cream Sauce.

3. Fill the zucchini shells with the pork mixture, mounding slightly. Sprinkle with Parmesan cheese. Arrange in a lightly greased 2-quart baking dish. Bake uncovered 10 to 15 minutes in 450° oven, or until tops are golden brown. Sprinkle with minced parsley. Makes 6 servings.

PORK-STUFFED CABBAGE LEAVES

8 large cabbage leaves
4 quarts boiling salted water
½ cup minced onion
⅓ cup minced celery
1 tablespoon butter or
  margarine
▶ 1 to 1½ cups coarsely ground
  cooked pork
▶ ½ to ⅔ cup cooked rice

2 tablespoons minced fresh
  parsley
½ teaspoon paprika
½ teaspoon dried rosemary
  Salt and pepper to taste
1 teaspoon instant beef bouillon
  (optional)
1½ cups tomato purée

1. Cook the cabbage leaves in boiling salted water for 10 minutes, until leaves are wilted. Drain and set aside.

2. Sauté the onion and celery in the butter for 5 minutes, stirring occasionally. Remove and mix in a bowl with the pork, rice, parsley, paprika, and rosemary. Add salt and pepper to taste.

3. Place a generous ¼ cup of meat mixture on each cabbage leaf near the stem end. Fold stem end over onto filling, then both sides toward the middle. Roll and place, seam side down, in a well-greased 11 × 7-inch baking dish.

4. Mix the instant beef bouillon (if used) with the tomato purée. Pour over the cabbage rolls. Cover and bake in a 350° oven for 40 minutes.

5. Remove the cabbage rolls to a platter. Season the tomato purée to taste. Serve the cabbage with the sauce and with sour cream, passed separately. Makes 4 to 6 servings.

STUFFED ACORN SQUASH

4 acorn or butternut squash
1 cup butter or margarine (2 sticks)
Salt and freshly ground pepper to taste
▶ 4 cups chopped cooked pork
2 tart apples, peeled, cored and chopped

16 chestnuts, roasted, peeled and chopped, or 1 cup canned purée
2 medium onions, chopped, sautéed in 3 tablespoons butter for 5 minutes
2 tablespoons brown sugar
1½ teaspoons dried sage

1. Split the squash lengthwise and remove seeds and fibers. Butter the squash generously. Sprinkle each with salt and pepper; place them on a cookie sheet. Bake in a preheated 350° oven for 40 minutes. Remove from the oven and scoop out the pulp and melted butter, being careful not to break the skin.

2. Chop the pulp and put it in a large bowl. Stir in the pork, apples, chestnuts, onions, brown sugar and sage. Heap the stuffing mixture in each squash shell. Cover each serving loosely with foil. Return to the oven and bake for 30 minutes. Makes 8 servings.

PORK POT PIE

2 packages pie crust mix
▶ 2 cups coarsely chopped cooked pork
▶ 2 cups diced cooked potatoes
▶ ½ cup cooked green peas
▶ ½ cup cooked green beans
1 tablespoon minced parsley
Dash of ground cloves

Dash of ground nutmeg
½ cup chopped onion
¼ cup chopped mushrooms
3 tablespoons butter
2 tablespoons flour
▶ 1½ cups chicken broth
1 tablespoon milk

1. Prepare pie crust mix according to package directions; roll to ⅛-inch thickness. Line a 8-cup baking dish with the pie crust, reserving enough for a top crust. Partially prebake pie crust. (See Basics).

2. In a large bowl, combine the pork, potatoes, peas, beans, parsley, cloves, and nutmeg. In a skillet, sauté the onion and mushrooms in the butter until the onion is soft. Add the flour and cook, stirring, for 1 minute. Gradually stir in the broth and cook, stirring constantly, until thick and smooth. Add to the pork and vegetable mixture.

3. Fill the baking dish with the mixture. Cover with the top crust; slash center. Pinch the edges of the crust together; brush the top with the milk. Bake in a preheated 400° oven for 40 to 45 minutes. Makes 4 servings.

EGG ROLL SQUARES

▶ ⅔ cup finely chopped cooked shrimp
▶ ⅓ cup finely chopped cooked pork
⅓ cup finely chopped scallions (with the green)
⅓ cup finely chopped water chestnuts
⅓ cup shredded cabbage

¼ cup thinly sliced celery
Soy sauce and pepper to taste
10 sheets egg roll or wonton wrappers (available in supermarket or Oriental grocery)
2 eggs, beaten
Peanut oil, for deep-frying

1. In a large bowl, mix together the shrimp, pork, scallions, water chestnuts, cabbage, celery, soy sauce, and pepper.

2. Lay out the wonton wrappers on a counter; brush each with the beaten egg. Spoon equal amounts of the shrimp mixture onto the centers of the wrappers. Bring two opposite corners of the rectangles up over the filling. Seal with the beaten egg. Fold up the remaining two corners, one at a time, sealing with the egg.

3. Bring the peanut oil to 375° in a large skillet or wok. Fry egg rolls in oil until golden brown, about 3 to 4 mintues. Drain on paper towels. Serve hot with the mustard. Makes 10 egg rolls.

PORK AND SWEET POTATO PIE

2 tablespoons minced onion
⅓ cup diced celery
3 tablespoons butter or margarine
3 tablespoons flour
½ teaspoon salt
¼ teaspoon poultry seasoning
⅛ teaspoon pepper
Dash of nutmeg
Dash of allspice

2 cups milk
▶ 1½ cups diced cooked sweet potatoes
▶ 2 cups diced cooked pork
1 package prepared pastry mix or pastry for one-crust pie (see Basics)
1 egg yolk
2 teaspoons water

1. In a medium-sized skillet sauté onion and celery in butter for 3 minutes. Blend in flour, salt, poultry seasoning, pepper, nutmeg and allspice; stir and cook for 1 minute. Gradually add milk and cook over medium heat, stirring constantly, until thickened, about 3 minutes. Put sweet potatoes and pork in 1½-quart baking dish. Pour sauce over mixture.

2. Prepare pastry; roll to ¼-inch thickness; cut in strips ¾ inch wide. Arrange, lattice-fashion, on pie. Beat egg yolk with water; brush on pastry. Bake in a preheated 450° oven for 10 minutes. Reduce heat to 350° and bake 15 minutes longer. Makes 6 servings.

WONTON APPETIZERS

2 cups flour
1 egg
⅓ cup chilled water
1 tablespoon vegetable oil
2 scallions, chopped
½ cup chopped mushrooms
▶ 1 cup minced cooked pork

▶ 4 cooked shrimp, chopped
    (optional)
2 teaspoons soy sauce
Pepper to taste
1 egg, beaten
Shortening for frying
Hot mustard

1. In a medium-size bowl, combine the flour, egg, and water. Mix quickly with your hands until the mixture forms a dough. Turn onto a lightly floured board. Knead until smooth. Cover; let stand 20 minutes. Roll out dough paper thin. Cut into 2-inch squares; set aside.

2. Heat the oil in a heavy skillet; add the scallions and sauté 5 minutes. Add the mushrooms and pork. Sauté 5 minutes, stirring occasionally. Add the shrimp, soy sauce, and pepper; cook over low heat 5 minutes.

3. Place 1 teaspoon of the filling in the middle of each wonton square. Moisten the edges with the beaten egg. Bring the ends to the center to enclose the filling; press to seal. Melt the shortening in a large skillet or wok and deep-fry the wontons 4 or 5 at a time at 365° until golden. Drain on paper towels; keep warm in the oven. Serve with hot mustard. Makes 4 dozen.

Note: Packaged wonton wrappers are available in supermarkets.

PORK AND CHEESE PANCAKES

2 tablespoons peanut oil or
    butter
4 scallions, thinly sliced
1 clove garlic, minced
1 large rib celery, sliced very
    thin
½ teaspoon salt
⅛ teaspoon freshly ground black
    pepper

½ teaspoon ground ginger
⅓ cup chopped mushrooms
▶ ½ cup finely minced cooked
    pork
3 eggs, separated
¼ cup unsifted all-purpose flour
¾ cup creamed cottage cheese

1. Heat a medium-size skillet or wok over moderate heat, then swirl in the oil and quickly sauté the scallions, garlic, and celery. Mix in the salt, pepper, ginger, mushrooms, and pork. Sauté briefly, then remove the skillet from the heat. In a mixing bowl, beat the egg whites to soft peaks. In a separate bowl, beat the egg yolks until frothy; blend in the flour and cottage cheese, then fold in the meat mixture, then the beaten egg whites.

2. Drop the mixture by tablespoonfuls onto a hot, lightly greased griddle or skillet set over moderately high heat. Flatten each pancake slightly with the back of the spoon, then brown lightly on each side. Makes 4 servings.

OMELETTES FOO YOUNG

2 tablespoons chopped scallions
¼ cup thinly sliced celery
3 tablespoons corn oil
¼ cup thinly sliced water chestnuts
▶ ½ cup finely shredded cooked pork
2 tablespoons soy sauce

1 teaspoon sugar
▶ ¾ cup chicken stock, homemade or canned
1 clove garlic, minced
2 tablespoons dry sherry
2 teaspoons cornstarch, dissolved in 1 tablespoon water
6 eggs

1. In a large saucepan, sauté the scallions and celery in 2 tablespoons of the corn oil for 1 minute. Add the water chestnuts, pork, 1 tablespoon of the soy sauce, and the sugar. Blend well, remove from heat, and set aside until cool.

2. In a small saucepan, mix together the stock, garlic, sherry, the remaining soy sauce, and the cornstarch. Simmer gently 3 to 4 minutes. Set aside.

3. Beat the eggs until frothy and combine with the cooled pork mixture. Heat a bit of the remaining 1 tablespoon of corn oil in a medium-size skillet. Pour in about 1/6 of the egg mixture. Cook over medium flame until underside is lightly browned. Turn and brown the second side. Transfer to a heated platter and repeat until all the egg mixture has been used. Serve the omelette cakes with a bit of the hot sherry/soy sauce mixture. Makes 6 servings.

EGG DROP SOUP

▶ ½ cup shredded cooked pork
1½ teaspoons sherry
1½ teaspoons soy sauce
1½ teaspoons cornstarch
2 tablespoons vegetable oil
▶ 6 cups chicken broth, homemade or canned

1 scallion, sliced (with the green)
1 cucumber, julienned
½ teaspoon salt
Pepper to taste
2 eggs, lightly beaten

1. Combine the pork, sherry, soy sauce, and cornstarch. Heat the oil in a large skillet or a wok. Add the pork mixture and brown quickly.

2. Bring the broth to a boil in a large saucepan, reduce the heat, add the pork mixture and cook for 10 minutes over very low heat. Add the scallion and cucumber and season with salt and pepper. Simmer for 5 more minutes.

3. Into the simmering broth, slowly add the eggs, stirring constantly. Remove from heat immediately. Makes 6 servings.

COMPANY PORK LOAF

▶ 4 cups coarsely ground cooked
pork
1 cup packaged savory stuffing
▶ ¾ cup pork gravy
2 eggs, well beaten
1 can (5-⅓ oz.) evaporated milk
or light cream
¼ cup minced celery
¼ teaspoon chopped capers

¼ cup minced green pepper
¼ cup minced red pepper
1 small onion, minced
4 tablespoons butter, melted
½ teaspoon salt
¼ teaspoon pepper
¼ cup dry bread crumbs
1 tablespoon chopped parsley

1. Mix together the pork, stuffing, gravy, eggs, evaporated milk, celery, capers, green and red peppers, onion, 2 tablespoons of the butter, salt, and pepper. Mix thoroughly.

2. Pat into a greased 1½-quart loaf pan; sprinkle top with bread crumbs and remaining 2 tablespoons butter. Bake in a preheated 400° oven for 45 minutes. Unmold on a heated platter and garnish with parsley. Makes 6 servings.

PORK BALLS PIQUANTE

▶ 3 cups minced cooked pork
2 eggs
½ cup soft bread crumbs
3 tablespoons minced scallion

½ cup chopped mushrooms,
sautéed in 1 tablespoon
peanut oil
½ teaspoon salt
½ teaspoon pepper
2 cups peanut oil

1. Mix together the pork, eggs, bread crumbs, scallions, sautéed mushrooms, salt and pepper.

2. Heat the oil to 375°. Form pork mixture into 2-inch balls and fry for 3 minutes, or until golden brown. Drain on paper towels. Serve with sauce.

Sauce

1 tablespoon peanut oil
1 clove garlic, minced
1 green pepper, cut into strips
▶ 1 cup chicken stock, homemade
or canned
2 tablespoons red wine vinegar
1 tablespoon soy sauce
1 tablespoon brown sugar

1 can (8 oz.) pineapple chunks
(reserve juice)
½ cup sweet mixed pickles,
coarsely chopped
1 tablespoon cornstarch,
dissolved in 1 tablespoon water
1 tomato, cut into 8 wedges.

3. Heat the oil in large skillet or a wok. Add the garlic and green pepper and stir-fry for 3 minutes.

4. Add the stock, vinegar, soy sauce, sugar, and the juice from the canned pineapple. Bring to a boil; add the pineapple chunks and the pickles. Cook 2 to 3 minutes. Stir in the cornstarch, blend and add the tomato wedges. Stir to heat through. Makes 4 servings.

DEVILED HASH

3 tablespoons butter
▶ 2 cups diced cooked pork
▶ 1 cup diced cooked potato
1 medium onion, coarsely chopped
1 tablespoon flour
½ teaspoon salt

½ teaspoon pepper
▶ ¾ cup thin leftover gravy, or ⅔ cup beef or chicken stock, homemade or canned
1 teaspoon vinegar
1 teaspoon prepared mustard

1. In a large skillet, melt the butter. Add the pork and potatoes and brown lightly on all sides. Remove and set aside.

2. Sauté the onion in the same pan until golden brown; sprinkle with the flour, add salt and pepper and stir well. Cook, stirring, over medium heat for about 4 minutes or until flour is light brown. Stir in the gravy or stock, vinegar and mustard, blending well, and cook until smooth and thickened. Add the pork and potatoes and mix well. Makes 4 servings.

ITALIAN PORK SALAD

2 cups julienned fennel, or julienned celery
▶ 4 hard cooked egg yolks
1 tablespoon prepared Dijon-style mustard
½ cup olive oil
1 tablespoon white wine vinegar

½ teaspoon lemon juice
1 teaspoon salt
Few dashes cayenne
1 to 2 tablespoons heavy cream
1 head romaine lettuce, shredded
▶ 2 cups julienned cooked pork

1. Crisp the fennel by soaking in ice water for an hour. Make the dressing by mashing the egg yolks and mustard together to a smooth paste; beat in the olive oil slowly about ½ teaspoon at a time. The mixture should be the consistency of a thin mayonnaise. Stir in the vinegar and lemon juice; season with salt and cayenne. Lastly, stir in 1 tablespoon of the heavy cream, adding more cream if the dressing seems too thick.

2. Assemble the salad in a serving bowl by first putting in the lettuce, then the pork, then the drained and dried fennel or celery. Pour on the dressing and mix at the table. Makes 4 servings.

CHINESE PORK SALAD

3 cups thinly sliced green or Chinese cabbage
▶ ¾ cup cooked rice
▶ ⅔ cup cooked peas
▶ 2 cups diced cooked pork
⅓ cup sliced water chestnuts

2 tablespoons sliced scallions
2 tablespoons sesame oil
½ teaspoon celery salt
1 tablespoon soy sauce
Pepper to taste

In a large serving bowl, toss together the cabbage, rice, peas, pork, water chestnuts, and scallions. Combine the sesame oil, celery salt, soy sauce, and pepper; add to the salad and toss. Makes 4 servings.

PORK AND VEGETABLE SALAD

1 teaspoon prepared mustard
⅓ cup olive oil
  Salt and pepper
1 tablespoon wine vinegar
  Dash of sugar
1 tablespoon heavy cream
▶ 1 cup diced cooked pork

1 bunch of watercress, chopped
▶ 1 cup diced cooked potatoes
▶ 1 cup diced cooked beets
2 large unpeeled red apples, diced
1 sweet pickle, minced
¼ cup capers (optional)

1. Put the mustard in a small bowl and gradually beat in the oil. Season with salt and pepper and add the vinegar. Add the sugar and cream and mix well.

2. In a large glass bowl, mix the pork, watercress, potatoes, beets, apples, pickle, and capers. Drizzle on the dresing, mix well, and chill thoroughly. Makes 6 servings.

CHINESE FRIED RICE

½ cup peanut oil
▶ 4 cups cold cooked rice
▶ 2 cups shredded cooked pork
2 tablespoons soy sauce

Pepper to taste
3 eggs, lightly beaten
3 scallions, cut into ½-inch pieces and slivered lengthwise

1. In a large frying pan or wok, heat ⅓ cup of the peanut oil until it smokes. Add the rice and stir over moderate heat until grains are thoroughly coated with oil and begin to color slightly. Add the remaining oil if the rice seems dry. Mix in the pork and cook 3 to 4 minutes or until it is heated through. Stir in the soy sauce and season with pepper.

2. Pour the eggs over the rice and pork mixture. Cook over high heat, stirring, until the eggs are cooked. Just before serving, sprinkle with the scallions. Makes 4 to 6 servings.

TACOS WITH MEXICAN PORK

2 tablespoons butter or margarine
½ cup chopped onion
1 can (8 oz.) tomato sauce
2 tablespoons chopped green chilies
⅛ teaspoon cayenne pepper
1 teaspoon brown sugar
1 tablespoon lemon juice
1 medium clove garlic, minced

1 teaspoon Worcestershire sauce
1 teaspoon chili powder, or to taste
▶ 2 cups chopped cooked roast pork
8 taco shells
½ cup shredded lettuce
½ cup shredded Cheddar cheese

1. Melt the butter in a saucepan and sauté the onion until golden. Add the tomato sauce, chilies, cayenne, brown sugar, lemon juice, garlic, Worcestershire sauce, chili powder, and pork. Simmer for 15 minutes, stirring occasionally. Add more chili powder if needed.

2. Divide the mixture into the prepared taco shells. Top with some lettuce and sprinkle with cheese. Put briefly under the broiler, if desired, to melt the cheese. Makes 4 servings.

BARBECUED PORK SANDWICH

2 tablespoons vegetable oil
⅓ cup chopped onion
1 can (8 oz.) tomato sauce
4 tablespoons brown sugar
1 tablespoon Worcestershire
    sauce
⅛ teaspoon cayenne pepper

2 teaspoons lemon juice
1 tablespoon vinegar
2 teaspoons prepared mustard
⅛ teaspoon paprika
▶ 2 cups cubed cooked pork
4 sandwich buns, split and
    warmed

1. Heat oil in a heavy medium skillet and sauté onion until tender. Gradually add the tomato sauce, then the brown sugar, Worcestershire sauce, cayenne pepper, lemon juice, vinegar, mustard, and paprika. Simmer for 20 minutes, uncovered.

2. Add the pork and simmer, stirring frequently, until the pork has absorbed the flavor of the sauce. Spoon into the buns. Makes 4 servings.

▸LAMB

LAMB CASSEROLE

4 tablespoons butter or
  margarine
½ cup chopped onion
2 ribs celery, chopped
1 cup fresh or frozen peas
▶ 2 cups diced cooked lamb
1½ teaspoons Worcestershire
  sauce

▶ 2 cups medium thick gravy or
  white sauce (see Basics)
Salt and pepper
1 tablespoon chopped parsley
½ teaspoon ground thyme
1 cup shredded sharp Cheddar
  cheese

1. Melt the butter in an ovenproof skillet and sauté the onion, celery, and peas for 5 minutes. Add the lamb and sauté for 3 or 4 minutes; stir in Worcestershire sauce.

2. Blend the gravy or white sauce into the lamb mixture; salt and pepper to taste. Add the parsley and thyme; heat for 10 minutes. Sprinkle the top with cheese and place under the broiler until the cheese is melted. Makes 4 servings.

LAMB ROMANA

¼ cup olive oil
1½ cups sliced onions
1 garlic clove, minced
▶ 2 cups diced cooked lamb
▶ 1 cup cubed cooked eggplant
1 teaspoon salt
1 teaspoon dried basil

½ teaspoon pepper
1 can (28 oz.) plum tomatoes
  (with juice), chopped
▶ 2 cups cooked elbow macaroni
8 ounces Mozzarella cheese,
  sliced thin

1. In a large saucepan, heat olive oil and add onions and garlic. Stir and cook over medium heat for 5 minutes.

2. Add lamb to saucepan; stir and cook until lamb is brown. Add eggplant, salt, basil, pepper and tomatoes. Bring to a boil and stir.

3. Remove from heat, stir in macaroni and turn into a 2-quart casserole. Top with cheese. Bake, uncovered, in a preheated 350° oven for 30 minutes. Makes 4 servings.

BAKED ZUCCHINI WITH LAMB

4 tablespoons olive oil
1 medium onion, minced
4 medium zucchini, unpeeled
  and chopped
▶ 1 cup diced cooked lamb
▶ ½ cup cooked rice

⅓ cup grated Swiss cheese
½ cup chopped parsley
1 medium egg, beaten
Salt and pepper to taste
2 tablespoons bread crumbs

1. Heat 3 tablespoons of the oil in a medium skillet. Sauté the onion until soft. Add zucchini and cook, covered, 10 minutes over low heat, stirring occasionally. Remove from heat and allow to cool slightly.

2. Combine the lamb, rice, cheese, parlsey, egg, salt, and pepper. Add zucchini and mix well. Pour into greased 1½-quart baking dish. Mix the bread crumbs with the remaining 1 tablespoon of olive oil and sprinkle over the top. Bake at 375° for 20 minutes. Makes 6 servings.

LAMB PILAF

2 tablespoons olive oil or butter
1 cup uncooked rice
2 tablespoons minced scallions
▶ 2 cups beef broth or stock, homemade or canned
½ teaspoon salt
¼ teaspoon black pepper
2 tablespoons butter
1 large sweet red onion, chopped
1 medium green pepper, cut into strips
1 clove garlic, minced

▶ 2 to 2½ cups diced cooked lamb
½ cup chopped pine nuts, almonds, or walnuts
½ cup currants or seedless raisins
⅛ teaspoon cinnamon
¼ teaspoon ground allspice
Salt and pepper to taste
▶ 2 to 3 tablespoons thin lamb gravy or broth
1 tablespoon chopped fresh mint leaves, or 1 teaspoon dried mint leaves

1. Heat the oil in a deep, heavy saucepan; add the rice and scallions and stir over low heat until the grains are coated with oil. Do not allow to brown. Add the broth, salt, and pepper. Bring to a boil, cover tightly, and lower heat. Cook over low heat until rice is tender and all liquid has been absorbed—20 to 25 minutes.

2. Heat the 2 tablespoons butter in a heavy skillet. Add the onion, green pepper, and garlic. Cook, stirring frequently, over medium heat until vegetables are soft, but not browned. Add the lamb, nuts, currants, cinnamon, allspice, salt and pepper, and just enough gravy or broth to moisten. Cover skillet and cook over very low heat for 10 to 15 minutes. Stir in the mint. Combine with the rice, toss lightly, and serve. Makes 4 to 6 servings.

PERSIAN LAMB MOLD

2 eggplants (about 2 lbs. total), peeled and cut into ½-inch slices
1 tablespoon plus 1 teaspoon salt
½ cup flour
¾ cup (approximately) olive oil
2 cups thinly sliced onions
6 tablespoons slivered almonds
½ cup long grain rice (not converted)

▶ 1 cup ground cooked lamb
1 teaspoon minced garlic
½ teaspoon pepper
¼ teaspoon dried thyme
¼ teaspoon allspice
▶ ¾ cup beef or chicken stock, homemade or canned
1 cup yogurt
½ cup chopped cucumber
1 tablespoon minced dill
Few dashes cayenne

1. Sprinkle the eggplant slices with the 1 tablespoon salt and lay side by side on a large platter. After 1 hour, pat the slices dry and dip lightly in the flour, shaking to remove excess. In large frying pan, heat 3 tablespoons of the olive oil, and sauté the eggplant until brown but not cooked through. Use more oil as necessary. Transfer to a platter and keep warm.

2. In the same frying pan, add 2 tablespoons of the olive oil and saute' onions until golden, about 5 minutes. Add almonds and sauté for 3 more minutes. Transfer to a small bowl.

(continued)

3. Cook the rice in boiling water for 8 minutes. Drain and run cold water through it to stop the cooking.

4. In a small bowl, combine the lamb with the garlic, ½ teaspoon of the salt, pepper, thyme, and allspice; mix thoroughly.

5. Grease with olive oil a 1-quart mold with straight sides. Layer in this way: eggplant on the bottom, a layer of meat, a layer of the onion/ almond mixture, another layer of eggplant, the remaining meat, the remaining onion/almond mixture, and finish with the remaining eggplant. Spread the rice evenly over the top of the mold.

6. In a small saucepan, bring the stock to a boil and pour into the mold without disturbing the layers. Cover mold with foil and set in a pan filled with water. Bake in a preheated 350° oven for 1 hour; the rice should be completely cooked. Let rest for 5 minutes before unmolding.

7. Make the sauce by mixing together the yogurt, cucumber, dill, the remaining ½ teaspoon salt, and cayenne. Serve this dish hot or cold with the sauce (chilled) on the side. Makes 6 servings.

LAMB MADRAS

5 tablespoons butter
2 cups thinly sliced onions
1 teaspoon minced garlic
▶ 2 cups cubed cooked lamb
4 tablespoons lemon juice
1 teaspoon salt

2 to 3 tablespoons curry powder, (to taste) mixed with 1 tablespoon flour
1 tablespoon peanut oil
▶ 1 cup chicken or beef broth, homemade or canned
Cucumber Sauce

1. In a heavy casserole, melt 2 tablespoons of the butter over moderate heat. Add onions and garlic and sauté, stirring, for 10 minutes. Transfer to a small bowl.

2. Dip the cubed lamb in the lemon juice, sprinkle with salt and coat heavily with the curry powder/flour mixture.

3. In the casserole, heat the remaining 3 tablespoons butter and the peanut oil over moderate heat. Sauté the lamb, stirring, until golden brown. Return the cooked onion/garlic mixture to the casserole, add the broth; bring to a boil. Cover, bake in a 325° oven for 1 hour, or until dish has thickened to the consistency of a stew. Serve with Cucumber-Yogurt Sauce (recipe follows) and rice, if you wish. Makes 4 servings.

Cucumber Sauce

1 cup chopped cucumber
2 tablespoons fresh dill, minced or 1 teaspoon dried dill
1 teaspoon salt

¼ teaspoon cayenne
2 cups plain yogurt
2 teaspoons white wine vinegar

Mix all ingredients and serve with curry dishes. Keeps about 1 week in the refrigerator. Makes 3 cups.

MOUSSAKA DELPHI

2 medium eggplants, peeled carefully so the skin is in big pieces
½ cup olive oil (more if needed)
1 large onion, finely chopped and sautéed in 4 tablespoons butter
► 2 pounds chopped cooked lamb

½ pound mushrooms, chopped
5 tablespoons fresh bread crumbs
1 clove garlic, finely chopped
2 tablespoons chopped parsley
3 eggs
Dash of nutmeg
Salt and pepper to taste
¾ cup tomato purée

1. Cut 10 slices, ½-inch thick, from the eggplants and chop the rest. Sauté the chopped eggplant in ¼ cup olive oil; remove from the frying pan and reserve, and sauté the eggplant slices in the remaining oil until brown on both sides.

2. In a bowl, combine the chopped eggplant, the onion, lamb, mushrooms, bread crumbs, garlic, parsley, eggs, nutmeg, salt and pepper, and tomato purée. Mix well.

3. Oil a deep, round ovenproof mold and line it with the skin of the eggplant, purple side down. Put in a layer of the mixed meat and eggplant and then a layer of eggplant slices, then the meat mixture, and continue the layers until the casserole or mold is filled. Cover the top with more eggplant skin and stand the casserole in a pan of hot water. Bake in a 350° oven for 1 hour and 15 minutes. Let the mold stand outside of the hot water for a few minutes and then unmold on a large hot platter. Serve with a rice pilaf, if you wish. Makes 4 servings.

DEVON SHEPHERD'S PIE

2 tablespoons minced onion
1 small clove garlic, minced
½ cup thinly sliced celery
2 tablespoons butter
► 2 cups cubed cooked lamb
► 1 cup cooked peas
► 1 cup cooked carrots, if desired
► 3 cups lamb or beef gravy, thickened

¼ cup chopped parsley
½ teaspoon dried marjoram
½ teaspoon salt
⅛ teaspoon pepper
2 egg yolks, beaten
► 2 cups mashed potatoes
¼ cup shredded Cheddar cheese

1. Preheat the oven to 350°. In a large skillet, sauté the onion, garlic, and celery in butter until tender. Stir in the lamb, peas, carrots, gravy, parsley, marjoram, salt, and pepper. Pour into a 2-quart baking dish.

2. In a bowl, add the egg yolks to the mashed potatoes; beat well. Spoon the potatoes around the edge of the baking dish. Sprinkle with the Cheddar cheese. Bake 30 to 35 minutes. Makes 4 servings.

RICE MALAGA

1 medium Spanish onion, peeled and chopped
2 cloves garlic, peeled and minced
½ cup minced green pepper
⅓ cup olive oil
½ pound mushrooms, sliced thin
▶ 2 cups cubed cooked lamb
1½ cups uncooked rice
¾ teaspoon salt
¼ teaspoon freshly ground black pepper
¼ teaspoon paprika
⅛ teaspoon cayenne
⅛ teaspoon powdered saffron
¾ cup tomato sauce or purée
2 cans (10½ oz. each) chicken broth or bouillon
1½ cups fresh or frozen green peas

1. Stir-fry the onion, garlic, and green pepper in the oil in a shallow, flame-proof 2-quart casserole until the onion is limp and golden. Add the mushrooms and sauté until they're lightly browned. Mix in the lamb, rice, salt, pepper, paprika, cayenne, saffron, tomato sauce, and broth; cover and bake 35 minutes at 325°.

2. Stir in the peas; recover and bake 10 to 15 minutes longer, until the peas are tender and the rice has absorbed almost all the liquid. Serve with chunks of hot, crusty bread. Makes 6 servings.

SLAVIC LAMB CASSEROLE

▶ ½ cup cooked rice
3 slices bacon, cut into 1-inch pieces, partially fried and drained
▶ 8 thin slices cooked lamb
2 potatoes, peeled and thinly sliced
1 green pepper, thinly sliced
1 onion, quartered and thinly sliced
2 cloves garlic, minced
3 tomatoes, peeled, seeded, and chopped
Salt and freshly ground pepper to taste
▶ ¼ cup beef stock, homemade or canned
1 cup shredded sharp Cheddar cheese
1 tablespoon butter

1. Heat oven to 350°. In a greased, shallow 1½-quart casserole, layer, in order, rice, bacon, lamb, potatoes, green pepper, onion, garlic, and tomatoes. Generously sprinkle with salt and pepper to taste.

2. Pour stock over top. Cover with cheese and dot with butter. Cover and bake for 1 hour. Makes 4 to 6 servings.

SOUTHERN LAMB CASSEROLE

3 tablespoons vegetable oil
½ cup chopped onion
½ cup minced celery
1 cup minced green pepper
1 clove garlic, minced
▶ 1 cup cooked rice
▶ 2 cups diced cooked lamb
2 cups canned tomatoes
¼ teaspoon nutmeg
Salt
Pepper
2 dashes of Tabasco sauce

1. Heat the vegetable oil in a skillet and sauté the onion, celery, green pepper, and garlic for 5 minutes over medium heat.

2. Preheat oven to 350°. In a bowl, mix together the sautéed vegetables, the rice, lamb, tomatoes, and nutmeg. Season to taste with salt, pepper, and Tabasco sauce. Pour into a 2-quart baking dish and bake 30 minutes or until hot. Makes 4 servings.

TURKISH EGGPLANT WITH LAMB

1 large or 2 small eggplants	1 teaspoon salt
1 teaspoon salt	½ teaspoon pepper
¼ cup butter or margarine, melted	1½ teaspoons allspice
2 medium onions, sliced	▶ ½ cup cooked or canned chopped tomatoes
1 small green pepper, chopped	1 tablespoon tomato paste
1 clove garlic, chopped (optional)	▶ ½ cup chicken or beef broth
	1 tomato, thinly sliced (optional)
▶ 2 cups ground cooked lamb	¼ cup chopped parsley

1. Cut the eggplant into 2-inch thick slices, sprinkle with 1 teaspoon salt, and let stand ½ hour. Dry thoroughly. Brush lightly with butter and place on a baking sheet. Bake at 450° for 15 minutes, or until lightly browned.

2. In a large skillet, heat the remaining butter, sauté the onions, green pepper, garlic, and meat, until the vegetables are tender. Season with salt, pepper and allspice.

3. Place the eggplant slices close together in one layer in a baking dish. Cut slits 1 inch deep in each slice. Fill with the lamb mixture.

4. Stir together the tomatoes, tomato paste, and broth. Pour over the meat and eggplant. If desired, top each eggplant slice with a tomato slice. Bake at 375° for 30 minutes. Sprinkle with chopped parsley before serving. Makes 4 to 6 servings.

FRENCH LAMB CASSEROLE

4 cups diced peeled potatoes	Fresh or dried mint
4 strips bacon, cut in 1-inch crosswise pieces	Olive oil to taste
	1 green pepper, chopped
▶ 2 cups cubed cooked lamb	1 tomato, chopped
1 medium onion, finely chopped	¼ cup chopped parsley
3 cloves garlic, minced	¼ cup grated Parmesan cheese
Salt and pepper to taste	

1. Soak the potatoes in ice water as you prepare the other ingredients.

2. Arrange half of the bacon over the bottom of an oiled shallow 2½-quart baking dish, then add all the lamb. Spread the onion and half of the garlic. Salt well, pepper lightly, and sprinkle on some of the mint. Drizzle over a bit of oil to moisten. Drain and pat the potatoes dry. Arrange over the onions, then give another light sprinkling of salt, pepper, and mint and the remaining garlic. The remaining bacon goes on top of the seasonings, then the green pepper and tomato, and more salt and pepper, with a light gilding of oil on top.

3. Lay foil loosely over the top and bake in a preheated 425° oven for 15 minutes. Lower heat to 300° and bake 45 minutes longer, or until potatoes are done and lamb is tender. Sprinkle parsley and cheese on top and bake, uncovered, 10 minutes longer. Makes 6 to 8 servings.

LAMB AND LENTIL CASSEROLE

¼ cup diced bacon or salt pork
¼ cup finely chopped onion
▶ 2 cups chicken broth
▶ 1 cup beef broth or consommé
1½ cups canned tomatoes
1½ cups dried lentils
1 teaspoon minced garlic

1 tablespoon chopped parsley
1 small bay leaf
⅛ teaspoon dried thyme
  Salt to taste
⅛ teaspoon Tabasco or more to
  taste
▶ 2 cups cubed cooked lamb

1. Brown the bacon or salt pork in a large saucepan. Add the onions and sauté lightly. Add the chicken and beef broth, tomatoes, lentils, garlic, parsley, bay leaf, thyme, salt, and Tabasco. Simmer until the lentils are tender, about 1 to 1½ hours.

2. Preheat the oven to 350°. Add the lamb and pour the mixture into a casserole. Bake uncovered for 20 to 30 minutes. Makes 6 servings.

PIQUANT LAMB CASSEROLE

▶ 2 cups diced cooked lamb
¾ cup prepared stuffing mix
3 tablespoons butter
2 medium onions, coarsely
  chopped
1 tablespoon curry powder
½ teaspoon coriander
1 tablespoon flour

2 medium green apples, pared,
  cored, and sliced
1 tablespoon lemon juice
1 teaspoon sugar
½ teaspoon salt
¼ teaspoon pepper
▶ 1 cup beef broth
¼ cup milk or cream

1. Preheat the oven to 350°. Combine the lamb and the stuffing in a buttered 1-quart casserole.

2. Heat the butter in a skillet and sauté the onions until transparent. Stir in the curry powder, coriander, and flour. Add the apples, lemon juice sugar, salt, pepper, and broth. Bring to a boil, stirring.

3. Stir the milk into the sauce, then pour it over the lamb/stuffing mixture. Cover and bake 30 to 40 minutes. Makes 6 servings.

MILANESE RICE AND LAMB

4 tablespoons butter
½ large onion, minced
½ cup sliced mushrooms
¼ cup minced celery
1 cup uncooked rice
▶ 2 cups lamb broth or consommé

▶ 2 cups chopped cooked lamb
  Salt and pepper to taste
¼ cup slivered almonds
¼ to ½ teaspoon powdered
  saffron
½ cup grated Parmesan cheese

1. Melt the butter in a large, heavy skillet; add the onion, mushrooms, and celery, and sauté until soft. Add rice and sauté 6 minutes, stirring constantly; add the broth and lamb and stir. Cover tightly and simmer over very low heat 35 minutes or until rice is tender. Season with salt and pepper to taste.

2. Mix in the almonds, saffron, and cheese. Continue cooking until cheese is melted. Makes 4 servings.

GREEK MOUSSAKA

3 medium-size eggplant
Salt
2 cups finely minced onion (2 large)
¾ cup butter or margarine
▶ 3 cups minced cooked lamb
1 clove garlic, finely minced
1 can (16 oz.) tomatoes, drained
1 can (8 oz.) tomato sauce

¼ cup chopped parsley
2 teaspoons salt
½ teaspoon ground cinnamon
¼ cup all-purpose flour
2 cups milk
Dash of nutmeg
1 cup ricotta or cottage cheese
3 eggs, beaten

1. Pare the eggplant and cut lengthwise in ½-inch-thick slices. Sprinkle with salt; set aside to draw out excess liquid.

2. In a skillet, cook the onion in 3 tablespoons of the butter over medium heat until soft. Add the lamb, garlic, tomatoes, tomato sauce, parsley, 1 teaspoon of the salt, and the cinnamon. Cook, stirring, until most of the moisture disappears.

3. Dry the eggplant. Brown on both sides in butter, using 2 tablespoons per batch. Blend the flour into 2 tablespoons melted butter in a saucepan. Cook 1 minute, stirring constantly. Add the milk, the remaining 1 teaspoon salt, and the nutmeg. Bring to boiling, stirring. Boil 1 minute; cool slightly. Stir in the cheese and the eggs.

4. Heat the oven to 375°. Layer half the eggplant in a 13 × 9 × 2-inch baking dish. Spoon half the meat mixture over the eggplant. Repeat layers. Spoon on the cheese sauce. Bake 30 minutes. Brown under the broiler. Let stand 15 minutes. Makes 6 to 8 servings.

SAUTÉED LAMB AND VEGETABLES MÉDITERRANÉE

▶2½ cups cubed cooked lamb
2 tablespoons olive or vegetable oil
1 tablespoon minced shallots or scallions
1 tablespoon chopped dill, or ½ teaspoon dillweed
2 cloves garlic, minced
2 teaspoons fresh lemon juice
4 leeks, cut into ¼-inch slices

2 small zucchini, sliced
1 green pepper, coarsely chopped
Salt and pepper to taste
4 tomatoes, peeled and cut into 6 wedges each
2 tablespoons minced fresh parsley
1 tablespoon chopped chives

1. Sauté lamb in hot oil in a large skillet until lightly browned. Reduce heat; mix in the shallots, dill, garlic, and lemon juice. Cook for 2 minutes; add leeks, zucchini, and green pepper; salt and pepper to taste.

2. Cover and cook for 8 to 10 minutes, stirring until zucchini is crisp-tender. Add the tomatoes, cover, and cook 2 to 3 minutes longer to heat through. Spoon meat and vegetables onto warm platter and pour pan juices over the top. Sprinkle with the parsley and chives and serve over hot rice. Makes 6 servings.

LAMB CACCIATORA MILANO

6 tablespoons olive oil
2 cups cubed cooked lamb
    Salt to taste
    Freshly ground black pepper
1 teaspoon dried marjoram
1 tablespoon flour
1 medium onion, chopped
1 large clove garlic, chopped

2 tablespoons red wine
    vinegar
¾ to 1 cup chicken stock,
    homemade or canned
2 anchovy fillets, drained,
    and finely chopped
1 tablespoon finely chopped
    parsley

1. Heat 4 tablespoons of the olive oil in a large saucepan; add the lamb, and quickly sauté over high heat until lightly browned. Add the salt, a few grindings of black pepper, the rosemary, and the flour; mix thoroughly. Cook the lamb over medium heat for 5 to 10 minutes.

2. Heat the remaining olive oil in a frying pan, add the onions and garlic and sauté, stirring constantly, until translucent. Add the vinegar, turn the heat up high, and boil the liquid away almost completely. Stir in ¾ cup of the stock and combine with the lamb. Turn mixture into a 1-quart casserole; cover tightly and put into a preheated 325° oven and cook for about 30 minutes, checking occasionally. If the sauce thickens too much, thin with a few tablespoons of stock.

3. Fifteen minutes before serving, remove 4 tablespoons of sauce from the casserole and combine with the chopped anchovies in a small bowl, beating until the anchovies almost completely dissolve. Stir the mixture into the saucepan and simmer 10 minutes longer. Serve the lamb arranged on a hot platter with buttered noodles, garnished with chopped parsley. Makes 4 servings.

LAMB SAVOURY

2 cups diced cooked lamb
2 hard-cooked eggs, chopped
2 tablespoons olive oil
1 tablespoon lemon juice
2 tablespoons butter

3 tablespoons flour
1 teaspoon dry mustard
2 cups milk
1 teaspoon Worcestershire sauce
    Salt to taste

1. Mix the lamb and eggs with the olive oil and lemon juice.

2. In a frying pan, melt the butter; stir in the flour and the mustard. Cook for 1 minute. Add milk; cook for 5 minutes. Add Worcestershire sauce and salt.

3. Add lamb mixture and heat through. Serve on toast. Makes 4 servings.

LAMB TUNIS

2 tablespoons butter
½ cup finely chopped onion
1 cup coarsely chopped celery
1 tablespoon minced parsley
▶ 3 cups cubed cooked lamb
▶ 1 cup lamb gravy or cream of
   mushroom soup

½ cup sliced mushrooms
1 cup water
½ cup chopped dried apricots
¼ teaspoon poultry seasoning
   Salt and pepper
1 tablespoon flour

1. In a medium saucepan, melt the butter and add the onion, celery, and parsley; cook for 5 minutes, stirring occasionally. Add the lamb, gravy, mushrooms, water, and apricots. Season with the poultry seasoning, and salt and pepper to taste. Cover and simmer 25 minutes.

2. Blend flour with a little cold water to form a paste; add to the lamb mixture. Cook and stir until thickened. Serve over rice or noodles. Makes 6 servings.

AFRICAN LAMB

1 large onion, chopped
1 clove garlic, mashed
2 tablespoons olive oil
1 medium eggplant, peeled, cut
   into 1-inch cubes
1 cup canned tomatoes
1 tablespoon tomato paste
1 bay leaf

½ teaspoon dried chervil
½ teaspoon dried basil
¼ teaspoon dried marjoram
1 teaspoon salt
½ teaspoon pepper
▶ 2 cups coarsely chopped
   cooked lamb
¼ cup pine nuts

1. Sauté onion and garlic in olive oil in a medium, heavy skillet. Add eggplant; cook 5 minutes, stirring frequently.

2. Add tomatoes, tomato paste, bay leaf, chervil, basil, marjoram, salt and pepper. Cover; simmer 12 minutes or until eggplant is soft. Stir in lamb and heat thoroughly. Serve over rice, if you wish. Garnish with pine nuts. Makes 4 servings.

LAMB POLSKI

1½ tablespoons butter
1 medium onion, thinly sliced
1 cup sliced mushrooms
▶ 2 cups cubed cooked lamb
1 tablespoon flour
1 tablespoon paprika

½ teaspoon pepper
▶ ½ cup beef or chicken stock,
   homemade or canned
½ cup sour cream
1 tablespoon minced parsley

1. Melt the butter in a large skillet, and sauté the onion for 5 minutes, until transparent. Add the mushrooms and sauté 5 minutes more. Set aside in a small bowl.

(continued)

2. Add the lamb to the skillet and brown lightly, about 10 minutes. Stir in the flour, paprika, and pepper; stir and sauté for about 3 minutes, until flour browns. Add the stock and bring to a boil. Reduce heat and simmer, stirring constantly, 10 minutes. Off the heat, stir in the sour cream until blended. Garnish with parsley. Makes 4 servings.

LAMB NAVARIN

2 tablespoons butter
2 medium onions, sliced
1 small clove garlic, minced
2 small green peppers, diced
¼ cup chopped celery
▶ 1 cup lamb gravy

▶ ½ cup diced cooked carrots
¼ cup dry white wine
Salt and pepper to taste
▶ 2 cups cubed cooked lamb, all
fat removed
1 tablespoon minced parsley

1. Heat the butter to sizzling in a medium-size skillet and add onions, garlic, green peppers, celery. Cook, stirring constantly, until light brown, about 10 minutes.

2. Add the gravy, carrots, and wine; season with salt and pepper. Add the lamb cubes; stir gently. Cover and heat to boiling over low heat. Sprinkle with parsley and serve. Makes 4 servings.

CURRY OF LAMB POONA

2 tablespoons olive oil
2 medium onions, sliced
1 green pepper, chopped
1 clove garlic, minced
2 medium cooking apples,
pared, cored, and sliced
▶ 2 cups diced cooked lamb
2 tablespoons flour
1¼ tablespoons curry powder
½ teaspoon salt

⅛ teaspoon dried thyme
▶1½ cup chicken broth, homemade
or canned
1½ teaspoons grated lemon rind
3 tablespoons lemon juice
½ cup raisins
⅛ teaspoon ground cloves
¼ cup shredded coconut
2 tablespoons chopped peanuts
Hot boiled rice

1. Heat the oil in a large skillet. Add the onions, green pepper, garlic, apples, and lamb. Sauté, stirring frequently, about 5 minutes or until onions are soft. With a slotted spoon remove lamb and set aside.

2. Combine the flour, curry powder, salt, and thyme. Stir into skillet. Cook over low heat, stirring frequently, about 5 minutes.

3. Stir in the chicken broth, lemon rind, lemon juice, raisins, and cloves. Cover and simmer over low heat, stirring occasionally, for 20 to 25 minutes.

4. Return meat to skillet. Stir in the coconut and peanuts. Heat through. Serve over hot boiled rice. Makes 6 servings.

SKILLET-QUICK LAMB AND EGGPLANT

¼ cup olive oil
1 medium-sized eggplant, pared and diced
1 tablespoon leaf oregano
2 cloves garlic, minced
2 teaspoons curry powder
1½ teaspoons dried thyme
1 teaspoon ground cardamom
½ teaspoon leaf sage

1 cup canned tomatoes, diced (with juice)
1 medium green pepper, diced
1 tablespoon lemon juice
4 tablespoons chopped parsley
▶ 2 cups ground or minced cooked lamb
Freshly cooked rice or noodles
2 tablespoons pine nuts

1. In a large skillet, heat olive oil and add eggplant, oregano, garlic, curry powder, thyme, cardamom, and sage. Cook over medium heat, stirring occasionally, about 10 minutes or until eggplant is tender.

2. Add tomatoes and green pepper; cook 5 minutes more. Stir in lemon juice and 2 tablespoons of the parsley. Stir in the lamb and heat through.

3. Serve over rice or noodles and sprinke with remaining parsley and pine nuts. Makes 6 servings.

SPANISH LAMB STEW

2 tablespoons butter or margarine
½ cup chopped onion
½ cup chopped celery
▶ 1 cup lamb broth, or consommé
▶ 1 cup cooked peas
▶ 2 cups cubed cooked lamb

▶1⅔ cups diced cooked potatoes
1 cup canned tomatoes
1 teaspoon chili powder
½ teaspoon salt (or to taste)
⅛ teaspoon paprika
Hot cooked rice
Parlsey sprigs

1. Melt butter in a large skillet; add onion and celery and cook over low heat 5 to 6 minutes. Add the broth, peas, lamb, potatoes, tomatoes, chili powder, salt, and paprika.

2. Cover and simmer over low heat for 15 minutes, stirring occasionally, until thoroughly heated. Serve over hot rice; garnish with parsley. Makes 4 servings.

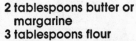

LAMB IN LEMON-DILL SAUCE

2 tablespoons butter or margarine
3 tablespoons flour
▶ 2 cups chicken or beef broth
1 teaspoon dried dillweed
2½ teaspoons sugar
2 tablespoons lemon juice
½ teaspoon salt

1 egg yolk
Salt and pepper to taste
▶ 2 cups cubed cooked lamb
▶ 1 cup cooked peas
Hot cooked noodles or rice
Parsley sprigs for garnish
Fresh lemon slices

1. Melt the butter in a saucepan over low heat. Stir in the flour. Cook, stirring constantly, until thick.

2. Gradually stir or whisk in the broth. Bring to a boil. Lower heat. Simmer, stirring, until smooth and thickened, about 8 to 10 minutes.

(continued)

3. Add the dillweed, sugar, lemon juice, and the ½ teaspoon salt.

4. Beat the egg yolk in a medium bowl. Stir or whisk in ¼ cup of the hot sauce until blended, then return mixture to pan, stirring constantly. Add lamb, peas, and salt and pepper to taste. Heat through (do not boil).

5. Serve on noodles or rice; garnish with parsley and lemon slices. Makes 4 servings.

 ## BARBECUED LAMB ON MASHED POTATO

1 large onion, chopped
¾ cup tomato sauce
▶ ½ cup chicken or beef broth
1 tablespoon brown sugar
1 tablespoon vinegar
2 tablespoons Worcestershire sauce

⅛ teaspoon dried thyme or oregano
½ teaspoon salt
⅛ teaspoon ground red pepper
▶ 2 cups cubed cooked lamb
Hot mashed potatoes

Combine the onion, tomato sauce, broth, sugar, vinegar, Worcestershire sauce, thyme, salt, and red pepper in skillet and cook over moderate heat for 5 minutes. Add the lamb; cover and simmer for 15 minutes. Serve over the potatoes. Makes 4 servings.

 ## QUICK LAMB CURRY

1 tablespoon vegetable oil
1 cup diced apple
¼ cup chopped onion
1 tomato, peeled and chopped
1 to 2 teaspoons curry powder
¼ teaspoon salt

½ cup milk
1 can (10½ oz.) condensed cream of chicken soup
▶ 2 cups cubed cooked lamb
1 cup sour cream
Hot cooked rice

1. In a medium-size skillet, heat the oil and sauté the apple, onion, tomato, curry powder, and salt for 5 minutes. Stir in milk and soup; blend until smooth. Add lamb and simmer 10 minutes.

2. Stir in sour cream; heat but do not boil. Serve over hot rice with the traditional curry accompaniments: chutney, raisins, french-fried onion rings, chopped hard-boiled eggs, diced bananas, chopped green pepper, sliced scallions, etc. Makes 4 servings.

 ## STUFFED LAMB ROLLS

½ cup prepared seasoned bread stuffing mix
▶ 6 large, very thin slices cooked lamb
▶ ½ cup lamb gravy, medium thick

2 tablespoons red currant jelly
¾ teaspoon salt
¼ teaspoon pepper
1 tablespoon chopped sour pickles

1. Heat the oven to 400°. Place a spoonful of the stuffing on each slice of meat. Roll up the slices, tie with string, or fasten with wooden picks. Place in a shallow, greased 1-quart baking dish.

2. Heat the gravy and the jelly in a saucepan; when jelly is dissolved, pour the mixture over the rolls. Season with the salt and pepper. Sprinkle the pickles over the rolls. Bake 15 minutes, basting several times. Makes 6 servings.

ACORN SQUASH STUFFED WITH PEANUT AND PEPPER PILAF

5 tablespoons butter
2 medium acorn squash
3 tablespoons olive oil
1 large Spanish onion, chopped
1 small green pepper, seeded and chopped
1 small red pepper, seeded and chopped
1 cup coarsely chopped roasted peanuts
3 tablespoons cider vinegar
2 tablespoons brown sugar
► 2 to 2½ cups cooked rice
►1½ cups diced cooked lamb
► Chicken or beef broth, homemade or canned
¼ cup grated Parmesan cheese

1. Melt 2 tablespoons of the butter. Cut the squash in half, remove the seeds, and brush the cut surface with the melted butter. Place the squash in a roasting pan filled with 1-inch hot water; cover pan tightly and bake in a preheated 350° oven for 45 mintues to 1 hour, until squash is tender.

2. When the squash is cooked, carefully scoop out some of the flesh, leaving shells about ¼-inch thick. Cube the squash pulp.

3. Heat the remaining butter with the oil in a large skillet, and sauté the onion and peppers until tender. Add the peanuts, vinegar, sugar, squash, rice and meat. Simmer, stirring, about 10 minutes until the mixture is hot. Add broth to moisten if mixture seems dry.

4. Divide the mixture among the 4 squash halves, heaping lightly. Sprinkle with the cheese and broil until light golden. Makes 4 servings.

EGGPLANT STUFFED WITH LAMB

3 small eggplants
3 tablespoons olive oil
1 medium onion, chopped
2 tomatoes, peeled and chopped
► 2 cups cooked rice
► 2 cups diced cooked lamb
2 tablespoons tomato sauce
Dash nutmeg
1 large clove garlic, minced
2 teaspoons chopped parsley
Salt and pepper to taste
1 egg
6 thin tomato slices
½ cup grated Parmesan cheese
¼ cup bread crumbs

1. Parboil eggplants, cut in half lengthwise, for 10 minutes in salted water. Drain, and scoop out the pulp; dice pulp and reserve shells. Heat the oil in a large heavy skillet and sauté onion until golden; mix in the tomatoes. Add the eggplant pulp, rice, lamb, tomato sauce, nutmeg, garlic, parsley, and salt and pepper to taste. Simmer over low heat for 10 minutes; remove from heat and gently mix in the egg.

2. Place the reserved eggplant shells in a large, shallow casserole dish. Mound the lamb mixture into the shells and place the tomato slices on top. Dust with cheese and bread crumbs. Bake at 350° for 25 minutes. Makes 6 servings.

ONIONS STUFFED WITH LAMB

4 large onions
► 2 cups finely chopped cooked lamb
► 1 cup cooked rice
1 tablespoon butter, melted
1 teaspoon minced parsley
¼ cup diced mushrooms

½ cup coarsely ground pine nuts or peanuts
¼ teaspoon salt
¼ teaspoon pepper
¼ teaspoon paprika
1 tablespoon tomato sauce
¾ cup consommé

1. Peel the onions and cut a thick slice from the top of each. Place the onions and the top slices in a saucepan and cover with water. Bring to a boil and cook until just tender. Drain and scoop out the centers of the onions; place onions in a 1-quart baking dish.

2. Combine lamb with rice, butter, parsley, mushrooms, nuts, salt, pepper, and paprika; mix well. Heap lamb mixture into onions, and cover with top slices. Mix together the tomato sauce and consommé; pour over lamb mixture. Bake at 350° for 20 minutes. Makes 4 servings.

LAMB-STUFFED GRAPE LEAVES IN LEMON-EGG SAUCE

1 jar (16 oz.) grape leaves
2 tablespoons olive oil
1 tablespoon butter
1 cup finely chopped onion
1 small clove garlic, minced
► 1 cup finely diced or ground cooked lamb
► 1½ cups cooked long-grain rice
1 teaspoon crumbled mint leaves

2 tablespoons coarsely chopped pine nuts or peanuts
⅛ teaspoon allspice
1 teaspoon chopped parsley
1 teaspoon salt
½ teaspoon pepper
► 2 to 2½ cups chicken stock
2 tablespoons melted butter
2 egg yolks
⅓ cup lemon juice
Salt to taste

1. Place grape leaves in colander and rinse under warm water to separate. Spread them out on paper toweling to dry. Heat the oil and butter in a large saucepan, add the onion and garlic, and sauté over moderate heat until vegetables are limp. Remove from heat and stir in the lamb, rice, mint, nuts, allspice, parsley, salt, and pepper.

2. Place grape leaves, glossy side down, on a flat surface and spoon no more than 2 teaspoons of the filling on each leaf; tightly fold edges in around the stuffing and roll toward point of leaf. Cover bottom of long shallow pan with crumbled grape leaves and place filled leaves in layers on top. In a saucepan, heat stock to boiling; pour the stock and the melted butter over the grape leaves. Place a heavy platter or plate directly on top of rolls, cover with aluminum foil and seal tightly. Place in a preheated 350° oven and bake for 30 minutes.

3. Transfer rolls from baking pan to heated platter and keep warm. In a mixing bowl, beat the egg yolks until very light, then beat in the lemon juice and beat a full minute. Add 3 tablespoons of the hot stock from the baking pan, blend well, season to taste with salt, and slowly stir into the stock remaining in the baking pan. Pour over the stuffed grape leaves. Makes 6 servings.

STUFFED ZUCCHINI IN CREAM SAUCE

6 medium zucchini or 6 3-inch slices of large zucchini
3 tablespoons olive oil
▶ 2 cups minced cooked lamb
1 large clove garlic, minced
½ cup chopped onion
½ teaspoon oregano
1 teaspoon salt

▶ 1½ cups cooked rice
2 tablespoons butter
2 tablespoons flour
1 cup light cream or evaporated milk
¼ teaspoon nutmeg
½ cup shredded Swiss cheese

1. Parboil zucchini and scoop out the pulp, leaving about ½-inch shell; reserve zucchini pulp. In large skillet, heat the olive oil and sauté the lamb, garlic, onion, oregano, and salt. Pour off fat. Add the zucchini pulp; simmer for 10 minutes, stirring occasionally. Stir in the rice and mix well.

2. Melt the butter in a medium saucepan; stir in the flour and cook until the mixture is smooth. Add the cream and nutmeg and stir, cooking until the sauce thickens. Mound meat mixture into zucchini shells and place in a greased baking dish. Pour the sauce over the zucchini and bake at 350° for 20 minutes. Sprinkle the cheese over the top and bake 5 more minutes. Makes 4 to 6 servings.

SAMOSAS (Curried Meat Turnovers)

¼ cup minced onion
2 tablespoons butter or margarine
¼ teaspoon each of garlic powder, ground cinnamon, ground ginger and cayenne
1 teaspoon ground coriander
¼ cup chopped fresh or canned, drained tomato
▶ 1½ cups ground cooked lamb

1¼ teaspoons salt
1 tablespoon lemon juice
2 cups sifted all-purpose flour
1 teaspoon salt
¼ cup melted butter or margarine
7 tablespoons yogurt
Egg white, beaten slightly
Vegetable oil for frying

1. In a large skillet, sauté the onion in butter with the garlic powder, cinnamon, ginger, cayenne, and coriander until tender. Add the tomato, lamb, salt, and lemon juice. Cook a few minutes to blend flavors. Cool.

2. Sift the flour and salt into a bowl, Blend in the melted butter. Mix in the yogurt to make a dough; knead until smooth.

3. Roll the dough very thin on a lightly floured board. Cut into circles with a 2½-inch cookie cutter. Brush the edges lightly with beaten egg white. Place a rounded ½ teaspoon of the lamb mixture in the center of each. Fold over the dough and crimp the edges with a fork, being sure they are well sealed.

4. Fry in hot deep fat (360° to 375° on a frying thermometer) until golden-brown. Drain on absorbent paper. Or, if desired, place on baking sheets and bake at 400° until brown. Makes about 60 turnovers.

LAMB AND SAUSAGE PIE

1 tablespoon butter
2 sweet Italian sausages, sliced
▶1½ cups cubed cooked lamb
2 carrots, chopped
2 medium onions, chopped
1 stalk celery, chopped
½ cup chopped fresh parsley
½ cup shredded red cabbage

3 tablespoons flour
▶1½ cups chicken broth
1 cup white wine
1 teaspoon salt
½ teaspoon pepper
½ teaspoon dried thyme
Pie dough for 1-crust pie (see Basics)

1. Heat the butter in a large skillet and brown the sausage pieces. Add the lamb, carrots, onions, celery, parsley, and cabbage and sauté, stirring, for 5 minutes more.

2. Sprinkle on the flour and stir well. Add the broth, wine, salt, pepper, and thyme. Bring to a boil; simmer 10 minutes, stirring occasionally.

3. Preheat the oven to 375°. Pour the mixture into a shallow 1½-quart baking dish. Roll out the pie dough to cover the dish. Lay the dough over the dish and seal the edges. Bake until the top is browned, 20 to 30 minutes. Makes 4 to 6 servings.

LAMB TURNOVERS

¼ cup finely chopped green pepper
¼ cup minced scallions
2 tablespoons minced celery
1 clove garlic, minced
1 tablespoon vegetable oil
▶ 1 cup finely chopped cooked lamb
¾ cup chopped well drained canned Italian tomatoes
¼ cup dry bread crumbs
2 tablespoons tomato paste

2 tablespoons minced fresh parsley
2 teaspoons minced fresh mint or ½ teaspoon dried mint, or ½ teaspoon dried basil
Salt and Tabasco sauce to taste
2 eggs, lightly beaten
Pie dough for 2-crust pie (see Basics)
1 egg white
1 tablespoon water

1. Sauté the green pepper, scallions, celery and garlic in oil for 1 or 2 minutes. Cool slightly.

2. Add the lamb, tomatoes, bread crumbs, tomato paste, parsley, mint or basil, salt, Tabasco sauce, and eggs. Stir well.

3. Preheat the oven to 425°. Roll out the dough and cut 12 5-inch squares. Place about 2½ tablespoons of the lamb mixture in the center of each. Moisten the edges lightly with the egg white beaten with the water. Fold over diagonally into triangles and crimp the edges well with a fork.

4. Place on baking sheets and brush the tops with the egg white mixture. Cut slits in the tops to let steam escape. Bake until browned, about 20 minutes. Makes 12 turnovers.

ARMENIAN LAMB PIES

1 package dry yeast
½ cup lukewarm water
¼ cup vegetable shortening,
   melted and cooled to
   lukewarm
½ teaspoon salt
½ teaspoon sugar
2 cups flour
1 tablespoon butter, softened
► 1 cup firmly packed ground
   cooked lamb
¼ cup finely chopped onions
1 teaspoon minced garlic
3 tablespoons finely chopped
   green pepper

2½ tablespoons minced parsley
1 tablespoon minced fresh mint,
   or 1 teaspoon dried mint
1 teaspoon ground coriander
4 teaspoons tomato paste
¾ cup fresh tomatoes, peeled,
   seeded, and finely chopped;
   or ¾ can (8 oz.) tomatoes,
   drained and finely
   chopped
½ teaspoon dried red pepper
   flakes or ¼ teaspoon Tabasco,
   or to taste
½ teaspoon salt, or to taste

1. Dissolve the yeast in the lukewarm water and stir in the shortening, salt, and sugar. Combine slowly with the flour in a large mixing bowl. On a floured board, knead the dough until it is smooth, shiny, and elastic. Form into a ball and cut a cross into the top.

2. Set it back into the bowl, sprinkle lightly with flour, and cover with a damp dish towel. Let the dough rise in a warm place for about 2 hours, or until the dough doubles in bulk. Punch it down and let it rest for another 10 minutes, then roll the dough out, about ¼-inch thick, on a floured board. Cut it into 2½-inch rounds for cocktail snacks, or 5-inch rounds for meals. Place the rounds on a buttered baking sheet.

3. Mix the ground lamb, onion, garlic, green pepper, parsley, mint, coriander, tomato paste, tomatoes, red peppers, and salt until they are thoroughly combined. Cover each round of pastry with approximately a ½-inch layer of filling and bake at 425° for about 20 minutes, or until crisp and brown. Slide them under a hot broiler for a few seconds, just before serving. Makes 4 to 6 servings.

LAMB-MACARONI QUICHE

► 1 cup cooked macaroni
► 1 cup finely chopped cooked
   lamb
1 teaspoon minced onion
2 teaspoons minced parsley
⅛ teaspoon celery salt

⅛ teaspoon garlic salt
½ teaspoon Worcestershire sauce
1 cup milk
½ cup light cream
3 eggs, lightly beaten
¼ cup grated Parmesan cheese

1. Spread macaroni in a well-greased 1½-quart baking dish. Mix the lamb with the onion, parsley, celery salt, garlic salt, and Worcestershire sauce. Arrange in a layer over macaroni.

2. Combine milk, cream, and eggs and pour over meat. Bake for 25 minutes in a preheated 350° oven. Sprinkle with the cheese; bake 5 minutes longer or until firm. Makes 4 servings.

LAMB BISCUIT ROLL

½ cup minced onion
3 tablespoons butter or oil
½ cup chopped mushrooms
▶ 2 cups ground cooked lamb
2 tablespoons chopped stuffed olives
2 tablespoons chopped sweet pickles

1 tablespoon chopped parsley
¼ teaspoon dry mustard
¾ teaspoon salt
¼ teaspoon pepper
Biscuit dough made with 2 cups flour (see Basics)
1 tablespoon milk
▶ Leftover gravy

1. In a large skillet, sauté the onion in the butter until nearly tender. Add the mushrooms and sauté another 3 to 4 minutes. Stir in the lamb, olives, pickles, parsley, mustard, salt and pepper. Cook 5 minutes, then cool.

2. Roll out the biscuit dough into a rectangle ¼ inch thick. Spread the lamb mixture over the dough, leaving a 1-inch margin around the edges. Roll up like a jelly roll.

3. Preheat the oven to 425°. Place the roll in a greased, shallow baking pan, seam side down. Brush the top with milk. Bake for about 30 minutes, until brown. Serve with gravy seasoned with a little mustard. Makes 6 servings.

LAMB AND MUSHROOM CRÊPES

½ cup butter or margarine
6 tablespoons flour
▶ 2 cups chicken stock, homemade or canned
2 egg yolks
1 cup light cream
Salt and white pepper to taste
1 teaspoon fresh lemon juice
3 tablespoons chopped shallots or scallions

1 cup chopped mushrooms
¼ cup dry white wine
▶ 2 cups chopped cooked lamb
1 tablespoon minced parsley
½ teaspoon dried rosemary
16 to 20 crêpes (see Basics)
4 tablespoons grated Swiss or Parmesan cheese

1. Melt 4 tablespoons of the butter in a saucepan and stir in the flour. Cook 1 minute. Add stock and bring to a boil. Lower heat to a simmer and cook 5 minutes. In a bowl, combine the egg yolks with ½ cup of the cream and mix well. Stir in a few tablespoons of the hot sauce. Pour the egg mixture back into the saucepan, stirring. Simmer for 1 minute. Add salt and pepper and lemon juice. Remove pan from heat.

2. Melt 2 tablespoons of the butter in a small frying pan and add the shallots. Sauté for 1 minute; mix in the mushrooms. Cook over low heat, stirring, for about 5 minutes. Pour in the wine, stirring constantly, and cook for another 5 minutes. Place in a mixing bowl.

3. Add to the mushrooms, the lamb, parsley, rosemary, and 1 cup of the reserved sauce. Spread a scant 2 tablespoons of the chicken mixture across the lower third of each crêpe and roll up. Lay side by side in a buttered baking dish. Thin the remaining sauce with the remaining ½ cup cream and pour over the crêpes. Sprinkle the grated cheese over the top and dot with the remaining 2 tablespoons butter. Bake in a 375° oven for 20 minutes, until sauce begins to bubble. Makes 4 to 6 servings.

POTATO AND LAMB FRITTERS

½ cup corn or peanut oil
2 cups peeled and minced
 baking potatoes
¼ cup minced shallots or onions
1 clove garlic, minced
▶ 1 cup finely ground cooked
 lamb

2 large eggs
¾ teaspoon salt
¼ teaspoon ground pepper
⅓ teaspoon fresh grated ginger
¼ teaspoon fresh grated nutmeg

1. Heat 2 tablespoons of the oil in a large skillet over moderate heat; add the potatoes, shallots, and garlic, and cook, stirring constantly, until the potatoes are lightly browned, but not crisp. Remove from the heat and cool for 5 minutes. Add the lamb, 1 egg, salt, pepper, ginger, and nutmeg, and stir to form a batter.

2. Shape the mixture into round balls, about 1-inch in diameter, and then flatten them into discs about ½-inch thick. Beat the remaining egg in a small dish. Heat the remaining oil in the skillet over moderate heat. Dip the fritters, one at a time, into the egg and fry them, taking care not to crowd them, for about 2½ minutes on each side, turning them carefully. Drain on paper towels. Serve with rice. Makes 4 servings.

CREAMED LAMB IN PUFF SHELLS

Puff Shells

½ cup water
¼ cup butter
¼ teaspoon salt
½ cup flour
2 eggs

Sauce

2 tablespoons butter or
 margarine

¼ cup all-purpose flour
2 cups milk
½ teaspoon salt
 Dash of pepper
1 teaspoon Worcestershire sauce
½ green pepper, minced
2 tablespoons chopped
 pimiento
▶ 2 cups cubed cooked lamb

1. To make the shells: combine the water, butter, and salt in a saucepan and bring to a boil. Add the flour all at once and cook, stirring constantly, until the mixture leaves sides of pan. Remove from the heat and cool 5 minutes. Add the eggs, one at a time, beating thoroughly after each addition.

2. Heap the dough in 6 mounds on a greased cookie sheet. Bake in a preheated 450° oven for 15 minutes, then turn the heat to 375° and bake 20 to 30 minutes more, until the shells are brown and crisp.

3. To make the sauce: melt the butter in a saucepan; blend in the flour and cook for 1 minute. Gradually stir in the milk; cook, stirring constantly, until smooth and thickened. Add the salt, pepper, Worcestershire sauce, green pepper, pimiento, and lamb. Cook until heated through.

4. Cut a small piece from the top of each of the puff shells. Fill with the creamed lamb. Makes 6 servings.

LAMB AND RATATOUILLE ALEXANDRIA

2 tablespoons butter
1 cup shredded Romano cheese
1 cup shredded Mozzarella cheese
2 cloves garlic, peeled and finely chopped
1 small onion, peeled and cut in half
1 tablespoon vegetable oil
▶ 2 cups coarsely chopped cooked lamb

1½ teaspoons dried oregano
1 teaspoon cinnamon
4 large eggs
1 cup heavy cream
½ teaspoon salt
⅓ cup plain yogurt
▶ 3 cups Ratatouille, well drained
¼ cup lightly packed, minced fresh parsley leaves
6 large scallions, sliced

1. Grease a 7-cup ovenproof baking dish with the butter. Mix the shredded cheeses together and press against the bottom and sides of the buttered baking dish to form a crust. In a medium-size skillet, sauté the garlic and onion in the oil until they are soft; add the lamb, oregano, and cinnamon and cook for 10 minutes, stirring frequently to prevent sticking. In a mixing bowl, beat together the eggs, cream, and salt until blended. Stir in the yogurt.

2. Carefully spread the Ratatouille over the cheese in the baking dish. Sprinkle the lamb mixture evenly over the Ratatouille. Pour the egg mixture on top. Sprinkle top with the parsley and scallions. Bake in the middle of the oven at 375° for 40 minutes, until the top is lightly browned. Let cool for at least 15 minutes before cutting into wedges to serve. Makes 6 servings.

OMELETS PROVENÇALE

2 tablespoons olive oil
1 small garlic clove
½ large onion, peeled and sliced
1 sweet green pepper, cut into strips
½ cup diced peeled tomatoes
▶ ½ cup diced cooked potatoes

▶ 1½ cups diced cooked lamb
Salt and freshly ground pepper
8 eggs
2 tablespoons milk or light cream
¼ teaspoon dried thyme
¼ cup chopped chives

1. Heat the oil in a large skillet, sauté garlic briefly then discard; add the onion slices and cook, stirring, until wilted. Add the green pepper strips, tomatoes and potatoes; toss them well, and continue to cook, uncovered, until the green pepper is crisp-tender. Stir in the lamb; season with salt and pepper to taste.

2. Lightly beat the eggs, milk and thyme in a mixing bowl. Melt enough butter in an omelet pan or skillet to coat. Make 4 individual omelets, filling each with some of the vegetables/lamb mixture. Serve immediately, garnished with chives. Makes 4 servings.

SCOTCH BROTH

- Bones from lamb roast
  4 tablespoons butter
- 2 cups diced cooked lamb
  3 leeks, thinly sliced
  1 large onion, peeled and diced
- 2 quarts chicken broth
  1 bay leaf
  ½ teaspoon salt
- ⅛ teaspoon pepper
  ½ cup barley
  ½ cup chopped parsley
  1 cup diced carrots
  1 cup chopped celery with
  leaves
  ½ cup diced rutabaga or turnip

1. Crack or break the lamb bones to fit the pot. Heat the butter in a large, heavy pot and add the bones and meat. Sauté 5 to 10 minutes to lightly brown the meat. Add the leeks and onions and sauté another 2 minutes.

2. Add the broth, bay leaf, salt, and pepper. Simmer 1 hour. Add the barley and simmer another 30 minutes. Add the parsley, carrots, celery, and rutabaga; simmer until the barley and vegetables are tender. Remove the bones before serving. Makes 6 to 8 servings.

BEAN AND LAMB SOUP

- 5 cups chicken broth
  ¾ cup diced carrot
  ½ cup chopped onion
  ½ cup diced celery
  1 clove garlic, minced
  ¼ cup diced turnip (optional)
  1 can (16 oz.) cannelini (white beans)
- ¼ teaspoon dried thyme
  ½ teaspoon curry powder
- ½ to 1 cup cubed cooked lamb
  Salt and Tabasco sauce to taste
  1 tablespoon chopped fresh parsley

Combine the broth, carrot, onion, celery, garlic, and turnip in a 2½-quart saucepan. Simmer 10 minutes. Add the beans, thyme, and curry powder. Continue to simmer until the vegetables are nearly tender. Add the lamb and simmer 10 minutes. Season to taste with salt and Tabasco sauce. Sprinkle with chopped parsley before serving. Makes 4 servings.

COUNTRY LAMB HASH

- 2 cups minced cooked lamb
- 1½ cups minced boiled potatoes
  ½ cup minced onion or scallion
  1 tablespoon chopped celery
  1 tablespoon minced fresh parsley
- ½ teaspoon dried rosemary
  Salt and pepper to taste
  2 tablespoons butter
  1 clove garlic, minced
- ¾ cup milk or leftover lamb gravy

1. Mix the lamb, potatoes, onion, celery, parsley, and rosemary together in a bowl. Season with salt and pepper to taste. Heat the butter in a skillet; add garlic and sauté for 2 minutes, stirring.

2. Add the meat mixture and sauté until it begins to brown lightly. Stir in the milk or gravy. Cook, uncovered, over medium heat without stirring until the bottom is crisp and the liquid almost evaporated, 10 to 15 minutes. Makes 4 servings.

ITALIAN LAMB HASH

½ cup minced onion
1 clove garlic, minced
2 tablespoons olive oil
1 cup diced eggplant
2 cups drained canned
   tomatoes
▶ ½ cup lamb gravy
▶ 1½ cups chopped cooked lamb

1 teaspoon salt
⅛ teaspoon pepper
⅛ teaspoon dried thyme
⅛ teaspoon rosemary
2 tablespoons butter
1 teaspoon grated lemon rind
▶ 1 cup hot cooked rice

1. Sauté the onion and garlic in the olive oil for 2 minutes in a large skillet. Add the eggplant and continue to cook for 5 minutes, stirring occasionally.

2. Add the tomatoes, gravy, lamb, salt, pepper, thyme, and rosemary. Cover and simmer for 15 minutes.

3. Mix the butter and lemon rind into the rice and serve with the hash. Makes 4 servings.

LAMB HASH CREOLE

⅓ cup coarsely chopped onion
⅓ cup diced green pepper
1 tablespoon chopped celery
1 tablespoon olive oil
▶ 2 cups diced cooked lamb
▶ 1 cup diced cooked potato
▶ 1 cup lamb gravy
½ cup tomato sauce

¼ teaspoon salt
¼ teaspoon dried basil
1 tablespoon steak sauce or
   Worcestershire
3 tablespoons diced pimiento
½ cup grated Cheddar cheese
1 tablespoon butter

1. Heat the oven to 375°. In a saucepan, sauté the onion, green pepper, and celery in the olive oil. Combine the lamb and potato with the gravy, tomato sauce, salt, basil, steak sauce, and pimiento. Blend well.

2. Divide among 4 individual ramekins, sprinkle with cheese and dot with butter. Bake 20 to 25 minutes or until lightly browned. Makes 4 servings.

LAMB FRIKADELLER

1 cup finely chopped onion
1 tablespoon butter
▶ 2 cups chopped cooked lamb
½ pound sausage meat

½ cup cracker crumbs
½ teaspoon salt
1 egg, well beaten
¼ cup milk

1. Sauté the onion in butter until tender. Cool thoroughly.

2. In a bowl combine the lamb, sausage meat, onion, crumbs and salt. Add the egg and milk and mix until the liquid is absorbed.

3. Shape into 6 patties and brown slowly in a greased skillet 30 minutes, turning occasionally. Serve with applesauce mixed with lemon juice and a pinch of ground nutmeg, if desired. Makes 6 servings.

DILLED LAMB CROQUETTES

3 tablespoons butter
2 tablespoons finely chopped
  onions
½ cup plus 3 tablespoons flour
▶ ¾ cup beef broth (include any
  unthickened lamb juice)
1 egg yolk
2 tablespoons heavy cream
▶ 2 cups ground or minced
  cooked lamb

2 teaspoons dried dill
1 tablespoon chopped parsley
¼ teaspoon dried thyme
½ teaspoon salt
  Black pepper to taste
2 teaspoons lemon juice
1 whole egg
¼ cup milk
½ cup dry bread crumbs
  Deep fat for frying

1. Melt 3 tablespoons of butter in a small saucepan. Over moderate heat, sauté the onions for 4 to 5 minutes until soft but not browned. Stir in 3 tablespoons of flour. Gradually stir in the broth. Bring to a boil, stirring constantly, until the mixture is very thick; simmer for 1 or 2 minutes.

2. Combine the egg yolk with the cream and stir in 2 tablespoons of the hot sauce. Beat the egg mixture into the rest of the sauce in the pan and cook for 5 seconds. Transfer sauce to a large mixing bowl; add the ground lamb, dill, parsley, thyme, salt, black pepper, and lemon juice; with a large spoon, beat the mixture until smooth as possible. Taste for seasoning. Spread the mixture out on a platter, cover it with plastic wrap, and refrigerate at least 4 hours.

3. In a shallow bowl, beat the whole egg with the milk. Put the ½ cup flour in a second bowl and the bread crumbs in a third. Form large spoonfuls of the chilled lamb mixture into large balls or cones. Roll lightly in the flour and shake off the excess. Dip, one at a time, in the egg mixture, then roll in the bread crumbs, coating completely. Chill again for 1 hour before frying.

4. Fry the croquettes, 2 or 3 at a time, in deep fat heated to 375°, until golden brown; drain on paper towels. Serve immediately or keep warm, uncovered in a slow oven. Serve with lemon quarters or with cream sauce flavored with dill, mustard, or chopped capers. Makes 4 to 6 servings.

SALMAGUNDI SALAD

▶ 1½ cups diced cooked lamb
▶ ½ cup diced cooked potato
▶ ½ cup diced cooked carrots
▶ ½ cup cooked peas or diced
  green beans
¼ cup chopped sweet pickle
1 tablespoon wine vinegar

3 tablespoons olive oil or salad
  oil
½ teaspoon salt
¼ teaspoon pepper
▶ 1 hard-cooked egg, chopped
½ cup mayonnaise
  Salad greens

1. In a bowl, combine the lamb, vegetables, and pickle. In another bowl, mix the vinegar, oil, salt and pepper; add to the lamb mixture, stir well, and chill 30 minutes.

2. Fold the chopped egg and mayonnaise into the chilled mixture. Serve on a bed of salad greens. Makes 4 servings.

MOLDED MEAT SALAD

1 package (3 oz.) lemon-
flavored gelatin
1 cup boiling water
½ cup cold water
½ cup mayonnaise
2 tablespoons vinegar
¼ teaspoon salt

Pepper, to taste
½ cup chopped celery
1 tablespoon chopped parsley
1 tablespoon grated onion
▶ 2 cups chopped cooked lamb
Salad greens

Dissolve the gelatin in the boiling water. Stir in the cold water, mayonnaise, vinegar, salt, and pepper. Chill until syrupy but not set. Whip the
gelatin until fluffy. Fold in the celery, parsley, onion, and lamb. Pour into
a 1-quart mold. Chill until firm. Unmold on salad greens. Makes 4 to 6
servings.

LAMB SUPPER SALAD

▶ 2 cups chopped cooked lamb
▶ ½ cup cooked peas
½ cup diced celery
¼ cup chopped walnuts
½ cup (or more) mayonnaise

1 teaspoon prepared mustard
½ teaspoon dried tarragon or
mint
Salt and pepper
Lettuce

Toss the lamb, peas, celery and walnuts in a bowl. Season the mayonnaise with the mustard, tarragon, and salt and pepper to taste. Mix into
the meat mixture. Serve on lettuce leaves. Makes 4 servings.

MIDDLE EASTERN LAMB AND APPLE SALAD

1 cup lentils (6½ oz.), soaked 8
hours and drained or 1 cup raw
brown rice
1 cup minced parsley
1 large apple cored, peeled
and cut into eighths
½ cup peanut oil
¼ cup fresh lemon juice
1 teaspoon salt
¾ teaspoon curry powder

½ teaspoon cumin
1 medium cucumber, peeled,
seeded, halved lengthwise
and sliced thin
1 large celery rib, sliced thin
4 medium-size scallions, minced
▶ ¾ pound chopped cooked lamb
(about 2 cups)
½ cup raisins
Boston lettuce leaves

1. Bring 1 quart water to rapid boil over high heat. Add lentils or rice. Reduce heat to medium-low, cover and simmer just until tender, about 20
minutes; do not overcook. Drain, set aside, and cool.

2. In a blender, make dressing by puréeing parsley, apples, oil, lemon
juice, salt, curry powder, and cumin.

3. Transfer mixture to large bowl. Add lentils, cucumber, celery, scallions, lamb and raisins and toss to blend. Line salad bowl with lettuce
leaves. Spoon lentil mixture into lettuce and serve immediately. Makes 4
servings.

LAMB-AND-EGG MOUSSE PERSILLADE

2 envelopes unflavored gelatin
1¼ cups water
► ¾ cup chicken stock or bouillon
► 2 cups finely chopped cooked
  lamb
1½ tablespoons brandy
1¼ cups finely chopped parsley

½ cup chopped scallions
1 clove garlic, peeled and
  minced fine
Freshly ground white pepper
► 7 hard-cooked eggs
1 cup chilled heavy cream

1. In a small bowl, sprinkle the gelatin into ¼ cup of the water and let it soften for about 5 minutes. In a small saucepan, mix the remaining water with chicken stock. Add the softened gelatin and stir over low heat until gelatin dissolves. Cool until syrupy and thick but not set. In a large bowl, combine the lamb, brandy, parsley, scallions, garlic, and white pepper to taste. Coarsely chop 5 of the hard-cooked eggs and the whites of the remaining 2 eggs; mix with the lamb. Whip the cream until soft peaks form. Stir the lamb into the gelatin mixture thoroughly and fold into the cream carefully.

2. Rinse an 8-cup ring mold or soufflé dish with cold water. Pour in the mousse and refrigerate for 3 hours or until set. Unmold onto a chilled serving plate. Sprinkle the 2 reserved hard-cooked egg yolks, sieved over the top of the mousse. Serve with rye thins or toast points. Makes 12 servings as an hors d'oeuvre.

LAMB IN ASPIC

2 tablespoons unflavored gelatin
3 cups tomato juice
4 beef bouillon cubes
2 teaspoons Worcestershire
  sauce
¼ teaspoon Tabasco
1 tablespoon grated onion

► 2 cups cooked lamb, cut in thin
  strips
½ cup diced celery
► 1 cup cooked lima beans or
  peas
Lettuce greens

1. Stir the gelatin into ½ cup of the tomato juice. Let stand 5 minutes.

2. Bring the remaining tomato juice to a boil in a medium saucepan. Add the bouillon cubes and gelatin mixture and stir until both are dissolved. Stir in the Worcestershire, Tabasco and the onion.

3. Chill until thick but not set. Stir in the lamb, celery, and beans.

4. Pour into a 1½-quart ring mold which has been rinsed in cold water. Chill until firm. Unmold on a bed of lettuce greens; serve with mayonnaise, if desired. Makes 8 servings.

HINTS FOR UNMOLDING

1. Rinse mold in water just before filling, leaving a "wet" mold.
2. When ready to unmold:
   a) Dip a small pointed knife in warm water and run tip of it around edge of mold to loosen. Or moisten tips of fingers and gently pull gelatin from top edge of mold.
   b) Moisten top of gelatin and a chilled plate with cold water—the moist surfaces make it easier to center the gelatin on the plate after it has been unmolded.
   c) Dip mold in warm water (do not use hot water) just to rim of mold—hold about 10 seconds. Lift from water, hold upright, and shake slightly to loosen gelatin from mold.
   d) Invert moistened plate on mold. Then invert mold and plate together and shake again. Lift off mold carefully. If gelatin does not release easily, dip again in warm water.

▸VEAL

AUSTRIAN VEAL STEAKS

¾ cup white wine, or chicken
   bouillon
Juice of 1 lemon
Salt and pepper to taste
▶ 6 to 8 slices cooked veal
¼ cup butter

1 egg, beaten
½ cup fine dry bread crumbs
6 to 8 slices Swiss cheese, cut in
   strips
Slivered blanched almonds
Paprika

1. Mix the wine with the lemon juice, and the salt and pepper. Pour the mixture over the veal slices. Marinate for 1 hour. Drain.

2. Heat the butter to sizzling point. Dip veal into the beaten egg and then into bread crumbs on one side only. Brown just the breaded side. Arrange the veal slices in a single layer, the unbrowned side up, and cover with the cheese strips, the slivered almonds, and sprinkle with paprika. Bake in a shallow pan in preheated hot oven (400°) until cheese sizzles, about 10 minutes. Makes 4 to 6 servings.

VEAL AND TOMATO SLICES À LA SUISSE

▶ 6 to 8 slices cooked veal
   Salt and pepper to taste
6 tablespoons butter
6 to 8 slices tomato
6 to 8 large mushrooms, thinly
   sliced lengthwise

2 to 3 shallots, thinly sliced, or 1
   tablespoon chopped scallions
1 tablespoon lemon juice
¼ cup dry sherry or Madeira
6 to 8 thin slices Swiss cheese

1. Sprinkle veal slices with salt and pepper, pressing the seasoning into the meat. Place in a shallow ovenproof dish.

2. In a heavy skillet, melt 2 tablespoons of butter and quickly sauté the tomato slices; lay over the veal slices. Sauté the mushrooms and the shallots in the remaining butter, over medium heat, for 2 or 3 minutes. Add the lemon juice. Cook, stirring gently, 1 to 2 minutes. Add the sherry, bring to a boil, and pour over the meat and tomato slices in the baking dish.

3. Cover meat, tomato, and sauce with overlapping slices of cheese. Bake in a preheated 350° oven until cheese is melted, sauce bubbly. Makes 4 servings.

Casserole topping
If the recipe calls for, but time doesn't permit, making fresh biscuits, use the refrigerator biscuits sold in supermarkets. Just flatten a bit and sprinkle with parsley or another herb.

VEAL QUITO

½ cup butter or margarine
1 medium onion, chopped
1 medium green pepper, chopped
½ cup chopped mushrooms
½ clove garlic, minced
6 tablespoons flour
► 3 cups chicken broth
► 3 cups diced cooked veal

¼ cup chopped, pitted ripe olives
► 2 hard-cooked eggs, coarsely chopped
1 teaspoon chili powder
½ teaspoon salt
¼ teaspoon pepper
1½ cups soft bread crumbs

1. Melt 6 tablespoons of the butter in a skillet; sauté onion, green pepper, mushrooms, and garlic for 5 minutes; blend in flour. Cook over low heat, stirring constantly, until mixture browns. Slowly add the chicken broth, stirring constantly until thickened.

2. Add veal, olives, eggs, chili powder, and salt and pepper, and blend well. Pour mixture into a 2½-quart baking pan. Melt the remaining 2 tablespoons of butter; toss with bread crumbs. Top veal mixture with crumbs. Bake in preheated 350° oven for 30 to 35 minutes. Makes 6 to 8 servings.

SCALLOP OF VEAL ORLOFF

6 tablespoons butter or margarine
2 cups coarsely chopped onion
3 tablespoons raw rice (not the converted type)
► ⅓ cup plus 1½ cups chicken stock, fresh or canned
1 egg yolk
Salt
⅛ teaspoon cayenne pepper

⅛ teaspoon lemon juice
⅓ to ⅔ cup heavy cream
4 tablespoons flour
Salt and white pepper to taste
¼ cup grated imported Swiss cheese
► 6 to 8 thin (¼- to ½-inch) slices cold braised veal, well trimmed
½ cup bread crumbs

1. To prepare the onion sauce, melt 2 tablespoons of butter in a casserole. Add the onion, stirring continuously; cook 3 to 4 minutes until they wilt slightly. Mix in the rice and ⅓ cup of the chicken stock and bring to a boil. Cover the casserole tightly; place in the middle of a preheated 325° oven and bake undisturbed for 30 minutes or until the rice and onions are tender. Force the mixture through a food mill, or purée in a blender. Beat in the egg yolk, salt, cayenne, and lemon juice. The purée will be very thick; thin with enough heavy cream that the sauce just holds its shape in the spoon. Set aside.

2. To prepare the Mornay (cheese) sauce, melt 3 tablespoons of butter in a saucepan. Remove from heat, and stir in the flour. Add 1½ cups of the chicken stock, stirring vigorously. Return to heat; continue to beat until sauce begins to thicken. With heat to a bare simmer, add ¼ cup heavy cream. Sauce should flow fairly easily off the spoon. Thin with the remaining cream, as necessary. Season with salt and pepper to taste and add the grated cheese.

3. In a shallow baking dish spread a thin layer of the Mornay sauce. Spread the veal pieces, one at a time, with a fairly thick layer of the on-

(continued)

ion sauce and lay them down the center of the dish, one slightly overlapping the other; spread the remaining sauce on top and around the sides of the loaf. Over this, spoon the cheese sauce, covering the onion sauce almost completely. Sprinkle the veal with the bread crumbs and dot with remaining tablespoon of butter.

4. Preheat oven to 375°. Place the baking dish in the center of the oven for 15 to 20 minutes, or until the sauce begins to bubble. Slide it at once under the hot broiler for a few seconds to brown its surface. Serve at once. Makes 4 servings.

VEAL CASSEROLE PARMA

2 cups spinach noodles	½ teaspoon salt
1 cup sour cream	¼ teaspoon pepper
½ cup heavy cream	½ teaspoon paprika
1½ cups grated Swiss cheese	1 tablespoon butter or
▶ 2 cups coarsely chopped	margarine
cooked veal	2 tablespoons chopped parsley

1. Cook noodles in salted boiling water for 8 mintues or until just tender; drain.

2. Combine sour cream with heavy cream; heat in medium saucepan to just below boiling. Stir in half of the cheese and all of the veal. Season with salt, pepper, and paprika.

3. In a well-greased 1½-quart baking dish, alternate layers of noodles and veal mixture. Top with remaining cheese, and dot with small bits of butter. Sprinkle the parsley over all. Bake in preheated 375° oven for 20 to 25 minutes or until top is lightly browned. Makes 4 servings.

VEAL ORLÉANS

▶ 3 cups diced cooked veal	3 cloves
½ cup coarsely chopped onion	1 bay leaf, crushed
2 ribs celery, cut up	3 tablespoons flour
3 carrots, cut into 1-inch pieces	4 cups consommé
3 medium potatoes, peeled and	½ teaspoon salt
cubed	Dash pepper
1 tablespoon chopped parsley	Baking powder biscuit dough
1 small clove garlic, minced	(see Basics)

1. Combine in a 2-quart casserole, the veal, onions, celery, carrots, potatoes, parsley, garlic, cloves, and bay leaf. Make a paste using the flour and 1 cup of the consommé; season with salt and pepper. Stir into the casserole and add the remaining consommé.

2. Bake, covered, in a preheated 350° oven for 30 minutes or until vegetables are tender. Remove from oven. Cover top with biscuit dough rolled to ½-inch thickness; slash center for steam to escape. Increase heat to 425°. Bake 12 to 15 minutes, or until biscuit topping is golden brown. Makes 4 servings.

VEAL AND HAM EN CASSEROLE

- 2 tablespoons bacon drippings
  ½ medium onion, coarsely chopped
- 2 cups diced cooked veal
- 1 cup diced cooked smoked ham
  ¼ pound mushrooms, sliced
- 1½ cups veal or ham gravy

1 teaspoon prepared mustard
1 teaspoon Worcestershire sauce
- ½ cup cooked diced potatoes
- ½ cup cooked mixed vegetables
  (peas, carrots, broccoli, etc.)
  ½ cup sour cream
  1½ cups packaged biscuit mix
  ½ cup milk

1. Heat 1 tablespoon of the bacon drippings in a large skillet, and sauté the onion and veal lightly over high heat. Turn into a 2-quart casserole. Add the remaining bacon drippings and sauté the ham and mushrooms briskly. Add to the casserole.

2. Reduce the heat under skillet, and stir in the gravy, mustard, and Worcestershire sauce; add the potatoes and mixed vegetables and heat briefly. Stir in the sour cream. Combine with the meat.

3. Preheat the oven to 450°. Prepare the biscuit mix with the milk, and roll out on lightly floured board. Cut into rounds and put on mixture in casserole. Bake for 15 minutes. Makes 4 servings.

VEAL AND ZUCCHINI CASSEROLE

½ cup tomato sauce
3 shallots, minced
1 teaspoon dried basil
- 1½ cups diced cooked veal
  1½ tablespoons melted butter mixed with 1 tablespoon olive oil

1 large onion, sliced
½ pound mushrooms, sliced
3 medium zucchini, sliced
¼ cup grated Parmesan cheese

1. In a saucepan, simmer the tomato sauce with the shallots and basil for 5 minutes. Spread in a thin layer over the bottom of a 1½-quart shallow casserole.

2. Sauté veal in 1 tablespoon of the butter/oil mixture for 1 minute in a skillet. Spread over the sauce in the casserole. In the same skillet, sauté the onion, mushrooms, and zucchini in the remaining butter/oil mixture for 6 or 7 minutes. Arrange in the casserole over the veal.

3. Pour the remaining tomato sauce over all. Sprinkle the top with the Parmesan cheese. Bake in a 350° oven for 20 minutes. Makes 4 servings.

VEAL PARMIGIANO

1 cup cracker crumbs
¼ cup Parmesan cheese
1 teaspoon oregano
1 teaspoon salt
¼ teaspoon pepper
▶ 8 thin slices cooked veal
2 small eggs, beaten with 1
   teaspoon cold water

3 tablespoons olive oil mixed
   with 3 tablespoons shortening
2 cloves garlic, halved
2 cans (8 oz.) tomato sauce,
   heated with 1 teaspoon dried
   basil
½ pound Mozzarella cheese,
   thinly sliced

1. Combine the crumbs, Parmesan cheese, oregano, salt, and pepper. Dip the veal slices in the crumb mixture, then in the beaten egg and again in the crumbs.

2. Heat half of the olive oil/shortening mixture and sauté half the garlic. When almost brown, remove from the pan. Then, brown half the veal slices quickly on both sides. Repeat with the remaining oil/shortening mixture, garlic, and veal slices. Place the browned veal slices in a warmed, shallow baking dish; pour the hot tomato sauce over them, and top with the cheese. Broil for 3 minutes or until cheese melts and is lightly brown. Makes 4 servings.

BLANQUETTE DE VEAU

4 tablespoons butter
▶ 2 tablespoons veal or chicken
   stock, homemade or canned
12 small white onions, peeled
1 tablespoon lemon juice
2 cups small whole mushrooms
3 tablespoons flour
2 egg yolks

½ cup heavy cream
Salt
⅛ teaspoon cayenne
▶ 2 cups cubed cooked veal
2 tablespoons parsley, finely
   chopped
Hot fluffy rice

1. In a saucepan with a tight cover, heat 1 tablespoon of butter with ½ cup of the stock. Add the onions; bring to a boil, cover the pan and reduce the heat. Simmer for about 20 minutes, turning the onions occasionally, adding stock if needed. When tender, remove them with a slotted spoon to a small bowl.

2. Stir ½ teaspoon of lemon juice into the stock remaining in the pan, bring it to a boil and add the mushrooms. Cook them over high heat for about 5 minutes, stirring almost constantly. Remove from pan with a slotted spoon to the bowl with the onions. Reserve stock for the sauce.

3. In a saucepan, melt the remaining butter, remove from heat, and stir in the flour. Gradually, add all the stock, hot and cold, and stir briskly. Increase the heat, stirring constantly until thickened. Reduce the heat and simmer for about 5 minutes.

4. Stir the egg yolks and the cream together, just enough to combine. Add a few tablespoons of the hot sauce, then pour the egg mixture back into the pan of sauce. Stir briskly, and season with the remaining lemon juice, salt, and cayenne.

5. Add the veal and the cooked white onions and mushrooms, with no liquid from the bowl. Cook gently until heated through; sprinkle with parsley and serve with rice. Makes 4 to 6 servings.

VEAL MAIGRET

4 tablespoons butter or
margarine
1 large sweet onion, sliced
¾ teaspoon curry powder
1 clove garlic, chopped
▶ 2 cups cubed cooked veal
½ cup boiling water
2 tablespoons crisp bacon,
crumbled

½ cup condensed tomato soup
¾ cup sliced mushrooms
¼ cup beer
½ cup sour cream
2 cups hot cooked noodles,
buttered
1 teaspoon poppy seed
2 tablespoons chopped toasted
almonds

1. Melt 2 tablespoons of butter in a medium, heavy skillet; add the onion, curry powder, and garlic, and sauté about 5 minutes. Add the veal and brown lightly. Gradually stir in the boiling water, the bacon and tomato soup. Cover and simmer for 15 minutes.

2. In a small skillet, melt the remaining butter, and sauté the mushrooms for 4 or 5 minutes over medium heat. Add the mushrooms to the veal mixture; stir in the beer and simmer for 5 minutes more.

3. Just before serving, stir in sour cream. Lightly toss noodles with poppy seed and almonds. Serve veal mixture over the noodles. Makes 6 servings.

ROBERTO'S VEAL AND KIDNEY BEANS

▶ 2 cups ground cooked veal
▶ 2 tablespoons bacon drippings
1 cup sliced onion
¼ cup chopped parsley
1 clove garlic, minced
2 cups canned tomatoes,
drained

½ bay leaf
½ teaspoon salt, or to taste
2 teaspoons chili powder
2 cans (20 oz. each) kidney
beans, rinsed and drained

1. In a large skillet, brown meat in bacon drippings for 1 minute. Add onion, parsley, and garlic, and sauté for 5 minutes. Add tomatoes, bay leaf, salt and chili powder. Stir in the beans. Cover; simmer for 40 to 45 minutes.

Double Cornbread

1 cup flour
1 cup yellow cornmeal
4 teaspoons baking powder
1 teaspoon salt
¼ cup sugar

2 eggs, lightly beaten
1 cup milk
3 tablespoons butter, melted
1 can (8¾ oz.) cream-style corn

2. Grease a 9-inch square pan. Combine flour, cornmeal, baking powder, salt and sugar; set aside. In a medium bowl, combine eggs, milk, butter, and corn; add flour mixture, stirring only until flour mixture is moistened. Spoon batter into the prepared pan. Bake in preheated 425° oven 25 to 30 minutes or until a knife inserted in center comes out clean and top is golden brown. Cut into squares.

3. Serve the hot corn bread with the veal and kidney beans. Makes 4 to 6 servings.

VEAL PAPRIKA

4 tablespoons butter
▶ 3 cups cooked veal, cut in strips
½ cup finely chopped onion
1 medium green pepper, slivered
1 tablespoon paprika
▶1½ cups leftover gravy

1 tablespoon tomato paste
¾ cup sour cream
¼ teaspoon lemon juice
2 cups cooked noodles, hot
Toasted slivered almonds, sautéed in frothy, hot butter

1. In a deep skillet, melt 2 tablespoons of butter. Add the veal and gently sauté. When brown, remove from pan. Add to the pan, 1 tablespoon of butter and cook the onion, green pepper, and paprika for about 5 minutes. Then add the gravy and the tomato paste. Cook for 5 minutes, stirring frequently. Return the veal to the mixture, add ½ cup sour cream, blend, and heat gently (do not boil) for about 3 minutes. Stir in the lemon juice.

2. Arrange hot noodles on a platter. Spoon the Veal Paprika over all; top with remaining sour cream and sprinkle with the toasted almonds. Makes 6 servings.

VITELLO TONNATO

¼ cup olive oil
1 can (3½ oz.) tuna fish (in olive oil)
2 flat anchovies, cut up
1 egg yolk
1 tablespoon lemon juice
Cayenne to taste
3 tablespoons heavy cream
▶ 3 tablespoons veal or chicken stock, homemade or canned
1 tablespoon capers, drained and chopped

Salt
▶ 6 to 8 slices braised veal, about ¼-inch thick
1 tablespoon finely chopped parsley
3 to 4 scallions, sliced
4 tomatoes, sliced or quartered
▶ 2 hard-cooked eggs, sliced
Black olives, Italian
1 lemon, sliced

1. Combine the olive oil, tunafish, anchovies, egg yolk, lemon juice, and cayenne in an electric blender. Blend long enough to turn into a thick, smooth purée. Scrape it into a small mixing bowl; stir in heavy cream and veal stock until the sauce has the consistency of a medium cream sauce. Add the capers, and also a little salt and more lemon juice, if needed.

2. Spread a thin layer of the tunafish sauce in a baking dish. Lay the cold veal on it and cover with the remaining sauce. Cover the dish tightly with plastic wrap and refrigerate at least overnight.

3. To serve, arrange the slices of veal, slightly overlapping, down the center of serving platter, cover with the sauce and sprinkle with the combined chopped parsley and scallions, and surround with the tomatoes, hard-cooked eggs, olives, and lemon. Makes 4 servings.

STRATFORD CREAMED VEAL

6 tablespoons butter or
  margarine
2 cups sliced mushrooms
½ green pepper, chopped
¼ cup chopped onions
¼ cup flour
½ cup cream
► 1 cup veal or chicken stock
½ teaspoon salt

⅛ teaspoon pepper
► 2 cups diced cooked veal
► ½ cup cooked peas
1 tablespoon minced pimiento
¾ cup dry white wine
⅛ teaspoon dried thyme
¼ cup minced parsley
4 cups hot cooked noodles

1. In a saucepan, melt 4 tablespoons of the butter, and sauté mushrooms, green pepper and onions for about 5 minutes. Add the flour and stir well. Add the cream and the stock gradually, blending thoroughly, and cook the mixture until thickened. Season with salt and pepper.

2. Add the veal, peas, and pimiento to the sauce; stir in the wine. Simmer for about 5 minutes longer.

3. Melt the remaining 2 tablespoons of butter, and combine with the thyme, and minced parsley. Add to the hot noodles; mix well. Press noodles into an oiled 6-cup ring mold. Unmold in 5 minutes on a hot serving plate; fill center with veal mixture. Garnish with parsley. Makes 4 servings.

VEAL MARENGO

3 tablespoons butter or
  margarine
24 small mushrooms
8 to 12 very small boiled white
  onions
► 2 cups diced cooked veal
1½ tablespoons flour
½ cup dry white wine

► 1 cup chicken stock, homemade
  or canned
3 tablespoons tomato sauce
Salt
Freshly ground black pepper
½ teaspoon thyme
2 tablespoons chopped parsley
Cooked white rice

1. Heat butter in large skillet. Add mushrooms and onions, and sauté for 3 to 4 minutes. Remove from pan and reserve.

2. Put veal in pan and cook, stirring, for 1 to 2 minutes. Stir in flour. When flour is lightly browned, add wine and chicken stock and stir until smooth. Blend in tomato sauce, salt and pepper to taste, and thyme. Cook, stirring frequently, until sauce is thickened and smooth.

3. Add reserved chopped parsley and blend well. Serve over freshly cooked white rice. Makes 4 servings.

ITALIAN SPAGHETTI SAUCE WITH VEAL

3 tablespoons olive oil
⅓ cup chopped onions
1 clove garlic, chopped
6 large tomatoes, peeled and chopped; or 1 can (16 oz.) imported tomatoes, drained and chopped
1 teaspoon oregano
½ teaspoon dried basil
Salt and pepper

Tabasco, 1 or 2 dashes
▶ 1 cup chopped cooked veal
▶ 2 to 3 tablespoons veal gravy (optional)
½ can (8 oz.) tomato sauce
1 package (16 oz.) thin spaghetti
1 cup shredded Mozzarella cheese
2 tablespoons chopped parsley

1. Heat the olive oil in a deep skillet, and sauté the onions and garlic. Add the tomatoes and cook over moderate heat, frequently stirring, until mixture is reduced to a thick sauce. Season with oregano, basil, salt and pepper, and Tabasco. Add the veal, veal gravy, and tomato sauce. Blend well and simmer over low heat while cooking spaghetti.

2. Cook spaghetti according to package directions. Drain, place in large serving bowl. Add sauce, Mozzarella cheese, and parsley. Blend well and serve. Makes 4 servings.

STUFFED PEPPERS ACAPULCO

4 green peppers
▶ 2 cups chopped cooked veal
▶ 1 cup cooked rice or buckwheat groats
½ teaspoon salt
⅛ teaspoon pepper
1½ tablespoons grated onion
1½ tablespoons chopped parsley
1 tablespoon chopped celery
2 cups canned tomatoes, chopped and drained

Pinch of dried thyme
Pinch of dried marjoram
⅛ teaspoon dried basil
1 teaspoon chili powder
1½ teaspoons Worcestershire sauce
1½ tablespoons grated Parmesan cheese
¼ teaspoon paprika

1. Cut off tops of peppers; remove seeds and fibers. Parboil for 10 minutes. Invert on paper towel to drain thoroughly.

2. In a large bowl, combine the veal, rice, salt, pepper, onion, parsley, celery, 1 cup of the tomatoes, thyme, marjoram, basil, chili powder, and Worcestershire sauce. Stuff the peppers with this mixture. Arrange in a greased 1½- or 2-quart baking dish. Sprinkle tops of peppers with the cheese and paprika. Pour the remaining tomatoes around them. Bake in a preheated 350° oven for 30 minutes. Makes 4 servings.

GOLDEN ACORN SQUASH

2 medium acorn squash
1½ teaspoons salt
¼ teaspoon pepper
2 tablespoons plus 1 teaspoon butter
3 tablespoons chopped onion
1 tablespoon plus 1 teaspoon flour

¾ cup light cream
► 1½ cups finely chopped cooked veal
► ½ cup cooked peas
1 teaspoon minced parsley
2 tablespoons chopped walnuts
⅛ teaspoon ground nutmeg
1 cup buttered bread crumbs

1. Cut squash in half crosswise; scoop out seeds and membrane. Season with half the salt and pepper. Turn upside down on a greased baking sheet; bake at 375° for 15 minutes. Spread 1 tablespoon butter on cut surfaces. With cut sides up continue baking for 15 to 20 minutes longer or until just tender.

2. Melt the remaining butter in a saucepan and sauté the onion until tender; add the flour to make a smooth paste. Cook for 2 or 3 minutes. Add the cream, and cook, stirring, until the mixture is smooth and thickened. Stir in the veal, peas, parsley, and walnuts. Season with the remaining salt and pepper, and the nutmeg.

3. Mound the veal mixture in the cavities of the squash. Cover with the bread crumbs and bake for 15 minutes longer. Makes 4 servings.

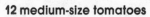

VEAL FLORENTINE SOUFFLÉED TOMATOES

12 medium-size tomatoes
1 package (10 oz.) frozen chopped spinach
3 tablespoons butter or margarine
1 tablespoon grated or minced onion

3 tablespoons flour
½ teaspoon salt
Dash of ground nutmeg
¾ cup milk
3 egg yolks
► ½ cup minced cooked veal
3 egg whites

1. Cut tops from tomatoes; scoop out seeds and pulp. Turn tomatoes upside down on paper towels to drain; let stand at least ½ hour.

2. Cook spinach according to package directions; drain well; cool. Squeeze out excess water. Chop finely.

3. Melt butter or margarine in saucepan; sauté onion for 2 minutes. Stir in flour, salt, and nutmeg. Cook over a medium heat, stirring constantly, until mixture bubbles. Remove from heat; gradually stir in milk. Cook over medium heat, stirring constantly, until mixture thickens and bubbles. (Sauce will be very thick.) Remove from heat.

4. Beat egg yolks until smooth and lemon colored. Add a few tablespoons of the hot sauce, blend well and stir back into the sauce mixture. Beat in the spinach and the veal, combining thoroughly.

5. Heat oven to 350°. Beat egg whites until stiff but not dry. Fold in veal/spinach mixture gently. Place tomatoes in a buttered baking pan; spoon mixture into tomatoes, dividing evenly. Pour about ½ inch boiling water into the pan around the tomatoes. Bake 25 minutes or until soufflé mixture is puffed and done and tomatoes are tender. Serve at once. Makes 6 servings, two each.

NEW ZEALAND VEAL TARTS

2 tablespoons butter or
  margarine
⅓ cup chopped onion
1 clove garlic, minced
2 tablespoons flour
¼ teaspoon ground marjoram
1 teaspoon salt

¼ teaspoon celery salt
⅛ teaspoon pepper
1 cup milk
► 2 cups diced cooked veal
2 tablespoons chopped parsley
½ package pie crust mix

1. Melt butter in a skillet; cook onion and garlic over low heat for 5 minutes. Blend in flour, marjoram, the two salts, and pepper and cook for 2 minutes. Gradually add milk and cook over low heat, stirring constantly, until mixture thickens. Add veal and parsley. Heat thoroughly, and keep warm.

2. Prepare ½ package pie crust mix as directed on package, substituting lemon juice for liquid called for. Place pastry on a 12-inch square of heavy aluminum foil. Flatten pastry and cover with a sheet of wax paper. Roll pastry into a 9-inch square. Remove wax paper.

3. Trim foil to edge of pastry; cut pastry and foil into four 4½-inch squares. Pinch together the corners of each square and shape a 1-inch standing rim all around to form a square tart shell inside the foil. Carefully prick pastry with a fork. Place on cookie sheet and bake in a preheated 425° oven for 5 minutes. Prick pastry again and bake 10 minutes longer, until golden brown. When cool, carefully remove shells from foil.

4. Spoon hot veal mixture into pastry tart shells and serve. Makes 4 servings.

CORN AND VEAL QUICHE

1 cup whole kernel corn, drained
¼ cup grated Swiss or Parmesan
  cheese
1 unbaked 9″ pie crust (see
  Basics)
5 eggs
1½ cups light cream

1 teaspoon minced onion
► 1 cup minced cooked veal
⅛ teaspoon cayenne
¼ teaspoon dried thyme
⅛ teaspoon pepper
4 slices crisp bacon, crumbled

1. Mix together the corn and cheese and put in the bottom of the pie crust. Beat the eggs with cream, and add the onion, veal, cayenne, thyme, and pepper. Pour over the corn; sprinkle with bacon.

2. Bake at 400° for 25 minutes. Reduce heat to 350° and bake about 20 minutes longer. Makes 6 servings.

VEAL CRÊPES

3 eggs
1 cup milk
¼ cup cold water
3 tablespoons melted butter
1¼ cups flour
1 teapoon salt
⅓ cup chopped onion
1 tablespoon butter or
  margarine

▶ 2 cups chopped cooked veal
⅓ cup chopped pimiento
½ teaspoon paprika
⅛ teaspoon pepper
▶ ¼ cup leftover gravy
1 cup cheese sauce (see Basics)
¼ cup sautéed slivered almonds

1. To prepare crêpe batter, beat eggs, milk, water, butter, flour, and ½ teaspoon salt until smooth. Let stand for 1 hour.

2. For filling, sauté onion in butter or margarine in a medium skillet. Add the veal, pimiento, paprika, remaining salt, and pepper. Add enough gravy to moisten mixture, and set aside.

3. Heat a 6-inch skillet and brush it with butter. Pour about 2 tablespoons of batter into the pan for each new crêpe, tipping this way and that, so batter covers bottom. After a few seconds, turn over. Remove when done and keep warm. Continue until batter is used up.

4. Fill each crêpe with about 2 tablespoons of the veal mixture and roll up. Place seam side down, in a buttered shallow baking dish. Cover with cheese sauce, and the almonds. Bake in preheated 400° oven for 10 minutes or until brown and bubbly. Makes 6 servings.

CREAMED VEAL PROFITEROLES

2 tablespoons butter
2 tablespoons flour
▶ ½ cup chicken broth, homemade
  or canned
½ cup light cream
Salt and pepper to taste

Dash nutmeg
Pinch of cayenne pepper
1 teaspoon dried thyme
▶ 1½ cups diced cooked veal
24 puff shells (see Basics)

1. Melt the butter in a saucepan; stir in the flour and cook for 1 minute. Add the broth, stirring constantly, until thickened and smooth, then add the cream. Season with the salt and pepper to taste, and the nutmeg, cayenne, and thyme. Add the veal and stir; bring to a boil.

2. Slice off the tops of the puff shells. Spoon an equal portion of the veal mixture into each shell. Replace the tops and serve. Makes 24 profiteroles.

VEAL SOUFFLÉ

6 tablespoons butter
6 tablespoons flour
1½ cups milk
½ cup cream
▶ 1 cup minced cooked veal
¼ cup minced celery
¼ cup minced parsley
½ teaspoon curry powder

1 can (4 oz.) finely chopped
  mushrooms
1 tablespoon minced onion
½ teaspoon salt
⅛ teaspoon pepper
4 egg yolks, slightly beaten
5 egg whites

1. Melt butter in a medium saucepan; blend in flour until smooth. Gradually add milk and cream and cook, stirring constantly, until thick.

2. Blend in veal, celery, parsley, curry powder, mushrooms, onion, salt, and pepper, and gradually beat in egg yolks. Remove from heat; cool slightly. Beat egg whites until stiff but not dry. Gently fold veal mixture into the egg whites. Turn into a thoroughly buttered 2-quart soufflé dish. Bake in a preheated 350° oven for 35 to 40 minutes or until firm. Makes 6 servings.

VEAL AND CHEESE FRITTATA

2 tablespoons butter
2 tablespoons olive oil
8 eggs, lightly beaten
1 can (4 oz.) pimientos, drained
  and diced
½ cup finely chopped scallions

1¼ cups shredded Swiss cheese
▶ ½ cup finely chopped cooked
  veal
2 tablespoons chopped parsley
½ teaspoon salt
¼ teaspoon pepper

1. Heat butter and oil over low heat in an ovenproof, straight-sided 9 to 10-inch skillet.

2. Combine eggs, pimientos, scallions, ½ cup cheese, veal, parsley, salt, and pepper; pour into skillet and cover. Cook over low heat 15 to 20 minutes until eggs are set except for the top half inch or so which will still be uncooked.

3. Sprinkle remaining cheese over frittata and broil about 4 inches from heat for 3 to 4 mintues, or until the top of eggs are set, and the cheese is melted and light golden. Makes 4 to 6 servings.

"Cooked" rice

To reheat cooked rice without loss of texture or flavor, place in a strainer or colander over simmering water in a covered pan for just a few minutes. (The cover on the pan need not fit tightly.) Or, you can reheat it in a covered dish in a microwave oven.

CORN, VEAL, AND CHEESE TIMBALES

▶ 1 cup minced cooked veal
3 beaten eggs
½ cup cream
¼ teaspoon salt

⅛ teaspoon paprika
1 teaspoon prepared mustard
1½ cups canned cream-style corn
½ cup grated Cheddar cheese

1. Grind or mince the veal as finely as possible. In a large bowl, beat the eggs and mix with the cream, salt, paprika, and mustard. Stir into the veal, adding the corn and cheese.

2. Butter the sides of 4 individual timbale or soufflé dishes, or a single 1½-quart baking dish. Put the dishes in a baking pan on a rack or a double thickness of paper, and pour water around the dishes as high as the filling in the molds. Bake in a moderate oven, about 325°, for 20 to 30 minutes. Timbales are done when knife inserted in center comes out uncoated. Makes 4 servings.

SCALLOPED VEAL

▶ 2 cups diced cooked veal
1½ cups fine soft bread crumbs
▶ ¾ cup cooked rice
⅓ cup chopped onion
⅓ cup chopped celery
¼ cup chopped pimiento
Salt to taste

¾ teaspoon poultry seasoning
▶ ¾ cup chicken broth, homemade or canned
¾ cup milk
2 eggs, slightly beaten
Creamy Mushroom Sauce

1. In a bowl, stir together the veal, bread crumbs, rice, onion, celery, and pimiento. Season with the salt and poultry seasoning. In another small bowl, combine the chicken broth, milk, and eggs; mix well then stir into the veal mixture. Spoon into a buttered shallow 1½-quart baking dish. Bake at 350° for 50 to 55 minutes, or until a knife inserted comes out clean. Serve with Creamy Mushroom Sauce. Makes 4 servings.

Creamy Mushroom Sauce

1 can (10½ oz.) cream of mushroom soup

¼ cup milk
1 cup sour cream

2. Combine the soup, milk, and sour cream and heat in saucepan until hot through, but do not boil.

UKRAINIAN SOUP

▶ Leftover cooked veal and beef bones
1 medium onion, quartered
2 cloves garlic
1 bay leaf
4 whole cloves
3 celery tops (leaves)
1 medium carrot, diced
1 sprig parsley
½ teaspoon salt
▶ 2 cups cubed cooked veal
2 medium onions, sliced
2 stalks celery, sliced

3 carrots, sliced
½ small head cabbage, cut in chunks
1 can (16 oz.) tomatoes
1 can (16 oz.) beets, drained, chopped, and liquid reserved
1 teaspoon sugar
¼ cup vinegar
½ teaspoon celery salt
¼ teaspoon white pepper
½ cup sour cream
3 tablespoons grated cucumber

1. Cover the veal and beef bones with 3 quarts of cold water in a large soup kettle. Add onion, garlic, bay leaf, cloves, celery tops, diced carrot, parsley, and salt. Bring to boil; skim well. Simmer partially covered for 2 hours. Strain; measure 2 quarts stock and return to kettle.

2. Add the veal, onions, celery, carrots, cabbage, tomatoes, and liquid from beets. Cover; simmer 1 hour. Add sugar, vinegar, celery salt, pepper, and drained beets; simmer 15 minutes. Top each serving with a dollop of sour cream mixed with the grated cucumber. Makes 8 servings.

SWISS VEAL CROQUETTES

3 tablespoons butter
⅓ cup flour
½ cup milk
½ cup light cream
▶1½ cups ground cooked veal
¼ cup minced mushrooms, sautéed

¼ cup shredded Swiss cheese
2 teaspoons salt
2 tablespoons minced onion
1½ cups fine bread crumbs
Shortening for frying

1. Melt the butter in a medium saucepan. Add the flour and stir until blended. Gradually stir in the milk and cream, and cook, stirring constantly, to make a smooth, thick sauce. Add the veal, mushrooms, cheese, salt, and onion. Chill for 30 minutes.

2. Shape into 8 croquettes. Roll in bread crumbs. Fry croquettes in hot shortening until well browned. Drain on absorbent paper. Serve with a cream or tomato sauce. Makes 4 servings.

HAWAIIAN VEAL PATTIES

▶ 2 cups ground cooked veal
¼ cup fine dry bread crumbs
¼ cup ketchup
¼ cup minced onion
½ teaspoon salt
⅛ teaspoon pepper
¼ teaspoon dried marjoram

¼ teaspoon dried rosemary
2 eggs, lightly beaten
2 tablespoons butter, melted
4 tablespoons brown sugar
½ cup pineapple tidbits and syrup
¼ cup wine vinegar

Combine veal, bread crumbs, ketchup, onion, seasonings, and eggs; mix well. Shape into four large patties. Place in a greased shallow pan. Combine butter, brown sugar, pineapple, and vinegar, and spoon over patties; cover. Bake in preheated 350° oven for 20 minutes. Uncover, and bake for 10 minutes longer, basting occasionally. Makes 4 servings.

FRICADELLES OF VEAL
(Fried Meatballs)

6 tablespoons butter
⅔ cup minced onion
1 teaspoon minced garlic
▶ 1 cup mashed potatoes, whipped with 1 tablespoon cream
▶ 2 cups ground or minced veal
4 flat anchovy fillets, washed, dried, and finely chopped (about 3 teaspoons)

1 teaspoon lemon juice
3 tablespoons minced parsley
1 egg, lightly beaten
2 tablespoons heavy cream
Freshly ground black pepper
Salt to taste
3 tablespoons vegetable oil
½ cup flour

Caper Sauce

2 tablespoons flour
▶ 1 cup veal broth or chicken stock, homemade or canned
1 egg yolk
½ cup heavy cream
2 tablespoons coarsely chopped capers

¼ teaspoon lemon juice
1 tablespoon finely chopped parsley
Salt to taste
⅛ teaspoon cayenne

1. Melt 2 tablespoons of the butter in a skillet; add the onions and garlic, and slowly cook until soft but not brown. Put in a large bowl and add the mashed potatoes, veal, anchovies, 1 teaspoon lemon juice, and parsley. Beat vigorously until the mixture is smooth; beat in the egg and 2 table-spoons cream. Season highly with freshly ground black pepper; taste before adding salt. Beat in 2 tablespoons softened butter. Form the meat into balls about 1-inch in diameter and place on a plate. Cover with waxed paper and chill for at least 1 hour.

2. To cook the fricadelles: slowly heat the vegetable oil and 1 table-spoon butter in a large heavy frying pan. Roll the fricadelles in ½ cup flour until thoroughly coated. When the fat in the pan is almost smoking, add 8 to 10 meatballs and shake the pan so they roll around almost con-

(continued)

stantly, keeping their shape and browning evenly. Cook for 3 or 4 minutes, and remove with a slotted spoon to a heated platter. Keep warm in
low oven. Continue the frying, adding more oil and butter to the pan, if
necessary.

3. To make the sauce: pour off all but 2 tablespoons of fat from the pan
and stir in the flour; mix thoroughly. Add the stock and cook, stirring constantly, until the sauce becomes smooth and thickened; simmer for 1 or 2
mintues. Combine the egg yolk with the cream; stir into it 3 tablespoons
of the hot sauce and return the egg mixture to the sauce in the pan. Add
the capers, lemon juice, parsley, salt, and cayenne. Taste for seasoning.
Pour sauce over the fricadelles and serve. Makes 30 meatballs.

 ## SOUTHERN-STYLE VEAL LOAF

▶ ¾ cup veal gravy
  1 cup herb stuffing mix
▶ 3 cups ground cooked veal
  ½ cup chopped celery
  2 tablespoons chopped ripe
    olives
  ½ cup chopped green pepper
  1 tablespoon chopped parsley
  1 small onion, minced

2 eggs, well beaten
1 can (5⅓ oz.) evaporated milk
2 tablespoons butter, melted
½ teaspoon salt
¼ teaspoon paprika
½ teaspoon dried tarragon
½ cup dried bread crumbs
1 tablespoon butter

1. Mix the gravy with the stuffing mix, and set aside.

2. In a large bowl, combine the veal, celery, olives, green pepper,
parsley, onion, and the stuffing mixture. Mix together the eggs, evaporated milk, and melted butter, and add to the veal mixture. Season with
the salt, paprika, and tarragon and mix well.

3. Place in a greased 1½-quart loaf pan; sprinkle with the bread crumbs,
and dot with butter. Set in a pan of hot water and bake the loaf in a 350°
oven for about 45 minutes. Makes 4 to 6 servings.

 ## VEAL MONT BLANC

  ½ cup sliced mushrooms
    Lemon juice
  5 tablespoons butter or
    margarine
▶ 2 cups ground or finely chopped
    cooked veal

¾ cup condensed cream of
  chicken soup
  Salt and pepper to taste
▶ 2 cups mashed potatoes
  ¼ cup grated Parmesan cheese
  ¼ cup fine dry bread crumbs

1. Sprinkle mushrooms with lemon juice. Melt 2 tablespoons of the butter
in a saucepan and sauté the mushrooms for 4 to 5 minutes. Add the
meat, stir in the soup, add salt and pepper, and heat thoroughly.

2. Melt 1 tablespoon of butter in a pan and mix the mashed potatoes
briskly to fluff up; add 2 tablespoons of the grated cheese and beat well
to blend.

3. In a buttered square baking dish, shape the veal mixture into a
mound. Cover the mound with a thick layer of mashed potatoes. Melt the
remaining 2 tablespoons of butter and pour over mound. Top with the
bread crumbs mixed with remaining 2 tablespoons grated cheese. Bake
in 425° oven for 20 minutes. Makes 4 to 6 servings.

SCANDINAVIAN VEAL AND HERRING SALAD

⅔ cup of ½" pieces of herring
(bottled imported herring in
wine sauce, or pickled in sour
cream)
► 2 cups cubed cooked veal
► 2 cups diced boiled potatoes
► 1 cup diced cooked or canned
beets, drained and patted dry
½ cup coarsley diced apple
⅓ cup minced onion
3 tablespoons minced dill pickle
4 tablespoons white wine
vinegar

4 tablespoons minced fresh dill
or 2 teaspoons dried dillweed
Salt to taste
Freshly ground black pepper
► 3 hard-cooked eggs
1 tablespoon prepared mustard
4 tablespoons vegetable oil
2 to 4 tablespoons heavy cream
½ pint sour cream
3 tablespoons beet juice from
canned beets
½ teaspoon lemon juice

1. Place herring in a sieve, rinse well in cold running water; drain and dry thoroughly. In a large bowl, combine the cut-up herring with the veal, potatoes, beets, apples, onions, dill pickle, 2 tablespoons of the vinegar, and most of the dill, and toss carefully but thoroughly. Add salt and a few grindings of black pepper.

2. Rub the yolks of the hard-cooked eggs through a fine sieve into a small bowl. Stir in the mustard, and mash to a paste; gradually beat in the remaining vinegar and the oil. Beat in enough heavy cream so the dressing will run thickly off the spoon. Pour over the salad and mix together lightly. Refrigerate for at least 3 hours before serving.

3. When ready to serve, mound the salad in a bowl and sprinkle with the chopped egg whites and the remaining dill. In a small bowl, gradually stir into the sour cream, the beet juice and lemon juice. Serve separately in a saucedish. Makes 4 to 6 servings.

VEAL SALAD BOULESTIN

¼ cup olive oil
2 tablespoons red wine vinegar
½ teaspoon Dijon mustard
1 clove garlic, minced
Salt and pepper to taste
► 2 cups cooked rice
½ cup diced green or red bell
pepper

►1½ cups cooked veal, cut into
strips
½ cup mayonnaise
4 scallions, chopped
2 tablespoons chopped fresh
chives
1 tablespoon chopped fresh
basil or parsley
► 2 hard-cooked eggs, sliced

In a small bowl, mix together the olive oil, vinegar, mustard, garlic, salt, and pepper. Pour over the rice and toss well. Add the diced pepper to the rice and mix well. In another bowl, mix together the veal, mayonnaise, scallions, chives, and basil or parsley. To assemble the salad, make a ring of the rice on a small platter, mound the veal into the center of the dish and garnish with the eggs. Makes 4 servings.

VEAL SALAD ALGIERS

1 cup mayonnaise
1 teaspoon dried tarragon
1 tablespoon lemon juice
▶ 2 cups diced cooked veal
¼ cup chopped shallots or
   scallions

¼ cup chopped celery
1 tablespoon ripe olive slivers
½ cup toasted blanched
   almonds
Crisp lettuce leaves
Cherry tomatoes

Mix the mayonnaise with the tarragon and lemon juice, and blend well. Combine the veal with the shallots, celery, olives, and almonds. Then, add just enough of the mayonnaise mixture to the veal mixture to bind it together. Heap onto the lettuce leaves and garnish with the cherry tomatoes. Serve with the remaining mayonnaise mixture. Makes 4 servings.

RUSSIAN VEAL AND CUCUMBER SALAD

▶ 2 cups diced cooked veal
▶ 2 cups diced cooked potatoes
1 cup diced peeled cucumbers
2 tablespoons chopped scallions
½ cup diced dill pickles

1 cup diced peeled tart apples
1 teaspoon celery seed
½ cup mayonnaise
½ cup sour cream
1 teaspoon Worcestershire sauce

Combine the veal, potatoes, cucumbers, scallions, pickles, apples, and the celery seed in a large bowl. Then, blend well together the mayonnaise, sour cream, and Worcestershire sauce. Add the sauce mixture to the veal mixture and toss gently with 2 forks. Chill before serving. Makes 6 servings.

VEAL SANDWICHES NAPOLI

⅓ cup butter or margarine
¾ teaspoon dry mustard
¾ teaspoon anchovy paste
¾ teaspoon oregano

8 slices Italian bread, toasted
▶ 8 thin slices cooked veal
8 thin slices Mozzarella cheese
8 tomato slices

Cream the butter with the mustard, anchovy paste, and oregano. Spread the mixture on each slice of bread. Top with a slice of veal, and slice of cheese. Broil 5 inches from heat until cheese melts. Top with tomatoe slices and serve. Makes 4 servings.

►FISH

NARRAGANSETT NOODLE RING

1½ cups milk
1 cup grated Cheddar cheese
½ cup finely chopped or grated onion
½ teaspoon salt
½ teaspoon paprika
⅛ teaspoon black pepper
3 eggs
1 cup soft bread crumbs
1 pimiento, chopped

6 mushrooms, chopped
2 tablespoons chopped parsley
▶ ¼ cup chopped cooked green beans
▶ ¼ cup chopped cooked carrots
▶2½ cups cooked medium egg noodles,
▶ 2 cups flaked cooked codfish or halibut

1. In top of a double boiler, heat the milk; stir in the cheese, onion, and seasonings. In a large bowl, beat the eggs well. Add the milk/cheese mixture to the eggs, stirring constantly.

2. Stir in the crumbs, pimiento, mushrooms, parsley, green beans, and carrots. Carefully stir in the noodles and the fish.

3. Spoon into a greased 8-cup ring mold. Set mold in pan of hot water. Bake in a preheated 350° oven for 25 to 30 minutes. Turn out onto heated platter; serve immediately. Makes 4 to 6 servings.

MEDITERRANEAN FISH CASSEROLE

1 medium onion, chopped
4 tablespoons butter or margarine
1½ tablespoons flour
Pinch sage
⅔ cup milk
⅔ cup light cream
2 tablespoons grated Parmesan cheese
1 tablespoon capers

¼ teaspoon lemon juice
½ teaspoon salt
4 medium potatoes, pared, thinly sliced, about 2 cups.
▶ 2 cups flaked firm cooked fish (cod, haddock, pollack, etc.)
1½ tablespoons fine dry bread crumbs
½ teaspoon paprika

1. Sauté onion in 3 tablespoons butter for 3 minutes or until soft but not brown. Stir in flour and sage and cook 3 minutes. Combine the milk and cream and gradually add to the flour, cooking over low heat and stirring frequently until sauce thickens. Add cheese, capers, lemon juice, and salt.

2. In a 1½-quart baking dish, alternate layers of potatoes and fish, ending with potatoes. Pour the sauce over the contents. Shake dish gently so sauce filters down throughout. Combine bread crumbs and paprika; sprinkle over the casserole and dot the top with bits of remaining butter. Bake 1 hour or until potatoes are tender. Makes 4 to 6 servings.

SCALLOPED FISH AND POTATOES

1 large onion, chopped
3 tablespoons butter or
  margarine
4 medium potatoes, peeled
▶ 2 cups cooked haddock or
  halibut

2 tablespoons minced parsley
  Salt and pepper
2 eggs
¾ cup sour cream
  Soft bread crumbs

1. Sauté onions in butter until golden brown. Boil the potatoes for 10 minutes. Drain and slice.

2. In a greased casserole, alternate a layer of fish with a layer of potatoes, sprinkling each layer with the browned onions, parsley, and salt and pepper. End with a layer of potatoes.

3. Beat eggs with ½ teaspoon salt. Add sour cream, and pour over the layers. Sprinkle with bread crumbs. Bake in preheated 350° oven for about 35 minutes. Makes 4 servings.

SOHO FISH PIE

2½ tablespoons butter
2 onions, sliced
▶ 2 cups flaked cooked fish
▶ 4 hard-cooked eggs, sliced
3 tomatoes, peeled and sliced
1 teaspoon salt

¼ teaspoon pepper
1 large egg, well beaten
▶ 2 cups mashed potatoes
1 tablespoon chopped parsley
2 tablespoons chopped almonds

1. Melt 1 tablespoon of the butter in a skillet; add onions and sauté until lightly browned. Stir in fish; mix gently.

2. With ½ tablespoon of the butter, grease a 1-quart baking dish and arrange a layer of egg and tomato slices. Top with half the fish mixture, and repeat until all these ingredients are used up. Season to taste with salt and pepper.

3. Mix ¾ of the beaten egg with the mashed potatoes, parsley, and almonds. Spread over the fish mixture. Dot with the remaining butter and brush with the remaining beaten egg. Bake in preheated 400° oven for 25 minutes or until top is well browned. Makes 4 to 6 servings.

KEDGEREE

3 tablespoon butter
2 tablespoons minced onion
▶ 2 cups cooked rice
1 tablespoon chopped parsley
1 teaspoon curry powder
▶ 3 hard-cooked eggs, chopped

¾ cup light cream
  Salt and pepper
▶ 2 cups flaked cooked fish,
  preferably salmon
1½ tablespoons fresh lime juice

1. Melt butter in medium skillet. Add onion and sauté until tender. Stir in rice, parsley, and curry powder. Blend well and cook 2 minutes. Remove from heat. Add eggs and cream; salt and pepper to taste and add melted butter. Let stand for 15 minutes.

(continued)

2. Heat oven to 400°. Arrange fish in a greased 1-quart baking dish. Pour lime juice over it. Top with the rice mixture. Bake for 20 minutes or until heated through. Makes 4 to 6 servings.

FISH FLORENTINE

4 ounces wide egg noodles
(makes about 2 cups cooked)
3 tablespoons butter or
margarine
¼ cup mushrooms
1 tablespoon minced scallions
2 tablespoons flour
¾ teaspoon salt
⅓ teaspoon pepper

1½ cups milk
2 tablespoons dry sherry
⅔ cup sour cream
1 teaspoon dillweed
1 package (10 oz.) frozen
chopped spinach, thawed and
squeezed dry
▶ 2 cups flaked cooked firm fish
2 tablespoons bread crumbs

1. Cook noodles as directed on package, but omit salt; drain and set aside.

2. Melt butter in a saucepan, over medium heat. Add mushrooms and scallions and cook until tender, about 5 minutes. Push vegetables to side of the pan and stir in flour, salt, and pepper, blending thoroughly; cook for 1 minute. Gradually stir in milk and sherry; cook until mixture is slightly thickened and smooth, stirring frequently. Remove ½ cup of the sauce and reserve. Add the noodles to the remaining sauce in the saucepan and combine well.

3. Preheat oven to 350°. Mix the sour cream and dill into the spinach. Mix the fish into the reserved sauce. Spread half the noodle mixture on the bottom of a greased 1½-quart baking dish. Layer the spinach over the noodles, then the fish, and then top with the remaining noodles. Sprinkle with bread crumbs, and bake for 20 minutes. Brown crumbs quickly under the broiler just before serving. Makes 4 servings.

BROCCOLI-SALMON AU GRATIN

¼ cup butter
¼ cup flour
¼ teaspoon dry mustard
2 cups milk*
1 teaspoon salt or to taste
2 tablespoons dry sherry or
Madeira

1 egg yolk, beaten
▶ 2 cups flaked cooked salmon
2 packages (10½ oz. each)
frozen chopped broccoli,
cooked
½ cup grated Parmesan cheese
½ cup buttered bread crumbs

1. Melt the butter in a saucepan, stir in the flour and dry mustard, and blend until smooth over low heat. Slowly stir the milk into the flour mixture, and cook 5 minutes. Add salt and sherry and cook, stirring constantly, until sauce thickens. Blend egg yolk with small amount of sauce and stir into the sauce in the pan. Add salmon and remove from heat.

2. Spread broccoli in the bottom of a lightly buttered shallow baking dish. Pour salmon mixture over surface. Sprinkle with grated cheese and bread crumbs. Bake in a preheated 350° oven for 20 minutes, or until surface is lightly browned. Makes 4 servings.
*Note: If salmon poaching liquid is available, substitute it for a portion of the milk, up to ¾ cup of the milk.

FISH EN CASSEROLE

▶ 1 cup flaked cooked fish
▶ 3 hard-cooked eggs, diced
▶ 1 cup cooked peas
3 tablespoons butter or margarine
3 tablespoons all-purpose flour
1½ cups milk mixed with ¼ cup half-and-half cream
1 teaspoon Worcestershire sauce

Tabasco to taste (by drops)
½ teaspoon salt
1 egg yolk, beaten
2 tablespoons sherry
3 tablespoons grated Parmesan cheese
¼ teaspoon paprika
Hot biscuits

1. Arrange the fish in the bottom of a buttered 1-quart baking dish. Scatter the eggs and the peas on top.

2. In a small saucepan, melt the butter; add the flour and cook, stirring, for 3 minutes. Whisk in milk/half-and-half mixture, Worcestershire sauce, Tabasco, and salt, and continue to cook and stir until the sauce has thickened, about 5 minutes.

3. Remove about ⅓ cup of the sauce and mix well with the egg yolk. Return to saucepan; cook, stirring, for 1 minute. Add sherry.

4. Pour sauce over fish, eggs, and peas. Sprinkle top with Parmesan cheese and paprika. Bake in preheated 350° oven for 20 minutes or until heated through and bubbling. Serve immediately over biscuits. Makes 4 to 5 servings.

CHILLED FISH ALSACIENNE

1 egg yolk
¼ teaspoon salt
½ teaspoon Dijon-type mustard
⅛ teaspoon cayenne
½ cup olive oil
2 teaspoons lemon juice
1 tablespoon heavy cream
3 tablespoons cucumber, peeled and shredded
1½ tablespoons finely chopped scallions

2 tablespoons finely chopped parsley
▶ 4 to 6 substantial pieces chilled, cooked fish (sole, scrod, trout, flounder, halibut, whiting, bluefish, etc.)
2 medium tomatoes, peeled and sliced
8 to 12 black olives
Crisp watercress

1. With a small whisk, or electric mixer, beat the egg yolk for 1 or 2 minutes until it thickens; add the salt, mustard, and cayenne, and beat for a few seconds longer. Beat in the ¼ cup olive oil very gradually. Thin the sauce with 1 teaspoon of the lemon juice. Continue beating, pouring in the remaining oil in a thin stream. Stir in the remaining teaspoon of lemon juice and the heavy cream. Then, blend in the cucumber, scallions, and parsley; taste for seasoning.

2. Arrange the pieces of fish on an attractive chilled platter and cover them completely with the sauce. Surround with the sliced tomatoes, intersect with the olives, and ring with sprays of watercress. Serve at once. Makes 4 servings.

SEAFOOD À LA KING

½ cup sliced fresh mushrooms
3 tablespoons chopped green
  pepper
1½ tablespoons chopped
  pimiento
¼ cup butter or margarine
1½ tablespoons all-purpose flour
1½ cups light cream

½ teaspoon salt
  Dash of paprika
► 2 cups flaked cooked cod,
  haddock, shrimp, sole, etc.
2 egg yolks
2 tablespoons sherry or Madeira
  (optional)

1. In a large skillet or saucepan, sauté the mushrooms, green pepper, and pimiento in butter for 5 minutes over low heat. Remove vegetables and reserve. Stir flour into pan liquid; cook 1 minute. Gradually stir in cream and cook until smooth and thick, stirring constantly. Return the vegetables to the pan, season with salt and paprika, add the seafood, and cook, over low heat, for 2 minutes, stirring gently.

2. Beat egg yolks slightly; stir some of the hot sauce into them. Blend well. Stir egg mixture into remaining hot sauce. Cook for 1 minute longer over low heat, stirring constantly. Remove from heat and stir in sherry, if desired. Serve on rice, noodles, or in heated pastry shells. Makes 4 to 6 servings.

NEW ORLEANS FISH CREOLE

¼ cup butter or margarine
¼ cup chopped onion
1 cup chopped celery
2 tablespoons chopped green
  pepper
1 clove garlic, minced
¼ cup flour
2½ cups canned tomatoes,
  chunked and undrained

¼ cup water
1 bay leaf
1 teaspoon chopped parsley
¼ teaspoon dried thyme
► 2 cups cooked rice
► 2 cups cooked fish, in chunks or
  flaked

1. Melt the butter in a medium, heavy skillet; add the onion, celery, green pepper, and garlic and sauté 5 minutes or until almost tender, stirring frequently. Blend in flour; cook over low heat for 2 minutes.

2. Stir in tomatoes and water; cook, stirring constantly, until thickened. Add bay leaf, parsley, thyme, rice, and blend well. Cook over low heat for 10 minutes. Remove bay leaf; add fish, simmer gently another 5 minutes. Makes 4 servings.

Egg sauces

Remember when making sauces with egg yolks, the primary problem is keeping the heat of the egg low (thereby avoiding scrambling the eggs). The simplest way is to prepare the sauce in a double boiler *over*, not *in*, hot water. This means that the water in the lower pan does *not* touch the bottom of the upper pan containing the sauce.

SEAFOOD NEWBURG

2 tablespoons butter
1 teaspoon finely chopped
shallots
¼ cup Madeira
3 egg yolks
1 cup light cream

Salt and pepper
Dash of cayenne
▶ 2 cups sliced cooked seafood
(shrimp, halibut, cod, sole,
crab, etc.)
Hot toast or pastry shells

1. Melt butter in saucepan; add shallots, and sauté gently until tender and translucent. Add Madeira, and cook over low heat for 2 minutes.

2. Beat egg yolks into the light cream; stir into the saucepan and heat slowly without boiling, stirring constantly, until it thickens. Season with salt and pepper and cayenne. Add the seafood and heat thoroughly. Serve immediately on hot toast or in 4 pastry shells. Makes 4 servings.

CREAMED FISH RUSSIAN STYLE

¼ cup minced onion
2 tablespoons butter or
margarine
1 teaspoon paprika
1 cup sour cream
2 egg yolks, lightly beaten
1 teaspoon salt

¼ teaspoon pepper
▶ 2 cups cooked fish, broken in
chunks
1 tablespoon lemon juice
Hot fluffy rice
2 tablespoons chopped parsley

1. In a large skillet, over medium heat, sauté onion in butter until lightly browned; stir in paprika. Add sour cream and heat almost to boiling, stirring constantly. Remove skillet from heat.

2. Stir a little of the sauce mixture into the egg yolks; blend well. Add the egg yolk mixture to the sauce in skillet. Add the salt and pepper and the fish. Just before serving, heat lemon juice and stir into the sauce. Serve immediately over hot fluffy rice, with parsley sprinkled on top.

CODFISH OPORTO

1 finely chopped onion
1 clove garlic, crushed
1 tablespoon olive oil
¼ cup coarsely chopped parsley
Dash of thyme

3 peeled, seeded and coarsely
chopped tomatoes, or 1½ cups
drained and coarsely
chopped canned Italian plum
tomatoes
½ cup dry white wine
▶ 2 cups flaked cooked codfish
1 teaspoon butter

1. In a heavy saucepan, cook the onion, and garlic briefly in olive oil. Add the parsley, thyme, tomatoes, and wine. Bring to a boil, reduce the heat, and simmer gently, covered, for about 10 minutes to blend flavors.

2. Uncover, and cook to reduce the liquid a bit, about 5 minutes. Add the fish, and stir gently. Simmer for 3 minutes, to heat the fish thoroughly. Just before serving, drop bits of butter into the sauce, and rotate the pan in a circular motion until melted. Ladle the fish and sauce over hot fluffy rice. Makes 4 servings.

CALIFORNIA FISH WITH AVOCADO

2 tablespoons butter
2 teaspoons chopped scallions
1 tablespoon chopped celery
2 tablespoons flour
1 teaspoon curry powder
1½ cups milk
1 egg yolk

2 teaspoons sherry
¼ teaspoon salt
⅛ teaspoon pepper
2 medium avocados
▶ 2 cups flaked cooked fish (sole, halibut, haddock, etc.)
Freshly made hot toast or rice

1. Melt the butter in a heavy saucepan; cook the scallions and celery for 3 to 4 minutes. Add the flour and curry powder and blend well; cook for 2 minutes more. Gradually stir the milk into the mixture; continue cooking, stirring constantly, until smooth. When sauce thickens, remove from heat. Beat the egg yolk and add 3 tablespoons of the hot sauce, mixing well; add the egg yolk mixture to the sauce in the pan. Return pan to low heat, add the sherry, salt, and pepper, and cook until hot.

2. Cut avocados in half, remove seeds, and peel. Cut into bite-size pieces and add to sauce with the fish, stirring gently to avoid breaking up the avocado. Spoon over toast or rice. Makes 4 servings.

SEAFOOD-STUFFED EGGPLANT

2 large eggplants, halved lengthwise
¼ cup (½ stick) butter, or more
5 tablespoons chopped green pepper
5 tablespoons chopped scallions
5 tablespoons chopped celery
5 tablespoons chopped parsley
½ teaspoon dried thyme
1½ cups uncooked shrimp, shelled, deveined and cut into ¼-inch pieces

▶ 2 cups cooked rice
1½ teaspoons Worcestershire sauce
▶ 1½ cups flaked cooked fish
Salt and pepper
¾ cup fine bread crumbs
5 tablespoons melted butter
5 tablespoons grated Parmesan cheese

1. With a sharp knife carefully remove the pulp from the eggplant halves, leaving a ¼-inch shell. Reserve the pulp. Blanch the eggplant shells by boiling in slightly salted water for 5 minutes, or until tender. Drain, the cut side down, on paper toweling.

2. Melt the butter in a large skillet. Sauté the green pepper, scallions, celery, parsley, and thyme until softened, about 5 minutes. Chop the eggplant pulp, and add to the skillet with additional butter if needed, and sauté for 5 minutes. Reduce heat and cook covered for 10 minutes or until eggplant is tender.

3. Stir in the shrimp, rice, and the Worcestershire sauce, raise the heat, and sauté the mixture for 2 minutes to cook the shrimp. Carefully fold in the fish flakes; cover the pan and turn off the heat.

4. Arrange the eggplant shells in a lightly greased, shallow baking dish. Sprinkle with salt and pepper before piling the seafood/rice mixture into the shells, mounding on top. Combine the bread crumbs, butter, and Parmesan cheese. Sprinkle over the eggplants. Place under preheated broiler for 2 or 3 minutes or until lightly browned. Makes 4 servings.

FISH-STUFFED POTATOES

4 large Idaho baking potatoes, about ½ pound each
3 tablespoons butter
1 cup coarsely diced fresh mushrooms
1 tablespoon chopped scallions
2 tablespoons dry sherry

▶ 1 cup flaked cooked fish
¼ cup heavy cream
Salt
Freshly ground pepper
A few drops Tabasco
1 tablespoon freshly grated Parmesan cheese

1. Arrange the potatoes on a baking sheet and place them in a preheated 400° oven. Bake 1 hour or until done.

2. Heat 1 tablespoon of the butter in a saucepan and add the mushrooms and the scallions. Cook, stirring, about 1 minute. Add the sherry and the fish; stir and remove from heat.

3. Slice off the top of each potato and scoop out the pulp into a saucepan. Reserve the shells. Mash the potato pulp well. Add the cream and 1 tablespoon of the butter, and cook briefly, stirring. Add salt, pepper, and Tabasco to taste; blend. Carefully combine this with the fish mixture.

4. Fill the potato shells with the mixture, piling it up lightly.

5. Arrange the potatoes on a baking dish. Sprinkle tops with cheese. Melt the remaining tablespoon of butter and pour it over the potatoes. Bake in the oven for 15 minutes. Makes 4 servings.

SEAFOOD-STUFFED TOMATOES

4 large ripe tomatoes
1 tablespoon butter or margarine
1 teaspoon curry powder
4 tablespoons chopped scallions
▶1½ cups cooked long-grain rice, (½ cup raw)
Pinch dillweed (optional)

▶ 1 cup cooked seafood (flaked fish, shrimp, crabmeat)
⅓ cup white wine vinegar
⅔ cup oil (olive and vegetable oils combined)
¼ teaspoon salt
⅛ teaspoon pepper
Lettuce

1. Cut tomatoes into 6 sections with a sharp knife, cutting about half way down. Scoop out the seeds and pulp with a spoon. Carefully turn upside down on paper toweling to drain.

(continued)

2. Melt the butter in a small skillet. Add the curry powder and cook 1 minute over low heat. Add 2 tablespoons of the scallions and sauté until tender, about 2 minutes.

3. In a medium-size bowl, combine rice with the sautéed scallion mixture, the remaining scallions, and add dillweed, if desired. Carefully fold in the fish.

4. Combine the wine vinegar, the oil, and salt and pepper in a screwtop jar and shake well. Pour ⅔ of the dressing over the rice mixture and toss to coat thoroughly. Set aside for 15 to 20 minutes to allow flavors to blend.

5. Stuff the tomatoes gently with the rice/fish mixture; serve on crisp lettuce with the remaining dressing. Makes 4 servings.

SEAFOOD QUICHE

2 tablespoons butter
¼ cup minced onion
1 tablespoon tomato paste
¼ cup Marsala wine
▶ 1 cup flaked cooked fish
▶ ½ pound diced, cooked scallops
   or shrimps (about 1 cup)
2 tablespoons minced parsley
   Salt and pepper
4 large eggs, lightly beaten

1 cup whipping cream
½ cup half-and-half cream
½ teaspoon dried basil
¼ teaspoon ground fennel
   Dash cayenne
1 9-inch pastry shell, partially
   baked 8 to 10 minutes at 400°
1¼ cups grated Gruyère or Swiss
   cheese

1. In a large skillet, melt butter. Add onion and sauté until soft. Stir in tomato paste. Add wine and cook over high heat for 1 to 2 minutes, until sauce is reduced to about 2 tablespoons. Add the fish, scallops, parsley, and season with salt and pepper to taste.

2. Beat the eggs with the creams and combine well with the basil, fennel, cayenne, and salt and pepper to taste.

3. Spoon the seafood mixture into the partially baked pastry shell, and sprinkle with the cheese. Pour the cream mixture over the cheese. Bake in a preheated 375° oven for 35 to 40 minutes until a knife inserted in the center comes out clean. Cool on rack for about 10 minutes before serving. Makes 6 to 8 servings.

"Preheating" oven

Before putting a quiche, pie, soufflé, or casserole in the oven, always allow sufficient time for the oven to reach the temperature specified in the recipe.

INDIVIDUAL FISH QUICHES

Pastry sufficient for 2-crust pie
▶ ¾ cup flaked cooked fish
 ¼ cup sliced scallions
 4 ounces grated Swiss cheese
 (1 cup)

2 eggs
⅓ cup milk
½ cup mayonnaise
¼ teaspoon salt
¼ teaspoon dried dillweed

1. On floured surface, roll half of the pastry into a 12-inch circle. Cut six 4-inch circles from it. Repeat with the remaining pastry. Fit the twelve circles into twelve 2½-inch muffin pan cups.

2. Distribute into each pastry cup a portion of the flaked fish, the scallions and the cheese.

3. Beat eggs with the milk, mayonnaise, salt, and dillweed. Pour over the filling in each pastry cup. Bake in 400° oven for 15 to 20 minutes or until browned. Makes 4 to 6 servings.

NANTUCKET HALIBUT PIE

⅓ cup butter, melted
3 cups fresh bread crumbs
1½ tablespoons grated onion
1 teaspoon salt
¾ teaspoon celery salt
¼ teaspoon pepper
¼ teaspoon rubbed sage
3 tablespoons butter or
 margarine
⅓ cup chopped onion
⅓ cup chopped celery

2 tablespoons chopped green
 pepper
3 tablespoons flour
1 cup milk
¼ teaspoon dill weed
▶ ½ cup cooked peas
▶ 1 cup flaked cooked halibut or
 haddock
1 cup dry bread crumbs,
 buttered

1. In a mixing bowl, combine the melted butter, fresh crumbs, grated onion, ½ teaspoon salt, ½ teaspoon celery salt, ⅛ teaspoon pepper, and ⅛ teaspoon sage; mix well. Butter a 1½-quart baking pan (8-inch square, or 11 x 7-inch) and press the crumb mixture onto the bottom and sides. Bake 25 minutes in a preheated 375° oven; let cool slightly.

2. Increase oven temperature to 425°. Melt the 3 tablespoons of butter in a medium skillet. Sauté onion, celery, and green pepper for 5 minutes; blend in the flour. Gradually stir in the milk. Cook over medium heat, stirring constantly, until thick and smooth. Remove from heat. Stir in the remaining salt, celery salt, pepper, and sage, and the dill, peas, and fish. Pour onto prepared crust. Top with buttered bread crumbs. Bake 20 minutes or until lightly browned. Makes 4 servings.

FISH ROLL FANTASTIQUE

Filling

2 tablespoons butter or
  margarine
2 tablespoons chopped onion
1 tablespoon chopped celery
2 tablespoons flour
¾ cup light cream
1 tablespoon minced parsley
1 tablespoon minced pimiento
▶ 3 tablespoons finely chopped
  cooked carrots
▶ 1 cup flaked cooked haddock
¾ teaspoon salt
⅛ teaspoon pepper

¼ teaspoon powdered mace
⅛ teaspoon paprika

Herbed Biscuit Dough

1 cup flour
1½ teaspoons baking powder
½ teaspoon salt
⅛ teaspoon dry mustard
¼ teaspoon powdered mace
¾ teaspoon caraway seeds
2 tablespoons shortening
6 tablespoons milk

Lemon Sauce (see Basics)

1. In a skillet, melt butter and sauté the onion and celery until lightly browned. Stir in flour and cook for 1 minute. Gradually add cream, stirring constantly until thickened and smooth. Remove from heat. Add parsley, pimiento, carrots, haddock, salt, pepper, mace, and paprika. Set aside and let cool.

2. To make the biscuit dough: combine the flour with the baking powder, salt, dry mustard, mace, and caraway seeds in a bowl. Use a pastry blender or two knives to cut in the shortening until mixture looks like coarse cornmeal. Make a well in the center and add the milk. Stir until it is fairly free from the sides of the bowl (about ½ minute). Turn the dough onto a lightly floured board. Knead gently and quickly 20 times or about ½ minute.

3. Roll or pat out the dough into a rectangle ½-inch thick. Spread the fish mixture over the dough. Roll up like a jelly roll. With a greased sharp knife, cut roll into 1-inch slices. Lay slices on a greased baking sheet. Bake in a preheated 425° oven for 12 to 15 minutes or until well browned. Serve with a bowl of Lemon Sauce (Avgolemono). Makes 4 servings.

FISH PUFF PIE

1 9" unbaked pie shell (see
  Basics)
2 tablespoons butter or
  margarine
2 tablespoons minced scallions
1 tablespoon chopped celery
1 tablespoon chopped green
  pepper
1 can (3 oz.) sliced mushrooms,
  drained; reserve liquid
4 eggs, beaten

¾ cup light cream
½ teaspoon salt
  Dash cayenne
⅛ teaspoon dried tarragon
¼ teaspoon dried marjoram
⅛ teaspoon pepper
▶ ¾ cup flaked cooked mild white
  fish
½ cup grated Swiss cheese
  Paprika

1. Partially bake pie shell in a very hot, 450° oven for about 7 minutes. Cool.

2. Melt butter in a small skillet, and sauté the scallions, celery, and green pepper for 5 minutes. Add the canned mushrooms, reserving about 10 slices. Cook 2 to 3 minutes more, until hot.

3. Combine the eggs, cream, reserved mushroom liquid, salt, cayenne, tarragon, marjoram, and pepper, beating well. Fold in, thoroughly, the sautéed onion mixture and flaked fish. Pour into the pie shell.

4. Sprinkle the pie with the cheese and bake 35 minutes in preheated 375° oven (350° if using glass baking dish). After baking 20 minutes, place the reserved 10 slices of mushrooms around the top, and return to oven. Bake 15 minutes longer or until the mixture is puffed and brown. When done, knife inserted into the center will come out clean. Sprinkle with paprika. Let pie stand for 5 minutes before cutting. Makes 6 servings.

 ## SIMPLE SIMON FISH CRÊPES

▶ 1 cup flaked cooked fish
▶ 2 hard-cooked eggs, chopped
1 tablespoon chopped chives
6 tablespoons mayonnaise
½ cup sour cream
2 teaspoons lemon juice, fresh or reconstituted

¼ teaspoon dried chervil
Salt and freshly ground pepper
8 crêpes (see Basics)
2 tablespoons melted butter
2 tablespoons grated Parmesan cheese

1. Combine the fish, eggs, and chives. Next, mix together the mayonnaise, sour cream, lemon juice and chervil. Fold carefully into the fish mixture; add salt and pepper to taste.

2. Divide the filling among the 8 crêpes, roll them up and place seam side down in a generously buttered oblong baking dish. Drizzle the melted butter over all, and sprinkle with the grated cheese. Bake in a preheated 350° oven for 20 minutes, or until heated through. Makes 4 servings.

 ## BAKED CRÊPES WITH FISH MORNAY

3 tablespoons butter
3 tablespoons flour
1½ cups milk
¼ cup dry white wine or sherry
¼ teaspoon salt
1 cup grated Gruyère or Swiss cheese
▶ 1 cup flaked cooked fish (sole, trout, haddock, halibut, etc.)

⅓ cup slivered blanched almonds
1 small pimiento, chopped
16 small cooked crêpes (see Basics)
2 egg yolks
2 tablespoons dry fine bread crumbs
Parsley
Lemon wedges

1. In a 2-quart saucepan, melt butter over medium heat. Mix in flour; cook and stir 1 minute. Gradually whisk in milk, wine, and salt; cook and stir until smooth and thickened. Gradually add cheese. Cook and stir until smooth, about 8 minutes. Remove from heat and add 1 cup of the sauce to the flaked fish. Add the almonds and pimiento and blend well.

(continued)

2. Place a generous tablespoon of this filling on each cooked crêpe. Fold crêpes over and place seam side down in a single layer in a long shallow baking dish.

3. Add the egg yolks to the remaining sauce, blend, and cook, stirring, over low heat for about 5 minutes (until sauce is very hot and quite thick). Pour over crêpes in baking dish. Sprinkle surface with bread crumbs and place dish in a preheated 375° oven until heated through and the edges of the crêpes begin to curl, about 10 minutes. Transfer to heated serving plates. Garnish with parsley sprigs and lemon wedges. Makes 4 servings.

SALMON BEIGNETS (French Fritters)

¼ cup plus 2 tablespoons butter
  or margarine
1 cup water
1 cup flour
4 eggs
▶ 1 cup flaked cooked salmon (or
  sole, flounder, cod, etc.)
3 or 4 anchovy fillets, chopped

4 tablespoons Parmesan
  cheese, freshly grated
1 teaspoon salt
  Cayenne to taste
  Deep fat for frying

1. Combine the butter and water in a saucepan and bring to a rolling boil. When the butter is melted, remove pan from heat. Add flour all at once and quickly mix together. Cook over low heat for about 5 minutes, stirring constantly, until the paste becomes smooth and doughy. Remove from heat.

2. Add the eggs one at a time, beating vigorously after each addition. Beat entire mixture for 3 to 4 minutes until smooth and shiny.

3. Stir in the salmon, anchovies, grated cheese, salt, and cayenne. Beat for 1 or 2 minutes more so ingredients will be thoroughly combined. Taste for seasoning and add more salt and cayenne if mixture is too bland.

4. Heat the deep fat—at least 3 inches in depth—to a temperature of 375°. Drop by heaping teaspoonfuls into the fat without crowding. Cook until they double in size and are deep brown all over, turning them periodically with a slotted spoon. Place each in a paper-towel-lined baking dish to drain and keep warm in the oven until all the *beignets* are done. Serve with cocktails, soups, and salads. Makes 6 servings.

FISH TIMBALES

¼ cup butter or margarine	½ cup finely chopped almonds
1 tablespoon minced celery	3 eggs, beaten
2 tablespoons minced green pepper	1 cup milk
	½ teaspoon salt
1 tablespoon minced scallions	⅛ teaspoon pepper
½ cup soft stale bread crumbs	⅛ teaspoon ground mace
▶1¼ cups flaked cooked fish	1 teaspoon Worcestershire sauce

1. Melt the butter and sauté, for 1 minute, the celery, green pepper, and scallions. Remove from the heat and add the crumbs, fish and almonds. Beat the eggs into the milk thoroughly, season with the salt, pepper, mace and Worcestershire sauce, and combine with the fish mixture.

2. Pour into 4 individual buttered soufflé molds, filling them three-quarters full. Place in a pan of warm water and bake in a preheated 350° oven for 20 to 25 minutes or until firm.

3. Unmold and serve with a rich cream or cheese sauce. Makes 4 servings.

COLD SALMON MOUSSE

2 teaspoons vegetable oil	2 teaspoons tomato paste
1 envelope unflavored gelatin	1 teaspoon paprika
¼ cup dry white wine	1½ tablespoons finely grated onion
▶ ¾ cup chicken stock, homemade or canned, thoroughly degreased	
	1½ teaspoons salt
	1 tablespoon lemon juice
▶ 2 cups chilled cooked salmon (firmly packed)	⅛ teaspoon Tabasco sauce
	¼ cup heavy cream
	Lettuce or watercress

1. Brush a 3- or 4-cup decorative mold with the vegetable oil; invert the mold into paper toweling to drain.

2. Soften the gelatin in the wine for 5 minutes. Heat the chicken stock to a simmer and add the softened gelatin. Cook for 1 or 2 minutes until the gelatin dissolves, then pour it into the jar of an electric blender. Add the salmon and blend at high speed until the mixture is an absolutely smooth purée. Scrape it out of the jar into a small mixing bowl; stir in the tomato paste, paprika, grated onion, salt, lemon juice, and Tabasco. Taste for seasoning.

3. Whip the cream in a chilled bowl until it is firm, not quite stiff. Set the bowl of puréed salmon into a larger bowl filled with ice and a little cold water. Stir the purée for a few minutes until it begins to stiffen. Remove from the ice and gently fold the whipped cream into the salmon mixture until no streaks of cream remain. Pour at once into the oiled mold, smooth the top, cover with plastic wrap, and refrigerate for 2 hours or until firm.

4. To serve, run a small sharp knife around the inside edge of the mold, dip the bottom of the mold into hot water for a second or two, and wipe it dry with a towel. Place a chilled platter on top of it, invert it, and rap it smartly on the table once or twice to dislodge it. Surround with crisp lettuce or watercress. Serve it with plain or curry mayonnaise. Makes 4 to 6 servings.

NORDIC SOUFFLÉ

3 tablespoons butter
4 tablespoons flour
1 cup milk
2 teaspoons lemon juice
½ teaspoon grated onion
½ teaspoon Worcestershire sauce

¾ teaspoon salt
3 egg yolks
►1½ cups flaked cooked fish
4 egg whites, stiffly beaten
Pecan sauce (see below)

1. Melt butter in saucepan. Add flour and stir until blended. Add milk gradually and cook until the mixture is thickened, stirring constantly. Remove from heat. Add lemon juice, onion, Worcestershire sauce and salt. Beat the egg yolks until they are thick and lemon colored; add to the sauce with the flaked fish.

2. Fold in ⅔ of the beaten egg whites into the sauce very thoroughly. Fold in the remaining egg whites very gently. Pour into ungreased 1½-quart baking dish. Place in pan of hot water and bake in moderate oven (350°) for 1 hour or until firm. Serve at once with pecan sauce. Makes 4 to 6 servings.

Pecan Sauce

2 tablespoons butter
¼ cup chopped pecans
2 tablespoons flour

1 cup light cream
¼ teaspoon salt

Melt butter in a saucepan; brown pecans lightly, stirring frequently. Blend in flour; gradually stir in cream. Cook over low heat, stirring constantly, until thickened. Remove from heat; season with salt. Makes 1½ cups.

FISH AND VEGETABLE SOUFFLÉ

►1¼ cups chopped cooked
   vegetables
¼ cup minced green pepper
2 tablespoons minced pimiento
1 tablespoon minced onion

►1½ cups flaked cooked fish
►1½ cups mashed potatoes
½ cup mayonnaise
½ teaspoon dry mustard
4 eggs, separated

1. Combine the cooked vegetables, green pepper, pimiento, onion, and fish in a large mixing bowl.

2. Whip mashed potatoes a minute to fluff them; fold in the mayonnaise, and the dry mustard. Beat egg yolks into the potatoes, one at a time; beat potato/egg mixture until fluffy. Stir into vegetable mixture.

3. Beat egg whites until stiff but not dry and fold into vegetable mixture. Pour into greased 1½-quart casserole. Bake in preheated 350° oven for 1 hour or until knife inserted in center comes out clean. Serve at once. Makes 6 servings.

STUFFED EGGS BRITTANIA

2 tablespoons butter
2 tablespoons flour
½ cup light cream
½ cup milk
½ teaspoon salt
⅛ teaspoon pepper
¼ cup grated sharp Cheddar
  cheese

1 egg yolk, lightly beaten
▶ 6 hard-cooked eggs
▶ ¼ cup flaked cooked fish
1 teaspoon prepared mustard
¼ teaspoon curry powder
Dash cayenne
1 to 2 tablespoons mayonnaise
Paprika

1. Melt butter in a saucepan; stir in the flour and cook for 2 to 3 minutes. Gradually add the cream and milk, stirring constantly; season with salt and pepper, and cook until thickened. Add cheese and egg yolk. Stir in thoroughly. Set aside.

2. Cut eggs in half lengthwise; remove the yolks and mash. Combine with the fish, prepared mustard, curry powder and the cayenne, and mix well. Add enough mayonnaise to bind the mixture together. Stuff the egg whites with the egg mixture. Place in a greased, shallow baking dish.

3. Pour the sauce over the stuffed eggs. Sprinkle with paprika. Bake in a preheated 375° oven for 15 minutes or until lightly browned. Makes 4 servings.

DOUBLE CHEESE SOUFFLÉ
WITH SHRIMP SAUCE

8 tablespoons butter
▶ 1½ cups cubed cooked shrimp
¼ cup cognac
2 tablespoons finely chopped
  shallots or scallions
2 teaspoons tomato paste
5 tablespoons flour
▶ ½ cup chicken stock, homemade
  or canned
¼ cup dry white wine
6 tablespoons heavy cream

Salt
¼ teaspoon cayenne
½ teaspoon lemon juice
1 cup grated Parmesan and
  Gruyère cheeses, mixed
1 cup milk
4 egg yolks
1 teaspoon mustard,
  preferably Dijon
5 egg whites

1. In a small frying pan, melt 2 tablespoons of the butter; add the shrimp and, stirring constantly, cook briskly for about 1 minute; remove from heat. Warm the cognac in a ladle or a small saucepan, light it with a match, and pour it over the shrimp. Shake the pan back and forth until the flame dies out. Transfer the shrimp and any pan juices to a small bowl and reserve.

2. Add 2 tablespoons of butter to the pan and sauté the chopped shallots until soft. Remove pan from the heat, stir in the tomato paste, and 2 tablespoons flour, and stir until smooth. Pour in the chicken stock and white wine. Mix together with a whisk, bring the sauce to a boil, stirring almost constantly. Simmer over low heat for 1 minute; thin with the cream, a tablespoon at a time. Season with salt to taste, ⅛ teaspoon cayenne, and the lemon juice. Return the shrimp to the sauce and set aside.

(continued)

3. Generously butter a 6-cup soufflé dish or casserole and sprinkle 2 table-spoons of cheese evenly over all surfaces. In a saucepan, melt 3 tablespoons of butter, stir in the remaining 3 tablespoons of flour and cook, stirring over low heat for 2 minutes. Pour in the milk, stir until smooth and thick and simmer for 3 to 4 minutes to remove the raw taste of flour. Remove from the heat and, using a whisk, beat in, one at a time, the egg yolks. Add salt to taste, the remaining cayenne, the mustard and ¾ cup of the grated cheese. Mix thoroughly and let cool at least ½ a minute.

4. Beat the egg whites until they are shiny and stiff enough to hold a good peak when the beaters are lifted out of the bowl. Thoroughly fold ¼ cup of the beaten whites into the warm cheese sauce, then pour the sauce over the remaining egg whites. Fold in gently and quickly until almost com-bined. Pour the mixture into the soufflé dish and sprinkle with the remaining cheese. Place the dish in the center of a pre-heated 375° oven. Bake for 25 to 35 minutes. Reheat the shrimp sauce and serve immediately with the soufflé. Makes 4 servings.

NEW BEDFORD FISH BISQUE

2 tablespoons butter
1 teaspoon minced onion
2 tablespoons flour
▶ 1 cup chicken broth
1½ cups light cream
½ teaspoon salt

⅛ teaspoon white pepper
1 teaspoon Worcestershire sauce
▶ 1 cup flaked cooked fish
Dash cayenne
1 teaspoon minced parsley

1. Melt butter in a medium skillet; add onion and sauté until soft but not brown. Stir in flour; cook 2 minutes. Slowly add combined chicken broth and cream; stir until smooth. Season with salt, pepper, and Worcestershire sauce.

2. Add fish to the soup. Turn into the top of a double boiler. Heat over boiling water for 15 minutes. Pour into a soup tureen; sprinkle with cay-enne and parsley. Makes 4 servings.

CHILLED SEAFOOD BISQUE

1 can (10½ oz.) tomato soup
1 cup milk
¼ cup light cream
▶ ½ cup chopped cooked shrimp
▶ ½ cup flaked cooked fish

Salt and pepper to taste
1 teaspoon dried dill
Lemon juice
Chopped chives

Beat soup and milk and cream together until smooth. Add the chopped shrimp and flaked fish. Season to taste with salt and pepper, dill and lemon juice; chill for 1 hour. Top with chives before serving. Makes 4 servings.

BRISTOL FISH SOUP

4 tablespoons butter or
  margarine
½ onion chopped
1 cup milk
½ cup chopped raw carrots
► 1 cup flaked cooked fish
3 tablespoons flour

► 2 cups chicken broth, fish stock
  or vegetable stock
½ teaspoon thyme, crumbled
Salt and pepper to taste
Dash nutmeg
Herb croutons

1. Melt 1 tablespoon of butter in a heavy saucepan; sauté the onion but
do not let brown. Combine the onion with milk, and carrots, and simmer
for 10 minutes. Purée the fish in the blender with the milk/vegetable mixture. Put aside.

2. Melting the remaining 3 tablespoons of butter in the saucepan, stir in
flour until smooth. Cook slowly, stirring constantly, for about 2 minutes. Do
not brown. Remove from heat; add the heated chicken broth, stirring until well blended. Cook over medium heat, whisking constantly, until the
sauce boils 1 minute. Remove from heat and season with thyme, and salt
and pepper to taste.

3. Combine the fish and milk mixture with the velouté sauce in the
saucepan, and bring just to a boil. Add the nutmeg, and more salt if desired. If too thick, add more milk or broth. Serve with toasted herbed
croûtons. Makes 4 servings.

 CAPE COD FISH CHOWDER

► 2 tablespoons bacon drippings
1 onion, chopped
¼ cup chopped green pepper
► 2 cups diced cooked potatoes
1 cup water
1 can (10½ oz.) condensed
  cream of celery soup
1 can (10½ oz.) condensed New
  England-style clam chowder
1 cup milk

1 cup light cream
1 teaspoon salt
¼ teaspoon pepper
½ teaspoon thyme
► 2 cups coarsely chopped
  cooked fish
► ½ cup cooked mixed
  vegetables, optional
5 strips crisp bacon, chopped
3 tablespoons minced parsley

1. In a deep saucepan, heat the bacon drippings and cook the onion
and green pepper until tender but not browned. Add the potatoes and
fry for 2 or 3 minutes. Add the water, soups, milk, and cream; stir until well
blended. Season with the salt, pepper, and thyme.

2. Gently stir in the fish, vegetables, and chopped bacon, and heat 2
minutes. Stir in half of the parsley. Heat until piping hot. Pour into a large
soup tureen; sprinkle with the remaining parsley and serve hot. Makes 6
servings.

FISH CROQUETTES

3 tablespoons butter
4 tablespoons flour
½ teaspoon salt
⅛ teaspoon pepper
1 cup milk
▶ 2 cups flaked cooked fish

2 tablespoons minced parsley
2 tablespoons minced onion
1 teaspoon dillweed
¾ cup fine dried bread crumbs
1 egg, beaten with 1 tablespoon water

1. Melt butter and blend in flour, salt, and pepper. Gradually add milk and cook, stirring constantly, until smooth and thickened. Stir in fish flakes, parsley, onion, and dillweed.

2. Spread mixture on a flat dish and cool. Divide mixture into 12 equal parts. Shape each into a roll about 2 inches long. Roll in crumbs, then in egg beaten with the water. Roll again in crumbs. Chill for 30 minutes.

3. Fry in hot deep fat (375° on a frying thermometer) until golden brown, about 3 minutes.* Drain on absorbent paper. Serve with a creamed vegetable. Makes 12 croquettes. Makes 4 servings.
*Note: Can also be baked in 350° oven for 20 minutes or sautéed in frying pan in oil.

SCANDINAVIAN FISH CAKES

4 medium baking-type potatoes, freshly boiled (about 1 cup mashed)
▶ 1 cup finely flaked cooked fish (firmly packed)
5 anchovy fillets, drained, washed, dried and finely chopped (about 1 tablespoon)
2 egg yolks
1 tablespoon finely grated onion
1 tablespoon softened butter

1 tablespoon finely chopped fresh dill, or 1 teaspoon dried dill
½ teaspoon salt
⅛ teaspoon cayenne
1 to 3 tablespoons fine dry bread crumbs (optional)
6 tablespoons butter, melted and combined with 2 tablespoons vegetable oil
½ cup cornstarch or flour, sifted

1. Dry the potatoes thoroughly over low heat in an ungreased frying pan before you peel and mash them. If available, use a potato ricer for the mashing.

2. In a large mixing bowl combine the mashed potatoes, fish, and anchovies, beating vigorously until thoroughly combined and smooth. Beat in the egg yolks, one at a time, then the grated onion, softened butter, dill, salt, and cayenne. If mixture is not solid enough to hold its shape in a spoon, beat into it up to 3 tablespoons of bread crumbs to give the mixture the proper density. Chill for 1 hour or so if time permits. Form the fish mixture into patties* about 3 inches in diameter.

3. In a large heavy frying pan heat the butter-oil mixture until the fat begins to sizzle. Quickly dip the cakes into the sifted cornstarch, shake free of any excess, and fry the cakes over fairly high heat until they are a crisp, deep brown on both sides. Add a little more fat to the pan, if necessary, when you turn them over. Serve at once. Makes 4 servings.
*Note: These fish cakes may be formed into small balls and either sautéed or deep-fried at 375° until golden brown and crisp. They make fine hors d'oeuvres with or without a sauce.

RED HADDOCK HASH

1 medium onion
1 tablespoon chopped green
  pepper
► 1 tablespoon melted bacon
  drippings
► 1 cup coarsely flaked cooked
  haddock
► 1 cup chopped boiled potatoes
► ½ cup chopped cooked beets

1 teaspoon chopped parsley
1 teaspoon salt
¼ teaspoon pepper
  Dash cayenne
  Dash Tabasco
  Pinch nutmeg
½ cup milk
1 tablespoon butter

1. In a skillet, sauté onion and green pepper in melted bacon drippings until tender, about 5 minutes. Remove with a slotted spoon.

2. In a large bowl, mix fish, potatoes, and beets lightly; add parsley, salt, pepper, cayenne, Tabasco, nutmeg, milk, and the onion and green pepper.

3. Add butter to drippings in skillet; add fish mixture, and brown lightly over medium heat, stirring with a fork. Pat mixture lightly, cover and continue cooking until well browned on bottom. Fold over and slide onto a heated platter. Makes 4 servings.

BAKED FISH LOAF

1 egg
¼ cup evaporated milk, or light
  cream
1 tablespoon butter or
  margarine, melted
► 2 cups chopped cooked fish
¾ cup soft bread crumbs

3 tablespoons minced parsley
2 tablespoons minced onion
2 tablespoons minced olives
½ teaspoon salt
⅛ teaspoon pepper
¼ teaspoon nutmeg
1 teaspoon Worcestershire sauce

1. Beat the egg into the milk and melted butter. Add the fish, bread crumbs, parsley, onion, and olives, and mix thoroughly. Season with the salt, pepper, nutmeg, and Worcestershire sauce. Beat mixture well.

2. Pour into greased loaf pan. Bake in a preheated 400° oven for 30 to 40 mintues. Serve hot with a white sauce or cheese sauce, or cold with curry mayonnaise. Makes 4 servings.

CHESAPEAKE COLESLAW

2 cups finely shredded crisp
  cabbage
½ cup chopped unpared apple
½ cup chopped celery
¼ cup chopped walnuts

► 1 cup flaked cooked fish
½ teaspoon salt
⅛ teaspoon pepper
½ cup mayonnaise
2 tablespoons chili sauce

Combine the cabbage with the apple, celery, walnuts, flaked fish, salt, and pepper. Mix the mayonnaise with the chili sauce, and toss with fish/vegetable mixture thoroughly to blend. Makes 4 servings.

SEAFOOD AND POTATO SALAD

▶ 3 large cooked potatoes,
  quartered and sliced ½-inch
  thick
▶ ½ cup cooked flaked fish
▶ ¾ cup sliced cooked scallops
  ¼ cup chopped red onion
  ½ cup dry white wine
  ½ cup mayonnaise

1 egg yolk, beaten
1½ teaspoons olive oil
  A few drops grated onion
1 teaspoon lemon juice
1 teaspoon chopped chives
1 teaspoon parsley

1. Place the sliced potatoes, fish, scallops and red onion in a bowl; cover with the wine and set aside.

2. In another bowl, combine the mayonnaise, egg yolk, oil, onion juice, and lemon juice, and beat vigorously together until smooth.

3. Drain the potatoes and seafood. Combine with the mayonnaise mixture. When ready to serve, sprinkle with chives and parsley. Makes 4 to 6 servings.

CARIBBEAN FISH SALAD

▶ 2 cups cold cooked rice
  ½ cup chopped celery
  1 tablespoon chopped chives or
  scallions
▶ ½ cup cooked peas
  1 tablespoon chopped almonds
  1 tablespoon chopped chutney

  Dash paprika
▶ 1½ cups flaked cooked fish
  2 tablespoons lemon juice
  ⅔ cup mayonnaise
  ½ teaspoon curry powder
  Crisp lettuce leaves

1. Combine the rice, celery, chives, peas, almonds, chutney, paprika, and the fish, and toss with lemon juice.

2. Mix the mayonnaise and the curry powder. Combine with the rice/fish mixture. Toss lightly to blend. Mound onto crisp lettuce leaves. Makes 6 servings.

DILLED FISH SALAD

  3 tablespoons olive oil
  1 tablespoon lemon juice
  ½ teaspoon salt
  ⅛ teaspoon cayenne
  2 tablespoons minced shallots or
  scallions
  2 tablespoons minced fresh dill
  or 1 teaspoon dillweed
▶ 2 cups poached sole, chilled
  and cut into 1-inch pieces

  1 cup mayonnaise
  ¼ cup minced celery
  2 to 3 cups romaine or Boston
  lettuce, shredded and chilled
  4 tomatoes, peeled and sliced
▶ 3 hard-cooked eggs, sliced
  2 tablespoons capers, drained,
  washed and dried

1. Mix together the olive oil, lemon juice, salt, cayenne, shallots or scallions, and half the dill. Pour over the cold fish and toss together gently. Let the fish marinate in this mixture for about 1 hour, turning the pieces over occasionally.

2. Combine ½ cup of the mayonnaise carefully with the fish and its marinade, and the celery. Arrange this mixture on the chilled lettuce in a large glass bowl. Stir the remaining dill into the remaining mayonnaise and spread it over the fish, covering it completely. Alternately overlap the sliced tomatoes and hard-cooked eggs around the edge of the bowl and sprinkle the capers over the fish. Serve chilled. Makes 4 servings.

SEAFOOD SALAD CONSTANTINE

▶ 1 cup cooked diced shrimp
▶ 1 cup cooked flaked fish
½ cup diced celery
⅓ cup peeled chopped tomato
½ teaspoon minced parsley
1 cup mayonnaise
1 teaspoon prepared mustard
⅛ teaspoon Worcestershire sauce

1 tablespoon minced sweet
  gherkins
1 teaspoon chopped capers
1 teaspoon dried chervil
½ teaspoon anchovy paste
1 teaspoon salt
¼ teaspoon pepper
¼ teaspoon paprika
Crisp lettuce cups

1. Combine the shrimp, fish, celery, tomato, and parsley. In a separate bowl, mix the remaining ingredients. except the lettuce cups, beating vigorously to blend well.

2. Toss the dressing with the fish mixture and blend thoroughly. Chill 1 hour and serve in the crisp lettuce cups. Makes 4 servings.

MOLDED FISH SALAD

1 envelope (1 tablespoon)
  unflavored gelatin
2 cups tomato juice
½ teaspoon salt
  Dash of pepper
  Dash of Worcestershire sauce
1 teaspoon sugar
1 teaspoon prepared
  horseradish

1½ teaspoons grated onion
1 tablespoon lemon juice
⅓ cup mayonnaise
▶ 2 cups cooked fish, flaked
¼ cup finely chopped dill pickle
½ cup finely chopped celery
▶ 2 hard-cooked eggs, sliced

1. Combine gelatin and ¼ cup of the tomato juice in mixing bowl. Heat remaining tomato juice, add to gelatin, and stir until gelatin is dissolved. Then add salt, pepper, Worcestershire sauce, sugar, horseradish, onion, lemon juice, and mayonnaise; blend together. Chill until slightly thickened. Fold in fish, dill pickle, and celery.

2. Arrange egg slices in bottom of wet 1½-quart ring mold. Turn the gelatin mixture into the mold. Chill until firm. Unmold on crisp lettuce. Serve with mayonnaise. Makes 8 servings.

QUICK FISH SALAD

▶ 2 cups flaked cooked fish
▶ 1½ cups cooked macaroni shells
  ½ cucumber, diced
  ¼ cup minced celery
  2 tablespoons chopped scallions
▶ 3 hard-cooked eggs, diced

▶ ¼ cup chopped cooked broccoli
  or carrots
  Salt and pepper
  ½ cup mayonnaise
  ½ teaspoon prepared mustard
  Lettuce leaves
  Tomato slices

1. In a large bowl, combine the fish, macaroni shells, cucumber, celery, scallions, eggs, broccoli or carrots, and salt and pepper to taste.

2. Mix the mayonnaise and the mustard. Fold the dressing into the fish/vegetable mixture. Chill and serve on crisp lettuce leaves in a circle of tomato slices. Makes 4 servings.

AVOCADO FISH DIP

  1 large ripe avocado
  ½ cup heavy cream
  ¼ cup dry white wine
  ½ teaspoon lemon juice
  ½ teaspoon dillweed

▶ ½ cup flaked cooked fish (sole,
  halibut, haddock, etc.)
  Cayenne pepper
  Salt
  Minced chives

Cut the avocado in half, remove seed and skin. Scoop out fruit and mash until smooth. Beat until light. Slowly blend in the cream; add the wine, lemon juice, dill, and flaked fish. Blend well, season with cayenne pepper and salt to taste. Pile into serving dish and sprinkle surface with chives to taste. Serve with crisp crackers or melba toast rounds. Makes 1½ cups.

SALMON PÂTÉ

  ⅓ pound sweet butter, softened
▶ 2 cups cooked flaked salmon
  (or other fish), firmly packed
  1½ teaspoons finely chopped
  onion

  1 tablespoon lemon juice
  1 teaspoon salt
  Cayenne to taste
  4 tablespoons chives, minced

1. In a large mixing bowl, cream the butter by beating until smooth and pale in color. In a heavy bowl, mash and pound the salmon until it is perfectly smooth and pasty; then beat it, bit by bit, into the creamed butter. Beat in the onions, lemon juice, salt, cayenne, and chives.

2. Transfer the pâté to a 2-cup crock or two 1-cup crocks. Chill for at least 3 hours, or overnight. Serve the pâté as a spread on crisp French or Italian bread, pumpernickel, or crackers. Makes 2 cups.

BROILED FISH BURGERS

▶ 1 cup cooked flaked fish (trout, halibut, or other firm white fish)
1½ tablespoons minced celery
1 tablespoon sweet pickle relish
1 tablespoon minced scallions
½ teaspoon fresh lemon juice, or to taste

Freshly ground pepper
2 to 3 tablespoons mayonnaise
Butter or margarine
2 hamburger buns, or English muffins
4 slices bacon
4 slices Cheddar cheese

1. Combine fish, celery, sweet pickle relish, scallions, lemon juice, pepper to taste, and enough mayonnaise to moisten. Lightly toast and butter bun halves and spread with fish mixture.

2. Cut bacon slices in half and partially fry to remove most of fat. Top each fish mixture with a slice of cheese and 2 bacon strips. Broil 5 inches from heat for 4 minutes or until cheese melts and bacon crisps. Makes 4 servings.

Hints for cooking with cheese

To prepare cheese to melt readily, hard cheeses should first be grated, semi-hard should be shredded, and softer cheeses should be cut into small cubes. This should be done when the cheese is cold. When the cooking process begins, of course, all cheese should be at room temperature.

Always add cheese to a sauce after the sauce is cooked and heat only until melted, over the lowest possible heat.

Bake casseroles containing cheese at moderate or low temperatures. When mixed with crumbs, or used alone as a topping, add shortly before casseroles come out of oven.

Hints for cooking with wine

1. Always use a "drinking" wine rather than a "cooking" wine, and always use rather sparingly.

2. Warm wine before adding it to a hot liquid or pan, unless you want to reduce it in order to increase its flavoring effect. Reduce wine quickly using high heat (1 cup down to ¼ cup in 10 minutes), but when cooking food in wine, keep heat at a bare simmer, and keep pan covered.

3. To get a stronger wine flavor, add reduced wine at the end of the cooking period; otherwise, wine should be added early in the cooking.

4. To avoid curdling a sauce, add any wine to a dish *before* including any eggs, milk, cream, or butter, which should be added with the pan off the heat.

5. Use salt with caution, since wine enhances the flavor of salt.

Steaming vegetables

Preparing fresh vegetables properly—by steaming over hot water only until crisp-tender—will ensure great vegetables the first time, and perfect vegetables for your leftovers dishes.

►VEGETABLES

For leftover vegetables, too, each recipe is identified by the symbol of the type of dish made with it.

 CASSEROLES

 SAUCED COMBINATION DISHES

 STUFFED VEGETABLES

 PIES, TARTS, TURNOVERS & QUICHES

 PANCAKES, CRÊPES & FRITTERS

 EGGS & SOUFFLES

 SOUPS

 CROQUETTES & HASH

 SALADS

 OTHERS

ASPARAGUS À LA PROVENCE

3 strips bacon, chopped
1 onion, chopped
1 clove garlic, minced
4 large fresh tomatoes, chopped
½ teaspoon grated orange rind

1 cup dry white wine
½ cup minced parsley
Salt and pepper to taste
▶ 12 to 16 drained, cooked
asparagus

1. Cook the bacon in a saucepan until crisp. Remove and set aside.

2. Add the onion, garlic, tomatoes, orange rind and wine to the pan. Cook, stirring often, until mixture is reduced to a sauce. Stir in the bacon, and parsley; season with salt and pepper.

3. Add the asparagus to the sauce and simmer just until asparagus are warmed through. Makes 4 servings.

COLD CREAM OF ASPARAGUS SOUP

▶ 2 cups diced cooked asparagus
stalks
▶ ½ cup chicken broth
½ cup dry white wine
½ cup heavy cream

1 teaspoon curry powder
⅛ teaspoon ground mace
½ cup sour cream
Salt and pepper to taste

Purée the asparagus with broth, wine, and heavy cream. Stir in the curry powder, mace and sour cream. Season with salt and pepper. Serve cold. Makes 4 to 6 servings.

To serve hot: before adding sour cream, salt and pepper, bring soup to a boil; reduce heat. When soup is just simmering, stir in sour cream, salt and pepper. Remove soup from heat and serve immediately.

IVY LEAGUE BEETS

5 tablespoons orange juice
2 teaspoons lemon juice
2 tablespoons butter
1 teaspoon salt

▶ 2 cups chopped cooked beets
2 teaspoons cornstarch
½ teaspoon grated orange rind
(optional)

1. Combine 4 tablespoons of the orange juice with the lemon juice, butter, and salt in a saucepan. Bring to a simmer over very low heat, and add the beets. Gently cook until the beets are heated through, about 5 minutes.

2. Mix the cornstarch with the remaining orange juice. Stir into the beets and continue stirring until the sauce is thickened and clear. Add, if you wish, the orange rind. Makes 4 servings.

BORSCHT

2 tablespoons butter
1 small onion, diced
▶ 3 cups clear chicken broth, homemade or canned
▶ 1 cup diced cooked beets
½ cup tomato purée

1 tablespoon lemon juice
½ teaspoon sugar
Salt and pepper to taste
2 egg yolks, lightly beaten
1 cup sour cream

1. Heat the butter in a saucepan; sauté the onion until tender. Add the broth, beets, tomato purée, lemon juice, sugar, and salt and pepper to taste. Simmer 30 minutes.

2. Vigorously beat 2 tablespoons of the hot soup into the egg yolks, then beat the egg yolks into the soup in the saucepan; immediately remove from heat but keep beating until the soup thickens.

3. Serve hot or cold with a dollop of sour cream on each portion. Makes 4 servings.

BEET SALAD

▶ 2 cups cold sliced cooked beets
1 red onion, thinly sliced
1 tablespoon superfine sugar
2 tablespoons cider vinegar

⅓ cup salad oil
Salt and freshly ground pepper to taste

1. Arrange the beet and onion slices in overlapping circles in a shallow bowl.

2. In another bowl or jar, mix the sugar with the vinegar, oil, and salt and pepper. Pour over the beets and onions, making sure all the vegetables are coated. Cover, and let stand at room temperature 1 hour. Serve as a colorful go-along salad to accompany tuna salad, egg salad, bowls of olives and celery sticks. Makes 4 servings.

BEET AND POTATO SALAD

▶ 2 cups cubed cooked peeled beets
▶ 2 cups cubed cooked peeled potatoes
½ cup minced scallions
1 stalk celery, diced
¼ cup sour cream

½ cup mayonnaise
¼ cup plain yogurt
½ teaspoon dry mustard
1 teaspoon vinegar
Salt and pepper to taste
▶ 1 cup cooked peas (optional)

1. Place the beets, potatoes, scallions, and celery in a large mixing bowl.

2. In a smaller bowl, combine the sour cream, mayonnaise, yogurt, mustard, vinegar, salt and pepper; toss gently with the salad ingredients.

3. Put the salad into a serving bowl; garnish with the peas. Makes 4 servings.

BROCCOLI CASSEROLE FIRENZA

4 tablespoons butter
3 tablespoons flour
1 cup milk
½ cup shredded Cheddar
  cheese
½ teaspoon dried oregano
⅛ teaspoon pepper

1 cup chopped stewed
  tomatoes, drained
2 eggs, lightly beaten
▶ 2 to 2½ cups coarsely chopped
  cooked broccoli, drained
⅓ cup grated Parmesan cheese

1. Heat 3 tablespoons butter in a saucepan; add flour and stir until *roux* is smooth; gradually pour in milk, stirring constantly. Add Cheddar cheese to sauce and simmer for 10 minutes; remove from heat, and let cool to lukewarm. Stir oregano, pepper, tomatoes, eggs and broccoli into sauce.

2. Turn this mixture into a buttered 10 × 6 baking dish, and sprinkle the Parmesan cheese over the top. Bake in a preheated 350° oven about 30 minutes or until very hot and bubbly. Makes 4 to 6 servings.

BROCCOLI AU GRATIN

4 tablespoons butter
3 tablespoons flour
1½ cups milk
½ teaspoon salt
⅛ teaspoon each: nutmeg,
  pepper, and allspice
2 tablespoons dry sherry

½ cup shredded Cheddar
  cheese
1 egg yolk, slightly beaten
▶ 2 cups drained chopped
  cooked broccoli
¼ cup fine dry bread crumbs
Paprika to taste

1. Melt 3 tablespoons of the butter in a saucepan, add the flour, and stir until the mixture is smooth; slowly add the milk, stirring constantly. Cook, stirring over low heat until sauce thickens.

2. Add the salt, nutmeg, pepper, allspice, sherry, and cheese. Stir until the cheese is melted. Beat a little of the hot sauce into the egg yolk; beat the egg mixture back into the sauce, and remove pan from heat.

3. Stir the broccoli into the sauce and transfer the mixture to a shallow greased baking dish. Sprinkle with the bread crumbs and paprika. Bake in a preheated 375° oven until the sauce is bubbly hot and the surface is lightly browned. Makes 4 servings.

Storage of herbs and spices

Herbs and spices lose flavor if kept in light and near heat. They should be kept in tightly sealed containers in a dry place that is cool and dark.

BROCCOLI QUICHE

Pastry for 9" single-crust pie
(see Basics)
½ cup grated Parmesan cheese
▶ 2 cups drained diced cooked
broccoli
1 cup shredded Swiss cheese
½ cup thin-sliced scallions

3 eggs
▶ ¼ cup chicken broth, homemade
or canned
1 cup heavy cream
½ teaspoon salt
4 drops Tabasco

1. Line a 9" pie pan or quiche dish with pastry. Generously prick bottom and sides with fork. Bake in a preheated 450° oven for 5 minutes. Remove from the oven (leave oven on) and sprinkle with 2 tablespoons of the Parmesan cheese.

2. Combine 2 tablespoons of the Parmesan cheese with the broccoli, Swiss cheese, and scallions in a mixing bowl.

3. Beat the eggs, broth, cream, salt, and Tabasco together and stir into the broccoli mixture; pour into the prepared pie shell.

4. Sprinkle the remaining Parmesan cheese over the quiche. Bake in the 450° oven 10 minutes; reduce heat to 325° and bake 30 to 35 minutes or until a knife inserted in the center comes out clean. Let stand 10 minutes before cutting. Makes 6 servings.

CREAM OF BROCCOLI SOUP

1 leek, washed and thinly sliced
1 stalk celery, sliced
1 tablespoon butter or
margarine
▶1½ cups chicken broth,
homemade or canned
Salt and pepper to taste

2 tablespoons uncooked long-
grain rice
▶ 2 cups cooked, drained broccoli
¾ cup dry white wine
2 tablespoons lemon juice
½ cup cream

1. Combine the leek, celery, butter and ½ cup of the chicken broth in a large saucepan. Simmer 2 minutes; stir in salt, pepper, rice, and the remaining broth. Bring to boiling; lower the heat; cover; simmer 15 minutes or until the rice is tender.

2. Whirl the vegetable-broth mixture in the container of an electric blender until smooth. Return mixture to saucepan.

3. Whirl the broccoli, wine, and lemon juice in blender until smooth. Stir into the mixture in the saucepan. Stir in the cream; heat, stirring constantly, until hot. Makes 4 to 6 servings.

BROCCOLI, ENDIVE, AND WALNUT SALAD

¼ cup mayonnaise
1 teaspoon lemon juice
3 tablespoons heavy cream
2 tablespoons crumbled
  Roquefort cheese
¼ teaspoon pepper

▶ 1 cup coarsely chopped cooked
  broccoli
2 heads Belgian endive, trimmed
  and coarsely chopped
½ cup coarsely chopped walnuts
  Lettuce leaves
4 walnut halves

1. Blend the mayonnaise with lemon juice, cream, cheese, and pepper. Stir the broccoli, endive, and chopped walnuts into the dressing.

2. Spoon the salad onto lettuce leaves and garnish with the walnut halves. Makes 4 servings.

BROCCOLI-CAULIFLOWER SALAD

⅓ cup vegetable oil
2 tablespoons vinegar
1 tablespoon honey
¼ teaspoon salt
  Freshly ground pepper to taste
▶ 1 cup cooked broccoli flowerets
▶ 1 cup cooked cauliflowerets

½ cup slivered carrots
3 scallions, sliced
  Crisp lettuce leaves
6 to 8 cherry tomatoes, cut in
  half
2 strips crisp, crumbled cooked
  bacon

1. In a medium bowl, whisk together oil, vinegar, honey, salt, and pepper to taste. Add the broccoli, cauliflower, carrot, and scallions; toss gently. Cover and chill for 2 hours.

2. Pour into a lettuce-lined bowl; surround with cherry tomatoes,and sprinkle bacon on top. Makes 4 servings

CARROT PIE

▶1½ cups puréed cooked carrots
½ cup firmly packed light brown
  sugar
1 tablespoon cornstarch
½ teaspoon salt
¼ teaspoon ground cinnamon
¼ teaspoon ground ginger

¼ teaspoon ground allspice
¼ teaspoon ground nutmeg
1½ cups milk
2 eggs, well beaten
½ teaspoon vanilla extract
1 9-inch pie crust, unbaked (see
  Basics)

1. In a mixing bowl, combine the carrots, sugar, cornstarch, salt, cinnamon, ginger, allspice, nutmeg, milk, eggs, and vanilla; beat until well blended. Pour mixture into the pie shell.

2. Bake in a preheated 350° oven for 50 to 60 minutes, or until filling is set. Cool before cutting into wedges. Makes 6 to 8 servings.

CARROT SOUFFLÉ

▶ **1 cup bread crumbs from stale bread**
1 cup milk or light cream
¾ cup melted butter or margarine
3 egg yolks

1 teaspoon salt
▶ **1 cup puréed cooked carrots**
⅓ cup slivered almonds
Dash nutmeg
4 egg whites

1. In a large mixing bowl, mix together the crumbs and milk; beat in ¼ cup of the butter. Beat the egg yolks and add to the crumb mixture. Add the salt, and stir in the carrots, almonds, and nutmeg.

2. Beat egg whites until stiff but not dry. Fold egg whites into carrot mixture. Grease a 2-quart baking dish; set in shallow pan of hot water. Bake at 350° for 30 to 45 minutes, until risen, and lightly browned. Pour the remaining butter on top. Makes 6 servings.

CARROT PUDDING RING

▶ **2 cups mashed cooked carrots**
2 teaspoons minced onion
4 tablespoons butter, melted
2 eggs, well beaten
1 cup bread crumbs
1 tablespoon flour
1 cup light cream
2 tablespoons chopped parsley

1 cup grated Swiss cheese
½ teaspoon salt
¼ teaspoon pepper
⅛ teaspoon ground nutmeg
⅛ teaspoon ground ginger
Sprigs of watercress, or purée of spinach or peas

1. Combine the carrots, onion, 2 tablespoons of the butter, eggs, bread crumbs, flour, cream, parsley, cheese, salt, pepper, nutmeg, and ginger in a large bowl.

2. Use the remaining butter to thoroughly grease a 1-quart ring mold. Spoon the carrot mixture into the mold, and place the mold in a larger pan; fill the larger pan with 1-inch hot water.

3. Bake the mold in a preheated 350° oven 40 to 50 minutes until pudding is firm. Cover with aluminum foil during baking time if top starts to brown too much. Unmold onto a round platter and serve with sprigs of watercress in the center of the ring, or with a purée of peas or spinach. Makes 4 servings.

CARROT AND SPINACH FRITTATA

1 onion, minced
4 tablespoons butter or margarine
1 tablespoon olive oil
6 eggs
¼ teaspoon salt

⅛ teaspoon pepper
▶ **¾ cup drained cooked spinach**
▶ **½ cup diced cooked carrots**
6 tablespoons grated Parmesan cheese

1. In a small oven-proof skillet, sauté the onion in butter and olive oil. Beat together eggs, salt, and pepper. Stir the spinach and carrots into the beaten egg mixture; add 4 tablespoons of the Parmesan cheese. Pour over the onions.

(*continued*)

2. Cook, covered, over low heat until eggs are set (except for the top surface). Sprinkle with the remaining Parmesan cheese. Broil until the eggs are set and top of frittata is light golden. Cut into wedges to serve. Makes 4 servings.

CURRIED CARROT SOUP

1 medium-size onion, chopped
1 teaspoon crumbled leaf thyme
1 bay leaf
2 teaspoons vegetable oil
▶ 4 medium carrots, cooked and sliced
1 tablespoon curry powder
½ teaspoon cumin
½ teaspoon coriander
▶ 4 cups beef stock or vegetable bouillon
3 ounces cream cheese, cubed
3 tablespoons chopped parsley
Dash cayenne

1. Sauté the onion, thyme, and bay leaf in the oil in a large saucepan, stirring often, until onions are tender. Stir in the carrots, curry powder, cumin, and coriander; add the stock and bring to a boil. Lower the heat; simmer, uncovered, about 10 minutes. Remove from heat and discard bay leaf.

2. Pour the carrot/stock mixture and cream cheese in a blender or food processor; whirl until smooth. Return mixture to saucepan; heat to serving temperature. Stir in parsley and cayenne. Makes 4 servings.

CARROT RAISIN SQUARES

1 cup melted butter or margarine, cooled
1¼ cups sugar
4 eggs
▶ 1½ cups mashed cooked carrots
½ cups raisins
2 cups flour
1 teaspoon baking powder
1½ teaspoons vanilla extract
1 teaspoon almond extract
2¼ teaspoons lemon extract
Dash ground cinnamon
Dash ground nutmeg
2¼ cups confectioners' sugar
¼ cup water
½ teaspoon grated lemon rind

1. Pour the butter into a large mixing bowl; gradually beat in the sugar. Add the eggs, one at a time, beating thoroughly after each one. Add the carrots, raisins, flour, and baking powder; stir; add the vanilla and almond extracts, ¾ teaspoon of the lemon extract, the cinnamon, and nutmeg.

2. Spread in a greased 10 × 15 × 1-inch baking pan. Bake 25 minutes at 350°. Cool on a rack. Beat together the remaining 1½ teaspoons lemon extract, the confectioners' sugar, water, and lemon rind. Spread on the cooled cake. Makes 6 to 8 servings.

CURRIED CAULIFLOWER CASSEROLE

½ cup light cream
½ cup sliced mushrooms
1 cup shredded Cheddar
  cheese
⅓ cup mayonnaise
¼ teaspoon dry mustard
  Dash cayenne
1 teaspoon curry powder

▶ 1 large head cauliflower, broken
  into flowerettes, cooked,
  drained
▶ 1 cup diced cooked potatoes
¼ cup fine dry bread crumbs
2 tablespoons butter or
  margarine, melted
¼ cup snipped chives

1. In a medium bowl, stir together cream, mushroooms, cheese, mayonnaise, mustard, cayenne, and curry powder until well blended. Place cauliflower and potatoes in a greased 2-quart casserole; pour sauce over cauliflower.

2. In a small bowl mix together bread crumbs and butter; sprinkle over top. Bake, uncovered, in a 350° oven 30 minutes, until hot and bubbly. Sprinkle casserole with the chives and serve. Makes 6 to 8 servings.

CAULIFLOWER AU GRATIN

3 tablespoons butter
3 tablespoons flour
1½ cups milk
¼ teaspoon salt
¼ teaspoon Tabasco sauce
2 tablespoons dry sherry, or
  Madeira

½ cup sharp crumbled Cheddar
  cheese
1 egg yolk, slightly beaten
▶ 1½ to 2 cups chopped cooked
  cauliflower
⅓ cup celery
  Fine dry bread crumbs
  Paprika

1. Melt the butter in a saucepan, stir in flour until smooth; slowly add milk. Cook, stirring, over low heat until sauce thickens. Add salt, Tabasco sauce, sherry, and cheese. Stir until cheese is melted. Add a little of the hot cheese sauce to the egg yolk, blend, and stir egg mixture back into the cheese sauce.

2. Add the cauliflower and celery and transfer to a shallow greased baking pan. Sprinkle with bread crumbs and paprika. Bake at 375° until sauce is bubbly and surface is lightly browned. Makes 6 servings.

PURÉE OF CAULIFLOWER SOUP

▶ 2 cups cooked cauliflower
  flowerets
▶ 1½ cups sliced cooked potatoes
¼ cup butter
1 small onion, sliced
2 tablespoons grated celery
2 tablespoons all-purpose flour

▶ 4 cups hot chicken stock or
  bouillon
2 cups hot milk or light cream
  Salt and white pepper
1 egg yolk
¼ cup heavy cream
2 tablespoons Madeira or sherry

1. Reserve ¼ of the cauliflower flowerets; purée the remaining cauliflower and the potatoes in a blender or food mill. Melt the butter in a large saucepan and sauté the onion and celery. Stir in the flour; gradu-

(continued)

ally add the stock and puréed vegetables. Stir in the milk and season to taste with the salt and pepper.

2. Cook over medium heat, stirring constantly, until sauce thickens. Beat the egg yolk with the heavy cream in a large soup tureen or serving bowl. Remove the soup from the heat and gradually stir into the egg yolk mixture; add the Madeira and the reserved cauliflowerets. Makes 4 to 6 servings.

TOMATOES STUFFED WITH CORN

4 large tomatoes	2 tablespoons diced celery
Salt	½ cup bread crumbs
4 slices bacon, chopped, cooked until crisp	2 tablespoons cream
	⅛ teaspoon pepper
▶ 1 cup drained cooked corn	¼ teaspoon paprika
1 pimiento, diced	¼ cup grated Cheddar cheese

1. Hollow out the tomatoes, (reserve centers for soups, etc.) Salt lightly and invert on paper toweling for 15 minutes.

2. In a bowl, combine the bacon, corn, pimiento, celery, ½ teaspoon salt, bread crumbs, cream, pepper and paprika. Heap mixture into tomato centers, top with Cheddar cheese and place in a greased baking pan. Bake in a preheated 350° oven for 15 minutes, or until filling is hot. Makes 4 servings.

CORN CHEESE FRITTERS

2 eggs, lightly beaten	¼ teaspoon crumbled, dried oregano
4 tablespoons flour	
3 tablespoons Parmesan cheese	▶ 1 cup mashed cooked corn, drained
½ teaspoon baking powder	
¼ teaspoon salt	3 cups vegetable oil, approximately
Freshly ground black pepper	

1. Combine eggs, flour, cheese, baking powder, salt, pepper and oregano in a mixing bowl. Stir in the corn.

2. Heat 2 inches oil in a skillet to 375°; drop batter into pan by the tablespoonful and fry until golden on both sides, turning once. Drain fritters on absorbent paper; keep warm until all the batter is used. Makes about 4 servings.

HOME-STYLE CORN FRITTERS

▶ **2 cups drained and chopped
  cooked corn**
  ½ cup flour
  1 teaspoon baking powder
  ½ teaspoon salt

⅛ teaspoon pepper
2 eggs, beaten
Butter
Vegetable oil
Maple syrup

1. Combine the corn, flour, baking powder, salt, pepper, and eggs.

2. Heat enough butter to coat a skillet, adding 1 tablespoon oil for every 3 tablespoons butter. Drop the fritter batter into the skillet by the tablespoonful and cook on both sides until golden. Keep warm until all the batter is used. Serve with maple syrup. Makes 4 servings.

VEGETABLE-TUNA SOUFFLÉ

4 tablespoons butter
4 tablespoons flour
1 cup milk
4 egg yolks
▶ **1 cup cooked corn**
▶ **½ cup cooked peas**
2 tablespoons chopped onion

¼ cup chopped tomato, drained
½ cup drained flaked tuna
**2 tablespoons grated Parmesan
cheese**
⅛ teaspoon cayenne
Salt and pepper
5 egg whites

1. Heat butter in a pan and stir in flour; add milk, stirring constantly, until smooth and thick. Remove from heat and beat in the egg yolks, one at a time.

2. In a bowl, combine the corn, peas, onion, tomato, tuna, cheese, cayenne, salt and pepper to taste; add the sauce mixture and thoroughly stir.

3. Beat egg whites until stiff; fold lightly into the vegetable/tuna mixture. Pour into a buttered 8-cup soufflé dish. Bake at 350° until puffed and golden brown, about 35 minutes. Makes 4 servings.

CORN PUFF

1 cup milk
1 bay leaf
2 whole cloves
1 garlic clove
3 sprigs parsley
**3 tablespoons butter or
  margarine**
2 tablespoons chopped onion

2 tablespoons flour
¼ teaspoon salt
¼ teaspoon Tabasco
▶ **2 cups cooked whole kernel
  corn, drained**
3 eggs, separated
Paprika

1. In a saucepan combine the milk with bay leaf, cloves, garlic and parsley; scald and strain into a bowl. Melt the butter in the saucepan and sauté onion until golden. Blend in flour, salt and Tabasco. Add the milk, stirring constantly, until thickened. Remove from heat; stir in corn and beaten egg yolks.

2. Beat the egg whites until stiff and fold into the corn mixture; pour into shallow 1½-quart baking dish. Sprinkle with paprika. Bake at 350° about 25 minutes. Makes 4 to 6 servings.

QUICK CORN CHOWDER

6 to 8 tablespoons butter
1 medium onion, thinly sliced
► ½ cup sliced cooked potatoes
► 1 cup chopped cooked carrots
½ cup light cream
► 2 cups cooked corn

1 can (10½ oz.) cream of
mushroom soup
2 cups milk
½ bay leaf
Salt and pepper to taste
2 tablespoons chopped parsley
Paprika

1. In a soup kettle or large saucepan, melt 2 tablespoons of the butter and sauté the onions until golden. Add the potatoes, carrots, cream, corn, mushroom soup, milk, bay leaf, salt and pepper to taste. Stir until smooth and simmer just to the boiling point.

2. Remove the bay leaf. Place a pat of butter in each bowl before pouring the soup in. Sprinkle the top with chopped parsley and paprika. Makes 6 to 8 servings.

CHEESE AND CORN SPOON BREAD

2 cups milk
¾ cup yellow cornmeal
½ teaspoon salt
2 tablespoons butter
2 tablespoons minced green
pepper

► 1 cup cooked whole-kernel corn
1 cup shredded sharp Cheddar
cheese
4 eggs, separated

1. In a saucepan heat the milk until hot. Gradually add the cornmeal; stirring constantly; then add salt and butter and stir until butter melts. Remove from heat and stir in green pepper, corn, and cheese. Gradually stir the hot mixture into slightly beaten egg yolks. Beat egg whites until stiff but not dry, and gently fold into the corn mixture.

2. Turn into a buttered 1½-quart baking dish. Bake at 350° for 45 minutes, or until golden brown. Makes 6 to 8 servings.

CORN MUFFINS

1⅓ cups unsifted all-purpose flour
3 teaspoons baking powder
½ teaspoon salt
2 tablespoons sugar
¾ cup yellow cornmeal
2 eggs, beaten
1 cup milk

¼ cup melted butter or
margarine
¼ teaspoon crushed dried
rosemary
► ½ cup cooked whole-kernel corn
¼ cup bacon bits

1. Sift together the flour, baking powder, salt,and sugar into a large bowl. Stir in the cornmeal,eggs, milk, butter, rosemary, corn, and bacon, until the dry ingredients are damp.

2. Grease a 12-section muffin pan and fill each section ⅔ full with batter. Bake at 400° for 25 minutes. Makes 12 muffins.

BAKED GREEN BEANS CREOLE

1 green pepper, minced
1 medium onion, minced
2 tablespoons butter or
  margarine
1 tablespoon flour
¾ cup tomato juice
▶ 2 cups cooked green beans

½ cup shredded Cheddar
  cheese
Dash of cayenne
¼ teaspoon salt
¾ cup fresh buttered bread
  crumbs

1. In a small skillet, sauté the pepper and onion in butter until tender. Add flour and tomato juice. Stir until thickened; set aside. In a baking dish combine the beans, cheese, cayenne and salt.

2. Pour the tomato mixture over the beans. Sprinkle bread crumbs over top. Bake, uncovered, at 350° for 20 minutes, or until mixture is hot and crumbs are golden. Makes 4 to 6 servings.

SWEET-SOUR GREEN BEANS

2 strips bacon
2 tablespoons vegetable oil
1 cup chopped scallions
1 tablespoon flour
▶ ⅔ cup liquid from vegetables or
  ⅔ cup vegetable bouillon
1 teaspoon soy sauce

¼ cup vinegar
2 tablespoons brown sugar
1 teaspoon grated fresh ginger
  or ¼ teaspoon ground ginger
¼ teaspoon pepper
▶ 2 cups cooked green beans

1. Cook the bacon strips in a skillet; drain and crumble into bits. Wipe the skillet clean, add the oil and heat. Sauté the scallions until lightly browned. Stir in flour. Add vegetable liquid, soy sauce, vinegar, sugar, ginger, and pepper; bring to a boil. Reduce heat and simmer until sauce thickens.

2 Stir in beans; heat until warm. Sprinkle with crumbled bacon before serving. Makes 4 servings.

SWISS BEANS

2 tablespoons butter or
  margarine
6 to 8 medium mushrooms, sliced
½ cup chopped onions
2 tablespoons flour
½ teaspoon salt
¼ teaspoon dried marjoram

¼ teaspoon dried thyme
⅛ teaspoon pepper
¾ cup milk
▶ 2 cups cooked green beans
1 cup shredded Swiss cheese
2 crisp bacon strips, crumbled

1. In a medium-size skillet melt the butter; sauté mushrooms and onions until tender. Stir in flour, salt, marjoram, thyme, and pepper. Gradually stir in milk; heat, stirring frequently, until mixture is thick. Stir in the beans and the cheese.

2. Cover and heat gently until beans are heated through and cheese is melted. Sprinkle with crumbled bacon. Makes 4 servings.

PARMESAN GREEN BEANS

3 tablespoons olive oil
▶ 2 cups diced cooked green
  beans
1 cup sliced mushrooms
1 tablespoon vinegar
2 teaspoons minced onion

¼ teaspoon salt
½ cup plain or flavored croûtons
1 tablespoon slivered almonds
2 tablespoons grated Parmesan
  cheese

1. In a medium skillet heat 2 tablespoons oil, add the green beans and mushrooms and sauté gently. In a small mixing bowl beat together the vinegar, remaining oil, onion, and salt; pour over warmed beans and toss gently.

2. Place the beans in a serving bowl and toss with the croûtons and almonds, and sprinkle with Parmesan cheese. Makes 4 servings.

MARINATED GREEN BEAN
AND WATER CHESTNUT SALAD

▶ 2 cups crisp-cooked green
  beans
¾ cup thinly sliced water
  chestnuts
6 tablespoons olive oil
2 to 3 tablespoons white wine
  vinegar
¼ teaspoon salt

⅛ teaspoon pepper
2 teaspoons minced onion
1 teaspoon dried, crumbled
  basil
2 tablespoons minced parsley
1 small head Boston lettuce,
  washed and dried

1. Combine the green beans and water chestnuts in a large bowl.

2. Combine the oil, vinegar, salt, pepper, onion, basil, and parsley in a jar with a tight lid. Cover and shake until well blended. Pour the dressing over the beans and water chestnuts. Cover and marinate in the refrigerator for three hours.

3. Arrange the lettuce leaves in a shallow serving bowl. Spoon the vegetables into the bowl on top of the lettuce. Makes 4 to 6 servings.

VEGETABLE FIESTA

▶ 1 cup cooked green beans, cut
  in 1-inch pieces
1 cup thinly sliced zucchini,
  halved
½ cup minced green pepper
1 cup slivered carrots
½ cup thinly sliced radishes
¼ cup minced red onion

1½ cups chopped seeded
  cucumber
▶ 2 cups cooked thin spaghetti
1 cup mayonnaise
2 tablespoons chopped parsley
1 tablespoon lemon juice
1 teaspoon dried basil leaves
½ teaspoon salt
¼ teaspoon pepper

1. In a large bowl, combine the green beans, zucchini, green pepper, carrots, radishes, red onion, cucumber, and spaghetti.

2. Mix the mayonnaise, parsley, lemon juice, basil, salt, and pepper. Add to the vegetable mixture; toss to coat well. Chill before serving. Makes 6 to 8 servings.

GREEN BEANS AND MUSHROOM SALAD

1 tablespoon vinegar
3 tablespoons oil
½ cup minced scallions
1 teaspoon Dijon mustard
½ teaspoon salt
⅛ teaspoon pepper

1 cup sour cream
½ pound fresh mushrooms, sliced
▶ 3 cups cooked green beans, cut into 2" pieces
1 pint cherry tomatoes

1. Combine the vinegar, oil, scallions, mustard, salt, and pepper in a jar with a tight lid. Shake well until blended; stir in the sour cream.

2. Combine the mushrooms and green beans with the dressing; toss lightly. Chill the salad thoroughly.

3. Serve the salad at room temperature on a small serving platter garnished by a border of cherry tomatoes. Makes 4 to 6 servings.

GREEN BEAN AND RED ONION SALAD

▶ 2 cups cold cooked green beans
1 large red onion, chopped
¼ teaspoon honey
2 teaspoons wine vinegar

1 tablespoon prepared mustard
¼ cup olive oil
Salt
Freshly ground black pepper
Lettuce

1. In a mixing bowl, combine the beans and onion. Mix together the honey, vinegar, mustard, oil, and salt and pepper to taste. Pour over the beans and onion, and blend. Cover and chill for at least 1 hour.

2. Line a salad bowl with large lettuce leaves. Spoon salad into the middle. Makes 4 servings.

LEEK SOUFFLÉ

3 tablespoons flour
3 tablespoons butter
1 cup milk
Salt and pepper to taste
Dash of Tabasco sauce

▶ 1 cup chopped cooked leeks
¾ cup grated Cheddar cheese
4 egg yolks, beaten
5 egg whites

1. Combine the flour and butter in a skillet and cook for a few minutes. Gradually stir in the milk, salt, pepper and Tabasco sauce; continue stirring until thickened. Add the leeks and cheese; remove from heat; stirring continuously, carefully add the egg yolks. Cook, still stirring, over low heat for 5 minutes, or until the cheese is melted. Cool.

2. Beat the egg whites until stiff but not dry. Stir half of the whites into the sauce. Gently fold in the remainder. Pour into a buttered 1½-quart soufflé dish and bake in a 375° oven for 25 to 30 minutes. Makes 6 servings.

LIMA BEAN SALAD

▶ 1 cup cooked lima beans
½ cup thin-sliced celery
¼ cup minced scallions
⅓ cup mayonnaise
1 to 2 tablespoons ketchup
½ teaspoon salt

⅛ teaspoon pepper
2 tablespoons finely chopped
  parsley
Crisp lettuce greens
▶ 2 hard-cooked eggs, sliced

Combine the lima beans, celery, and scallions in a mixing bowl. Combine the mayonnaise, ketchup, salt, pepper, and parsley. Add to the mixing bowl and lightly toss with the salad ingredients. Arrange a bed of lettuce in a small shallow bowl. Heap the salad on the lettuce. Garnish with the egg slices. Makes 4 servings.

PEAS AND SHELL MACARONI

¼ cup butter
¼ cup olive oil
1 medium-size onion, minced
1 garlic clove, minced
▶ ½ pound drained cooked shell
  macaroni (4 cups)

▶ 3 cups cooked peas
¼ cup chopped parsley
▶ 1 cup finely chopped cooked
  ham
Salt and pepper
Grated Parmesan cheese

1. In a large skillet, melt the butter and add the oil. Sauté onion and garlic until the onions are transparent. Add the macaroni, peas, parsley and ham; season to taste with salt and pepper. Simmer, covered, for 10 minutes, stirring occasionally.

2. Pour the mixture into a serving bowl and sprinkle the cheese over the top of the macaroni. Makes 4 to 6 servings.

PEAS AND WHITE ONIONS IN ROQUEFORT CREAM SAUCE

▶ 1 cup cooked peas
▶ 1 cup cooked small white onions
▶ ¼ cup liquid from cooked
  vegetables
1 tablespoon butter

2 tablespoons crumbled
  Roquefort cheese
½ cup sour cream
1½ tablespoons minced chives
Freshly ground pepper

1. In a medium-size saucepan, heat the peas and onions in the vegetable liquid and the butter. In a mixing bowl, combine the cheese with the sour cream and the chives; pour in just enough of the liquid from the vegetables to make a smooth sauce. Pepper to taste.

2. Pour the sauce over the vegetables in the pan. Cook briefly, stirring gently. Makes 4 servings.

PEAS AND CELERY IN CREAM SAUCE

2 cups thinly sliced celery
2 tablespoons minced onion
▶ ½ cup chicken broth or bouillon
2 teaspoons flour
¼ cup light cream

▶1½ cups cooked peas
1 tablespoon butter
¼ teaspoon salt
⅛ teaspoon pepper
Dash nutmeg

1. Mix together the celery, onion, and chicken broth in a medium saucepan; cover and simmer for 10 minutes. Blend in the flour and cream, and stir constantly until slightly thickened.

2. Add the peas and butter to the sauce. Heat 2 minutes; season with salt, pepper,and nutmeg. Makes 4 servings.

SKILLET SOUFFLÉ

4 eggs, separated
¼ teaspoon salt
Dash pepper
▶1½ cups cooked peas
▶ ½ cup shredded cooked carrots
1½ tablespoons chopped parsley
1½ tablespoons chopped celery

2 tablespoons minced onion
3 tablespoons grated Parmesan
cheese
½ teaspoon dried thyme
½ teaspoon dried oregano
2 tablespoons vegetable oil

1. Beat egg yolks with salt and pepper in a large mixing bowl until thick. Mix in the peas, carrots, parsley, celery, onion, cheese, thyme and oregano. Beat egg whites until stiff; fold into vegetable mixture.

2. Heat the vegetable oil in a large, ovenproof skillet until hot. Pour in mixture and bake 20 minutes at 350°. Makes 4 servings.

MACÉDOINE OF VEGETABLES

1½ tablespoons wine vinegar
¼ teaspoon parsley
¼ teaspoon dried thyme
⅛ teaspoon prepared mustard
⅓ cup olive oil
▶1½ cups cooked peas
1 cucumber, peeled and thinly
sliced

4 scallions, minced
1 cup shredded carrots
1 ripe avocado
Juice of 1 lemon
Lettuce leaves
1 can (16 oz.) sliced pickled
beets, drained

1. In a small bowl place the vinegar, parsley, thyme, and mustard; beat in the olive oil. Toss the peas, cucumbers, scallions, and carrots in a large bowl with half the dressing.

2. Peel and slice the avocado. Immediately dip the slices in lemon juice. Arrange lettuce leaves on a round platter. Pile the vegetable mixture in the center; encircle with the beet slices and edge with the avocado slices. Makes 6 servings.

SPICY VEGETABLE DIP

▶ ½ cup cooked peas
½ cup chopped onion
1 can (8¾ oz.) whole-kernel corn
with liquid
½ teaspoon dried oregano
¼ teaspoon minced garlic
2 tablespoons seeded and
chopped green chili peppers

⅛ teaspoon Tabasco
½ cup sour cream
½ cup plain yogurt
Raw cauliflower and broccoli
flowerets, zucchini slices,
mushroom slices, etc.

1. In a blender container or food processor bowl, combine the peas, onions, corn, corn liquid, oregano, garlic, chili peppers, and Tabasco; process until smooth, scraping sides as necessary. Stir in the sour cream and yogurt. Cover and chill.

2. Pour the dip into an attractive serving bowl. Serve with the raw cauliflower and broccoli flowerets, zucchini slices, mushroom slices, etc. Makes about 2½ cups.

POTATOES CHANTILLY

¼ cup milk
4 tablespoons butter
▶ 4 to 5 cups mashed potatoes
Salt and pepper to taste

½ cup heavy cream, stiffly
beaten
¼ cup grated Cheddar cheese

1. Heat the milk with 2 tablespoons of the butter in a large saucepan. Add the potatoes. Blend, over low heat, until smooth. Season with salt and pepper.

2. Thoroughly butter six 1-cup ramekins and divide the potatoes among them, or shape the potatoes in a mound in a greased pie pan. Lightly spread the whipped cream over the potatoes and sprinkle with the grated cheese. Bake in a preheated 350° oven until cheese is melted and topping is lightly browned. Makes 4 to 6 servings.

POTATO SAUSAGE BAKE

3 tablespoons butter or
margarine
½ cup finely chopped onion
1 can (10½ oz.) condensed
cream of celery soup
⅓ cup milk
1 tablespoon Dijon mustard
▶ 3 cups diced cooked potatoes

½ cup chopped green pepper
1 jar (2 oz.) pimiento, drained
and diced
1 package (12- or 16-oz.) ready-
to-eat smoked sausage links;
half of the links thinly sliced
1 cup shredded process
American cheese

1. Melt 2 tablespoons of the butter in a medium skillet and sauté the onion until tender; stir in the soup, milk, and mustard.

2. Butter a 1½-quart casserole; evenly arrange the potatoes, green pepper, pimiento, and sausage slices in the dish. Pour the soup mixture over the ingredients, top with the cheese, then the remaining whole sausage links. Bake in a preheated 350° oven 30 minutes. Makes 6 servings.

ELEGANT POTATO BAKE

▶ 3 large cooked potatoes,
  peeled
  3 tablespoons butter,
  approximately
▶ ½ cup diced cooked ham
  1 green pepper, chopped
  ¼ cup chopped onion

½ teaspoon salt
¼ teaspoon pepper
1 cup grated Cheddar cheese
1½ cups heavy cream
1 cup lightly toasted bread
  crumbs

1. Cut the potatoes in thick ½-inch lengthwise slices, and arrange in a lightly buttered 1½-quart shallow baking dish in one layer.

2. Sprinkle the potatoes with the ham, green pepper, onion, salt, pepper, and Cheddar cheese. Pour the cream over all the ingredients, top casserole with the bread crumbs, and dot with about 2 tablespoons butter.

3. Bake the casserole in a preheated 350° oven for about 30 minutes, until the potatoes are heated through. Makes 4 servings.

POTATOES ROMA

▶ 6 large cooked potatoes,
  peeled and cubed
  ½ pound Mozzarella cheese,
  shredded
  1 cup ricotta cheese
  2 cups (8 oz.) grated Gruyère
  cheese
  1 cup sour cream

½ cup finely chopped scallions
¼ cup finely minced parsley
1 teaspoon dried sweet basil
½ teaspoon salt
¼ teaspoon freshly ground
  pepper or to taste
¼ teaspoon paprika
2 to 3 tablespoons butter

1. Preheat the oven to 350°. In a large mixing bowl combine the potatoes, Mozzarella, ricotta, 1 cup Gruyère, sour cream, scallions, parsley, basil, salt, pepper and paprika.

2. Thoroughly butter a 9 × 13-inch casserole. Spoon ingredients into casserole, sprinkle with remaining Gruyère and bake at 350° about 30 minutes, until bubbly. Makes 6 to 8 servings.

POTATOES AU GRATIN

6 tablespoons butter
1 large onion, minced
2 cloves garlic, minced
3 tablespoons flour
1½ cups light cream
1 teaspoon salt

⅛ teaspoon cayenne
1 cup shredded Cheddar
  cheese
▶ 4 cups thinly sliced cooked
  potatoes

1. Melt 2 tablespoons of the butter in a skillet; sauté the onion and garlic until very tender. Remove and reserve.

2. Melt 3 tablespoons butter in the skillet; add the flour and stir until the *roux* is smooth. Gradually add the cream to the *roux*, stirring constantly, until sauce is thick and smooth. Simmer the sauce over very low heat, for

(*continued*)

10 minutes, add salt, cayenne, the cooked onions, and the cheese and cook until the cheese melts.

3. Butter a 1½-quart baking dish, arrange alternate layers of potatoes and sauce in the baking dish, finishing with the sauce. Bake in a preheated 350° oven for 30 to 45 minutes until bubbling hot. Makes 4 to 6 servings.

 ## SWEDISH CREAMED POTATOES

2 tablespoons butter or margarine
2 tablespoons flour
1¾ cups light cream
▶ 6 medium boiled potatoes, sliced or diced

▶ ½ cup shredded cooked beef or ham
1 teaspoon salt
½ teaspoon white pepper
1 tablespoon chopped fresh dill, chives, or parsley

1. In a saucepan, heat the butter and stir in flour, stirring constantly, until mixture forms a paste. Slowly add the cream and stir constantly over medium heat until mixture is smooth and thickened somewhat.

2. Add the potatoes, meat, salt, and pepper; heat thoroughly. Garnish with chopped herb. Makes 4 servings.

 ## POTATO PASTIES

1 cup sifted flour
½ teaspoon salt
¼ pound butter (1 stick)
3 tablespoons sour cream
4 tablespoons butter or chicken fat

½ cup chopped onion
▶ ¾ cup mashed potatoes
1 egg, separated
Salt and pepper to taste
¼ cup milk, approximately

1. To prepare the pastry: sift flour and salt into a bowl. Work in the butter by hand. Add the sour cream, mixing until a ball of dough is formed. Chill for at least 2 hours, or overnight if possible.

2. To prepare the filling: melt the butter in a skillet. Sauté the onions for 10 minutes. Add the potatoes, mixing well. Add the egg yolk, salt, and pepper.

3. Roll out the dough as thin as possible and cut into rounds with a cookie cutter. Place a teaspoon of filling on each round. Fold over the dough and seal edges with the egg white. Brush with milk, place on a lightly greased cookie sheet, and bake in a preheated 425° oven for 15 minutes, or until browned. Makes about 30 pasties.

POTATO PANCAKES WITH BACON

▶ 1 cup cold mashed potatoes
   1 egg
   ½ cup milk
   2 tablespoons butter or
     margarine, melted

2 cups baking mix
8 strips of bacon, grilled
Maple syrup or jelly

1. Combine the mashed potatoes, egg, milk, and butter in a medium-size bowl, and beat until smooth. Stir in the baking mix thoroughly.

2. Using a tablespoon, drop the batter onto a hot, greased skillet or griddle. Fry about 5 minutes on each side, or until golden brown. Serve hot with bacon and syrup. Makes 4 servings.

POTATO CHEESE PUFF

▶ 1 cup mashed potatoes
   2 teaspoons milk
     (approximately)
   3 tablespoons butter or
     margarine (approximately)
   1 cup small curd cream-style
     cottage cheese
   ½ cup sour cream

3 egg yolks
1 tablespoon chopped chives
¼ teaspoon celery salt
1 teaspoon paprika
1 teaspoon finely grated onion
2 tablespoons finely chopped
  parsley
4 egg whites

1. In a small saucepan, warm and fluff up the mashed potatoes with 1 or 2 teaspoons of milk and butter, stirring briskly with a fork.

2. In a large bowl, beat the mashed potatoes with the cottage cheese, sour cream, egg yolks, chives, celery salt, paprika, onion, and parsley.

3. Beat the egg whites until stiff peaks form; fold into the potato mixture. Pour into a greased 1½-quart casserole; dot with butter. Bake in a 350° oven for 1 hour or until top is lightly browned. Makes 6 to 8 servings.

SPANISH OMELETTE

   2 tablespoons margarine
   1 small onion, chopped
   1 medium tomato, chopped; or
     ½ cup chopped canned
     tomatoes, drained
▶ 2 baked or boiled potatoes,
     peeled and diced
▶ ½ cup cooked peas

4 eggs
2 tablespoons milk or light
  cream
½ teaspoon salt
¼ teaspoon pepper
⅛ teaspoon cayenne
¼ cup shredded Cheddar
  cheese

1. In a medium skillet melt the margarine and sauté the onion until limp; add the tomatoes, potatoes and peas. Cook 3 or 4 minutes more, stirring.

2. In a bowl, beat together the eggs, milk, salt, pepper, and cayenne. Pour into the skillet with the vegetables over low heat. Shake pan occasionally, spreading evenly, and cooking eggs till underside is browned. Sprinkle the top with the cheese and place under the broiler until top is brown and cheese is melted. Makes 4 servings.

ITALIAN SAUSAGE AND PEPPER OMELET

¾ pound sweet Italian sausage links
2 tablespoons olive oil
2 tablespoons butter
1 coarsely chopped medium-size red onion
2 cloves garlic, thinly sliced
¼ pound Italian peppers, seeded and cut into strips
▶ 1 large boiled potato, peeled and diced
1 large tomato, peeled and diced
1 teaspoon dried basil
1 teaspoon dried oregano
2 tablespoons minced parsley
Salt and pepper
6 eggs
2 tablespoons milk
½ cup grated Parmesan cheese
Parsley sprigs

1. Cover sausage with water in a pan and bring to a boil. Cook 5 or 10 minutes, turning the links frequently, until nearly all the water is evaporated and sausages are browned. Drain and slice sausages in rounds ½-inch thick.

2. Heat the oil and butter in 12-inch ovenproof frying pan. Sauté the onion, garlic, and peppers until soft. Add sausage slices, potato, tomato, basil, oregano, parsley, and salt and pepper to taste. Sauté for 2 minutes. Beat eggs lightly with the milk. Pour into the pan with the other ingredients and cook until the bottom of the omelet is set and browned.

3. Sprinkle the top with cheese. Place pan under the broiler until top is puffed and browned. Cut into wedges and garnish with parsley sprigs. Makes 6 servings.

POTATO SOUFFLÉ

½ cup light cream
1 tablespoon butter
▶ 2 cups mashed potatoes
¼ teaspoon salt
Dash nutmeg
¼ teaspoon white pepper
1 tablespoon chopped chives
2 tablespoons grated Parmesan cheese
4 eggs, separated

1. In a large saucepan, heat together the cream and butter until butter melts. Stir in the potatoes and cook, stirring, until mixture is smooth and hot. Add the salt, nutmeg, pepper, chives, and cheese; beat in the egg yolks one at a time. Beat the egg whites until stiff but not dry; fold into potato mixture.

2. Spoon into a well-buttered deep baking dish. Bake at 350° for 25 to 30 minutes until soufflé is puffed and lightly browned. Makes 4 to 6 servings.

VICHYSSOISE

2 tablespoons butter or
  margarine
3 leeks (white part only), well
  washed and thinly sliced
1 large onion, thinly sliced
▶ 4 cups chicken broth,
  homemade or canned

▶ 3 medium-size potatoes, cooked
  and diced or mashed (about
  1½ cups)
1 cup milk, warmed
Salt to taste
Dash of white pepper
½ cup heavy cream
Chopped chives

1. In a large saucepan, melt the butter and sauté the leeks and onion for 15 minutes, stirring occasionally, until vegetables are soft.

2. Stir in the chicken broth and potatoes; cook 10 minutes. Add the milk; bring the mixture to boiling and remove from heat. Season with the salt and pepper to taste. Purée soup through sieve, food mill, or in a blender. Chill several hours.

3. Stir the cream into chilled soup. Serve in chilled cups with a sprinkling of chopped chives on each. Makes 6 servings.

CORN CHOWDER

¼ pound salt pork, diced
1 large onion, diced
1 green pepper, diced
▶ 3 cups diced cooked potatoes
1 can (12 oz.) corn kernels, with
  the liquid
¼ teaspoon pepper

1 cup milk
1 cup heavy cream
1½ cups water
12 oysters, shelled and halved,
  and their liquor (optional)
Salt to taste
⅓ cup minced fresh parsley

1. Sauté the salt pork in a large saucepan over medium-high heat until crisp and brown. Remove the bits with a slotted spoon and set aside. Add the onion and green pepper to the fat in the pan and sauté until tender.

2. Add the reserved salt pork bits, the potatoes, corn, pepper, milk, cream, water, and the liquor from the oysters to the pan. Simmer 30 minutes. Add the oysters and simmer 3 to 5 minutes, just until the oysters are warmed through. Salt to taste and stir in the parsley. Makes 6 servings.

POTATO BROCCOLI SOUP

4 leeks
1¼ cups sliced fresh mushrooms
¼ cup butter
▶ 4 cups chicken broth, or
  bouillion
5 sprigs parsley
¼ teaspoon crushed bay leaf
½ teaspoon dried thyme

¼ teaspoon dried basil
▶ 2 cups diced or mashed cooked
  potatoes
▶ 1 cup cooked broccoli
½ teaspoon salt
¼ teaspoon white pepper
1 cup light cream
2 tablespoons chopped chives

1. Sauté the leeks with the mushrooms in butter, stirring frequently, until limp. Add broth, parsley, bay leaf, thyme, and basil. Bring to a boil; cook 5 minutes. Add potatoes, and broccoli; season with salt and pepper to taste. Cover and simmer 15 minutes or until vegetables are soft.

(continued)

2. Force the mixture through a food mill or purée in a blender or food processor. Return to saucepan and heat to boiling point. Stir in cream; heat gently 5 minutes. Sprinkle with chives. Makes 6 servings.

SPICY POTATO-BEEF PATTIES

▶ 1 cup mashed potatoes
½ pound ground beef
1 egg
¼ teaspoon salt
⅛ teaspoon pepper
¼ teaspoon dried oregano
¼ teaspoon dried thyme
1 teaspoon Worcestershire sauce

¼ teaspoon dried basil
2 tablespoons minced onion
1 garlic clove, mashed
¼ cup bread crumbs
Flour
2 tablespoons butter
1 cup ketchup
¼ cup water

1. In a bowl, mix together the potatoes, beef, egg, salt, pepper, oregano, thyme, Worcestershire sauce, basil, onion, garlic and bread crumbs. Form into 6 patties about 1 inch thick; coat with flour shaking off excess.

2. Brown patties on both sides in butter. Mix together the ketchup and water, then pour over the patties; simmer 25 minutes. Makes 6 servings.

SALADE NIÇOISE

▶ 1½ pounds cooked small new
  potatoes, quartered
▶ 2 cups cooked green beans
1 cup olive oil
⅓ cup white wine vinegar
1 teaspoon salt
½ teaspoon pepper
1 tablespoon Dijon mustard
3 cloves garlic, crushed
½ teaspoon each: dried thyme,
  sage, rosemary, and tarragon
2 to 3 heads Boston lettuce

3 ripe tomatoes, cored and
  quartered
▶ 6 hard-cooked eggs, peeled
  and quartered
18 pitted black olives
3 cans (7 oz. each) solid pack
  white tuna, drained and
  broken
1 can (2 oz.) anchovy fillets,
  drained
1 to 2 loaves, crisp, warm,
  buttered French bread

1. In a bowl, combine the potatoes and green beans. Mix, in a jar, the oil, vinegar, salt, pepper, mustard, garlic, thyme, sage, rosemary, and tarragon, and shake vigorously. Gently toss the potatoes and beans with ⅓ to ½ cup of the dressing.

2. Line a large flat platter with the lettuce leaves and pile the potato mixture down the center of the platter. Surround the potato mound with the tomatoes, eggs, olives, and tuna. Place the anchovy fillets over the potato mound. Drizzle the remaining dressing (or as much as you want) over the lettuce, tomatoes, eggs, olives, and especially the tuna. Serve immediately with the French bread. Makes 6 servings.

DOWN HOME POTATO SALAD

- 4 cups diced cooked potatoes
  1 cup diced celery
  ¼ cup chopped scallions
  ¼ cup sliced radishes
  2 tablespoons minced parsley
- 4 hard-cooked eggs, chopped
  ¼ cup sliced green olives
  (optional)

1 cup mayonnaise
1 tablespoon vinegar
2 teaspoons prepared mustard
½ teaspoon celery seed
1½ teaspoons salt
⅛ teaspoon pepper

1. Combine, in a large bowl, the potatoes, celery, scallions, radishes, parsley, eggs, and olives.

2. In a separate bowl, mix the mayonnaise, vinegar, mustard, celery seed, salt, and pepper. Stir the dressing into the vegetables to coat well, and chill for several hours. Makes 6 servings.

SALMAGUNDI SALAD WITH HAM AND SALAMI

  1 large garlic clove, halved
- 2 cups diced cooked potatoes
- 3 hard-cooked eggs, diced
  1 cup diced celery
  1 tablespoon minced onion
  ½ cup diced green pepper
  ½ cup cubed hard salami
- ½ cup cubed cooked ham
  ½ cup cubed sharp Cheddar
  cheese

1 cup shredded cabbage
⅓ cup olive oil
2 tablespoons lemon juice
Salt and pepper
½ cup mayonnaise
Lettuce leaves
4 large black olives, sliced
Paprika

1. Rub a large wooden salad bowl with the garlic clove, then discard. Mix together the potatoes, eggs, celery, onion, green pepper, salami, ham, cheese and cabbage. In a small bowl, mix the oil, lemon juice, salt and pepper, and mayonnaise; combine thoroughly and mix into the vegetables.

2. Line a serving plate with lettuce leaves. Pile the salad on top and garnish with olive slices and a dusting of paprika. Makes 4 servings.

POTATO VEGETABLE SALAD

- 4 cups diced cooked potatoes
  2 tablespoons thinly sliced
  scallions
- 2 cups cooked peas
- 1½ cups diced cooked green
  beans
  3 tablespoons wine vinegar
  ⅔ cup olive oil

¼ teaspoon dried tarragon
⅛ teaspoon pepper
¼ teaspoon dried thyme
⅛ teaspoon dry mustard
⅔ cup mayonnaise
¼ teaspoon salt
Lettuce leaves
2 black olives, sliced

1. In a salad bowl, combine the potatoes, scallions, peas and green beans. Mix together the vinegar, oil, tarragon, peppers, thyme and mustard; toss lightly with the potato mixture. Cover and chill several hours, stirring occasionally.

(continued)

2. Drain off dressing, reserving 2 tablespoons. Combine the reserved dressing with the mayonnaise and salt. Mix well with potato mixture. Pile on top of the lettuce leaves and garnish with olives. Makes 8 servings.

 ## POTATO ROLLS

1 yeast cake, or 1 package
  active dry yeast
¼ cup warm water
6 tablespoons butter or
  margarine, melted

▶ ½ cup mashed potatoes
½ cup warm milk
1 tablespoon sugar
1 teaspoon salt
2½ cups flour

1. Dissolve the yeast in the water and butter. In a large mixing bowl, combine the potato, milk, sugar and salt. Add the yeast and enough flour to make dough easy to handle. Knead until smooth.

2. Place in a greased bowl and let rise in a warm place about 1 hour. Shape into round 1-inch balls, and put in muffin pans. Let rise 30 minutes more. Bake at 400° for 15 minutes. Makes about 4 dozen rolls.

 ## SLAVIC SUGAR CAKE

4 to 4½ cups enriched flour
2 packages active dry yeast
½ cup water
½ cup sugar
½ cup butter
½ teaspoon salt
2 eggs

▶ ½ cup mashed potatoes
½ cup firmly-packed light brown
  sugar
2 teaspoons cinnamon
½ cup melted butter
Confectioners' sugar icing

1. In a large mixing bowl, stir together 2 cups flour and the yeast. In a small pan, heat the water, sugar, ½ cup butter and salt over low heat only until warm, stirring to blend. Add the liquid ingredients to flour-yeast mixture and beat until smooth, about 2 minutes on medium speed of electric mixer.

2. Blend in the eggs and mashed potatoes. Add 1 cup flour and beat 1 minute longer. Stir in additional flour to make moderately stiff dough.

3. Turn out on lightly floured surface and knead until smooth and satiny, about 8 to 10 minutes. Place in lightly greased bowl, turning to grease surface. Cover; let rise in warm place until doubled, about 1½ hours.

4. Punch down; divide in half. Let rest 10 minutes. Pat or roll each portion into a 9-inch square; fit into greased 9-inch square baking pan. Combine brown sugar and cinnamon; sprinkle half the mixture over each coffee cake. Drizzle cakes with melted butter. Let rise in warm place until doubled, about 1 hour.

5. Bake at 350° for 30 to 35 minutes. Remove from pan. Drizzle with confectioners' sugar icing while warm, if desired. Makes 2 9″ coffee cakes.

KNOCKWURST ROLLS

6 strips bacon
6 knockwursts
► 1½ cups mashed potatoes
1 egg, beaten
1½ tablespoons chopped onion
½ teaspoon minced celery

¼ teaspoon paprika
1 teaspoon prepared mustard
2 teaspoons prepared
horseradish
2 tablespoons Parmesan cheese

1. Fry bacon in a skillet until limp. Cut knockwursts almost through lenghwise; lay open. In a medium bowl, mix together the potatoes, egg, onion, celery, paprika, mustard, horseradish, and cheese. Spoon some of the potato mixture into the knockwursts, close the halves, wrap each with bacon, and fasten with a wooden pick.

2. Place in a shallow baking pan. Bake 10 to 15 minutes at 425° or until bacon is crisp. Makes 6 servings.

MASHED POTATO CHOCOLATE CAKE

½ cup milk
3 ounces (3 squares)
unsweetened chocolate
1 cup shortening
2 cups sugar
► 1 cup cooked, still hot mashed
potatoes*

4 eggs, separated
1¾ cups all-purpose flour, sifted
3 teaspoons baking powder
Salt to taste
1 teaspoon vanilla

1. In a medium saucepan, heat the milk slowly but do not boil. Add the chocolate, stirring to melt. Remove from the heat and cool to room temperature.

2. Cream together shortening and 1¾ cups sugar until fluffy. Combine the milk and chocolate mixture with potatoes, and add to creamed sugar and shortening. Beat in the egg yolks.

3. Sift together the flour, baking powder, and salt. Stir into the batter; add vanilla. Beat the egg whites until foamy. Add a pinch of salt. Gradually add remaining sugar, beating until stiff peaks form. Fold into the batter.

4. Turn batter into 3 greased and floured 8-inch cake pans. Bake in a preheated 350° oven for 30 minutes. Cool on racks.

Chocolate Frosting

½ cup butter or margarine
4 tablespoons cocoa
6 tablespoons milk

1 teaspoon vanilla
1 pound confectioners' sugar
½ cup chopped nuts

5. Combine the butter, cocoa, and milk in a saucepan and heat to boiling. Remove from the heat, add the vanilla, confectioners' sugar, and nuts. Beat well to combine. Spread on cooled cake.
*If starting with cold mashed potatoes, warm and whip up in a saucepan with a little butter and a teaspoon or two of milk.

POTATO DUMPLINGS WITH HAM

1 tablespoon vegetable oil
► ½ cup minced cooked ham
1 small onion, minced
► 1½ cups mashed potatoes
1 large or 2 small eggs
½ teaspoon salt
½ teaspoon pepper
½ teaspoon prepared mustard

2 to 2½ cups flour
4 beef bouillon cubes
Water
4 tablespoons melted butter or
margarine
2 tablespoons grated Parmesan
cheese

1. Heat the oil in a skillet and fry the onion until limp. Stir in the ham, cook another minute and set aside. In a mixing bowl, combine the potatoes, eggs, salt, pepper, mustard and 1 cup of the flour; blend until smooth. Turn out onto a lightly floured board; knead in enough of the remaining flour to form a light, smooth dough. Form dough into small balls. Make a hole in the center of each and stuff with a small amount of the ham mixture, close, and roll each ball in flour.

2. Mix the bouillon cubes with 1 cup boiling water in a large saucepan or stock pot. Add about 8 cups of water and bring to boil. Add potato balls a few at a time. Cook for 25 minutes. Remove with slotted spoon. Mix the melted butter with the Parmesan cheese and pour over the dumplings. Makes 4 to 6 servings.

RATATOUILLE PANCAKES

¼ cup loosely packed, chopped
fresh parsley leaves
4 large eggs
½ cup chopped chives
½ cup unbleached flour
¾ teaspoon salt
¼ teaspoon freshly grated
nutmeg

¼ teaspoon dried basil
¼ teaspoon dried oregano
Freshly ground black pepper
► 2 cups chopped Ratatouille,
drained
2 to 3 tablespons butter
2 to 3 tablespoons vegetable oil
Sour cream

1. In a mixing bowl, beat together the parsley, eggs, half the chives, flour, salt, nutmeg, basil, oregano, and pepper; stir in the Ratatouille.

2. In a large, heavy skillet, heat 1 tablespoon of the butter and 1 tablespoon of the oil over moderate heat. Pour in heaping tablespoons of the batter to make 3-inch pancakes. Brown well on one side, then turn the pancakes over and brown the other side. Repeat until all the batter is used; add additional butter and oil whenever the pancakes begin sticking. Serve warm with a dollop of sour cream and sprinkle with the remaining chives. Makes 4 servings.

FISH BAKED WITH RATATOUILLE

2 tablespoons olive oil
2 tablespoons bread crumbs
1½ pounds scrod, flounder, or
striped bass fillets
Juice of 1 lemon

Salt and freshly ground black
pepper
▶ 3 cups Ratatouille, room
temperature
1½ tablespoons drained capers
Lemon wedges

1. Use some of the oil to grease a baking dish that is big enough to hold the fish. Sprinkle 1 tablespoon of the bread crumbs in the bottom of the dish. Arrange the fillets in the baking dish, sprinkle with lemon juice, and season with salt and pepper.

2. Coarsely chop the Ratatouille and mix with the capers. Spread over the fish, sprinkle with remaining bread crumbs, and drizzle with the remaining olive oil. Bake in a preheated 400° oven for 20 minutes. Garnish with lemon wedges before serving. Makes 4 servings.

Note: Ratatouille is a classic French vegetable dish made up mostly of eggplant, zucchini, tomatoes, onions and garlic braised together. Check any basic cookbook for a recipe.

SPINACH-CHEESE DUMPLINGS IN TOMATO-WINE SAUCE

2 tablespoons butter
½ cup chopped onion
1 clove garlic, crushed
1 tablespoon flour,
1 cup tomato purée
▶ 1 cup beef broth, homemade or
canned
½ cup white wine
1 teaspoon salt
¼ teaspoon pepper
½ teaspoon dried oregano
1½ cups ricotta cheese
1½ cups grated Parmesan cheese

1½ cups Italian-flavored bread
crumbs
▶ 1 cup chopped cooked and
drained spinach
2 eggs, lightly beaten
2 teaspoons baking powder
1 clove garlic, pressed
1 teaspoon salt
¼ teaspoon pepper
1 teaspoon dried basil
¼ teaspoon ground nutmeg
A large pot of simmering water

1. To prepare the sauce; heat butter in a skillet, sauté onion and garlic until tender. Sprinkle flour over onions and garlic; stir thoroughly. Add tomato purée, broth, wine, salt, pepper and oregano to skillet; simmer sauce while you prepare dumplings.

2. To prepare the dumplings; combine the cheeses, bread crumbs, spinach, eggs, baking powder, garlic, salt, pepper, basil and nutmeg. Divide the mixture into about 36 balls, 1½ inches in diameter. Drop into simmering water without crowding, and poach 5 to 7 minutes until they float to the top of the water. Remove the dumplings with a slotted spoon to a serving dish; spoon warm sauce over and serve immediately. Makes 4 to 6 servings.

STUFFED ZUCCHINI FLORENTINE

4 medium-size zucchini, halved
  lengthwise
1 tablespoon olive oil
6 to 8 mushrooms, chopped
1 clove garlic, minced
2 shallots or scallions, minced
¾ teaspoon leaf oregano
1 teaspoon leaf thyme
¼ teaspoon ground nutmeg
¼ teaspoon pepper
▶ 2 cups cooked and drained
  spinach
1½ cups shredded Monterey Jack
  cheese
▶ ½ cup cooked rice
  Red pepper strips for garnish

1. Fill a large saucepan with water and bring to a boil; add the zucchini, cover, and boil until tender. Drain and scoop out the center, leaving a ¼-inch shell; chop pulp coarsely and reserve.

2. Heat the olive oil in a skillet, and sauté the mushrooms, garlic, shallots, oregano, thyme, nutmeg, and pepper; cook over medium heat, stirring often, until mushrooms are soft. Stir in the spinach and 1 cup of the cheese; cook, stirring constantly, until the cheese is melted. Remove from heat; stir in the rice and reserved zucchini pulp.

3. Spoon the mixture into the zucchini shells. Place the stuffed shells in a buttered baking dish and sprinkle with the remaining cheese. Bake at 350° for 10 minutes. Garnish with the red pepper strips. Makes 4 servings.

SURPRISE PIE INDIENNE

1 teaspoon grated onion
▶ 4 potatoes, cooked, mashed,
  and seasoned (about 2 cups)
▶ 6 hard-cooked eggs, cut into
  chunks
▶ ½ cup diced cooked ham
▶ ½ cup drained, cooked spinach
2 tablespoons butter or
  margarine
1 tablespoon all-purpose flour
½ teaspoon salt
½ teaspoon curry powder
  Dash cayenne
¼ teaspoon ground coriander
⅛ teaspoon pepper
¾ cup milk
½ teaspoon chopped parsley

1. Mix the onion with the potatoes, and line a shallow 1½-quart buttered baking dish with the mixture. Spread the center of the potato shell with the eggs, ham, and spinach.

2. In a saucepan, melt the butter and blend in the flour, salt, curry powder, cayenne, coriander, and pepper, and cook 2 minutes. Gradually add the milk, and cook, stirring constantly, until thickened. Add the parsley, and pour the sauce over the eggs, ham and spinach. Bake at 375° for about 30 minutes. Makes 6 servings.

SPINACH FRITTERS

▶ 2 cups chopped, drained
   cooked spinach
2 eggs, well beaten
½ cup fine cracker crumbs
¼ cup grated Parmesan cheese

3 tablespoons finely minced
onion
Salt and pepper to taste
Vegetable oil (about 3 cups)

1. In a large bowl, combine the spinach, eggs, cracker crumbs, Paremsan cheese, onion, salt, and pepper.

2. Heat 2 inches of vegetable oil in a large skillet to 360° (or until a 1-inch cube of bread browns in the hot oil in about 50 seconds). Drop the spinach mixture by rounded tablespoonfuls into the hot oil and fry a few at a time, turning once, until fritters are light golden on both sides. Drain on absorbent paper. Keep the cooked fritters covered and warm until all the batter is used. Makes 4 servings.

SPINACH SOUFFLÉ

5 tablespoons butter
½ cup minced onion
3 tablespoons flour
1 cup light cream
4 eggs, separated

1 teaspoon salt
⅛ teaspoon pepper
¼ teaspoon ground nutmeg
▶1⅓ cups well drained, finely
   chopped cooked spinach

1. Melt 4 tablespoons of the butter in a saucepan. Sauté the onion until tender; blend in the flour; slowly add cream, stirring constantly, until mixture is smooth and thickened. Simmer gently 10 minutes over very low heat.

2. Beat the 4 egg yolks lightly; stir a little of the hot sauce into the yolks, then beat the yolk mixture into the hot sauce, vigorously stirring over low heat, so that the eggs do not curdle. Remove the pan from the heat and stir in the salt, pepper, nutmeg, and spinach.

3. Lightly butter a 5-cup soufflé dish. Beat the egg whites until stiff but not dry, and gently fold into the spinach mixture; carefully spoon into the soufflé dish, and bake in a preheated 350° oven 40 minutes until puffed and browned. Makes 4 servings.

SQUASH PUFF

▶ 3 cups cooked squash
½ teaspoon salt
½ teaspoon grated onion
⅛ teaspoon pepper
½ teaspoon sugar
¼ teaspoon ground nutmeg

2 tablespoons melted butter
2 tablespoons flour
2 teaspoons baking powder
¾ cup light cream or milk
1 egg, beaten
¼ cup dry bread crumbs

1. In a medium bowl, mash the squash; add the salt, onion, pepper, sugar, nutmeg and butter; mix well. In another bowl, combine the flour and baking powder. Gradually stir in the cream and blend well. Add the egg and blend the liquid into the squash mixture.

2. Turn into a greased 1½-quart casserole; sprinkle top with crumbs. Bake, uncovered, at 325° for 35 minutes. Makes 6 servings.

SWEET POTATO PIE

▶ 2 cups mashed cooked sweet
  potatoes
1 cup firmly packed brown
  sugar
2 eggs, separated
½ teaspoon ground cloves
½ teaspoon ground cinnamon
½ teaspoon ground nutmeg

Salt to taste
8 tablespoons soft butter or
  margarine
½ cup evaporated milk or light
  cream
1 tablespoon sugar
1 9" unbaked pie crust (see
  Basics)

1. In a bowl, combine the sweet potatoes with the brown sugar, egg
yolks, cloves, cinnamon, nutmeg, and salt to taste. Beat in the butter and
stir in the milk. Beat the egg whites until almost stiff. Gradually add the
sugar, beating until stiff. Fold the whites into the potato mixture.

2. Spoon the filling into the unbaked pie crust. Place in preheated 400°
oven and bake 10 minutes. Reduce oven temperature to 350° and continue baking about 45 minutes longer. Remove to a rack and let cool before slicing. Makes 6 servings.

PISTACHIO YAM MERINGUE PIE

▶ 2 cups cold mashed cooked
  yams
3 eggs, separated
¾ cup sugar
  Dash nutmeg
2 tablespoons butter, melted
¼ teaspoon salt

1 cup milk
½ cup shelled, chopped
  pistachio nuts
1 9" unbaked pie shell (see
  Basics)
½ teaspoon vanilla extract
¼ cup shredded coconut

1. In a large bowl, beat the yams and egg yolks together until light and
fluffy. Beat in ½ cup sugar, nutmeg, the butter, salt and milk; stir in the
nuts. Pour into the pie shell and bake at 350° for 40 minutes, or until set.

2. Beat egg whites until foamy. Gradually beat in remaining sugar and
continue beating until stiff. Add vanilla; pile meringue lightly on pie.
Sprinkle with coconut. Bake at 425° until peaks are brown. Cool before
serving. Makes 6 to 8 servings.

SWEET POTATO SPICED PUDDING

¼ cup butter or margarine
¼ cup firmly packed brown
  sugar
2 eggs, separated
¼ cup milk
¼ cup orange juice

1 tablespoon rum
¼ teaspoon ground nutmeg
⅛ teaspoon ground cinnamon
⅛ teaspoon ground ginger
▶ 1 cup mashed cooked sweet
  potatoes

1. Cream butter and sugar together in a bowl; add well-beaten egg
yolks, milk, orange juice, rum, nutmeg, cinnamon, ginger and sweet potatoes. Beat egg whites until stiff and fold into mixture.

2. Turn into a 1½-quart casserole. Bake at 350° for 40 minutes. Makes 4
servings.

SWEET POTATO CHEESE SOUFFLÉ

2 tablespoons melted butter
2 tablespoons flour
½ cup milk
¼ cup light cream
½ teaspoon grated lemon rind
½ cup grated Swiss cheese

½ cup grated Parmesan cheese
3 eggs, separated
¼ teaspoon salt
¼ teaspoon nutmeg
▶ 2 cups mashed cooked sweet
   potatoes

1. Melt the butter in a saucepan, blend in the flour, and cook for 1 minute. Gradually stir in the milk, cream, and lemon rind, and cook, stirring constantly, until sauce is smooth and thickened. Add the cheeses and cook until melted. Beat in the egg yolks, one at a time. Season with salt and nutmeg. Blend in the sweet potatoes. Beat egg whites until stiff, but not dry; fold into the sweet potato mixture.

2. Turn into a buttered 1-quart baking dish. Bake at 375° for 45 minutes, or until puffed and lightly browned. Makes 6 servings.

SWEET POTATO PUFF

1 cup milk
¼ teaspoon salt
2 teaspoons sugar
2 tablespoons butter or
   margarine
1 tablespoon brandy, heated

▶ 2 cups mashed sweet potatoes
2 eggs, separated
½ cup raisins
½ teaspoon ground nutmeg
½ cup chopped walnuts

1. In a saucepan, scald the milk together with salt, sugar, and butter. Stir in the brandy and add to the potatoes in a mixing bowl; beat well. Beat egg yolks, then add to the potatoes, and stir in the raisins, nutmeg and walnuts.

2. Beat the egg whites until stiff but not dry; fold gently into the potato mixture. Pour into a well greased 1½-quart casserole. Bake at 325° for 45 minutes. Makes 6 servings.

SWEET POTATO AND APPLE MUFFINS

2 cups flour
2 teaspoons baking powder
1 teaspoon ground cinnamon
¼ teaspoon freshly grated
   nutmeg
⅛ teaspoon salt
½ cup raisins
2 eggs

▶ 1 cup mashed cooked sweet
   potatoes
⅓ cup honey
4 tablespoons butter or
   margarine, melted
¼ cup unsweetened applesauce
¼ cup milk

1. Sift the flour, baking powder, cinnamon, nutmeg, and salt into a large bowl; stir in the raisins, thoroughly coating them with the flour mixture. Beat together the eggs, sweet potatoes, honey, butter, applesauce, and milk in a separate bowl; quickly stir wet ingredients into dry ingredients just until flour is moistened.

2. Spoon batter into a well-greased 12-cup muffin pan; bake at 400° until golden, about 30 minutes. Makes 12 muffins.

YAM SPICECAKE

2 cups sifted cake flour
¾ teaspoon salt
2 teaspoons baking powder
¼ teaspoon baking soda
1 teaspoon ground cinnamon
1 teaspoon ground nutmeg
⅛ teaspoon ground cloves

½ cup butter or margarine,
    softened
¾ cup sugar
2 eggs
►1¼ cups cold mashed cooked
    yams
¼ cup coarsely chopped nuts
½ cup milk

1. In a bowl, sift together the flour, salt, baking powder, baking soda, cinnamon, nutmeg, and cloves. In a separate large mixing bowl, cream the butter; add the sugar, and cream until light and fluffy. Add the eggs one at a time, beating thoroughly after each, then beat in the yams; stir in the nuts. Add the sifted dry ingredients and the milk; beat only until smooth.

2. Grease and flour a 13 × 9-inch baking pan (or 2 8-inch layer cake pans). Pour batter into the pan and bake at 350° for about 35 minutes. Turn out on a rack and cool. Sprinkle top with confectioners' sugar.

 CREAMED VEGETABLES

4 tablespoons butter
3 tablespoons flour
1 cup milk
¼ cup heavy cream

1 teaspoon Worcestershire sauce
Salt and pepper to taste
► 2 cups chopped cooked
    vegetables

1. Melt the butter in a saucepan, add the flour and stir until *roux* is thick. Gradually stir in the milk, cream, Worcestershire sauce, salt, and pepper and simmer over low heat for 10 minutes.

2. Add the vegetables and continue to simmer until mixture is hot. Makes 4 servings.

 VEGETABLE PUDDING

4 tablespoons butter
4 tablespoons flour
1 cup milk
► ½ cup chopped cooked broccoli
► ½ cup cooked whole-kernel corn
► ½ cup diced cooked carrots
► ½ cup diced cooked string
    beans

1 tablespoon grated onion
1 tablespoon lemon juice
¼ teaspoon salt
⅛ teaspoon ground nutmeg
3 eggs, well beaten

Melt the butter in a saucepan, blend in the flour and cook for 1 minute. Gradually add the milk, stirring constantly, until sauce thickens. Remove from the heat and blend in the broccoli, corn, carrots, string beans, onion, lemon juice, salt, nutmeg and eggs. Pour into a lightly greased 1½-quart baking dish. Bake at 350° until firm, about 25 minutes. Makes 4 to 6 servings.

QUICK CREAM OF VEGETABLE PURÉE SOUP

3 tablespoons butter or margarine
1 onion, coarsely chopped
▶ 2 cups cooked vegetables (such as carrots, cauliflower, celery, spinach, peas, broccoli, asparagus, summer squash)

▶ 1½ cups rich stock, vegetable or chicken
½ to 1 cup cream
Salt and pepper to taste
Croutons or sliced almonds

Heat the butter in a skillet; add onion and cook until tender. Put the onion, vegetables, stock and cream in blender or food processor and process until mixture is smooth. Season with salt and pepper. Serve hot or chilled. Garnish with croutons or almonds. Makes 4 to 6 servings.

OLD-FASHIONED VEGETABLE SOUP

▶ 6 to 8 cups homemade beef broth
½ cup diced carrots
½ cup diced celery
½ cup diced onions
1 small turnip, chopped
1 small parsnip, chopped
½ medium white cabbage, sliced thin

1 cup canned tomatoes, chopped
1 teaspoon Worcestershire sauce
1 teaspoon dried thyme
1 teaspoon salt
¼ teaspoon pepper
▶ 1 cup mixed cooked vegetables
2 tablespoons fresh minced parsley

Heat broth in a large saucepan. Add carrots, celery, onions, turnip and parsnip and simmer 10 minutes, or until vegetables are crisp-tender. Add cabbage, tomatoes, Worcestershire sauce, thyme, salt and pepper, and simmer 5 to 6 minutes. Add the cooked vegetables and simmer 2 to 3 minutes longer. Sprinkle with parsley. Serve hot. Makes 4 to 6 servings.

RUSSIAN VEGETABLE SALAD

¼ cup wine vinegar
¼ teaspoon dried tarragon
⅛ teaspoon pepper
¼ teaspoon dried thyme
¼ teaspoon paprika
1 small clove garlic, minced
¾ cup olive oil
▶ ½ cup diced cooked green beans
▶ ¼ cup diced cooked beets

▶ ½ cup diced cooked carrots
¼ cup diced celery
1 medium red onion, thinly sliced
▶ 1 cup diced cooked potatoes
½ cup mayonnaise, approximately
Crisp lettuce leaves
▶ 8 thin slices cold cooked lamb
▶ 2 hard-cooked eggs, sliced
4 black olives, sliced

1. In a small bowl, stir together the vinegar, tarragon, pepper, thyme, paprika, garlic, and oil. In a large glass salad bowl, combine the green beans, beets, carrots, celery, onion, and potatoes; pour the dressing over the vegetables and blend well. Marinate for 1 hour.

2. Drain the marinated vegetables well; gently stir in enough mayonnaise to coat vegetables. On a serving plate, arrange the lettuce leaves and lamb slices in alternating layers. Mound the salad on top. Garnish with the eggs and olives. Makes 4 servings.

JAVANESE VEGETABLE SALAD

¾ cup peanut butter
1¾ cups milk
 2 cloves garlic, pressed
 ½ teaspoon sugar
 ⅛ teaspoon cayenne pepper or
 to taste
▶ 2 cups cooked whole green
 beans

▶ 2 cups sliced cooked carrots
 1 medium cucumber, peeled
 and sliced
▶ 1 cup chopped cooked
 cauliflower
 6 large mushrooms, sliced
 1 small green pepper, julienned
▶ 4 small potatoes, cooked and
 sliced

1. In a medium saucepan over low heat, stir together the peanut butter and ½ cup milk until well blended and warm. Gradually beat in the remaining 1¼ cups milk, the garlic, sugar and cayenne. Cook, stirring, until thickened; cool.

2. In a large mixing bowl combine the beans, carrots, cucumber, cauliflower, mushrooms, green pepper and potatoes; mix well with the peanut sauce. Arrange the salad on a large serving platter and chill for no more than 1 hour. Makes 4 servings.

SALADE PARISIENNE

▶ 4 cups mixed, cooked
 vegetables: choose from green
 beans, peas, cauliflower, corn,
 green pepper strips, quartered
 turnips, broccoli, etc.
 3 raw carrots, shredded
 ½ cup sliced raw mushrooms
▶ 1 cup diced cooked chicken
 livers

▶ 1 cup diced cooked shrimp
 1 cup olive oil
 ⅓ cup vinegar
 Salt, pepper, and sugar to
 taste
 ⅓ cup minced fresh parsley
 1 cup small black olives

1. Combine the cooked vegetables with the carrots, mushrooms, livers, and shrimp in a large mixing bowl.

2. Combine the oil, vinegar, salt, pepper, sugar, and parsley and stir vigorously.

3. Toss the salad ingredients with the dressing until well blended. Spread the salad out on a small pretty platter and garnish with the olives. Makes 4 to 6 servings.

HAM AND VEGETABLE SALAD

1 head Romaine lettuce, well
  drained
▶ 2 cups cooked green peas
▶ ½ cup diced cooked carrots
▶ 1 cup diced cooked ham
  ½ cup pitted and sliced black
  olives
▶ 2 hard-cooked eggs, halved

¼ cup olive oil
2 tablespoons white wine
  vinegar
Dash prepared mustard
1 teaspoon salt
¼ teaspoon freshly ground black
  pepper

1. Combine in a salad bowl, the lettuce torn into bite-size pieces, and the peas, carrots, ham, and olives.

2. Mash the egg yolks with the olive oil and vinegar in a small bowl. Season with mustard, salt, and pepper. Pour over the mixture in the salad bowl, and toss until well blended. Chop the egg whites and sprinkle over the surface of the salad. Makes 4 to 6 servings.

SCALLOPED ZUCCHINI AND CORN

▶ 3 to 4 cups sliced cooked
  zucchini
  1 can (16 oz.) cream-style corn
  ½ cup chopped celery
  4 eggs, beaten
  1 teaspoon salt
  Dash pepper

2 tablespoons butter or
  vegetable oil
½ cup chopped onion
1 green pepper, chopped
1 cup shredded Cheddar
  cheese
2 tablespoons parsley
¼ teaspoon paprika

In a bowl, mix together the zucchini, corn, celery, eggs, salt, and pepper. Melt the butter in a skillet and sauté the onions and green pepper until golden; pour into a 2-quart casserole; add the zucchini mixture and blend well. Sprinkle the top with the cheese, parsley, and paprika. Bake uncovered at 350° for 40 minutes. Makes 4 servings.

ZUCCHINI AND TOMATO QUICHE

  ½ cup minced onion
  2 tablespoons butter or
  margarine
▶ 1 cup minced cooked zucchini
  ½ teaspoon salt
  ½ teaspoon dried oregano
  ¼ teaspoon dried basil
  ¾ cup shredded Swiss cheese

1 baked 9-inch pie shell (see
  Basics)
1½ cups light cream
3 eggs
  Pinch ground nutmeg
  Dash Tobasco sauce
1 large tomato, sliced

1. In a medium-size skillet, sauté the onion in the butter until golden. Add the zucchini, half the salt, the oregano, and the basil, and simmer for 3 minutes, stirring gently, until almost all the liquid has evaporated. Remove from heat. Distribute the cheese evenly on the bottom of the pie shell. Spread the zucchini mixture over the cheese.

(continued)

2. In a bowl, beat the cream with the eggs, nutmeg, Tabasco, and the remaining salt. Pour into the pie shell and arrange the tomato slices on top. Bake at 400° until set, about 25 minutes. Serve hot or at room temperature. Makes 6 servings.

 # ZUCCHINI AND CAULIFLOWER SALAD

½ cup mayonnaise
1 tablespoon lemon juice
1 tablespoon capers
½ teaspoon summer savory
2½ tablespoons minced chives
¼ cup chopped black olives

1 cup thinly sliced zucchini
▶ 2 cups cold cooked cauliflower
   flowerets
   Romaine lettuce
¼ cup toasted slivered almonds

In a large bowl mix together the mayonnaise, lemon juice, capers, summer savory and chives. Add the olives, zucchini and cauliflower and toss to blend. Place salad in a serving bowl lined with lettuce leaves. Garnish the top with almond slivers. Makes 4 servings.

▶RICE/PASTA/BEANS

SPANISH RICE

6 slices bacon
1 medium onion, minced
1 green pepper, minced
1 medium garlic clove, minced
¼ cup diced celery
▶ 2 cups cooked, or canned
tomatoes

1 teaspoon salt
⅛ teaspoon pepper
▶ 2 to 3 cups cooked rice
⅛ teaspoon cayenne or saffron
1 teaspoon paprika

1. In a medium skillet, sauté the bacon until crisp; remove bacon from pan and pour off all but 2 tablespoons fat. Cook the onion, green pepper, garlic and celery in the bacon fat until onion is translucent. Add the tomatoes, salt and pepper and simmer for 5 minutes.

2. Stir in the rice, cayenne and paprika; simmer for 5 minutes. Crumble bacon over the top. Makes 4 to 6 servings.

QUICK RICE AND BEANS

2 slices of thick smoked bacon,
diced
½ cup sweet red onion, diced
1 green pepper, diced
1 clove garlic, minced
1 can (14 oz.) Italian-style
tomatoes with basil
1 can (1 lb.) kidney beans,
drained

½ teaspoon salt
¼ teaspoon freshly ground black
pepper
⅛ teaspoon Tabasco sauce
⅓ teaspoon dried oregano
Dash cayenne
▶ 3 cups boiled rice
⅓ cup grated sharp Cheddar
cheese

1. In a large heavy skillet, over medium heat, cook the bacon until done but not overcrisp; set aside and pour all but 1 tablespoon of bacon fat from the skillet. Add the onion, green pepper, and garlic; sauté until they are limp. Sprinkle in the bacon. Add tomatoes, beans, salt, pepper, Tabasco sauce, oregano and cayenne.

2. Cover and simmer for about 20 minutes. Add the rice, stir to blend, and cook a final 2 minutes. Stir in the cheese until melted. Makes 6 servings.

INDONESIAN FRIED RICE (Nasi Goreng)

⅓ cup peanut or salad oil
4 medium onions, chopped
2 cloves garlic, minced
▶ 3 cups cooked rice, cold and
dry
½ teaspoon ground chili pepper
1 teaspoon ground cumin
2 teaspoons ground coriander

¼ teaspoon mace or nutmeg
⅛ teaspoon black pepper
2 tablespoons peanut butter
▶ 1 cup cubed cooked ham
▶ 1 cup chopped cooked shrimp
▶ 1 cup shredded cooked chicken
▶ ¼ cup chicken broth

1. Heat oil in large skillet. Cook onions and garlic until golden. Add cold rice, chili pepper, cumin, coriander, mace, black pepper, and peanut

butter. Mix well. Fry rice mixture, stirring often, until lightly browned. Add ham, shrimp, and chicken; toss to mix well.

2. Add 2 to 4 tablespoons chicken broth if rice mixture appears dry. Cover and heat in 300° over for 30 minutes. This dish improves on standing. Cook ahead, refrigerate, and reheat. Serve with regular curry accompaniments: chutney, crumbled bacon, soy sauce, sliced cucumber, chopped egg, peanuts, and broiled bananas. Makes 6 servings.

RICE-STUFFED TOMATOES

4 medium tomatoes
¼ teaspoon salt
▶ ½ cup cooked rice
2 tablespoons chopped mushrooms
▶ ¼ cup minced cooked lamb or pork
1 small clove garlic, minced

2 teaspoons minced onion
1 teaspoon capers
1 teaspoon dried parsley flakes
¼ teaspoon dried oregano
1 egg, lightly beaten
Dash black pepper
1 tablespoon oil

1. Slice off the stem end of each tomato; reserve. Scoop out the pulp (reserve for soups, etc.) and sprinkle the insides with salt; turn upside down and drain. Combine the rice, mushrooms, lamb, garlic, onion, capers, parsley, oregano, egg, and pepper; mix well.

2. Fill the tomatoes and replace the tops. Place in a shallow buttered baking dish and drizzle the oil over the tops of the tomatoes. Bake at 350° for 15 to 20 minutes, or until filling is hot. Makes 4 servings.

MEXICAN STUFFED ZUCCHINI

3 medium zucchini
2 slices bacon, cut up
¾ cup chopped mushrooms
½ cup chopped green pepper
2 green chilies, seeded and chopped
⅓ cup chopped onion
1 small clove garlic, crushed
1 cup whole-kernel corn, drained

1 can (8 oz.) tomato sauce
⅛ teaspoon cayenne
¼ cup sliced black olvies
▶ 2 cups cooked rice
Salt
Dash pepper
1 egg, slightly beaten
¾ cup grated Monterey Jack cheese

1. Wash the zucchini; cut off and discard stems. Cut each in half lengthwise; scoop out and discard pulp. In a medium skillet with a cover, bring 2 cups water and 1 teaspoon salt to boiling; add zucchini shells, cut side down; cook, covered, until crisp-tender. Drain well.

2. In a medium skillet, sauté the bacon until crisp. Stir in mushrooms, green pepper, chilies, onion, and garlic; sauté until onion is tender. Remove from heat; add the corn, tomato sauce, cayenne, olives, rice, salt to taste, pepper, and egg; mix well.

3. Fill the zucchini halves with the rice mixture, dividing evenly. Sprinkle with the cheese. Arrange in the bottom of a baking dish and bake at 350° for 15 to 20 minutes, until the cheese melts. Makes 4 to 6 servings.

SPANISH ONIONS WITH CURRANT PECAN STUFFING

6 Spanish onions, each about ¾ pound
6 tablespoons butter, approximately
½ cup minced mushrooms
▶ 1 cup cooked rice
⅓ cup dry currants

½ cup finely minced pecans
¼ teaspoon crumbled leaf thyme
⅛ teaspoon nutmeg
¼ to ½ teaspoon salt
¼ teaspoon pepper
1 extra large egg, lightly beaten

1. Cut 1 inch off the top of each onion; peel the onions; gently boil them in lightly salted water for about 20 minutes, or until tender. Drain the onions well, then scoop out the insides, leaving onion shells about ⅜-inch thick (2 layers of onion).

2. Chop the scooped-out onion and measure out 1 cup of it (the remainder can be used in soups or stews). Heat 3 tablespoons of the butter in a skillet; cook the 1 cup of chopped onion and the mushrooms until tender.

3. In a mixing bowl, combine the onion and mushrooms (with their pan juices), with the rice, currants, pecans, thyme, nutmeg, salt, pepper, and egg. Stuff the hollowed out onions with the mixture, packing it in lightly and piling it up on top. Melt the remaining butter; lightly butter a baking dish and arrange onions in it; use remaining melted butter to lightly brush over the onions. Bake in a preheated 350° oven for about 30 minutes until onions are heated through. Makes 6 servings.

SALMON CHEESE PIE

5 tablespoons butter
3 tablespoons flour
1½ cups milk
▶ 2 cups cooked rice
2 medium onions, thinly sliced
9" Double-crust pie shell, unbaked (see Basics)

1 can (16 oz.) salmon
▶ 2 hard-cooked eggs, finely chopped
⅓ cup grated Cheddar cheese
⅓ cup mayonnaise

1. In a saucepan, melt 3 tablespoons butter and gradually beat in the flour to form a paste; cook for 1 minute. Slowly stir in the milk and simmer until smooth and thick. Mix the rice with ½ cup of the sauce. In a skillet, sauté the onion in the remaining butter until golden.

2. Line a deep 9" pie plate with one pastry circle; pour ½ the rice mixture in the pie shell; crumble the salmon on top and cover with the onions and egg. Cover with the remaining rice. Moisten edges and lay the other crust over the salmon mixture; crimp the edges; cut steam vents in the top crust. Bake at 450° for 15 minutes.

3. Melt the cheese in the remaining sauce. Remove from heat and fold in the mayonnaise. Serve sauce alongside the pie. Makes 4 to 6 servings.

SWEET RICE FRITTERS

▶ 1 cup cold boiled rice
2 tablespoons golden raisins
½ teaspoon grated lemon rind
2 tablespoons finely chopped almonds
½ teaspoon vanilla
3 tablespoons flour

2 eggs
4 tablespoons butter, approximately
1 tablespoon light oil (safflower or corn), approximately
Powdered sugar
Jam or jelly

1. Combine the rice, raisins, lemon rind, almonds, and vanilla in a bowl; mix well. Sprinkle the flour over the rice mixture and stir. Add the eggs and mix well.

2. Heat the butter and oil in a small skillet over moderate heat. Drop the rice batter by the tablespoonful into the hot fat and fry on both sides. Remove the fritters from the pan and drain on absorbent paper; keep warm until all the batter is used.

3. Sprinkle the fritters with the powdered sugar and serve with jam or jelly. Makes 4 servings.

RICE PUDDING

▶ 2 cups cooked rice
½ cup water
2 cups warm milk
2 eggs, beaten
⅓ cup sugar
Pinch salt

1 teaspoon vanilla
2 tablespoons Madeira or sherry
2 teaspoons cinnamon
Black Cherry Sauce, optional (see below)

1. In a saucepan, combine the rice with the water and simmer 2 to 3 minutes, until liquid is absorbed. Add the milk and simmer for 5 minutes or until the milk looks creamy. Let cool until lukewarm.

2. Combine the eggs, sugar, salt, vanilla, Madeira, and 1 teaspoon of the cinnamon. Slowly stir the egg mixture into the rice, then pour the pudding into a buttered 5-cup casserole.

3. Place the casserole dish into a larger pan filled with hot water; bake in a preheated 350° oven 45 to 50 minutes or until a knife inserted in the center comes out clean.

Black Cherry Sauce

1 can (16 oz.) pitted dark sweet cherries, drained (reserve syrup)

1 tablespoon sugar
2 teaspoons cornstarch

4. Combine the reserved cherry syrup with the sugar and cornstarch in a saucepan. Cook, stirring until mixture comes to a boil and thickens. Add the cherries, and remove the sauce from heat. Serve warm or at room temperature on the Rice Pudding. Makes 4 to 6 servings.

RICE SOUFFLÉ

3 tablespoons butter	1 cup grated Swiss or sharp
3 tablespoons flour	cheese
1 cup milk	▶ 1 cup cooked rice
4 eggs, separated	½ teaspoon salt
	¼ teaspoon pepper

1. Melt the butter in a large saucepan; add the flour and stir constantly until *roux* is smooth. Gradually add the milk and continue to stir until sauce is thick and smooth. Simmer the sauce for 10 minutes; remove from heat.

2. Beat a little sauce into the egg yolks, then beat the egg yolk mixture into the remaining sauce. Add the cheese, rice, salt, and pepper to the sauce.

3. Beat the egg whites until stiff but not dry; gently fold into the rice mixture. Pour the mixture into a greased 2-quart soufflé dish and bake in a preheated 325° oven for 1 hour. Makes 4 servings.

GREEK RICE SOUP (Avgolemono)

▶ 6 cups seasoned chicken broth	Juice of one lemon
▶ 1 cup cooked rice	Salt and pepper
3 eggs	Chopped parsley

Heat broth in a saucepan; add the rice, and simmer for 10 minutes. Beat the eggs well, then beat in about ½ cup of the hot liquid. Add lemon juice and pour into the remaining liquid and rice. Mix well, check seasoning, and serve at once. Garnish with chopped parsley. Makes 6 servings.

SURPRISE RICE PATTIES

▶ 2 cups cooked rice	1 tablespoon melted butter or
½ cup grated Parmesan cheese	margarine
1 egg, well beaten	2 cups (1 lb.) ½-inch cubes
2 tablespoons prepared mustard	Mozzarella cheese
¼ teaspoon dried basil	Fine bread crumbs
½ teaspoon salt	Vegetable oil for frying
⅛ teaspoon white pepper	

Mix together the rice and grated cheese. Add egg, mustard, basil, salt and pepper and melted butter. Blend well. Cover each cube of cheese with the rice mixture. Form into thick patties; cover with bread crumbs. Fry in oil in a deep skillet until light brown; drain thoroughly. Makes 4 to 6 servings.

ITALIAN RICE SALAD

▶ 2 cups cooked rice, room
   temperature
1 cup grated carrot
¼ cup minced celery
2 scallions, thinly sliced
   crosswise
¼ cup minced red onion
½ cup peeled, chopped, drained
   cucumber
2 anchovies, minced
6 pitted olives, chopped

2 tablespoons minced fresh
   parsley
4 large fresh mushrooms, thinly
   sliced
¼ cup olive oil
1 teaspoon basil
2 tablespoons white wine
   vinegar
Salt and pepper to taste
Lettuce
Lemon slices for garnish

1. In a large mixing bowl combine the rice with the carrots, celery, scallions, red onion, cucumber, anchovies, olives, parsley and mushrooms.

2. Combine the oil, basil, vinegar, salt and pepper to taste. Mix thoroghly with vegetables. Line a serving plate with crisp lettuce leaves and pile salad on top. Garnish with lemon slices. Makes 4 servings.

FRIED RICE WITH BEEF AND GREEN PEPPERS

▶ 2 cups shredded cooked beef
2 tablespoons soy sauce
½ teaspoon sugar
2 teaspoons cornstarch
2 teaspoons sherry
6 tablespoons salad oil
1 large onion, sliced

2 large green peppers, julienned
½ teaspoon salt
¼ cup chicken stock
▶ 4 cups cold cooked rice
1 scallion, sliced
Dash of freshly ground pepper

1. Place the shredded beef in a small mixing bowl. Add 1 tablespoon soy sauce, sugar, cornstarch and sherry and marinate for about ten minutes.

2. Heat two tablespoons salad oil in a large skillet and cook onions until soft. Add green peppers and salt and cook one minute; they should remain green and crisp. Add the meat, chicken stock and remaining soy sauce; stir-fry for one minute. Remove onions, peppers, and beef; set aside.

3. Heat 4 tablespoons oil; fry the rice. When thoroughly heated, stir in onions, green peppers and beef. Add scallions and a dash of pepper and mix well. Serve immediately. Makes 4 servings.

ORANGE RICE (for Roast Chicken)

2 tablespoons butter or
   margarine
½ cup sliced celery
½ cup chopped onion
▶ 3 cups cooked rice (cooked in
   chicken broth)

½ cup plumped raisins
1 tablespoon grated orange
   peel
Salt and pepper to taste

In a skillet, melt the butter and sauté the celery and onion until golden brown. Add the rice, raisins and orange peel; heat. Season with salt and pepper to taste. Mound the rice mixture into orange cups or in piles around roast chicken. Makes 6 servings.

FRIED RICE

8 slices bacon, chopped
⅓ cup chopped mushrooms
⅓ cup chopped green pepper
3 tablespoons vegetable oil
► 2 cups cold cooked rice

⅓ cup thinly sliced water
  chestnuts
⅓ cup finely chopped bamboo
  shoots
⅓ cup minced scallions
2 eggs, well beaten
1 teaspoon Worcestershire sauce

1. Cook bacon in a large skillet until crisp; remove and set aside. Pour off all but 2 tablespoons bacon fat; cook mushrooms and green pepper in the fat until tender and most of liquid in pan has evaporated. Add the oil and heat.

2. Add the rice, water chestnuts, bamboo shoots, scallions, and Worcestershire sauce to skillet. Heat, stirring, until rice is very hot; add eggs and reserved bacon. Stir fry until rice is covered with eggs, and dry. Makes 4 servings.

HAM CHEESE ROLLS

► 1½ cups cooked rice
⅓ cup chopped raisins
1 egg, beaten
¼ teaspoon paprika
½ teaspoon Worcestershire sauce
½ cup chopped scallions

¼ cup chopped celery
½ teaspoon dried basil
2 ounces cream cheese
► 8 thin slices ham
  Mustard

1. In a mixing bowl, combine the rice, raisins, egg, paprika, Worcester-shire sauce, scallions, celery, and basil. Spread the cream cheese over the ham slices. Spoon some of the rice mixture over each ham slice and roll tightly.

2. Spread mustard over the tops of the ham rolls and place in a buttered baking dish. Bake at 400° for 10 to 15 minutes. Makes 4 servings.

MALTESE PASTA OMELET

► 3 cups cooked spaghetti
3 eggs, beaten
⅓ to ½ cup grated Parmesan
  cheese
¼ cup diced scallions

► 1 cup cooked crumbled
  sausage
  Salt and pepper to taste
3 tablespoons butter or
  margarine

In a medium-size mixing bowl, combine the spaghetti, eggs, cheese, scallions, sausage, salt and pepper. Heat 2 tablespoons of the butter to sizzling in a 10-inch skillet; add the spaghetti mixture and press with a spatula to make a compact cake; sauté over medium heat 10 minutes, or until golden brown. Dot with remaining butter. Cut the pancake in half and turn each side over carefully to brown. Makes 4 to 6 servings.

MACARONI KUGEL

▶ 2 cups cooked macaroni or
   wide noodles
3 tablespoons melted butter
½ cup milk
3 eggs
½ cup sugar

1½ teaspoons grated lemon peel
1 teaspoon vanilla
¼ teaspoon nutmeg
½ cup seedless raisins
Sour cream for topping

1. Mix macaroni with butter. Heat milk (do not boil) in a heavy saucepan. Add macaroni and simmer uncovered for 3 to 4 minutes, stirring frequently.

2. Beat the eggs, add the sugar and cook over low heat, stirring constantly, until thick and lemon-colored. Combine the egg mixture with the milk/macaroni mixture. Add the lemon peel, vanilla, nutmeg, and raisins.

3. Pour into a lightly buttered 1-quart casserole. Bake at 300° for 45 to 50 minutes, or until a knife inserted in the center comes out clean. Serve warm or cold with sour cream. Makes 6 servings.

ROCKY MOUNTAIN CHOWDER

1 tablespoon butter or
   margarine
1 medium onion, sliced
1 clove garlic, minced
⅓ cup chopped green pepper
1 cup canned tomatoes,
   chopped (do not drain)
3 cups consommé

▶ 4 cooked frankfurters, coarsely
   chopped
▶ 2 cups leftover baked beans
1 stalk celery, chopped
2 tablespoons minced parsley
¼ teaspoon dried basil
¼ teaspoon dried rosemary
Salt and pepper to taste
3 tablespoons sherry

Melt butter in a heavy saucepan, and sauté the onion, garlic, and green pepper until tender but not brown. Add the tomatoes, consommé, frankfurters, beans, celery, parsley, basil, rosemary, salt, and pepper. Bring to a boil; reduce heat and simmer 30 minutes. Stir in sherry and serve. Makes 4 servings.

COLD PASTA SALAD

2 tablespoons wine vinegar
¼ teaspoon dillweed
1 medium garlic clove, pressed
¼ teaspoon dried basil
½ teaspoon dried oregano
½ cup olive oil

¾ teaspoon lemon juice
▶ 2 cups cooked pasta
▶ ¾ cup diced cooked broccoli
▶ ¾ cup julienned cooked beets
1 tablespoon sliced olives
⅓ cup grated Romano cheese

1. In a small bowl, mix together the vinegar, dill, garlic, basil and oregano; let sit for 1 hour, then strain into the olive oil; mix in the lemon juice.

2. Combine the pasta with the broccoli, beets, and olives; pour the dressing over the pasta and blend well. Chill for 1 hour. Sprinkle cheese on top before serving. Makes 4 servings.

"Perfect" Hollandaise

Too many cooks despair of preparing a "perfect" Hollandaise sauce. The next time you begin, just remember that it must be cooked over the lowest possible heat, preferably in the top of a double boiler over hot water (not in it), or in a heavy saucepan.

If the sauce begins to look grainy as you stir, be warned that it is beginning to curdle. Remove instantly from the heat, add 1 to 2 teaspoons of cold water, and beat the mixture vigorously until it is smooth.

If the sauce doesn't respond to this measure (and assuming you haven't "scrambled" the eggs), begin again by taking another egg yolk, heating it over the hot water very gradually, and adding the "broken" Hollandaise the same way you added the melted butter, drop by drop, adding the "eggy" part first, and beating vigorously.

It's generally a good idea to set out the cold water before beginning the sauce, to have it handy. Remember, controlling the amount of heat is the major trick.

Egg Yolks Storage and Freezing

Store leftover egg yolks, unbroken, in a small container or jar, covered with cold water. Cover container or jar tightly and keep refrigerated up to 3 days.

To freeze egg yolks, first stir lightly quantities of 7 or more, (about ½ cup), mixed with either ½ teaspoon salt or 1½ teaspoons sugar. Store full quantity in an airtight container sealed and labeled. Or, to enable use in smaller quantities, distribute by tablespoonfuls into ice cube trays (1 tablespoon of broken egg yolk equals 1 whole egg yolk). Transfer, when frozen, to freezer bags for easy storage. Thaw at room temperature in half an hour and use immediately.

Egg Whites Storage and Freezing

Store egg whites in an airtight container or a tightly covered jar in the refrigerator up to 1 week.

To freeze, pour single egg whites into individual ice cube cups. Store, when frozen, in a plastic bag and seal. In quantity, pour into an airtight container, leaving ½" air space. Label with number of whites and store up to six months. Thaw at room temperature and use immediately.

Hard-cooked egg whites do not freeze well, so do not freeze hard-cooked eggs.

►EGGS

EGG AND MUSHROOM CASSEROLE

▶ 6 hard-cooked eggs
4 tablespoons butter or
 margarine
⅓ pound mushrooms, sliced
¼ cup chopped onion
½ cup chopped celery
2 tablespoons flour
¼ teaspoon salt
⅛ teaspoon pepper

⅛ teaspoon cayenne
1 teaspoon Worcestershire sauce
½ can (10½ oz.) cream of
 mushroom soup mixed with ½
 can milk
½ cup shredded Cheddar
 cheese
¾ cup seasoned stuffing mix

1. Slice the eggs and arrange in a buttered shallow baking dish. Melt 2 tablespoons of the butter in a skillet and sauté the mushrooms, onion, and celery until mushroom liquid evaporates. Spread over the top of the eggs. Melt the remaining butter; stir in the flour, salt, pepper, cayenne, and Worcestershire sauce. Gradually stir into the soup and milk mixture; stir until smooth and thickened.

2. Pour the sauce into the baking dish. Mix together the cheese and stuffing, and sprinkle over the top of the casserole. Bake at 350° for 20 minutes until bubbly. Serve with rice or on toast points. Makes 4 servings.

EGGS À LA KING

4 tablespoons butter
½ pound fresh mushrooms, sliced
½ small green pepper, seeded
 and minced
3 tablespoons flour
1½ cups light cream
1 teaspoon Worcestershire sauce
1 small pimiento, minced

▶ ½ cup cooked peas
 Salt and pepper
▶ 4 extra large or jumbo eggs,
 hard-cooked and quartered
4 slices toast
2 tablespoons minced parsley
 Watercress
 Tomato wedges

1. Heat the butter in a saucepan; sauté the mushrooms and green pepper until they are tender and most of the pan juices have evaporated. Sprinkle the vegetables with the flour, stir in thoroughly, gradually add the cream, stirring constantly until sauce thickens. Add the Worcestershire sauce, pimiento, and peas to the sauce. Season with salt and pepper; heat the sauce until very hot.

2. Arrange 4 egg quarters on each slice of toast. Pour the sauce over all and sprinkle with the parsley. Garnish each plate with watercress and tomato wedges. Makes 4 servings.

CURRIED EGGS

4 tablespoons butter
2 onions sliced
1/3 cup minced celery
1 large apple, peeled, cored, and finely minced
1 to 2 tablespoons curry powder
3 tablespoons flour
1/2 cup heavy cream

1 cup milk
▶ 3 cups cooked, hot buttered rice
1/2 cup golden raisins
1/2 cup toasted slivered almonds
▶ 12 small eggs, hard-cooked, peeled and halved lengthwise
1/2 cup fresh minced coriander or parsley

1. Melt the butter in a large skillet. Sauté the onions, celery and apples until tender. Add curry powder and flour; blend well. Slowly pour in cream and milk, stirring constantly, until sauce thickens. Simmer 15 minutes.

2. Combine the rice with the raisins and almonds. Arrange a border of rice on a serving plate. Place the egg halves, yolk down, in center; pour sauce over eggs to serve. Sprinkle with coriander or parsley. Makes 6 servings.

SCOTCH EGGS

▶ 4 hard-cooked eggs, shelled
1 tablespoon flour
1/2 pound pork sausage meat
1/2 cup fresh soft bread crumbs
2 raw eggs

1/2 cup dry white bread crumbs
Vegetable oil for deep-frying
1 cup rich tomato sauce or 2 ripe tomatoes, cut into thin wedges

1. Roll the hard-cooked eggs in flour.

2. Combine the sausage meat, soft bread crumbs, and one raw egg; shape the mixture into 4 flat thin patties.

3. Place a hard-cooked egg in the center of each patty; smooth the meat around each egg to completely enclose it.

4. Dip each meat-covered egg in remaining lightly beaten raw egg, then in the dry bread crumbs to coat thoroughly.

5. Heat enough oil to deep-fry to 350°. Fry the eggs for 10 minutes; carefully remove the eggs from the oil and drain on absorbent paper. Cut each egg in half crosswise, place 2 halves on individual serving plates, yolk side up, and garnish with the tomato sauce or tomato wedges. Makes 4 servings.

EGG CROQUETTES

1½ tablespoons butter
3 tablespoons all-purpose flour
1 cup milk
▶ 6 hard-cooked eggs
¼ cup minced scallions
2 tablespoons minced parsley
3 tablespoons minced red
pepper

¼ cup grated Cheddar cheese
Salt and pepper to taste
Fine dry bread crumbs
1 egg, beaten with 2
tablespoons water
Fat for deep frying

1. In a saucepan, melt the butter; stir in the flour and gradually add the milk, stirring constantly, until thick. Finely chop the hard-cooked eggs and add to the sauce with the scallions, parsley, red pepper, cheese, and salt and pepper. Simmer for 20 minutes or until thick. Let stand until cool enough to handle.

2. Shape mixture into 8 croquettes, dip into crumbs, then into egg, and then again into crumbs. Fry in deep fat heated to 375° until croquettes are golden. Makes 4 servings.

EGGS À LA RUSSE

1 cup mayonnaise
4 tablespoons chili sauce
1 teaspoon tarragon vinegar
4 drops Tabasco sauce
2 teaspoons lemon juice
▶ 4 hard-cooked eggs peeled,
halved lengthwise

4 large lettuce leaves
4 teaspoons black caviar
4 teaspoons red caviar
1 small cucumber, peeled,
sliced very thin

1. Combine the mayonnaise, chili sauce, vinegar, Tabasco sauce and lemon juice in a bowl.

2. Place 2 egg halves, yolks down, on each of 4 lettuce-lined plates. Cover the eggs with sauce. Sprinkle caviar over the sauce—on one half, the red, and on the other half, the black. Garnish the plate with cucumber slices. Serve immediately. Makes 4 servings.

STRAWBERRY CHIFFON PIE

1½ cups crushed vanilla wafer
crumbs
⅓ cup softened butter or
margarine
¾ cup sugar
1 pint firm, ripe strawberries,
washed, hulled, and sliced
(reserve 3 whole berries for
garnish)

1 envelope unflavored gelatin
¼ cup water or 2 tablespoons
water plus 2 tablespoons Kirsch
1 tablespoon lemon juice
▶ 2 egg whites
½ cup heavy cream, whipped

1. Heat the over to 350°. Mix the crumbs, butter, and 2 tablespoons of the sugar thoroughly in a bowl. Press mixture firmly onto bottom and sides of lightly buttered 9-inch pie pan. Bake 8 minutes; cool.

2. Combine the strawberries and 6 tablespoons of the sugar; let stand 15 minutes or until very juicy. Strain the juice into a saucepan. Soften gelatin in the water and Kirsch for 5 minutes; add to the strawberry juice; heat until gelatin is dissolved; cool. Stir in the lemon juice. Add the sliced strawberries to the cooled mixture; chill until the mixture mounds when spooned.

3. Beat the egg whites with the remaining sugar until stiff but not dry. Fold the thickened strawberry mixture into the egg whites; fold in the whipped cream and pour into the cooled crust.

4. Cut the 3 whole berries in half, garnish the pie in a circular design with the berry slices. Makes 8 servings.

SNOW PUDDING WITH RASPBERRY SAUCE

1 envelope unflavored gelatin
½ cup water
½ cup plus 2 tablespoons sugar
Dash salt
½ cup plus 2 tablespoons boiling water

¼ cup fresh lemon juice
1 teaspoon grated lemon rind
▶ 2 egg whites, room temperature
1 package (10 oz.) frozen raspberries in syrup

1. Sprinkle the gelatin over the water in a saucepan; add ½ cup of sugar, salt, and boiling water, stirring until gelatin is completely dissolved. Blend in lemon juice and rind. Chill until mixture begins to set and is the consistency of unbeaten egg whites. Stir occasionally.

2. Beat egg whites with 2 tablespoons of sugar until stiff but not dry. Gently fold egg whites into lemon mixture until no clumps of egg white streak the mixture. Pour into a 1½-quart mold. Chill for several hours or until firm.

3. Defrost raspberries according to package directions. Purée fruit and syrup in blender or food processor. Pass sauce through strainer to remove seeds.

4. Unmold the Snow Pudding and serve with raspberry purée. Makes 4 to 6 servings.

THREE FRUITS SOUFFLÉ

2 tablespoons confectioners' sugar
2 packages peach-flavored gelatin
1 cup boiling water
2 jars (7¾ oz. each) junior apricots with tapioca

1 tablespoon grated orange peel
¼ cup orange juice
▶ 4 egg whites
½ cup heavy cream
½ cup pulverized almonds

1. Make an aluminum foil collar around the top of 1-quart soufflé dish. Lightly oil inside of collar and dust with confectioners' sugar. In a medium-size mixing bowl, dissolve the gelatin in the boiling water; stir in apricots, orange peel and juice; blend with a whip. Chill until syrupy.

2. Beat egg whites in a large bowl until stiff but not dry. Whip the cream in a separate bowl. Fold egg whites and cream gently into gelatin. Pour into the soufflé dish. Chill 3 or 4 hours or until very firm. Remove collar carefully. Press almonds around sides of the soufflé. Makes 8 servings.

PEACH SHERBET

1 envelope unflavored gelatin
½ cup sugar
2½ cups skim milk
1 can (16 oz.) Elberta peach
halves, well drained

▶ 2 egg whites
2 teaspoons grated lemon rind
3 tablespoons lemon juice
2 teaspoons vanilla extract

1. In a medium saucepan mix the gelatin and sugar together. Stir in milk and put over low heat, stirring, just until gelatin and sugar are dissolved. Put in a freezing tray or metal bowl and freeze until frozen 1" from edge.

2. Purée peaches in blender or through a food mill, and put in a large bowl. Add semi-frozen mixture, egg whites, lemon rind, juice, and vanilla extract; beat until light and fluffy. Put back in tray and freeze until firm. Soften slightly at room temperature before serving. Makes 1 quart.

WHIPPED PRUNE CREAM

¾ cup prune juice
½ cup sugar
1 envelope unflavored gelatin
1 cup drained, finely chopped
stewed prunes

3 tablespoons lemon juice
▶ 2 egg whites, room temperature
½ cup heavy cream, whipped
Nutmeg

1. Heat ½ cup of the prune juice combined with ¼ cup of the sugar in a small saucepan. Soften the gelatin in the remaining prune juice; let stand for 5 minutes. Add the hot prune juice mixture and stir until gelatin is dissolved. Add the prunes and lemon juice.

2. Let the prune mixture cool over ice water or in the refrigerator until slightly thickened. Meanwhile, beat the egg whites with the remaining sugar until stiff but not dry. Gently fold the whites into the cooled prune mixture.

3. Spoon the whip into individual sherbet glasses. Chill until firm, about 3 hours. Serve with the whipped cream and a dusting of nutmeg. Makes 4 servings.

TUNA AU GRATIN

1 cup evaporated milk
1 tablespoon cornstarch
¼ teaspoon salt
¼ teaspoon white pepper
1 teaspoon tomato paste
½ cup finely minced green
pepper
▶ 2 egg yolks

1 tablespoon lemon juice
1 can (4 oz.) sliced mushrooms
2 tablespoons dry sherry
3 cans (6 ½ oz. each) water-
packed tuna, drained and
flaked
6 tablespoons grated Gruyère
or Swiss cheese

1. Combine the evaporated milk, cornstarch, salt, pepper, tomato paste, and green pepper in a saucepan. Cook over medium heat, stirring constantly, until mixture thickens and bubbles; lower heat and simmer 10 minutes.

2. Combine the egg yolks, lemon juice, and the liquid from the mushrooms in a small bowl. Beat in a little of the hot sauce; mix well. Beat egg yolk mixture into the sauce. Cook, stirring constantly, until thickened; do not boil. Add the mushrooms, sherry, and tuna; heat 2 minutes.

3. Spoon the tuna mixture into 6 shells or individual baking dishes; sprinkle with the cheese. Broil a few minutes, just until the cheese is browned. Serve with rice or toast points. Makes 6 servings.

ZABAGLIONE

▶ **4 egg yolks**   **½ cup Marsala wine**
   ¼ cup sugar   **2 tablespoons grated lemon rind**

1. Put egg yolks and sugar in the top of a double boiler or saucepan, and whip with wire whisk or beaters until pale yellow and creamy.

2. Place the pan over boiling water; add the Marsala and lemon rind and continue beating until it forms soft mounds. Serve warm alone or as a sauce over fruit.

3. To serve cold, take the saucepan off the boiling water and set it in a basin of cracked ice; beat until cool. Makes 4 servings.

FLOATING ISLAND

▶ **3 egg whites**   **½ cup light cream**
   ½ cup plus 2 tablespoons sugar ▶ **6 egg yolks, lightly beaten**
   1½ cups milk   **1 teaspoon vanilla extract**

1. In a medium bowl, beat the egg whites until foamy; gradually add ¼ cup plus 2 tablespoons of the sugar and continue to beat until the whites are stiff but not dry.

2. Drop the beaten egg whites by heaping tablespoonfuls into ½ inch of boiling water in a shallow baking pan. Bake in a preheated 325° oven for 10 minutes. Carefully remove meringues from water and let stand until cool.

3. Scald the milk and cream in the top part of a double boiler over hot water. Beat the egg yolks with the remaining sugar. Beat a little of the hot milk mixture into the egg yolks, then beat the yolks into the hot milk. Cook the sauce (do not boil), stirring constantly, until thick enough to coat a metal spoon. Cool; add vanilla. Cover and chill. Serve topped with the meringue "islands." Makes 4 servings.

CRÊME BRÛLÉE

   1 pint heavy cream   **1 teaspoon vanilla**
   1 tablespoon sugar   **¾ cup light brown sugar, sieved**
▶ **4 egg yolks**   **to remove all lumps**

1. Heat cream in a saucepan over very low heat, or in the top of a double boiler over boiling water, covered, until hot but not scalding. Remove from heat, add sugar, stirring until dissolved. Beat egg yolks thoroughly in a bowl and beat into cream with a wire whisk. Add vanilla and

(*continued*)

stir in well. Pour into a shallow 1-quart baking dish. Set in a pan of water and bake at 300° until set (50 to 60 minutes) or until knife inserted in the center comes out clean. Cool. Chill overnight.

2. Lightly but thoroughly sprinkle sieved brown sugar ¼ inch thick over entire top of the custard. Broil 4 to 5 inches from source of heat until sugar melts and forms a hard crunchy surface, about 3 or 4 minutes. Cool and chill in the refrigerator 1 to 2 hours. Makes 4 servings.

SOFT CUSTARD SAUCE

1½ cups milk
▶ 4 egg yolks, beaten
⅓ cup sugar

⅛ teaspoon salt
1 tablespoon butter, if desired
1 teaspoon vanilla

1. Place the top of a double boiler over direct heat, and bring 1 cup of the milk to scalding point. Put the top back on the bottom of a double boiler containing simmering water.

2. Combine the egg yolks, sugar, salt, butter, and the remaining milk. Beat a little of the hot milk into the egg mixture; beat the egg mixture back into the hot milk and continue to cook, stirring constantly, until the custard coats a spoon. Remove pan from over the water; stir in the vanilla. Chill. Serve over fruit cakes, puddings, stewed fruit. Makes 4 to 6 servings.

PLAIN BAKED CUSTARDS

1½ cups milk
½ cup half-and-half or light cream
▶ 4 egg yolks

⅓ cup sugar
¼ teaspoon salt
½ teaspoon vanilla extract
Nutmeg

1. Heat the milk and cream in a saucepan to scalding. In a large mixing bowl, beat the egg yolks slightly; add sugar, salt and vanilla. Gradually add milk, stirring constantly.

2. Divide into 4 custard cups. Set the cups in a pan of hot water; bake at 325° for 50 minutes, or until tip of inserted knife comes out clean. Dust the top with grated nutmeg. Makes 4 servings.

BASIC RECIPES

PIE PASTRY

Pastry for a 1-crust pie (9")

1¼ cups pre-sifted flour
½ teaspoon salt
½ cup shortening
3 tablespoons water

Pastry for a 2-crust pie (9") or 8 Tarts or 24 Tartlets

2¼ cups pre-sifted flour
1 teaspoon salt
1 cup shortening
5 to 6 tablespoons water

1. Combine flour and salt with shortening in a mixing bowl. Cut shortening into flour until mixture resembles coarse crumbs.

2. Sprinkle water over the mixture, a tablespoonful at a time, lightly mixing with a fork after each addition. If all the flour is moistened before you have used all the water, omit the remaining water.

3. Gather dough into a ball and refrigerate, covered with plastic wrap, for 1 hour.

For 2-Crust Pie: Cut dough into two pieces and roll out separately on a lightly floured board or between 2 sheets of waxed paper. Roll out dough so that it is about 2 inches larger than pie plate. Fit one pastry into pie plate, fill pie, place remaining pastry over pie. Trim edges and flute; pierce top of pie with fork to allow steam to escape. Bake pie according to recipe directions.

For 1-Crust Pie: Proceed as for 2-crust pie, trimming and fluting single edge; fill pie and bake according to recipe directions.

For a Partially-Baked 1-Crust Pie Shell:** After trimming and fluting edge of pie shell, pierce bottom of shell lightly with fork. Cover bottom and sides of pie shell with 1 sheet of waxed paper, cut to fit. Pour dried beans or rice into pie shell, about 1 inch deep, and bake pie shell in a preheated 425° oven for 7 minutes or until "set." Remove pie shell from oven, allow to cool for 5 minutes. Remove waxed paper and rice or beans (these cannot be used for food preparation but may be saved for future pie shell baking).

**This crust holds up well for wet fillings, such as quiche and custard pies.

For a Fully-Baked 1-Crust Pie Shell: Proceed as for partially baked 1-crust pie shell. After removing waxed paper and rice, put pie shell back in oven and allow to bake another 15 minutes or until pastry is light golden.

For a 10" 1-Crust Pie Shell: *Increase* the ingredients for 9" 1-crust pie by the following:

5 tablespoons flour	2 tablespoons shortening
Pinch of salt	2 teaspoons water

PÂTE À CHOUX PASTRY
FOR CREAM PUFF SHELLS

1 cup water	1½ cups flour
8 tablespoons butter	6 eggs
Pinch salt, optional	

1. Put the water, butter, and salt in a saucepan and bring to a boil.

2. Add the flour and stir vigorously until a ball of dough is formed and the mixture cleans the sides of the saucepan; remove the pan from the heat. Immediately add the eggs, one at a time, beating vigorously after each addition.

3. Spoon the mixture into a pastry bag fitted with a #6 pastry tube.* Pipe "puffs" about 1½ inches apart onto buttered, floured baking sheets and bake in a preheated 425° oven for about 30 minutes or until the cream puff shells are golden brown and cooked throughout. Remove the pan from the oven and let cool before cutting and filling. Makes about 30 to 36 small cream puff shells.

*Note: You may also drop the pastry mixture onto the baking sheets from a teaspoon.

BUTTERMILK BISCUITS

2 cups sifted flour	¼ teaspoon baking soda
1 teaspoon salt	⅓ cup chilled shortening
2 teaspoons baking powder	¾ cup cold buttermilk

1. Sift the flour, salt, baking powder, and baking soda together in a bowl. Cut the shortening into flour mixture until mixture resembles coarse crumbs. Add the milk, stirring lightly with a fork just until the dry mixture is moistened.

2. Knead the dough very gently on a lightly floured board—do 10 kneading strokes. Roll dough out to ½-inch thick.

3. Cut biscuits out with a floured biscuit cutter. Bake on a lightly greased baking sheet in a preheated 450° oven for about 12 to 15 minutes, until biscuits are lightly browned. Makes about 1½ dozen.

BAKING POWDER BISCUITS

2 cups flour	⅓ cup chilled shortening
1 teaspoon salt	¾ cup milk
2½ teaspoons baking powder	

Sift the flour, salt, and baking powder together in a bowl. Then, to continue, follow remainder of the directions for Buttermilk Biscuits (above) from #1 on, beginning with "Cut the shortening into etc."

CRÊPE BATTER

Makes 8 Crêpes	Makes 16 to 20 Crêpes
1 egg	3 eggs
½ cup flour	1¼ cups flour
Salt or sugar to taste, depending on recipe (i.e. entrée or dessert)	½ teaspoon salt
	1 cup milk
	¼ cup cold water
½ cup plus 2 tablespoons milk	3 tablespoons butter, melted and cooled (for batter)
1 tablespoon butter, melted and cooled (for batter)	4 to 5 tablespoons butter (for frying)
3 to 4 tablespoons butter (for frying)	

1. Combine the egg(s), flour, and salt or sugar in a bowl, and beat well. Add the milk (and water) and stir thoroughly. Stir in the melted butter. If flour lumps remain in the batter, press through a strainer to break up.

2. Melt a tablespoon of butter in a 6- to 7-inch frying pan, preferably one that is teflon-coated. When the butter is hot, pour 2 tablespoons of the batter into the pan, swirl so that batter covers the entire bottom of the pan, and let the crêpe cook over moderate heat for about 30 to 45 seconds. Crêpe should be light golden on the bottom. Turn crêpe, cook another 15 or 30 seconds, and remove to a plate. Continue making crêpes until all the batter is used, adding butter to the frying pan as necessary. The crêpes may be stacked one on top of another. Makes about 8 (16 to 20) crêpes.

BÈCHAMEL SAUCE
(White Sauce Made with Milk)

Medium White Sauce	Thick White Sauce
1½ tablespoons butter	2 tablespoons butter
1½ tablespoons flour	2 tablespoons flour
1 cup milk	1 cup milk
Salt and pepper to taste	Salt and pepper to taste

In a small saucepan, melt the butter over low heat; add the flour and stir constantly until mixture is smooth. Gradually add the milk; cook, stirring constantly, until the sauce is smooth and thick. Remove the sauce from the heat. Makes 1 cup sauce.

MORNAY SAUCE (Cheese Sauce)

1 cup Medium White Sauce	1 teaspoon Dijon mustard
¼ cup grated cheese (Cheddar, Gruyère, Parmesan, etc.)	(optional)

Heat the White Sauce. Stir the cheese and mustard into the sauce, over low heat, and cook just until cheese is melted. Immediately remove the pan from the heat. (Do not reheat the sauce or cheese will cook into strings.)

CREAM SAUCE

Add ¼ cup heavy cream to 1 cup Medium White Sauce, and simmer over low heat, stirring constantly, until sauce is desired consistency.

VELOUTÉ SAUCE
(White Sauce Made with Chicken or Fish Broth)

2 tablespoons butter
2 tablespoons flour

1 cup chicken or fish broth: homemade soup, canned broth, bouillon cubes (reconstituted), or bottled clam juice may be used
Salt and pepper to taste

In a small saucepan, melt the butter over low heat; add the flour and stir constantly until mixture is smooth. Gradually add the broth; cook, stirring constantly, until sauce is smooth and thick. Season with salt and pepper to taste. Remove the sauce from the heat. Makes 1 cup sauce. (A lighter or heavier Velouté may be made by adjusting the amount of butter and flour, as in Medium White Sauce and Thick White Sauce.)

HOLLANDAISE SAUCE

2 egg yolks
3 tablespoons lemon juice

½ cup (1 stick) butter, cut into 8 slices
Pinch of cayenne

Stir the egg yolks and lemon juice together in a small saucepan. Add 4 slices of the butter. Place pan over very low heat and cook, *stirring constantly,* until butter is melted and sauce thickened. Add the remaining butter, and cook, stirring constantly, until butter is melted. Remove pan from heat, stir in the cayenne, and serve the sauce immediately. Makes about ¾ cup.

BLENDER HOLLANDAISE SAUCE

3 egg yolks
2 tablespoons lemon juice
¼ teaspoon salt

Pinch of cayenne
½ cup (1 stick) butter, melted and hot (but not browned)

1. Place the egg yolks, lemon juice, salt, and cayenne in blender and process at high speed for 30 seconds, or just until ingredients are thoroughly combined. (Do not turn off blender.)

2. Uncover blender. With blender still running, slowly drizzle in the butter. Sauce should be thick and creamy by the time all the butter has been used. Immediately turn off the blender and serve the sauce. Makes about ¾ cup.

QUICK CHICKEN OR MUSHROOM CREAM SAUCE

1 can (10½ oz.) condensed
   cream of chicken or cream of
   mushroom soup
1 cup sour cream
2 tablespoons chopped parsley

1 teaspoon Worcestershire
   sauce, or 1 teaspoon Dijon
   mustard, or 1 to 2 tablespoons
   sherry or brandy

Combine the soup, sour cream, parsley, and Worcestershire sauce in a saucepan. Cook over low heat, stirring until sauce is hot—do not allow sauce to come to a boil. Remove pan from heat. (If adding sherry or brandy instead of the Worcestershire sauce or mustard, stir in after sauce has been heated.)

QUICK BEEF GRAVY

2 tablespoons butter
2 tablespoons flour

1 cup beef broth: homemade
   soup, canned broth, or bouillon
   cube (reconstituted)
Salt and pepper to taste

In a small saucepan, melt the butter over low heat; add the flour and stir constantly until mixture is smooth. Gradually add the broth; cook, stirring constantly, until smooth and thick. Season with salt and pepper to taste. Remove from the heat. Makes 1 cup.

QUICK MUSHROOM BEEF GRAVY

Add 1 can (4 oz.) sliced drained mushrooms to 1 recipe Quick Beef Gravy.

QUICK SAUCE BORDELAISE (Wine Sauce)

1 cup Quick Beef Gravy
½ cup red wine

¼ teaspoon dried thyme
1 tablespoon butter

Combine Quick Beef Gravy with red wine and thyme in a saucepan and cook, stirring, over medium heat, for about 5 minutes or until sauce is thickened to taste. Stir in the butter. Serve immediately. Makes 1¼ cups.

QUICK MADEIRA SAUCE

1 cup Quick Beef Gravy
⅓ cup Madeira

1 tablespoon butter

Combine Quick Beef Gravy with Madeira, and simmer until sauce is heated through. Stir butter into sauce, remove from heat, and serve immediately. Makes 1¼ cups.

TOMATO SAUCE

3 tablespoons olive oil
½ cup finely chopped onions
1 can (16 oz.) Italian plum
tomatoes, chopped
2 tablespoons tomato paste
½ cup white wine (optional)

1 teaspoon dried basil
1 teaspoon sugar
Salt to taste
Freshly ground black pepper
1 to 2 tablespoons minced fresh
parsley

In a saucepan, heat the olive oil and cook the onions for about 5 minutes, until they are soft and lightly colored. Add the tomatoes, tomato paste, wine, basil, and sugar. Bring to a boil, then reduce the heat and simmer the sauce, stirring occasionally, for about 20 minutes, until sauce is reduced and thickened. Season with salt and pepper to taste, and stir in parsley. Makes 2¼ cups.

LEMON SAUCE (Avgolemono)

3 egg yolks
1 tablespoon arrowroot
1 teaspoon salt
⅛ teaspoon cayenne
1 cup chicken stock, homemade
or canned

1 tablespoon lemon juice
1 tablespoon parsley, fresh dill,
or fresh tarragon, finely
chopped
1 to 2 tablespoons heavy cream
(optional)

1. In the top of a double boiler, combine the egg yolks, arrowroot, salt, and cayenne. Beat together lightly with a whisk, and stir in the chicken stock. Beating constantly, cook directly over moderate heat until the sauce begins to thicken. If it forms small lumps, remove from the heat, beat vigorously with a whisk, and return the pan to the heat; continue to whisk until the sauce thickens enough to cling heavily to the beater. Don't allow the sauce to come to a boil.

2. Stir in the lemon juice and the chopped herb. If necessary, thin the sauce with a little extra chicken stock or the heavy cream, and add a few more drops of lemon juice. Keep warm by placing pan over hot water. Makes 1½ cups.

BLENDER MAYONNAISE

1 egg
1 teaspoon Dijon mustard
½ teaspoon salt
2 tablespoons white wine
vinegar or lemon juice

1 small clove garlic, chopped
(optional)
1 cup corn, vegetable, or olive
oil

1. Put the egg, mustard, salt, vinegar, garlic and ¼ cup of the oil into a blender container.

2. Process the mixture at low speed; as soon as mixture is smooth, drizzle in the remaining oil through top of blender, with motor constantly running. As soon as all the oil is used, turn off the blender. Homemade mayonnaise will keep in a covered container in the refrigerator for 2 to 3 days. Makes about 1¼ cups.

Note: Additional flavorings may be added to the mixture in step #1: ¼ to ½ teaspoon dried herb of your choice; 1 to 2 teaspoons tomato paste; 1 tablespoon fresh minced parsley; 1 tablespoon chopped capers.

SIMPLE VINAIGRETTE DRESSING

¼ cup white wine vinegar
1 teaspoon salt
¼ teaspoon pepper

¼ teaspoon sugar
⅛ to ¼ teaspoon dry mustard
¾ cup vegetable oil

1. Combine the vinegar, salt, pepper, sugar, and mustard in a small bowl or jar and stir together.

2. Add the oil and beat or shake jar vigorously until dressing is well-blended. Makes 1 cup.

QUICK CHICKEN OR MEAT BROTH

1. The quick method for making chicken or meat broth calls first for accumulating in the freezer, leftover chicken or turkey carcasses; uncooked chicken necks, backs, wing tips, gizzards, and so forth; left-over bones of cooked beef, veal, ham, and lamb; frozen stems of parsley and other herbs; odd pieces of uncooked vegetables; pan drippings, gravies, and leftover sauces.

2. The accumulation of poultry carcasses and parts, or one or two of the different types of meat bones, is placed in a large pot together with accumulated odds and ends, and enough water to completely cover. To them, add:

1 bay leaf
4 to 5 parsley sprigs
½ onion, chopped
4 to 5 peppercorns
Pinch of salt

½ cup diced celery pieces and leaves
Piece of cinnamon stick (optional)

3. With a pot cover on, simmer for an hour or two, or until the soup begins to have a good tasty flavor. Then remove the pot cover, and cook until the soup is reduced and the flavor becomes stronger and more pronounced.

4. Strain the soup, and discard the carcasses, bones, vegetables, herbs, etc. The stock may be used immediately or frozen as a base for future sauces and soups.

WEIGHT AND VOLUME EQUIVALENTS

Beans/Peas/Lentils:	1 cup dried	= 2 to 2½ cups cooked
Beets:	1 pound	= 4 medium = 2 cups diced
Bread crumbs:	3 to 4 slices bread 1 slice bread	= 1 cup dry crumbs = ½ cup soft crumbs
Butter and solid fats:	1 pound ¼ pound	= 2 cups = ½ cup = 8 tablespoons
Cabbage:	1 pound	= 4 cups shredded
Celery:	1 pound	= 2 small bunches = 4 cups diced
Cheese:	¼ pound	= 1 cup shredded or grated
Cheese, cream:	8 ounces 3 ounces	= 1 cup = 6 tablespoons
Corn:	12 ears	= 3 cups cut kernels
Crackers, graham:	15 squares	= 1 cup fine crumbs
Crackers, saltine:	16 squares 22 squares	= 1 cup coarse crumbs = 1 cup fine crumbs
Cream, whipping:	1 cup	= 2 cups whipped
Eggplant:	1 pound	= 3 cups diced
Garlic:	1 large clove	= 1 teaspoon chopped
Lemon:	1 average	= 2 to 3 tablespoons juice
Lemon rind, grated:	1 lemon	= 2 to 3 teaspoons
Macaroni:	8 ounces dry	= 2 cups uncooked = 4 cups cooked
Meats:	1 pound cooked	= 3¼ cups chopped or diced = 4⅛ cups ground
Milk, evaporated:	5⅓ fluid ounces	= ⅔ cup
Mushrooms:	1 pound fresh ½ pound sliced	= 3 ounces dried = 2 cups cooked = 2½ cups
Noodles:	1 cup uncooked	= 1¾ cups cooked
Nuts, ground:	¼ pound	= 1 cup
Oil:	7½ ounces	= 1 cup
Onion:	1 medium 1 large	= ½ cup chopped = 1 cup chopped
Peanut butter:	1 pound	= 1¾ cups

(continued)

Peas:	1 pound in pod	= 1 cup shelled
Potatoes:	1 pound	= 4 average
		= 2½ cups diced
		= 2 cups mashed
	1 medium	= 1 cup sliced
Rice:	1 pound uncooked	= 2 cups uncooked
	1 cup uncooked	= 3 cups cooked
	1 cup instant	= 2 cups cooked
Tomatoes:	1 pound fresh	= 3 average
Walnut meats:	¼ pound	= 1 cup chopped
Zucchini:	2 medium	= about 3 cups sliced

INGREDIENT SUBSTITUTIONS

Beef broth:	1 cup	= 1 teaspoon beef-flavored concentrate or 1 beef bouillon cube dissolved in 1 cup boiling water
Biscuit mix:	1 cup	= 1 cup flour, 1½ teaspoon baking powder, ½ teaspoon salt, and 1 tablespoon shortening
Butter, clarified:	½ cup	= ¼ cup butter plus ¼ cup cup oil
Buttermilk:	1 cup	= 1 cup milk plus 1 tablespoon vinegar or lemon juice; let stand 5 minutes
		= 1 cup yogurt
Chicken broth:	1 cup	= 1 chicken bouillon cube or 1 envelope instant chicken broth dissolved in 1 cup boiling water
Cornstarch:	1 tablespoon	= 2 tablespoons flour
Cream, half & half (15% butterfat):	1 cup	= ½ cup light cream plus ½ cup milk
Cream, light (20% butterfat):	1 cup	= 3 tablespoons butter plus ¾ cup milk
Cream, heavy (40% butterfat):	1 cup	= ⅓ cup butter plus ¾ cup milk
Cream, sour:	1 cup	= 1 tablespoon lemon juice plus evaporated milk to make 1 cup
		= 3 tablespoons butter plus ¾ cup sour milk

Eggs:	1 whole egg	= 2 egg yolks plus 1 tablespoon water
Flour (as thickener):	1 tablespoon	= ½ tablespoon cornstarch or 2 teaspoons quick-cooking tapioca
Garlic:	1 small clove	= ⅛ teaspoon garlic powder
Ginger:	1 tablespoon chopped ginger root	= ⅛ teaspoon ground ginger
Herbs:	1 tablespoon fresh	= ½ teaspoon dried or ⅓ teaspoon ground
Milk, whole:	1 cup	= ½ cup evaporated milk plus ½ cup water
Mushrooms:	½ pound fresh	= 1 can (6 oz.) mushrooms
Mustard:	1 tablespoon prepared	= 1 teaspoon dry mustard plus 1 tablespoon white wine or vinegar
Onion:	¼ cup chopped raw	= 1 tablespoon instant dried
	1 tablespoon chopped raw	= ½ teaspoon onion powder
	Flavor of 1 medium raw	= 1 teaspoon onion salt
Shortening, hydrogenated:	1 cup	= 1⅛ cups butter or margarine, or ⅞ cup oil plus ½ teaspoon salt
Tabasco:	Few drops	= Dash of cayenne or red pepper
Tomato purée:	1 cup	= 2 tablespoons tomato paste plus enough water to make 1 cup
Tomato sauce:	1 can (8 oz.)	= 3 large fresh tomatoes, cooked
Tomatoes, canned:	1 can (16 oz.), 2 cups	= 6 large raw tomatoes cooked in ½ cup water or juice
	1 cup	= 1⅓ cups chopped fresh tomatoes simmered for 10 minutes
Yeast:	1 package active dry yeast	= 1 cake (0.6 oz.), compressed

THE STORAGE & FREEZING OF
ONCE-COOKED FOODS

The flavor of nutrients of cooked foods can be preserved for days, weeks, and even months with proper care. The two principal requirements are adequate packaging and storage that is sufficiently cold.

Most leftovers in airtight containers and wrappings keep well for a few days in the refrigerator. Longer storage requires freezing. The temperature in a freezer should be 0° F.

Equally important are container and wrappings materials. The longer a food is to be stored, the more important they are. The best materials available are those that are waterproof, moisture-proof, and vapor-proof. They are made of polyethylene, saran film, pliofilm, heavy duty foil, and laminated waterproof paper, and come in the form of wrapping papers, storage bags, rigid containers with tight lids, foil pie plates or partitioned trays.

To keep leftovers at their nutritious, flavorful best, they should be handled as follows:

In refrigerating:

1. Cool slightly and refrigerate soon after cooking in appropriate airtight containers. Bowls can be covered tightly with plastic film.
2. Meat and fish cooked in gravies and sauces should be stored covered as completely as possible with the gravies and sauces.
3. When packaging slices or pieces of meat in wrapping or storage bags, force out as much air as possible.

In freezing:

The same general directions apply as in refrigerating, with these important additions:

1. Foods should be rapidly and thoroughly cooled before freezing.
2. For convenience, foods should be stored in meal-size portions.
3. Slices and large pieces of meat should be wrapped with a double thickness of waxed paper between them so they can be separated easily for fast thawing.
4. Wrapping and bag edges should be sealed with freezer tape. Contents should be labeled, identifying the food, approximate weight or volume, and the date of freezing.
5. Foods that do not freeze very well are sauces made with eggs, milk, or cheese, fried foods, and potatoes.
6. Broths and stocks should be frozen in plastic containers in sizes (half-pint, pint, and quart) convenient for future use in all kinds of sauces and soups. Small quantities for use in gravies, for example, can be frozen in ice cube trays and muffin tins, removed and enclosed in heavy plastic storage bags with as much air squeezed out as possible.

RECOMMENDED STORAGE TIME PERIODS

1. MEAT. (beef, lamb, veal, and pork) Remove meat from bones: refrigerate 4 to 7 days; freeze 2 to 3 months.

2. HAM. Refrigerate up to 2 weeks; freeze up to 3 months.

3. POULTRY and STUFFING. Store stuffing separate from fowls; refrigerate 1 to 2 days; freeze pieces, wrapped in moisture-proof paper, 1 month; freeze in containers, covered in gravy, up to 3 months.

4. FISH. Remove skin and bones: refrigerate 1 to 2 days; freeze up to 6 weeks.

5. GRAVY and DRIPPINGS. Cool; remove fat from surface; refrigerate for up to 1 week; freeze up to 3 months.

6. VEGETABLES. Refrigerate 2 to 3 days; freeze with sauce or cooking liquid up to 6 weeks.

INDEX

Salad
  Beef-, 33
  Beet and, 241
  Boiled Beef and Vegetable Platter
    with Sour Cream Dressing, 33
  and Corned Beef, 40
  Down Home, 263
  Javanese Vegetable, 274
  Oliver, 82
  Pork and Vegetable, 163
  Russian, 138
  Russian Veal and Cucumber, 212
  Russian Vegetable, 273
  Salad Niçoise, 262
  Salmagundi (Chicken), 82
  Salmagundi (Lamb), 189
  Salmagundi with Ham and Salami,
    263
  Scandinavian Veal and Herring,
    211
  Seafood and, 234
  Vegetable, 263
Sausage Bake, 256
Soups
  Broccoli, 261
  in Cape Cod Fish Chowder, 231
  in Corn Chowder, 261
  in Purée of Cauliflower, 247
  in Quick Corn Chowder, 250
  Vichyssoise, 261
Stews
  Polish Pork and, (Bigos), 150
  Spanish Lamb, 177
  Swedish Creamed, 258
  in Turkey Roll-Ups, 88
  in Veal and Ham en Casserole, 197
Mashed Potatoes, uses for
  in Beef à la Burgundy, 4
  in Biscuits, Southern Chicken, 63
  Cakes
    Mashed Potato Chocolate, 265
    Slavic Sugar, 264
  Chantilly, 256
  Cheese Puff, 259
  Dumplings with Ham, 266
  in Fricadelles of Veal, 209
  in Knockwurst Rolls, 265
  in Loaf
    Glazed Ham, 132
    Veal Mont Blanc, 210
  Pancakes with Bacon, 259
  Pasties, 258
  in Patties
    -Beef, Spicy, 262
    Ham, 133

Pie
  Classic Shepherd's, 5
  Devon Shepherd's, 169
  Soho Fish, 225
  Surprise, Indienne, 268
Rolls, 264
Soufflé, 260
  in Fish and Vegetable, 228
Soup
  Broccoli, 261
  Vichyssoise, 261
  in Stuffed Tomatoes Riviera Style, 19

PUDDINGS
  Carrot Ring, 245
  Floating Island, 293
  Macaroni Kugel, 285
  Rice, 281
  Snow, with Raspberry Sauce, 291
  Sweet Potato Spiced, 270
  Vegetable, 272
  Whipped Prune Cream, 292

PUFFS
  Broccoli and Ham, 126
  Corn, 249
  Potato Cheese, 259
  Squash, 269
  Sweet Potato, 271
  Yorkshire Squares, 25

PUFF SHELLS, 297
  Chicken Puffs, 67
  Lamb in, Creamed, 185
  Veal Profiteroles, Creamed, 205

QUICHES
  Broccoli, 243
  Chicken-Spinach, 64
  Corn and Veal, 204
  Ham
    and Cheese, 120
    and Shrimp, 121
  Individual Fish, 223
  Lamb-Macaroni, 183
  Seafood, 222
  Zucchini and Tomato, 275

RATATOUILLE
  Chicken, au Gratin, 49
  Fish Baked with, 267
  Lamb and, Alexandria, 186
  Pancakes, 266

RICE
  Casserole
    Basque Chicken and, 45
    and Beans, Quick, 278

RICE

Casserole (continued)
  Chicken Livers with, Parmesan, 84
  Indonesian Fried Rice, 278
  in Kedgeree, 215
  in Lamb
    Baked Zucchini with, 166
    Slavic, 170
    Southern, 170
  in Pork and Pepper Moussaka, 147
  in Saturday Night, 3
  in Southern, 50
  Spanish, 278
in Chicken
  and Corn Custard, 71
  -Filled Crêpes in Cheese Sauce, 65
in Chop Suey, 51
in Eggs, Curried, 289
in Fish Creole, New Orleans, 218
Fried, 284
  with Beef and Green Peppers, 283
  Chinese, 163
  Indonesian (Nasi Goreng), 278
Fritters, Sweet, 281
in Ham Cheese Rolls, 284
in Lamb Hash, Italian, 188
Loaf
  Chicken and, 78
  in Dutch Ham, 133
Orange, 283
Patties
  in Beef, with Creamed Broccoli, 31
  Surprise, 282
Pie
  in Russian Chicken, 60
  in Salmon Cheese, 280
Pudding, 281
Salad
  in Beef, Japanese-Style, 34
  Chicken and, 79
  Chicken and, Italiano, 81
  Chicken and, with Tuna Mayonnaise, 80
  in Fish, Caribbean, 234
  Italian, 283
  in Pork, Chinese, 162
  Turkey, 103
  in Veal, Boulestin, 211
Soufflé, 282
Soup
  in Cajun Ham Gumbo, 129
  in Chicken Gumbo, 73
  in Creole, 29
  Greek (Avgolemono), 282
  in Mulligatawny, 72
Stuffed Vegetables
  Acorn Squash, with Peanut and Pepper Pilaf, 179

  Cabbage Leaves, Pork-, 156
  Eggplant, Classic, 16
  Eggplant with Lamb, 179
  Eggplant, Seafood-, 220
  Grape Leaves in Lemon-Egg Sauce, Lamb-, 180
  Onions with Lamb, 180
  Peppers Acapulco, 202
  Pepper Cups, Curried Chicken in, 59
  Spanish Onions with Currant Pecan Stuffing, 280
  Tomatoes, 279
  Tomatoes, Ham-, 118
  Tomatoes, Seafood-, 221
  Whole Cabbage, 17
  Zucchini in Cream Sauce, 181
  Zucchini Florentine, 268
  Zucchini, Mexican, 279
  Zucchini Rialto, 18
in Turkey
  Bombay, 93
  Cocktail Tidbits, 101
in Veal, Scalloped, 207

SALADS
(see listings under main ingredients—e.g. Beef, Chicken, etc.—and Salads entry in table of contents preceding each chapter)

SALAD DRESSINGS
Blender Mayonnaise, 301
Simple Vinaigrette, 301

SALMON
Beignets (French Fritters), 226
Broccoli-, au Gratin, 216
Kedgeree, 215
Mousse, Cold, 227
Pâté, 236

SANDWICHES
Chicken
  -Cheese, Toasted, 83
  Curried, Spread, 84
  Wessex, 84
Croque-Monsieur, 142
Fish Burgers, Broiled, 236
Ham
  Deviled, Spread, 142
  and Egg, Baked, 140
  Pita, with Chick Peas and, 142
  Salad Piquante, Hot, 141
  Soufflé, 141
Monte Cristo, 140
Pork, Barbecued, 164
Turkey
  Greek, 104

ADDITIONAL RECIPES

ADDITIONAL RECIPES

ADDITIONAL RECIPES

ADDITIONAL RECIPES

ADDITIONAL RECIPES

ADDITIONAL RECIPES

ADDITIONAL RECIPES

ADDITIONAL RECIPES

ADDITIONAL RECIPES

ADDITIONAL RECIPES